ROYAL HISTORICAL SOCIETY

STUDIES IN HISTORY

New Series

CIVIL WAR, INTERREGNUM
AND RESTORATION IN GLOUCESTERSHIRE
1640–1672

For Diane

CIVIL WAR, INTERREGNUM AND RESTORATION IN GLOUCESTERSHIRE
1640–1672

A. R. Warmington

THE ROYAL HISTORICAL SOCIETY
THE BOYDELL PRESS

First published 1997

A Royal Historical Society publication
Published by The Boydell Press
an imprint of Boydell & Brewer Ltd
PO Box 9   Woodbridge   Suffolk IP12 3DF   UK
and of Boydell & Brewer Inc.
PO Box 41026   Rochester   NY 14604–4126   USA

ISBN 0 86193 236 6

ISSN 0269–2244

A catalogue record for this book is available
from the British Library

Library of Congress Cataloging-in-Publication Data
Warmington, A. R. (Andrew Richard), 1963–
    Civil War, interregnum and restoration in Gloucestershire,
1640–1672 / A.R. Warmington.
        p.   cm. – (Royal Historical Society studies in history. New
series, ISSN 0269–2244
    Includes bibliographical references and index.
    ISBN 0–86193–236–6 (hardback : alk. paper)
    1. Great Britain – History – Civil War, 1642–1649. 2. Great
Britain – History – Commonwealth and Protectorate, 1649–1660.
3. Great Britain – History – Restoration, 1660–1688.
4. Gloucestershire (England) – History. I. Title. II. Series.
DA415.W33 1997
941.06'2 – dc21   97–16225

This book is printed on acid-free paper

Printed in Great Britain by
St Edmundsbury Press Ltd, Bury St Edmunds, Suffolk

Contents

List of Tables and Maps

Tables

Maps

Acknowledgements

Although a work like this is by definition a solitary pursuit, undertaking and completing it would not have been possible without the help of many others. My primary debt is to my supervisors, firstly Dr Gerald Aylmer, later Dr Clive Holmes. Whatever precision and accuracy it has is due to their help and patience. The staff at the Public Records Office, the British Library, the Gloucestershire Records Office, Gloucester Public Library and Durham University Computing Centre were unfailingly helpful. I am indebted to Dan Beaver and Paul Gladwish for several references and advice, to Leslie Zweigman for allowing me to consult his thesis at short notice towards the end of my study, to my parents for financial support, without which this project would not have been possible, and finally to Oxford United FC and Gloucestershire County Cricket Club for keeping me entertained.

A. R. Warmington
May, 1997

Publication of this volume was aided by a grant
from the Scouloudi Foundation.

Abbreviations

A&O	*Acts and ordinances of the Interregnum*, ed. C. H. Firth and R. S. Rait, London, 1911
BIHR	*Bulletin of the Institute for Historical Research*
BL	British Library
Bodl. Lib.	Bodleian Library, Oxford
CCAM	*Calendar of the Committee for the Advance of Money*, ed. M. A. E. Green, London 1888
CCC	*Calendar of the proceedings of the Committee for Compounding with Delinquents*, ed. M. A. E. Green, London 1892
CCSP	*Calendar of the Clarendon state papers*, ed. W. D. Macray and F. J. Routledge, Oxford 1876–1970
CJ	*Commons journals*
CSP	*Clarendon state papers*, ed. T. Monkhouse, Oxford 1786
CSPD	*Calendar of state papers, domestic*
CTB	*Calendar of treasury books*
DNB	*Dictionary of national biography*
EcHR	*Economic History Review*
EHR	*English Historical Review*
GBR	Gloucester Borough Records
GDR	Gloucester Diocesan Records
Glos. Pub. Lib.	Gloucester Public Library
GRO	Gloucestershire Records Office
HJ	*Historical Journal*
HMC	Historical Manuscripts Commission
JEH	*Journal of Ecclesiastical History*
JBS	*Journal of British Studies*
LJ	*Lords journals*
P&P	*Past and Present*
PRO	Public Records Office (Chancery Lane, except T51 [Kew])
TBGAS	*Transactions of the Bristol and Gloucestershire Archaeological Society*
TBR	Tewkesbury Borough Records
TSP	*A collection of the state papers of John Thurloe*, ed. J. T. Birch, London 1742
TRHS	*Transactions of the Royal Historical Society*
VCH	Victoria County History

1

Introduction

Historiographical

This introduction explores briefly the historiography of the English Civil War period, the key issues, and examines society, economy and county life in Gloucestershire prior to 1640, the year taken as the starting point for the narrative of events in chapter two. As research on almost every English county of the time has either been completed or is in progress, yet another county study may call for some justification. The best answer is that the work in the area has posed more new questions than it has answered old.

We should remember that the 'county community' school of historians is a recent phenomenon. For over two hundred years, the debate on the English Revolution had been constricted by the continued relevance, real or imagined, of the issues at stake in contemporary politics, and such assumptions continued to colour late nineteenth-century scholarship. These years did see an awakening of interest in local history, customs and folklore, and some works on the local dimension of the Civil War era emerged. But these works tended mainly to add colour to the old narrative of battles and great men. A second generation of county histories emerged in the 1920s and 1930s. Benefiting from the publication or calendaring of documents, and making more thorough use of local records, historians such as A. C. Wood on Nottinghamshire and Mary Coate on Cornwall demonstrated how different was each county's experience of the war.[1]

Such studies were still swamped by works of analysis which reflected greater historical controversies. The 'Storm over the Gentry', a series of increasingly acerbic articles and books, notably by R. H. Tawney, H. R. Trevor-Roper, J. H. Hexter and Lawrence Stone, reflected profound disagreements over the causes of the war, but all tended to rest on the assumption that long-term social and economic changes were at the root of it. 'Whig' and 'Marxist' interpretations of the war were never as crude as later detractors have suggested, but many still view the period as a crucial stage in the transformation of a feudal into a capitalist society, in a way that transcended provincial concerns. The many works of Christopher Hill also focused on society, economy and religion before the war, and the radical politics and religion that emerged from it.

---

[1] A. C. Wood, *Nottinghamshire in the Civil War*, London 1937; M. Coate, *Cornwall in the Great Civil War and Interregnum: a social and political study*, Oxford 1933.

Local studies such as J. T. Cliffe's work on the Yorkshire gentry somewhat undermined such grand schemes, but the first modern county study was A. M. Everitt's *The community of Kent and the Great Rebellion*, published in 1966. Everitt swept away the received notion that the economically 'advanced' south-east was naturally parliamentarian, showing that Kent was isolated from London, her inhabitants were not interested in constitutional matters and viewed public affairs through a stubbornly localist prism. Most viewed the war with dismay; the partisans on either side were an unrepresentative extremist fringe. The 1648 rebellion was not subdued Royalism boiling over but a local protest against a tyrannical county committee. Everitt stressed above all the harmony, stability and vertical integration of Kentish society. In the long-term development of the county community, the Civil War was merely a blip on the graph.[2]

Not all of this was new, but nobody had previously analysed the consequences of the obvious fact that the war itself was abhorrent to the vast majority of Englishmen. It is an ironic measure of Everitt's success that, despite his warnings that Kent's insularity and deep-rooted gentry society were in many ways atypical, it became the model for a new generation of studies. John Morrill's study of Cheshire, Antony Fletcher's of Sussex and David Underdown's of Somerset all owed much to Everitt in their use of local sources and in depicting the war as an intrusion into fundamentally harmonious societies which had been united in their dislike of Charles I's personal rule. These studies tied in with 'revisionist' work on the pre-Civil War period, which had generally downgraded the importance of long-term causes in favour of the unforeseen and coincidental in the years leading up to 1642.[3]

Neutralism and attempts to avoid the war became subjects of growing interest. Morrill showed how the choice of sides in the war was often arbitrary, depending on military circumstances as much as on any conscious preference. His work of synthesis, *The revolt of the provinces*, summarised a new orthodoxy. Whilst acknowledging that pre-war divisions – religious in Lancashire, factional in Leicestershire – were a factor, he held that the war was fought reluctantly by men who, whatever their preferences for one side, preferred peace to either. The war itself was a far worse burden on society than the unconstitutional taxation of the 1630s. The anguish and incomprehension with which most viewed the slow, chaotic drift to war was graphically demonstrated in Fletcher's second book, *The outbreak of the English Civil War*.

This tendency towards playing down causation, abstract principle and commitment begged questions about how the two sides managed to get armies

[2] J. T. Cliffe, *The Yorkshire gentry from the Reformation to the Civil War*, London 1964; A. M. Everitt, *The community of Kent and the Great Rebellion, 1640–1660*, Leicester 1966.
[3] J. S. Morrill, *Cheshire 1630–1660: county government and society during the Puritan revolution*, Oxford 1974; A. J. Fletcher, *A county community in peace and war: Sussex, 1600–1660*, London 1975; D. Underdown, *Somerset in the Civil War and Interregnum*, Newton Abbot 1973.

into the field and why Parliament won the war – or, conversely, why the king lost it. Morrill suggested that Parliament succeeded by suppressing localism in a centralised, arbitrary but better organised war machine. By contrast, the king tried to respect local feeling and customs, but was unable to prevent rapacious subordinates committing outrages against them time and again.[4]

Concentration of attention at county level often implies that the whole was only the sum of the parts. Much work remained to be done from larger and smaller regional perspectives. Clive Holmes's work on Parliament's main base, the Eastern Association, shows that this was not, as often assumed, a cohesive area united by Puritanism and common interests. On the contrary, it was riven by town and county particularism and its unity was enforced from above. Ronald Hutton's work on the main Royalist area, Wales and the West Midlands, shows that the Royalist war effort there was not based on widespread local support, but that this did not prevent the king from generating resources there which might have won him the war. Once his main field army was defeated, however, he could not hold the area down and the local communities turned against him 'not out of hatred of his cause, but from hatred of the war itself'.[5]

Just as recent years have seen an increasing emphasis on the importance of ideology and principle in pre-war politics and away from the idea of the Civil War as a freak accident, so there has been a swing away from the 'county community' school. Holmes sounded the first note of dissent in an article in 1980, in which he showed that local society operated at many different levels. Kinship and social and educational ties, far from reinforcing county isolationism, could draw the gentry into a far wider network. Often 'county' institutions, such as parliamentary elections and quarter sessions, were exactly those which most reminded local elites that they lived in a centralised nation state.[6]

Anne Hughes has shown how one county, Warwickshire, aligned itself ideologically before the war, and how this corresponded to real divisions in county society. Her work breaks down a division often taken for granted by historians between locally-minded moderates and nationally-minded extremists, with the latter usually of lower social origins (especially on the parliamentarian side). She also shows how local disputes over the conduct of the war were fought within the context of parliamentary politics. Her work is complemented by other Midland studies, notably that of Lynn Beats on Derbyshire, which show how unimportant 'county' feeling was to the gentry before and during the war. Hughes has also re-examined the two war machines, suggesting that Parliament triumphed not by suppressing localism but by incorporating local self-defence within the notion of allegiance to a cause, whilst the

[4] J. S. Morrill, *The revolt of the provinces: conservatives and radicals in the English Civil War, 1630–1650*, London 1974; A. J. Fletcher, *The outbreak of the English Civil War*, London 1981.
[5] C. Holmes, *The Eastern Association in the English Civil War*, Cambridge 1974; R. E. Hutton, *The royalist war effort, 1642–1646*, London 1982, 203.
[6] C. Holmes, 'The county community in English historiography', *JBS* xix (1980), 54–73.

intensely personal nature of Royalism made it fragile. This view is supported by Gloucestershire evidence.[7]

All these issues as they relate to Gloucestershire are addressed in chapter two, which covers the period from the controversial Short Parliament election of 1640, through the tentative moves towards a county defence scheme until the formation of sides in 1643, and the course of the war until the collapse of the local royalists in mid-1644. The pattern of gentry allegiance as the sides coalesced is examined in detail. The ways in which both sides continually adapted ramshackle administrative systems to changing circumstances, and the limited meaning of any 'county' feeling on either side in Gloucestershire, are recurrent themes throughout.

In chapter two and most other chapters, the issues are examined in a continuous narrative, so that the thread of what is an absorbing story in its own right should not be lost in a welter of analysis. However, the final pages of each chapter draw out the main conclusions and tie up loose ends. One county should not be regarded as a microcosm of England, and clearly Gloucestershire was often quite atypical. None the less, it is hoped that this fresh look at a county which was at once a cockpit of war and peripheral to regional strategy on both sides will add to our knowledge of a well-established but still fascinating subject.

Too often, county studies have concentrated on the Civil War itself, relegating the 1646–60 period to one chapter at the end. Questions remain about county government and relations between central government and the provinces during the Interregnum and then after the Restoration of Charles II. It is one of the aims of this work to redress the balance. Chapter three thus continues the story of the war until its end, and also examines in detail a serious feud of 1644 to 1645 between the governor of Gloucester, Colonel Massey, and some of the County Committee in the context of similar disputes over authority in the parliamentary command structure elsewhere. A wide variety of statistical and anecdotal evidence is also marshalled in a separate section to analyse the often grim effects of the war. Massey's slightly demented writings afford some light relief among the gloom.

Another important issue examined in chapter three is the changing composition of county government amid the absence of firm government and the proscription of most of the former ruling class – and all at an appallingly difficult time of poor harvests, poverty, economic dislocation and even starvation. Key sources for these years include state papers covering the work of the local sub-committees of accounts and the parliamentary Committee for Indemnity, as well as the better-known records of the Committees for Compounding and for Advance of Money. These throw much light on to the true

7 A. Hughes, *Politics, society and Civil War in Warwickshire, 1625–1660*, Cambridge 1987; L. N. Beats, 'Politics and government in Derbyshire, 1640–1660', unpubl. Ph.D. diss. Sheffield 1978; A. Hughes, 'The king, the Parliament and the localities in the English Civil War', *JBS* xxiv (1985), 236–63.

situation in the provinces, for it has too often been assumed that society in general and the defeated royalist gentry in particular were writhing helplessly under the military cosh. It will be argued that this was very far from being the case in the late 1640s, despite the heavy military presence.

Chapter four continues the political narrative up to the year 1659, interspersing it with analyses of several other important subjects of the time: the distinctive role played by the city of Gloucester, which is mostly based on city records; the well-documented work of the sequestration commissioners of 1650–5; above all, the remarkable domination of county life by a small group of minor gentry and radical pastors, who rose to hitherto unimaginable prominence through service to Parliament and membership of the gathered churches which flourished in the Cromwellian period. In relation to Gloucestershire, the Interregnum regime emerges as something very different from the centralising military dictatorship of traditional belief.

Much of the detail of chapter four is closely linked to chapter six, as both examine the relations between the county and the successive regimes of both Interregnum and Restoration, with particular reference to two issues which concerned both and where central policy was essentially the same: the prohibition of tobacco-growing in the Vale of Evesham and the state's aim to exploit for profit the resources of the Forest of Dean through ironworks and shipbuilding projects. A. M. Coleby's recent work on the relations between central government and the provinces in Hampshire in the period 1649 to 1689 is the starting point for these sections. Whilst many of the conclusions here differ radically from his, particularly in regard to the supposed superiority of the Restoration regime, it should be acknowledged that few of these vital questions had even been considered before his pioneering work.[8]

Chapter five is different in structure from the rest, in that it breaks away from the narrative to tackle a theme which was touched upon but not resolved in chapters two, three and four, that of popular culture and politics before, during and after the Civil War. This has been a subject of growing interest since the publication of David Underdown's *Revel, riot and rebellion* in 1987. Since this work was based on the adjacent counties of Somerset, Wiltshire and Dorset, Gloucestershire is a natural testing ground for his thesis.

At the risk of simplifying to excess a brilliant and complex work, then, Underdown argued that in the century before 1640 rural England became polarised between two different kinds of society with different cultures: the relatively closed, manorialised, nucleated, mainly arable 'chalk' downland settlements and the more open, dispersed, wood-pasture 'cheese' regions. Both felt the pressures of population growth, a market-oriented economy and growing divergences between rich and poor, but the impact was measurably greater in the 'cheese' areas, to which the migrant poor tended to drift, and where Puritanism was stronger among the ruling classes.

---

[8] A. M. Coleby, *Central government and the localities: Hampshire, 1649–1689*, Cambridge 1987.

The gentry and yeomanry of the 'chalk' regions, who had done well out of changing times, tended increasingly to diverge from the masses and assert their status and control in new ways, most notably in hostility, fortified by Puritanism, to drunken, disorderly or 'heathenish' festivity. By contrast, in the 'cheese' regions, manorial control was tighter, communities were more stable and popular culture was more often tolerated or even encouraged by Laudian clerics and paternalist landlords. Cultures differed markedly between the two types of society in many ways. For instance, football, a disorganised communal punch-up, was the game of the 'chalk' regions, whilst stoolball and other primitive forms of cricket, where the individual's role was more prominent, were more often played in the 'cheese' regions.

Much more importantly, it was the 'cheese' countries, far more directly vulnerable to the economic pressures of the early seventeenth century, which also saw the riots and revolts of the period and which, for this among other reasons, produced a general popular Parliamentarianism. Popular Royalism, notably among the Clubmen, occurred in downlands and small towns, where people banded together to defend their way of life against the threat of Puritan reformation. Underdown's work undermined traditional views of popular allegiance in the Civil War, be they those who thought the people had no real opinion and followed their masters blindly, those 'revisionists' who stressed a more positive indifference to the issues based on antipathy to both sides, or the strong and enduring tradition among left-wing historians in believing that the masses did hold their own, overwhelmingly Parliamentarian preferences.[9]

In chapter five, different patterns of popular activism – and passivity – in the strikingly different economic and cultural regions of Gloucestershire are examined. Plenty of evidence exists to illustrate that there was a real dichotomy (which events of 1640 showed to extend to the gentry as well), but issue is taken with the concept of popular Royalism. It will be argued that the real division was between politically conscious, pro-Parliament regions and the politically inert. However, the upheavals of the 1640s injected a measure of awareness into previously backward regions, in the form of radical religion, that altered the nature of the dichotomy prior to 1660. This is illustrated by evidence of non-violent conflicts which divided small town communities away from the Vales, the spread of different religious sects and then by an intensive study of the way all regions and all levels of county society reacted to the events from the crushing of an attempted revolt in July 1659 to the Restoration in May 1660.

Thus chapter five ties up many of the loose ends from previous chapters. Chapter six tackles many similar issues in taking the story on to the year 1672, when Gloucestershire, like the nation as a whole, reached several important turning points at once. Gloucester's independence was stripped away and the

---

9 D. Underdown, *Revel, riot and rebellion: popular culture and politics in England, 1600–1660*, New York 1987. See also B. S. Manning, *The English people and the English Revolution, 1640–1649*, London 1976; J. L. Malcolm, *Caesar's due: loyalty and Charles I*, London 1983.

city was integrated more into county life, tax-resistance encouraged by certain gentlemen had contributed to fiscal crisis and state attempts to manage the Forests of Dean and Kingswood were withering away in the face of local hostility. Above all, the gentry were eliminating alternative loci of power either above or below county level. Ironically perhaps, in view of all that has been said about the 'county community', it is one of this work's final contentions that if ever there was such a thing in Gloucestershire, it was not in 1640 but in the 1670s.

Geographic and economic

In what sense was Gloucestershire a united county, and what united or divided her? The county's size and shape had remained unchanged since the absorption of Winchcombeshire in the eleventh century, with 237 parishes in thirty hundreds in five divisions – Berkeley, the Seven Hundreds, Kiftsgate, Forest and the Inshire (see Map 1). She measured fifty-five miles by thirty-three at the widest extent.

However, counties were originally administrative, not geographical, units. Gloucestershire's form had been determined by many factors, of which logic was not one. In the west and north-west, the Wye and Warwickshire Avon formed natural boundaries, but much of the northern border with Worcestershire and Warwickshire was scarred by deep indentations of, and into, both, with many split parishes and 'islands'. Many parishes jutted into Worcestershire, while, further east, two Worcestershire islands and a large indentation, Broadway, left the upper part of Kiftsgate Division attached to the rest of the county by a chicken's neck of land.

The Warwickshire border again met the Avon in the far north-east, where the jigsaw was at its most complex. There were also two Gloucestershire parishes in Warwickshire and two in Oxfordshire. All four counties met at the famous Four-Shire Stone near Moreton-in-Marsh. Within Slaughter Hundred the picture became clearer, but even here there were islands of Worcestershire and Berkshire. The Wiltshire border snaked along the Cotswold plateau down to Marshfield, where the Somerset border ran along the course of the un-navigable Bristol Avon. Poulton and Kingswood were islands of Wiltshire in Gloucestershire, Minety the reverse.[10]

Bristol, a county in her own right, was England's third city and a burgeoning Atlantic port, with a population of some 15,000. Although Bristol had an impact in Gloucestershire as a market town and a source of new gentlemen, the reverse was rarely true. The city's politics had for a century revolved mainly around differences between the Merchant Venturers and smaller merchants

---

[10] C. S. Taylor, 'The northern boundary of Gloucestershire', *TBGAS* xxxii (1904), 109–11; VCH, *Worcs.* iii. 266–9, 279–86, 347–51, 468–71; iv. 33–40; *Warwicks.* v. 50–2, 157–9, 189–93; *Oxon.* ix. 189–93; *Glos.* vi. 2 and passim.

Map 1
Gloucestershire: divisions and towns

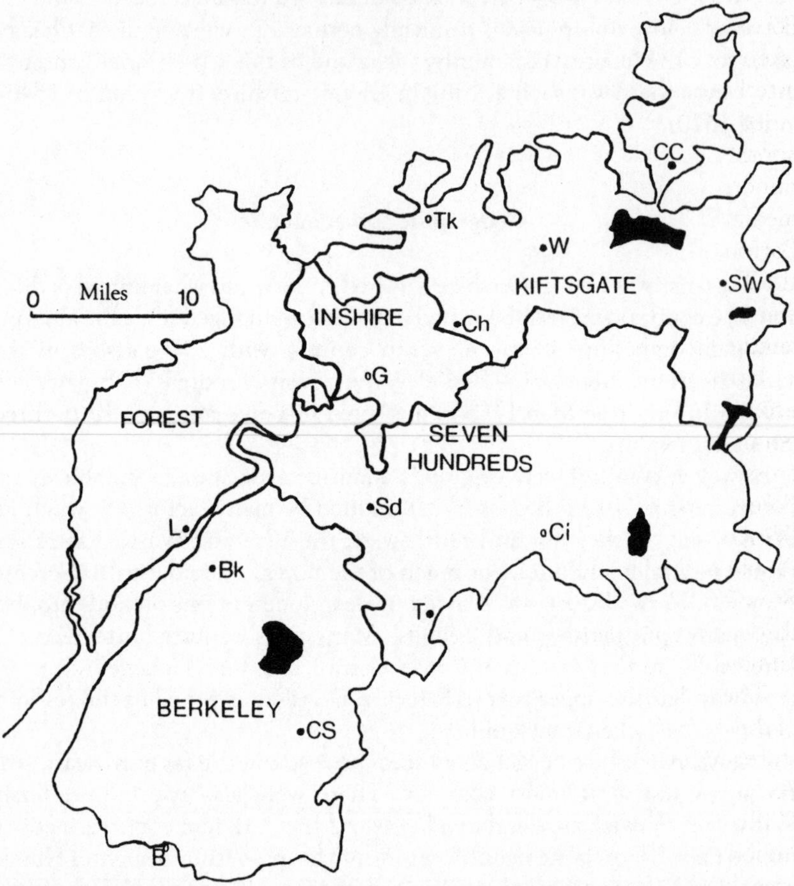

0   Miles   10

INSHIRE

FOREST

KIFTSGATE

SEVEN
HUNDREDS

BERKELEY

°Tk   •W
•Ch
CC
•SW
°G
•Sd
°Ci
L•
•Bk
T•
•CS
B•

Key:

■ islands of other counties
° Parliamentary boroughs:
   B – Bristol (not in Gloucester-
       shire)
   G – Gloucester
   Tk – Tewkesbury
   Ci – Cirencester

• Other major settlements:
   W – Winchcombe
   CC – Chipping Campden
   Ch – Cheltenham
   SW – Stow-on-the-Wold
   Sd – Stroud
   L – Lydney
   Bk – Berkeley
   T – Tetbury
   CS – Chipping Sodbury

and tradesmen. The latter had just lost a bitter battle over the right of non-members to trade abroad. Many of them were Puritans, and they were to be the backbone of the parliamentarian party in the Civil War.[11]

The hundreds of Gloucestershire were as fragmented as the divisions. In the Forest, the east and south they were generally coherent – although they were often divided into two parts in the south – but the north and north-east were utterly chaotic. Tewkesbury, Deerhurst and Westminster Hundreds were divided into many scattered parts. Vast, unwieldy Kiftsgate Hundred was yet another survival of ancient hideage arrangements. In a war which used the hundred as a unit of taxation, this was not a trivial point. Another contentious medieval relic was the 'Inshire', the two hundreds of Dudston and King's Barton, which had been placed under the jurisdiction of Gloucester by Richard III. The borough's authority there was resented by the gentry of Inshire and county alike. The 1620s had seen a fierce attack, led by the Cooke and Guise families, which Gloucester fought off with no little difficulty.[12]

If the county was not a naturally coherent unit, did communications or the economy make it more so? It is unlikely that the roads, bad even by contemporary standards, played any such role, although Gloucester was a major crossroads. From Gloucester, roads radiated to Bristol via Dursley, into the Forest of Dean, to Worcester via Tewkesbury, to Coventry via Cheltenham, Winchcombe and Chipping Campden, and to the Thames Valley via Lechlade. Another from Oxford to the West Midlands ran through Cirencester and Stow-on-the-Wold, which meant that Civil War armies frequently passed through both. In January 1643 Prince Rupert's first attack on Cirencester was fatally delayed by the 'extreme foulness' of the roads.[13]

The most obvious natural boundary, the Severn, flowed through the heart of the county. The river was navigable, with difficulty, throughout Gloucestershire, despite its tides, bores and a whirlpool at the mouth. The Warwickshire Avon had just been made navigable to Stratford at vast personal cost by Sir William Sandys, and a lively trade passed up and down the two rivers, bringing imports from Bristol up through the West Midlands and the produce of the area down.[14] However, the Severn did not unite the county. Quite apart from the many disputes between parishes on either side about fishing rights, its

---

11 D. Harris Sacks, 'Bristol's "Wars of Religion" ', in R. C. Richardson (ed.), *Town and countryside in the English Revolution*, Manchester 1992, 100–24.
12 *Autobiography of Thomas Raymond and memoirs of the family of Guise*, ed. G. E. Davies (Camden 3rd ser. xxviii), 104; VCH, *Glos*. iv. 87–8.
13 W. B. Willcox, *Gloucestershire: a study in local government, 1590–1640*, New Haven 1940, 1; Edward Hyde, earl of Clarendon, *The history of the rebellion and civil wars in England*, ed. W. D. Macray, Oxford 1969, vi. 237.
14 T. S. Willan, 'The river navigation and trade of the Severn valley, 1600–1750', *EcHR* 1st ser. viii (1937–8), 68–75; T. Fuller, *The history of the worthies of England*, London 1662, 351; *Guise memoirs*, 104–5.

ferries were so notoriously dangerous that even as late as 1725 Daniel Defoe did not care to try them.[15]

In any case, many of the county's rivers flowed not to the Severn but to the Thames, and most of those that did – the Wye, the Lugg and the Stroudwater streams – were not navigable. In 1641, John Taylor, the water poet, had a fraught journey trying to travel from east to west by river; unable to negotiate the Churn upstream beyond Cirencester, he had to hire wagons to rejoin the Stroudwater at Miserden and again at Stonehouse, where he made his way among 'suncke trees' and overhanging vegetation to Eastington before giving up and re-embarking on the Severn. The constructions of docks at Lechlade, at the south-eastern tip of Gloucestershire and the highest navigable place on the Thames, further aligned the Cotswolds away from the Severn Valley in the 1650s.[16]

Gloucestershire had been a byword for fertility and a dense population since the days of William of Malmesbury. The saying 'As sure as God's in Gloucestershire' derived not, as Thomas Fuller thought, from the number of abbeys there but from her extraordinary fertility – it was even used in a newssheet in 1654 after a bumper harvest.[17]

As none of the several censuses of the seventeenth century are complete, comparisons are rarely useful prior to Robert Atkyns's estimate of about 126,000 in the 1700s and Ralph Bigland's 130,000 in the 1730s.[18] But the population had clearly risen rapidly in the century before the Civil War, by 100 per cent in parts of the Vales of Gloucester and Berkeley and perhaps by even more in some clothing districts. Most of this occurred before 1603; a comparison of figures for communicants in the (almost contiguous) Gloucester diocese in 1603, for families in a church survey of 1650 and of the Compton Census of 1676 suggests a rise of between 10 and 18 per cent over the course of the years, though the figures are too imprecise to allow for regional comparisons.[19] The total population was probably over 100,000 for most of the century.

In 1608, the famous local antiquarian John Smyth of Nibley made a survey of the county militia. In theory, this listed the name, age, occupation and physique of every man of military age in the county. Though far from complete,

[15] John Smyth of Nibley, A description of the hundred of Berkeley, ed. Sir J. Maclean, Oxford 1885, 221–2; GRO, D326/L3; D. Defoe, A tour thro' the whole island of Great Britain, London 1725, ii, pp. ii, 49.

[16] J. Taylor, John Taylor's last voyage, London 1641.

[17] Fuller, Worthies, 352; BLE 814 (3) The weekly intelligencer, no. 3, 24–31 Oct. 1654.

[18] R. Atkyns, The ancient and present state of Gloucestershire, Gloucester 1712, 62–3; R. Bigland, Historical, monumental and genealogical collections relative to the county of Gloucester, Gloucester 1791, 36–42.

[19] L. J. Zweigman, 'The role of the gentleman in county government and society: the Gloucestershire gentry, 1625–1649', unpubl. D.Phil. diss. McGill 1987, 61–3; E. A. O. Whiteman, The Compton Census: a critical edition, London 1986, 524–31.

as it omits the unfit, those who failed to appear at musters and those outside the age limits, this is a valuable source and shows Gloucestershire to have been an atypical county in many ways. Of 17,046 men of given occupation, only 7,883 (46.2 per cent) worked in agriculture.

Yet this was not an urbanised county. Few towns were large enough to dominate an area, and some, notably Winchcombe, were predominantly agrarian. There were roughly equal numbers of agricultural workers and rural artisans, most of whom worked in textiles, and a high number of smallholders, independent producers and small employers. Above all, it was a highly differentiated society. There was a world of difference between sprawling Bisley, where ninety-nine of 140 men classified were textile workers, and feudal Sapperton, where only three were not agricultural workers, yet the two parishes were neighbours.[20]

Contemporaries, including Christopher Guise of Elmore, almost invariably divided Gloucestershire, like Gaul, into three parts: Vale, Wold and Forest. Another native observer, John Smyth, never ventured into the Forest of Dean, and preferred a three-fold division moving from Severn to Cotswolds. The banks of the Severn, he said, had wealth but no health (Guise also noticed the 'ill ayre' of Elmore and other river parishes), the Cotswolds had health 'in that sharpe aire' but no wealth, whilst his own beloved homeland in the heart of the Vale had both in abundance.[21]

Wartime commanders remarked on the differences between the regions too. In March 1643 Viscount Grandison was reluctant to commit his troops against Sir William Waller in the 'narrow inclosed waies of the vale [of Berkeley]'. After relieving Gloucester in August 1643, the earl of Essex avoided a battle by hiding in the 'Close country . . . woods and enclosed grounds' around Tewkesbury, whereas around Stow-on-the-Wold he found 'a brave champaign country', ideal for a pitched battle. Map 2 shows, in simplified form, the separate economic regions of the county.[22]

Smyth's pride in the rich soil, fruitful agriculture and eminent yeomanry of Berkeley Hundred was matched by that of the Cotswolds men in the beauty of their region and their image as plain, honest folk. However, these self-images should not be taken too much at face value. An apparently coherent region might contain many feuds, rivalries and competing allegiances. The hundreders of Berkeley described someone who promised much and delivered little as 'a man of Dursley', a clothing town in the hundred, and a vicar's casual use of this saying in a sermon at Berkeley in 1603 had nearly caused a riot among the Dursley men present. Vicious feuds between rival parishes persisted; on one

---

20 A. J. Tawney and R. H. Tawney, 'An occupational census of the seventeenth century', *EcHR* 1st ser. v (1934–5), 25–64. J. W. Wyatt, 'How accurate is "Men and Armour"?', *Gloucestershire Historical Studies* ix (1978), 19–30, suggests that the Tawneys were substantially correct in their conclusions.
21 *Guise memoirs*, 104–6; Bigland, *Gloucestershire collections*, 92; Smyth, *Description*, 10.
22 BL, MS Add. 18,980, fo. 48; E68 (4), *Mercurius Aulicus*, no. 37, 10–17 Sept. 1643; E69 (11), *A true relation of the marching of the trained bands of the city of London*, 1643.

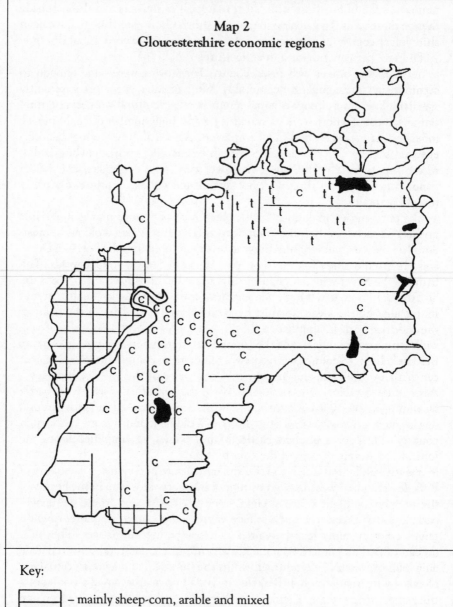

Map 2
Gloucestershire economic regions

Key:

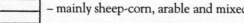
– mainly sheep-corn, arable and mixed

– mainly wood-pasture and dairying

– mainly forest, heath and waste

c – clothmaking parish, 1608

t – tobacco-growing location, 1627

famous occasion, the men of Chipping Campden descended on those of Winchcombe and beat them up so thoroughly that 'there was not a whole shirt left there'.[23]

Despite being the largest town and the hub of the transport network, Gloucester was not a true county town because of her jealously guarded separate status. Even during the Civil War, the sheriffs of Gloucestershire needed permission from Parliament to reside there. The town neither impressed nor depressed visitors very much. It was a chartered borough ruled by twelve aldermen, each serving as mayor (no more than twice) and elected for life from a common council of fluctuating numbers, with a recorder, a town clerk and numerous other officials.

Incorporated as a port in 1580, Gloucester was rapidly doomed by the increase in the size of ships. None of over 150 tons draught could continue up the shallow, tidal Severn beyond her downriver creek at Gatcombe and nothing of over thirty could pass beyond Gloucester. Imported goods were usually trans-shipped at Bristol to go upriver. Gloucester lagged far behind Bristol in overseas trade, and sometimes had to struggle not to be bypassed in inland trade in its rivalry with Tewkesbury.[24]

The city economy passed through crisis in the years before the Civil War. Its textile and capping industries almost collapsed in the face of Stroudwater's competition, and pinning could not as yet compensate. Poverty was widespread and budget deficits common. Nor, in view of the Inshire dispute, was the town a social magnet, though it was an important legal and religious centre. These problems fuelled a tendency to oligarchic rule by the aldermen through their control over poor relief and public order at the city's quarter sessions. Factionalism gradually gave way to self-discipline in the early seventeenth century. Many of the aldermen were strong Puritans and their promotion of Puritan clerics into city livings and lectureships – most notably John Workman – brought them into conflict with both crown and chapter in the 1630s.[25]

Both independence and oligarchy were precariously maintained, though the resentment of the 'many' against the 'few' spilled over several times at parliamentary elections when populist candidates tried to play on their grievances. The aldermen were aware enough of the problem in 1641 to lay on banquets for a famous son of the city in the hope of publicity. John Taylor duly obliged with an implausible scheme by which Gloucester could be converted into the nation's second city through expanding her fine quay and wharf for foreign trade. In reality the city's unique asset was its role as a central market town between all the regions and as an administrative and

---

[23] Smyth, *Description*, 3–6, 10; Willcox, *Gloucestershire*, 8; cited in E. Adlard, *Winchcombe cavalcade*, Cheltenham 1939, 86.

[24] Willcox, *Gloucestershire*, 204–10; HMC, 6th report, part i, appendix (MSS House of Lords 1644–7), 18; CJ, iv. 460.

[25] VCH, *Glos*. iv. 75–92.

social centre, but this niche was not to be found until later, when political independence was gone.[26]

John Smyth was not the only man to eulogise the fertile loams of the Vale of Berkeley. Defoe later called it 'the Richest, most Fertile and most agreeable part of England, the Bank of the Thames only excepted'. The reclaimed 'New Grounds' at Slimbridge and Frampton, scene of many enclosure riots, were particularly fertile. With its poor drainage, the area was not generally suitable for arable farming and little corn was grown. There was extensive pasture and the norm was small, enclosed family farms and market-oriented dairying.[27] In the seventy-three rural parishes and parts of others which made up the Vale, and which were on average the smallest in the county, manorial control was generally weak and settlements dispersed. The ship money assessments of the 1630s confirm that this was the richest area of the county, as it was taxed at 2s. 4d. per acre, compared with 2s. for the Vale of Gloucester, 1s. 8d. for the Cotswolds and 1s. 6d. for the Forest.[28]

The main reason for the area's rapidly rising population was the cloth industry, 'the heart and soul of the Gloucestershire economy'. Cloth employed 40 per cent of all able-bodied men in twenty-three Stroudwater parishes in 1608, and may have employed over 24,000 people in all. This was an ancient industry in the county, but in recent years it had shifted away from the north-eastern slope of the Cotswolds to the valleys of the Frome, Cam and Little Avon. This area alone had the fast streams and pure water needed to drive the multitude of fulling mills which grew up on the steep banks, and to produce the high quality red and white cloth. Here, too, were to be found the fuller's earth, teasels and dye plants, which all formed part of the complex process. Only recently had the industry outgrown the ulnager's seal, the traditional means of regulation and quality control.[29]

The recent ruralisation of the industry hastened the impoverishment of those towns, such as Thornbury, which were least able to profit from it, and the very success of the industry created problems, for it attracted droves of poor. Stroud, Dursley, Tetbury and Chipping Sodbury were all noted for their endemic poverty. When hit by the cyclical depressions to which the industry was prone, they had no other means of livelihood. From the 1620s, after the

[26] J. K. Gruenfelder, 'Gloucester's parliamentary elections, 1604–1640', *TBGAS* xcvi (1978), 53–9; Taylor, *Last voyage*, passim; P. J. Ripley, 'The city of Gloucester, 1660–1740', unpubl. M.Litt. diss. Bristol 1977.
[27] Defoe, *Tour*, ii, pp. ii, 60; Fuller, *Worthies*, 344; J. Thirsk (ed.), *The agrarian history of England*, London 1984, v. 187–91; Smyth, *Description*, passim.
[28] Zweigman, 'County government', 14, 59–60; P. Hamilton, 'Patterns of rural settlement in Gloucestershire, Herefordshire and Worcestershire', unpubl. MA diss. Reading 1960, 81–5, 163–5.
[29] Willcox, *Gloucestershire*, 162–5; R. Perry, 'The Gloucestershire woollen industry, 1100–1690', *TBGAS* lxvi (1945), 78, 81, 101, 108–10, 120; J. Tann, 'Aspects of the development of the Gloucestershire woollen industry', unpubl. Ph.D. diss. Leicester 1964, 101–67. For a long-term study of the area, see D. P. Rollison, *The local origins of modern society: Gloucestershire, 1500–1800*, London 1992.

disastrous Cockayne project, there were recurrent crises leading to massive unemployment and a major public order problem, which crown policy only made worse.[30] Thus the county's richest region also contained pockets of the direst misery. Mortality crises may have occurred in at least one cloth parish in over half of the years between 1560 and 1640, and were clearly recorded in Wotton-under-Edge, Minchinhampton, Tetbury, North Nibley and Stroud in the pre-war years.[31]

Berkeley Division was not monolithic, however. In the south and south-west lay a more exclusively agrarian area, and on the outskirts of Bristol, Kingswood Chase stretched across three Gloucestershire parishes. Here the manorial lords had been exploiting the rich coal seams for some years and fighting a long legal battle against crown attempts to establish it as a royal forest. The wood and game were rapidly falling victim to encroachment from the many poor cottagers moving into the area.[32]

The Vale of Gloucester, an area bounded by Gloucester, Cheltenham and Tewkesbury of about seventy-five parishes, only slightly larger on average than those of the Vale of Berkeley, was also an area of pasture, meadow, dairying and orchards, but was not quite as fertile. Much land had already been enclosed piecemeal. Cheltenham was still only a middling market and malting town. When contemporaries thought of Tewkesbury they thought of the proverbially sharp mustard balls made there. In reality, the county's second town (in terms of economy, but not population, which fluctuated at around 2,500 and was probably lower than Winchcombe's) made its living as a market town, river port and malting and tanning centre. Tewkesbury was incorporated in 1575, and, following the new charter of 1610, was governed by twenty-four principal and assistant burgesses and returned MPs, most of whom were well-connected non-resident gentlemen, such as Sir Dudley Digges and Sir Baptist Hicks, who could do financial favours for the troubled borough.[33]

Although anti-Laudian Puritanism was most pronounced in Gloucester during the reign of Charles I, it was also common in the Tewkesbury area, throughout the clothing region and in the Vales of Berkeley and Gloucester. Whether the poverty of the cures was to blame is less certain, but this was a major problem in a county with many impropriations and lay patrons. A leading Puritan minister, Humphrey Fox, was suspended from Forthampton, near Tewkesbury, but his sons, Hopewell and Help-on-High, continued the

30 Willcox, *Gloucestershire*, 9–10, 165–78; Tann, 'Gloucestershire woollen industry', 169–87; Perry, 'Woollen industry', 121–34.
31 Rollison, 'Bourgeois soul', 317; E. A. Wrigley and R. S. Schofield, *The population history of England, 1541–1871*, London 1981, 486, 676–80
32 B. Sharp, *In contempt of all authority: rural artisans and riot in the west of England, 1586–1660*, Berkeley 1980, 189–90.
33 Thirsk, *Agrarian history*, 273; J. Bennett, *A history of Tewkesbury*, Tewkesbury 1830, 200–1; VCH, *Glos*. vi. 240–3; M. F. Redmond, 'The borough of Tewkesbury, 1575–1714', unpubl. MA diss. Birmingham 1950, 2–6; W. R. Williams, *The parliamentary history of the county of Gloucester*, Hereford 1898, 232–6.

fight. John Geree, vicar of Tewkesbury, was also a prominent resister. Clothing towns such as Dursley, Stroud and Painswick were known for strong clerical and lay Puritanism, and radical gentlemen, such as Sir Robert Cooke of Highnam and Nathaniel Stephens of Eastington, were patrons of known anti-Laudian clerics. This region housed all the preachers who were to be so prominent on Stephens's behalf in the Short Parliament election of 1640.[34]

The most exclusively agrarian area, the Vale of Evesham, stretched away to the east of Tewkesbury. Here much land was owned by absentees, many manors had been sub-divided out of existence, and the few parish gentry lived close to their tenants. Both soil and society were ideally suited to market gardening and the cultivation of special crops: flax, woad, carrots and, above all, tobacco, which was widespread before and after the Civil War. As in the cloth region and the Forest of Dean, lax manorialism attracted swarms of poor, for tobacco was a labour-intensive crop which required close partnership between land-owner and cultivator, and one which could offer very high returns.[35]

The region around the main tobacco town, Winchcombe, was a byword for poverty, decay and crime; 'roguish Winchcombe', 'a poore beggarly town' occupied by 'neer foor-thousand beggars'. Some townsmen blamed the lord, Sir William Whitmore, for encouraging immigration and the splitting of tenements until ratepayers were outnumbered twenty to one by recipients. Whatever the case, from the 1620s, as the crown tried to prevent the cultiva-tion of tobacco in England and thus sparked off fifty years of periodic armed resistance, the closely-knit society of the Vale of Evesham drew even closer together.[36]

The largest town of the north-east was Chipping Campden, once a wool town and now a gloving, malting and market centre. Its prosperity was almost entirely due to the hundreds of thousands of pounds poured into the local economy by Sir Baptist Hicks. Between buying the manor in 1609 and his death in 1629, this wealthy London financier rebuilt large sections of the town, all emblazoned with his arms, and reputedly gave £100,000 to charity, as well as building his own mansion at a cost of some £30,000. None of Gloucester-shire's other poverty-stricken towns had this outrageous luck.[37]

Fewer travellers visited the proverbially cold and inaccessible Cotswold plateau than the Vale. 'Those poor sheep have nothing to shelter them but Bisley spire', it was said at the exposed market town of Stow-on-the-Wold. The Cotswolds' historic claim to fame had been their wool, but the region was as

[34] G. I. Soden, *Godfrey Goodman, bishop of Gloucester, 1583–1656*, London 1952, 185–296; SP 16/448/79.
[35] J. Thirsk, 'New crops and their diffusion in seventeenth century England', in *The rural economy of England*, London 1984, 259–85.
[36] BL, E842 (13), *Harry Hangman's honour: or, Gloucester-shire hangman's request to the smoakers or tobacconists in London*, 8; E. Adlard, *Winchcombe cavalcade*, London 1939, 32; GRO, D45/L19.
[37] Willcox, *Gloucestershire*, 10; C. Whitfield, *A history of Chipping Camden and Captain Robert Dover's olympick games*, Eton–Windsor 1958, 102–18.

varied as the Vale. Where the plateau dipped to the west lay a heavily arable region dominated by wheat and barley, whilst the limestone and clay belt from Chipping Campden to Marshfield was more mixed. In general, though, this was an arable, manorialised area, where the parishes were the largest in the county.[38] All but two of the settlements in the area bounded by Winchcombe, Moreton-in-Marsh, Lechlade and Tetbury were over 75 per cent nucleated. Industry was relatively scarce; between 54.2 and 68.5 per cent of men of recorded occupation in 1608 worked in agriculture in Kiftsgate, Brightwells Barrow, Rapsgate and Crowthorne and Minety Hundreds, where the folding system and the common fields still survived.[39]

Cotswold wool was generally woven in Cirencester and other Thames Valley towns, such as Tetbury, Fairford and Bisley, which looked to Wiltshire as much as Gloucestershire for customers. Cirencester, her economy long dominated by the closed weaver's company which, in the sixteenth century, had comprised some two-thirds of the county's weavers, had been hit particularly hard by the industry's shift to Stroudwater, and it was said that not a quarter of the area within the ancient walls was still occupied.[40]

The third distinctive region, the Forest of Dean, was sharply defined by the Severn and the Wye. It also gave its name to the division west of the Severn, although the two were not coterminous. The metes and bounds of the royal forest had varied over the years, but they were similar to those of St Briavel's Hundred. About half of the forest's 78,000 acres was still wooded in 1641. The rest, towards the Herefordshire border, consisted of heath and rough pasture, interspersed with mixed farming to the north-east.[41] Dean was not entirely a rural backwater, for there were market towns in Newent, Newnham, Westbury-on-Severn and Mitcheldean, and narrow cloths were made along the Hope Brook. Few contemporary travellers cared to visit notoriously lawless Dean. Thus they were prone to reproducing stock platitudes about the unique quality of the timber, the absurd myth that the Spanish Armada had been given special orders to burn it down and, later, that the iron industry was ruining the stock of timber.[42]

Although not exempt from county jurisdiction, the royal forest was a quasi-independent unit with its own officials, headed by the constable of St Briavel's and his verderers and regarders, who regulated its economic life through special courts. All men born within St Briavel's Hundred had the ancient prescriptive right to mine the rich coal and iron ore seams which lay under the forest, paying a token tax to the king and regulating themselves

[38] J. Johnson, Stow-on-the-Wold, Gloucester 1980, 364; Thirsk, Agrarian history, 177–8; Zweigman, 'County government', 15–16, 30–2.

[39] Hamilton, 'Patterns of settlement', 81–5, 124, 163–5; Tawney and Tawney, 'Occupational census', passim; Thirsk, Agrarian history, 177–8.

[40] Perry, 'Woollen industry', 93–5 and passim; Willcox, Gloucestershire, 11.

[41] Thirsk, Agrarian history, 177–8; C. E. Hart, 'The metes and bounds of the Forest of Dean', TBGAS lxvi (1945), 166–207.

[42] Fuller, Worthies, 349–51.

through the Minelaw Court. They defended their rights against all comers, and with increasing urgency, for, from the turn of the century, Dean had been transformed by the iron industry. With the development of the indirect method of casting, large, permanently operating furnaces and forges were erected for the first time and output increased rapidly. By 1641, some sixteen sites were operating in and around the forest and making about 6,000 tons of pig iron each year.[43]

This development inevitably drew in the cash-starved crown to seek ways of profiting from its hitherto neglected jurisdictional rights in the forest. Between 1611 and 1638, seven major concessions of varying quantities of woods, mines and ironworks were issued to, and withdrawn from, men of national and local importance, in a bewildering flurry of decrees, Exchequer suits, collusive actions and accusations. The net effect was certainly destructive of timber, though far less so than some contemporaries lamented. More impressively, all attempts at intensive exploitation were violently resisted by the small army of cottagers and squatters who lived in the forest and gleaned a meagre living from pasturing animals in the waste, selling their labour and taking wood. As Charles I's regime stepped up the pressure, so they responded with a series of semi-organised riots between 1628 and 1631, in which large crowds tore down enclosures, filled in charcoal pits and beat up the concessionaries' labourers.[44]

Exactly who the rioters were, the more 'respectable' inhabitants or the genuinely indigent artisans, is less clear than the effect of their continued defiance and the utter inability of county institutions to bring them to book. In the 1630s, concessions came and went quicker than ever; each was wrecked in part by the inhabitants' defiance and the crown executed a series of backflips in policy. In 1634, the first Forest Eyre in three centuries was held. Massive fines were levied on individuals of all social backgrounds for infringements of Forest Law, but the principle of protecting the timber was soon forgotten in what became yet another tawdry money-making expedient.[45]

Finally, in 1640, after violence had wrecked Edward Terringham's mines and grindstones concession, the government threw in its hand and agreed to a complete disafforestation in return for £10,000 and £16,000 per year for six years from the local Catholic courtier Sir John Wintour of Lydney, a long-time concessionary and ironmaster, who was bitterly detested in Gloucestershire. This grant was more important in terms of its effect on public opinion than on the Forest itself, for the outbreak of the Civil War prevented its full implementation, but the reaction in Gloucestershire and the nation demonstrated that

[43] Willcox, Gloucestershire, 179–92; C. E. Hart, The free miners of Dean forest, Gloucester 1975; G. F. Hammersley, 'The history of the iron industry in the Forest of Dean region, 1562–1660', unpubl. Ph.D. diss. London 1972, 10–40, 53.
[44] Willcox, Gloucestershire, 193–202; Sharp, In contempt, 175–219; Hammersley, 'Iron industry', 174–205.
[45] G. F. Hammersley, 'The revival of the Forest Laws under Charles I', History xlv (1960), 85–102.

over the course of one generation an area which had been quite marginal to county life under the Tudors had become the main concern, both in terms of public order and relations between 'court' and 'country'.

Social and political

Like every other county, pre-war Gloucestershire was governed mainly by resident gentlemen in their capacity as Justices of the Peace, sheriffs, deputy lieutenants and so forth. Exactly what defined a gentleman, particularly at the lower end of the scale where minor gentleman shaded into rich yeoman, is a matter of some dispute. Working from the common premise that a gentleman was anyone taken to be such by other people, Leslie Zweigman identifies 420 members of 325 families (excluding the Inshire) in the Caroline period. Of the 325, 132 lived in the Berkeley Division, about half that number in each of Seven Hundreds and Kiftsgate Divisions, and only twenty-four in the Forest Division. This was a historic trend, for in the fourteenth century most gentlemen had lived in the Vales, whilst two-thirds of all Cotswold vills had no resident lord.[46]

Since Norman times, the constant factor in county life had been the Berkeley barony, a concentrated bloc of manors around Berkeley Castle. Other medieval rivals – the Clare earls of Gloucester, the Beauchamps, the Giffords of Brimpsfield – had come and gone without ever eclipsing the Berkeleys for long. However, for nearly two hundred years prior to the Civil War, the ancient barony had been emasculated by a long-lived and sporadically violent feud against the Lisles and their heirs in a succession dispute, and by the folly of one marquis who bequeathed large tracts to the Tudors. The current Lord Berkeley hardly ever visited his estates and spent most of his life in London or abroad.[47]

Equally significantly, over half of the county's land, more than in any other, had belonged to monasteries. These included St Peter's Abbey in Gloucester, refounded as the dean and chapter in 1540, and others at Tewkesbury, Winchcombe, Cirencester and Hailes, beside priories at Llanthony and Kingswood, and a few smaller houses. The bulk of the land they owned was in the Cotswolds and the Vale of Evesham, with some around Gloucester and very little in the south. Inevitably, there was a major turnover in land over the course of the next century.[48]

---

[46] Zweigman, 'County government', 102–6, 743–4; N. E. Saul, 'The Gloucestershire gentry in the fourteenth century', unpubl. D.Phil. diss. Oxford 1978, 5–10; R. Hilton, A *medieval society*, London 1966, 90.

[47] Saul, 'Gloucestershire gentry', 8, 86–90; J. Johnson, *Tudor Gloucestershire*, Gloucester 1985, 60; J. N. Cooke, 'On the great Berkeley law suit of the fifteenth and sixteenth centuries: a chapter of Gloucestershire history', *TBGAS* iii (1878–9), 304–24.

[48] Hilton, *Medieval society*, 27–30; A. M. Moreton-Jackson, 'The dissolution of the monasteries in Worcestershire and Gloucestershire', unpubl. MA diss. Bristol 1978, 178, 201, 212.

The land was frequently resold and few descendants of the buyers still owned it in 1642 – the Tracys of Stanway being a prominent exception – and, of all the Caroline county gentry, only the Leighs of Adlestrop owed their position to monastic land alone. However, the dissolution did provide opportunities for enterprising gentlemen to add to their holdings. Most of the new gentry emerged from within the gentry class – the Tracys, for example, were a very ancient family, descended from one of the knights who murdered St Thomas à Becket.

The county was also a prime market for London money: Sir Thomas Leigh, lord mayor in 1558, Thomas Dutton, a surveyor of monastic lands, John Chamberlain, a diplomat, Nicholas Overbury, a judge, and Richard Master, Elizabeth I's physician, were some of those who acquired land, mostly in the Cotswolds, and whose descendants were still in the county elite in 1642. Others, such as the Brays of Great Barrington, moved in from other counties after acquiring the land.[49] The whole process militated against the development of a large gentry class in the Cotswolds, where large estates and absentee landlords remained the norm.

The market remained fairly lively into the Stuart period, not least because James I sold off much crown land in Gloucestershire. Families continued to settle here. Richard Colchester of Westbury-on-Severn, a former clerk in Chancery, arrived almost literally on the eve of the Civil War. Sir Robert Ducie, another former lord mayor of London, began buying manors soon after the heralds' visitation of 1623; his two sons played major roles in county life then died without heirs, leaving the estate to a Staffordshire junior line just before the 1682–3 visitation. And, of course, wealthy Bristol merchants were always buying land in the south.

Thus the century before the Civil War saw a change in the balance of the group of forty or fifty 'county' gentry families who filled the most prestigious offices. Their distribution over the shire became more even than that of the lesser gentry (who remained commoner in the Vales), and the greatest Cotswold men were at least on a par with their Vale counterparts; after the peers, the richest families were the Duttons of Sherborne and the Tracys of Toddington.[50]

Above all, with the permanent absence of George, Lord Berkeley, while John Smyth ran his estates, the county lacked a natural leader. The only resident peer, George, Lord Chandos of Sudeley, had barely achieved his majority in 1642. Sir Baptist Hicks's death had left a void, for his son-in-law and heir, Lord Noel, never lived in the county. The pre-war lords lieutenant were the Compton earls of Northampton – absentee courtiers, crippled by debt

[49] Johnson, *Tudor Gloucestershire*, 62; Moreton-Jackson, 'Dissolution', 229–30.
[50] VCH, *Glos*. x. 172–4; GRO, D36/A1; Willcox, *Gloucestershire*, 136–8, 199–200; Zweigman, 'County government', 136–8, 199–200.

and of limited influence as they tried vainly to exhort the county to obedience from London.

Much land in the north of the county was owned by Worcestershire men, such as Lord Coventry, Lord Craven and Lord Windsor, Richard Dowdeswell of Bushley, and, especially, the fabulously rich earl of Worcester and several junior branches of his family. Viscount Saye and Sele was a leading 'opposition' figure with lands at Norton, where his tenants paid for his grand gesture in opposing ship money. But no-one, resident or non-resident, was influential over the whole county or had any monopoly of contacts with the centre. Of the courtiers among the gentry, Sir Ralph Dutton of Standish and Henry Brett of Hatherley were not rich enough, and the only man whose wealth and influence made him a potential leading figure, Wintour, was ruled out by his Catholicism.[51]

County leadership thus devolved on a floating group of major gentry families. In terms of seats in Parliament, the most prominent were the Tracys, the Duttons, the Stephenses of Eastington, the Cookes of Highnam, the Poyntzes of Iron Acton, the Berkeleys of Rendcomb and Stoke Gifford, the Pooles of Sapperton and the Masters of Cirencester, but plenty of others were their near-equals. Most were *rentiers*, living off their lands and exploiting them increasingly intensively in the Caroline period, but, in a diversified county, the gentry also invested in timber and iron, cloth and tobacco. Many in the cloth-making region, including Nathaniel Stephens, maintained contact with the industry which had made their ancestors' fortunes. The leading gentlemen were closely inter-related. More than 50 per cent married Gloucestershire women and only 20 per cent looked beyond contiguous counties for brides. Even more of the lesser gentry married at home.[52]

W. B. Willcox's reliance on Star Chamber records in his study of pre-war Gloucestershire may lead him to overemphasise the violence and corruption in local society, but it is undoubtedly true that the county administration was often unable or unwilling to cope with the ever-increasing demands thrust upon it. A short survey such as this cannot probe the complexities of the issues of the 1620s and 1630s. However, the gentry of Gloucestershire had more reason than most to resent the Stuart regime. Most of the public order problems which they were expected to deal with as JPs and sheriffs were either the direct result of, or at least exacerbated by, crown policy.

James I's support for the Cockayne Project in 1621 had ended with thousands of unemployed clothworkers wandering the county, begging and stealing. In the 1630s, attempts to enforce quality control regulations, at the behest of

[51] Ibid. 94–100; R. P. Cust, *The forced loan and English politics, 1626–1628*, Oxford 1987, 117–18, 136–7; Willcox, *Gloucestershire*, 128–30.
[52] Williams, *Parliamentary history*, 49–53; Zweigman, 'County government', 231–300; Tann, 'Gloucestershire woollen industry', 137–8.

the Merchant Adventurers or others in the trade, by banning tenter frames, gig mills and mozing mills, or even casual spinners, brought that nightmare prospect close again. Likewise, the JPs were expected to risk their necks by cutting down the tobacco which some of them grew on their own lands and which kept the poor at work, for the sake of planters in far-off Virginia. Sheriffs and JPs were also required to lead the militia against violent rioters in Dean for the sake of Catholic and courtier entrepreneurs, and received nothing but scorn from the Privy Council for their efforts.[53]

The government also made heavy demands on the provinces during the wars of the late 1620s and the Personal Rule of Charles I. Gloucestershire was one of four counties where resistance to the forced loan of 1626-8 was strongest, and it was the major gentry, in their roles as commissioners, who led the county in obstruction or outright refusal to pay the loan. Nathaniel Stephens, Sir Robert Poyntz and John Dutton were among the most prominent resisters. For this reason, Stephens and Poyntz were sent to the 1628 Parliament as the county's MPs. Edward Stephens of Little Sodbury took his resistance to knighthood composition fines to a test case, and seven other leading gentlemen, including John Dutton, Nathaniel Stephens and Richard Berkeley of Rendcomb, also refused to compound. Billeting and the pressing of soldiers were added burdens.[54]

Resistance to the fiscal innovations of Charles I reached a high point after ship money was extended to the whole county in 1635. It is not proposed to summarise the course of the resistance here, as it has been dealt with at length in another study. But some points stand out. Again, the county gentry, other than the hapless sheriffs, used their offices and authority to lead the resistance. The method of assessment by traditional rating scales, but allowing sheriffs discretion to tax real wealth, was a minefield of potential disputes and resentment as communities tried to avoid the burden. All three major boroughs and Chipping Campden complained of unfair rating, and the Inshire dispute was predictably exacerbated.

Above all, while the county was not united in its response, the differences did not correspond to the future Civil War division. In 1635 the future Parliamentarian, Edward Stephens, was a conscientious sheriff, trying to deal with resistance led by Henry Poole, Sir William Master and Sir Edmund Bray, who were two future Royalists and the father of another. As Charles's regime collapsed after the failure of his Scottish wars in 1639-40, John Codrington of Didmarton, a future Parliamentarian, finished £1,200 short on his account in January 1640, and Sir Humphrey Tracy, one of the county's most zealous

53 Perry, 'Woollen industry', 121-34; Tann, 'Gloucestershire woollen industry', 173-87; Willcox, Gloucestershire, 158-71, 193-202; Thirsk, 'New crops', 279-81; Sharp, In contempt, 179-215.
54 Cust, Forced loan, 117-18, 136-7, 217-18, 230, 255, 289; Zweigman, 'County government', 470-89.

Royalists, collected barely £100 out of £6,000 assessed before the Long Parliament outlawed the tax. If there was any time when the county should have been united as a county, it was in early 1640, as excitement grew all over the nation about the meeting of the first Parliament in eleven years.[55]

[55] M. D. Gordon, 'The collection of ship money in the reign of Charles I', *TRHS* 3rd ser. iv (1910); Zweigman, 'County government', 500–37.

2

Cavaliers and Roundheads, 1640–1644

A county community?
From the Short Parliament election to the fall of Cirencester

There is an excellent account of the county's Short Parliament election of March 1640 in a letter from John Allibond, a Laudian prebendary of Gloucester Cathedral, to a colleague in London. Allibond was biased and regarded the divisions among the gentry with malicious glee but he was clearly well-informed. There was a tradition, followed in four of the five elections of the 1620s, that of the two shire MPs one should be of the Vale and one of the Cotswolds, and an attempt was made to arrange this again now, engineered by two prominent figures of Vale and Cotswold respectively, Sir Maurice Berkeley and John Dutton. At the assizes, the gentry, 'who, you know, usually sway the plebeians', chose Sir Robert Cooke, a well-known religious radical who lived at Highnam, near Gloucester, and Sir Robert Tracy, whose Toddington estates were in the heart of the Cotswolds. (It is quite wrong to regard Cooke as any sort of representative of a legal–mercantile interest. Like Tracy, he was a landed gentleman and had no ties with the city of Gloucester.)[1]

Several other candidates had already been suggested. In December 1639 Lord Berkeley, prodded by a courtier, suggested Sir Baynham Throckmorton of Clowerwall in Newland as a possibility, but left it to the discretion of John Smyth and Sir Maurice Berkeley. By February 1640 he was more insistent on Sir Ralph Dutton, the favoured choice of the earl of Pembroke and a man already notorious for his pro-court views. Sir Maurice Berkeley had written to Smyth at the outset, asking him not to declare his views until the candidates were known, so that they might 'join together in one voice'. But it seems that a contest was always feared. Cooke found '[th]e confidence of it much inter-rupted by iealousies and unexpected canvasings' and he went to Cirencester in February 1640, hoping to patch them over.[2]

On election day, with a large crowd present, a cry suddenly went up for Nathaniel Stephens, the popular hero who had been ejected from the commis-sion of the peace and imprisoned for opposing ship money, 'with . . . much zeale

---

[1] Allibond to Dr Peter Heylin, 24 Mar. 1640, SP 16/448 fo. 79 (*CSPD* 1639–40, 580–3); Williams, *Parliamentary history*, 51–3; Cooke to Smyth, 24 Feb. 1640, GRO, D2510/8; Rollison, *Local origins*, 138–48.
[2] Lord Berkeley to Smyth, 21 Dec. 1639, 18 Feb. 1640, Glos. Pub. Lib., Smyth of Nibley papers, x. 99, 100v; ii. 90; Sir Maurice Berkeley to Smyth, 2 Dec. 1639, ibid. ii. 89; GRO, D2510/8.

towards the zealous, so much indeared to the vulgar That now He is cryed up with no lesse Ardour and Fervencye then if He Had bene lately dropped out of the Clouds for the purpose'. Seeing some of Cooke's supporters 'stickling' for Stephens, Allibond was sure that Cooke had been party to a plot, or that he had at least failed to put in any effort to win their votes for Tracy. With Tracy absent ill, his allies duly voted for him and Cooke, whilst Cooke's second votes went to Stephens.

Thus Tracy brought Cooke 800 votes 'and receyved not twenty back agayne'. The first day ended in confusion. Next day Tracy himself came down and '[John] Dutton spares not to tell [Cooke] openly: That for his sake he would never more trust any Man that wore his Hayre shorter than his Eares.' Dutton then rounded on Stephens's cousin, Edward Stephens, 'of fayre esteem (but a favourer of the pretending holy side)', who explained – probably truthfully – that he had heard a rumour that Sir Ralph Dutton might stand with Tracy.

The present sheriff, however, was 'a nere kinsman' of Tracy's, Sir Humphrey Tracy of Stanway, who 'not onely putt backe divers of Stevens his voyces . . . but . . . continued the election to Winchcomb . . . well scituated for the apparancy of the rest of Tracyes strength & inconveneient for the repayre of Stevens his'. Here the election of Cooke and Tracy was steam-rollered through, even then by only 100 votes after four days, amidst continuing popular pressure, some of it violent, for Stephens.[3]

Taking their cue from Allibond, some historians have pronounced Cooke guilty of a trick.[4] They may be right, but the calendaring of the letter is misleading and underplays Allibond's cynicism. For instance, it omits to say that Cooke had written to Sir Maurice Berkeley beforehand to say that there was no need to bring his retinue as all was in hand. These men, freed from any obligation to their lord, duly went along to vote for Stephens. 'This perhaps might be a mistake & not malice in S[ir] Ro[bert] Cooke; but all his actions are now looked uppon by the other side with a not-Excusing Eye, it is apprehended not an oversight but a practice of Treachery.'[5]

We have seen that Cooke had already tried to smooth over some difficulties. He sent another letter to Smyth shortly before the election – it is endorsed 'late at night Tuesday', and Allibond says that polling began on a Wednesday – saying that he had been advised 'by my chiefe friends vpon some passages this night, not to lose any voyces [tha]t I may obteine in this streight of time', and begged Smyth to get as many as possible out.[6] Far from being in a plot, then, Cooke was worried that the popular tide for Stephens might damage his own prospects. Of course, Stephens's campaign could not be kept a secret –

3 SP 16/448, fo. 79.
4 A. J. Fletcher, 'National and local awareness in the county communities', in H. Tomlinson (ed.), Before the English Civil War, London 1983, 164–5; J. K. Gruenfelder, 'The election to the Short Parliament, 1640', in H. S. Reinmuth (ed.), Early Stuart studies, Minneapolis 1970, 211; Zweigman 'County government', 585.
5 SP 16/448, fo. 79.
6 Cooke to Smyth, undated, Smyth of Nibley papers, xvi. 13.

especially not if it was orchestrated by eleven Puritan clerics, as Allibond believed. Cooke may have done a last-minute deal. More significantly, popular pressure outweighed the gentry's wish for a closed contest. Since Tracy would have come a long way third on the first day with at least 800 votes, the overall turnout, allowing for single votes, may have been as high as 5,000.[7]

The essential problem was that, like Allibond, the Cotswold gentry behind Tracy did not understand that the Vale freeholders were not simply ballot-fodder like their own tenants. In the light of new evidence, it is impossible to see Sir Humphrey Tracy's act, as Mark Kishlansky apparently does, as an honest attempt to resolve the deadlock. It was *force majeure* pure and simple. Before adjourning, he had repeatedly postponed polls, taken only Tracy votes and told Stephens's supporters 'cry "Stephens" as long as you will, Stephens shall not have it'. His Cotswold allies were no more understanding. Sir Edward Bathurst of Lechlade threatened a troublemaker with conscription into the royal army and 'Cald one "cropeard knave" that said he was for Stephens and struck him'; John George of Baunton threatened to deny poor relief to Cirencester. Parliament was still debating Stephens's protest when it was dissolved in May.[8]

Superficially, the Long Parliament election of October looks like a return to normality, with Cooke tactfully standing elsewhere and Stephens and John Dutton being elected unopposed. In fact, there was almost as much election-eering as before. Stephens's win was taken for granted, but other candidates were again suggested. Cooke wondered if '[th]e Country may be perswaded to cast their vote upon S[i]r Maurice Berkly', or whoever else 'you [Smyth] incline to have ioyned wth Mr Stephens'.[9] Apparently they could not, but it is notable that at least Cooke, the man of the Vales, realised that votes had to be sought and won.

Another potentially very strong candidate was Sir Humphrey Tracy, who wrote to Smyth on 18 September asking for support and saying that he had been asked to stand by the gentry of Kiftsgate Division. Smyth kept a copy of his carefully worded reply. He assured Tracy of his affection but regretted that his support was already spoken for, 'and indeede had there bin noe such ingagement our parts . . . would not be p[er]swaded . . . to vote otherwise'. Tracy should not stand, if at all, with one of his own division, for he would find 'these parts out of former respects to oppose'. He might win with a Vale man 'by mutual castinge of voyces one uppon the other', but even then 'you will finde the p[ar]ty pertainige to Mr Stephens . . . strongly to oppose in these p[ar]ts . . . (with whom I mak question you will wyne . . .)'.[10] Tracy took the point and

[7]   D. Hirst, *The representative of the people? Voters and voting in England under the early Stuarts*, Cambridge 1975, 279n.
[8]   *The Short Parliament (1640) diary of Sir Thomas Aston*, ed. J. T. Maltby (Camden 4th ser. xxxv, 1988), 156; *CJ* ii. 4, 6, 7; M. A. Kishlansky, *Parliamentary selection: social and political choice in early modern England*, Cambridge 1986, 65 and passim; Rollison, *Local origins*, 138–48.
[9]   Cooke to Smyth, 28 Oct. 1640, GRO, D2510/10.
[10]   Tracy to Smyth, 18 Sept. [1640], Smyth of Nibley papers, xvi. 24.

stood down. He was wholly unsuitable in view of recent events. As late as 28 October, a week before the Long Parliament opened, Cooke was still looking for 'a suspension ere they come into the field', and on 18 November, Lord Berkeley was making a second recommendation of Sir Ralph Dutton, so the election must have ended very late indeed.[11] The vast cultural and religious gulf between the Vale and the Cotswolds had clearly brought about a state of mutual incomprehension. Allibond overheard many comments

> That Sir Ro[bert] Tracy should scorne to be webbed and loomed (in Relation to Stevens his pedigree; fetched not many generations from Clothiers) & Mr Dutton should complayne That Never was any Man so over-reached by Weavers; & receyved answer That Weavers might well enough ranke with Shephards ... they have divided the Countrey into Cotteswold-Shephards and the Vale Weavers.

The very falsehood of these stereotypes – for the Stephenses had been gentry for centuries and Dutton was the descendant of a Henrician official who bought monastic land – suggests their enduring strength.[12] It is certainly striking that the principle of unified choice, which was supposed to keep plebeians out of politics, prevailed in November to elect the man thrust on the gentry by popular pressure in March.

The borough elections were almost as lively, except in Cirencester where the Puritan John George of Baunton was returned on both occasions. Despite his court connections, he was an active Parliamentarian at first, but his capture at the sack of Cirencester forced him to change sides. Both of his colleagues, first Henry Poole of Sapperton and then Sir Theobald Gorges of Astley, Wiltshire, were Royalists. However, both George and Poole had resisted ship money and came from families with strong connections in the borough.[13]

Gloucester's long record of independence from aristocratic interference and her recurrent populist tradition were both reasserted. A local gentleman, Henry Brett of Hatherley, won each time with an alderman; firstly William Singleton, then the radical Thomas Pury, who had been rejected first time around. Pury was already a figure of loathing amongst local friends of the court. The recorder, William Lenthall, who was rejected both times, complained on the second occasion that despite the aldermen's assurances 'the Corporation is so great and the pace of election so popular that I have no assurance of election there' and he later claimed that a poll was denied him when he asked for it. Popular pressure evidently played a major part in both decisions.[14]

Tewkesbury's elections were peculiar. In March the Sussex Cavalier Sir

---

[11] GRO, D2510/10; Lord Berkeley to Smyth, 18 Nov. 1640, Smyth of Nibley papers, ii. 90.
[12] SP 16/448, fo. 79; VCH, Glos. x. 178; Johnson, Tudor Gloucestershire, 67; Rollison, Local origins, 138–48.
[13] Williams, Parliamentary history, 156–8.
[14] Berkshire Record Office, D/EL 10.5/12, cited in Gruenfelder, 'Gloucester's elections', 53–9; CJ ii. 43; SP 16/448, fo. 79.

Edward Alford and Sir Anthony Ashley Cooper, the future earl of Shaftesbury, were chosen. The latter was picked, by his own account, in gratitude for his gracious demeanour and his defence of the town bailiffs against some insulting remarks made by Sir Henry Spiller at a hunt and dinner given by the town magnates in honour of neighbouring gentry. Both were relatives of the powerful Hicks family, whose patronage in the borough was extensive, and Cooper was also the son-in-law of Lord Coventry. However the corporation rejected the son of their neighbour, the earl of Middlesex 'out of care for the common good'. The town clerk, William Hill, who was also Middlesex's steward, explained that 'an extraordinary care is taken in elections at this time, when religion is so much concerned and the good of the commonwealth never more so'. Middlesex's son-in-law, Lord Sheffield, might do better, Hill ventured, for he was 'seasoned timber'.[15]

In the event, even Hill misread the general feeling for Sheffield too was rejected. By November, popular pressure was mounting and there was a great dispute as one bailiff returned Alford and John Craven, the other Sir Robert Cooke and Edward Stephens. The problem arose because 'we admitted some freeholders to give voices and not resolved whether the election should be by freemen only or all the inhabitants (except almsmen)'. As a result, the Commons quashed both elections and imprisoned one of the bailiffs, Thomas Hale.[16]

In a second election in October 1641, the bailiffs returned Cooke and Alford, the inhabitants Cooke and Stephens, setting off a lively debate until Alford, who chose to serve for Arundel instead, was declared unelected in 1643. Cooke died in October 1643, and he was replaced, in 1645, by yet another Stephens, John of Lypiatt in Stroud. The struggle among the gentry to secure places and patronage in Tewkesbury, coupled with serious economic problems, caused the long-running battle between the corporation and the populace over the franchise to boil over, as the freemen chose distinctly more radical men on each occasion.[17]

In shire and boroughs alike the electors' attitudes towards the government hardened between the two elections, just as they did throughout the nation. It is far from clear that the elections were fought between established 'court' and 'country' parties under the Stephens and Tracy families, but hostility to men with any connections in government was fierce. Nathaniel Stephens and John Dutton were probably returned to the Long Parliament as the fiercest opponents of ship money, rather than as embodiments of particular religious outlooks.

15 Redmond, 'Tewkesbury', 233–4; K. H. D. Haley, *The first earl of Shaftesbury*, Oxford 1968, 33–7; HMC, 4th Report, appendix, 30; Hill to Middlesex, 15 Dec. 1639, 13 Feb. 1640, Kent Record Office, MSS Sackville (u).
16 GRO, D2688 (unfol.), 1640; CJ ii. 23, 32, 44, 333.
17 Williams, *Parliamentary history*, 237; CJ iii. 337, 352; *The journal of Sir Simonds d'Ewes*, ed. W. H. Coates, Yale 1970, 126–7; Hirst, *Representative of the people?*, 209–10.

It is of equal importance that all the MPs were locals, and all bar Gorges were from the county and supported the early measures of the Long Parliament. Their cohesiveness in Parliament until 1643 and the county's late entry into the war disguised just how seriously divided the gentry were. Many future Royalists – notably Sir John Wintour, Sir Ralph Dutton and the Tracys – were already marked out. The Tracys' position was very compromised. Sir Humphrey had been an energetic ship money sheriff, using his own men to collect the tax, though without success. Meanwhile, Sir Robert Tracy was communicating local events to the court via Viscount Conway. Both contributed to the cause before the battle of Edgehill signalled that the slide towards war was complete, and Sir Robert sent his son to the king's army soon after.[18]

Ship money was not Sir Humphrey's only problem as sheriff. Efforts to raise men for the Second Bishops War collapsed as coat-and-conduct money went unpaid and the men deserted. Those who actually marched twice came close to creating anti-Catholic disturbances in July, before mutinying and coming home.[19]

The first session of the Long Parliament was spent sweeping away the relics of Charles's Personal Rule, but there was also time for other business. Gloucester petitioned against Bishop Goodman in February 1641, as did some of his consistory court's victims, while Pury's speech against episcopacy not only catalogued many grievances against the chapter but also suggested a well-thought-out set of alternative uses for its revenues. Stow-on-the-Wold and Chipping Campden petitioned against oppressive lords, while Winchcombe, Painswick, Bisley and Minchinhampton brought actions against immoral, inadequate or Arminian clerics.[20]

The MPs of the 'Four Shires' (Gloucestershire, Herefordshire, Worcestershire and Shropshire), worked together to shake off the authority of the Council in the Marches of Wales. This was a longstanding grievance in the region, and two men who tried to serve a Council writ on Nathaniel Stephens were hauled up before the Commons. In Parliament itself, most of the county's MPs were busy, and the future parliamentarian leaders, Cooke, Nathaniel Stephens and Pury, were particularly active and radical.[21]

Most men at this time rarely distinguished 'local' from 'national' issues. For Gloucestershire men, they were often the same, as the county's chief concern was also one of John Pym's bêtes noires: Sir John Wintour and the bargain of 1640 which seemingly made the Forest of Dean his private fiefdom. Indeed, this matter was part of the Grand Remonstrance in November 1641. Wintour's

---

[18] CSPD 1640, 213, 302, 568, 617; 1640–1, 25, 83, 143.
[19] Ibid. 256, 492, 497.
[20] CJ ii 83; HMC, 4th Report, MSS House of Lords, 1640–1, 26, 110; BL, E198 (21), Mr *Thomas Pury Alderman of Glocester his speech.*
[21] CJ ii; LJ v passim; *The private journals of the Long Parliament, 3 January to 5 March 1642,* ed. W. H. Coates, A. S. Young and V. F. Snow, New Haven 1982, 120, 265, 439 and passim.

rival, Sir Baynham Throckmorton, feared that it enabled him 'to make a plantation of papists upon it and to have so great a power to command thereby over all that country'. There was also great general concern about the destruction of timber in the forest. Pury pursued the issue through the Commons until Wintour surrendered the bargain in March 1642.[22]

In June 1641 Nathaniel Stephens presented a petition from the inhabitants of Dean, who had intercepted two cartloads of arms leaving Wintour's house; he claimed he was sending them to an unnamed JP with the king's permission.[23] But this apart, Gloucestershire does not apppear to have shared the wilder aspects of the anti-Catholic mania that swept the country. Perhaps attention focused on Wintour and the earl of Worcester at Raglan Castle as more immediate, practical problems. Pury for one was scared that the Monmouthshire Catholics might have designs on Gloucester. Via Bristol, the county was open to first-hand accounts of the horrors of the Irish Catholic rebellion. Indeed, some Irish widows were found begging at Chipping Sodbury in 1641.[24]

Another major issue, which reflected national grievances and exacerbated local divisions, was the prosecution before the House of Lords of Sir Ralph Dutton for crimes committed as a deputy lieutenant when raising coat and conduct money. The case involved unjust levies, embezzlement and the taking of bribes. In July 1641 he was convicted before a panel of seven JPs, and the Lords' Committee of Petitions ordered a strict restitution to be made and new accounts rendered. Dutton alleged that witnesses were 'tampered with' and depositions 'unfairly taken' and it may well be that a feud with Cooke, whose relatives led the prosecution, lay at the root of it.[25]

Meanwhile, the county itself remained under the control of the major gentlemen in their roles as deputy lieutenants. It is unclear just how effective this control was. On a non-divisive issue, such as making donations to relieve Irish Protestants, they could tap popular enthusiasm to good effect. Returns survive only for Longtree Hundred but they seem generous. The average donation among more than 939 entries, even when omitting the gentry, is between 11d. and 2s. 6d. in every parish bar Rodmarton, Avening and Cherington (which did not have substantial resident gentlemen to give a lead), while the most generous were Shipton Moyne and Woodchester which did.[26]

In individual cases, the deputy lieutenants could move rapidly and effectively. When, at the assizes in May 1641, a minister was heard to say that the Commons had executed the earl of Strafford 'for feare he should doe some of [the]m hurt', an alert constable and the presence of John George saw him

22 Throckmorton to Thomas Smyth, 14 June 1641, Bristol Record Office, 36074/136e.
23 CJ ii. 489 and passim; Bodl. Lib., MS Rawlinson D1099, fo. 37v.
24 Fletcher, *Outbreak*, chs i–iii; *Private journals*, 120; GRO, D2071/A3, fo. 6.
25 LJ iv, passim.
26 SP 28/191 (unfol.).

30

packed off to the Committee for Scandalous Ministers in no time.[27] Popular action was sporadic and took many different forms, but enthusiasm for settling scores with unpopular supporters of the regime was clearly widespread. In Dean, Wintour's enclosures were torn down, and the commoners swore they would do this again as often as necessary and 'turn in their cattle as they were wont to do before'. At Forthampton, Middlesex's tenants seized the opportunity, starting in 1642, to destroy his deer park and withhold rents.[28]

G. A. Harrison praises the county defence scheme which led to regular meetings of the gentry and freeholders in each division to raise troops, arms and subscriptions, discuss important matters and keep an eye on the disaffected.[29] But in reality this system had barely come to life before 1642, and looks more like a partisan attempt to hold the lid down on a divided gentry community. John Smyth junior (whose father, the historian, died in the spring of 1641) was seriously alienated by the 'pulpit discourses' that labelled those who differed from the prevailing mood 'papists, common drunkards, base and lewde livers', and he alleged that certain Puritan clerics were taking the names of those who subscribed a counter-petition in the hope of seeing them brought to book.[30]

In other ways, popular activism outran the system's ability or willingness to use it. Smyth was amazed at the attendance at the Thornbury meetings and he was assured that there was equal enthusiasm in Kiftsgate and the Seven Hundreds, yet he failed to raise the small quota of dragoons required from Berkeley Division for the defence of Cirencester in December 1641. John George, for one, said that he was not surprised at the popular frustration with bad leadership, castigating '[th]e colde and dilatorie p[ro]ceedings' of those in charge, for exposing the county 'to ruyne & Slaverye'.[31]

Gloucestershire had been one of nineteen counties to present a 'root and branch' petition against episcopacy, now lost, with some 3,000 signatures, which Pury and Nathaniel Stephens delivered in February 1641.[32] By December a group of gentlemen who met at Cirencester were circulating a pro-episcopacy petition among their friends. Brushing aside the issue of *iure divino* episcopacy, it stated that it was sufficient that the present form of church government was ancient and called it the best since the apostles' times, asking that only the 'wittinglie and malitiousely guilty' be weeded out. Significantly, nine of the ten signatories were future Royalists. The two sides were already

[27] BL, MS Harleian 477, fo. 106; CJ ii. 159.
[28] LJ iv. 219; M. Prestwich, *Cranfield: politics and profits under the early Stuarts*, Oxford 1966, 569.
[29] G. A. Harrison, 'Royalist organisation in Gloucestershire and Bristol, 1641–1646', unpubl. MA diss. Manchester 1961, 29–55.
[30] Smyth to Mr Jones, undated, Smyth of Nibley papers, xi. 1.
[31] George to Smyth, 9 Dec. 1641, GRO, D2510/12.
[32] Fletcher, *Outbreak*, 92–3; *Two diaries of the Long Parliament*, ed. M. Jansson, Gloucester 1984, 33.

working separately; the signatories of a letter of 6 December about placing dragoons in Cirencester were almost all future Parliamentarians.[33]

Church government was not just an elite issue, for in Tewkesbury quite humble men were contending over it just as fiercely as their betters in 1642. Like the Gloucester man who abused the men who were removing pictures from his parish church and swore 'That the Parliament was not worth a Turd', some of them found themselves hauled up before the Commons and reminded in the most direct way that local issues were not divorced from national.[34] At the same time, between January and March 1642, weekly meetings were held and subscriptions taken to the Protestation. Although these do not survive, there is evidence of popular enthusiasm in that 400 are said to have subscribed at Tewkesbury alone.[35]

Between January and August 1642, all but two of forty English counties sent broadly similar petitions up to Parliament in defence of its achievements. The exceptions were Cumberland, which sent nothing, and Gloucestershire, which chose, in January, to address the king. There is no obvious reason for this, nor any telling whose views it represents, nor even that it is a genuine local document, although it does state that many of the subscribers had been ruined by the decay of trade. The writers lamented that they were still burdened with heavy taxes and ecclesiastical authority due to the continuing divisions between king and Commons. This they blamed squarely on 'whisperers and flatterers' for breeding the mistrust that caused the king's attempted arrest of the 'Five Members' on 4 January. They asked that the 'Five Members' might enjoy their privileges and that grievances be discussed.[36]

As a result of the deepening crisis, Gloucester's cautious rulers began to stockpile arms and repair the walls. But not until Charles's departure to York and rival attempts to raise forces did the provinces have a new issue to react to, and there were no more initiatives until the summer. From June, like their counterparts elsewhere, the county's MPs were being sent home to organise local forces, a double burden in an under-represented county. It was Gloucester, however, which began exercising the volunteer regiments raised from April onwards, although some 'did, with threatening words, discourage them'.[37]

Meanwhile, in June, Charles attempted to remodel the commissions of the peace, a move which could not be put into effect but which shows who were regarded as his enemies. In Gloucestershire he removed thirteen JPs, comprising the known opposition figures but also Sir William Master, and added three

[33] BL, MS Add. 11,055, fo. 130v; deputy lieutenants to Smyth, 6, 15 Dec. 1641, GRO, D2510/11, 13.

[34] *Private journals*, 418, 486; CJ ii. 442, 461, 486.

[35] Francis Creswicke to Smyth, 7 Feb. 1642, GRO, D2510/15; Harrison, 'Royalist organisation in Gloucestershire', 34.

[36] BL, E133 (7), *To the king's most excellent maiestie the humble petition of . . . Glocester*; CJ ii. 237, 589; Fletcher, *Outbreak*, 192, 223. Tewkesbury sent its own petition to the Commons in support of their measures.

[37] GRO, GBR, B3/2, fos 220–5; CJ ii. 516, 635, 641, 668, 673, 675, 719.

– George Kenn (who was insubstantial and no Royalist), Sir Robert Tracy and, with astonishing tactlessness, Sir Ralph Dutton.[38]

Even though conflict was raging in nearly every neighbouring county, the raising of the volunteers under professional commanders had been the limit of the deputy lieutenants' endeavours. The Militia Ordinance had not been executed nor much else done before August, when Lord Chandos came to Cirencester to enforce the king's Commission of Array. The first commission, published in June and proclaimed in several boroughs in July, was a roll-call of the county's leading Royalists, including both Tracys, both Duttons, Sir Robert Poyntz, Throckmorton, and Richard and Sir Maurice Berkeley. Chandos had been named lord lieutenant by Parliament in February. At first he had supported Parliament's measures, but concern soon grew about his unwillingness to go to London. However, a decision to replace him with Say and Sele had not been carried out before the news from Cirencester was known in London.[39]

The gentry were divided and uncertain, but some common people were already accustomed to taking the initiative; not a week before, 300 Bristol men and some 250 to 300 of the Gloucestershire volunteers had helped the Clubmen of Wiltshire and Somerset chase the marquis of Hertford from the Mendips.[40] Now Chandos called a gentry meeting at the Ram Inn, Cirencester. In response, about a thousand of the volunteers (including the tenants of some of Chandos's cohorts, whose estates dominated the area) turned out to help fortify the town with posts and chains. At length, Chandos was allowed in to dine with the JPs, having sworn he had not come to execute the commission, but trouble erupted again that evening. Some soldiers forced him and Sir Robert Tracy to sign a document swearing to 'maintaine the Power and Priviledge of Parliament and the Laws and Liberties of the Subject with his Life & Fortune'.

Even then, some were unsatisfied and pressed him further. Next day, the terrified Chandos had Sir William Master smuggle him out. The troops tore his coach to pieces, to the alarm of John Corbet, the Puritan minister who was to be the main historian of the unfolding drama. Indeed, those who knew these gentlemen best were the most violent, for 'the Townsmen were a meanes to save the Lord Chadoys life who else might have been torne in peeces by the inraged Country people'.[41]

This debacle set off a flurry of activity. Gloucester increased its vigilance, and was given permission to muster troops independently and to set up a

38 PRO, C231/5, fo. 528.
39 Northamptonshire Record Office MS, Finch-Hatton 133; A&O i. 1–4; HMC, 12th Report, part ix (records of the corporation of Gloucester), 490–5; CJ ii. 424, 667, 712.
40 BL, E111(5), *A perfect relation of all the passages and proceedings of the marquesse of Hartford*, 12 Aug. 1642.
41 John Corbet, *Historical relation of the military government of Gloucester*, 7, in *Bibliotheca Gloucestrensis*, ed. J. Washbourne, London 1823; BL, E113 (5), *A letter . . . concerning the Lord Shandois*, dates the incident to 15 August, but *LJ* v. 306, which is probably more reliable, places it on the 9th.

committee of defence.[42] Cooke and Nathaniel Stephens were despatched by Parliament to Gloucester with Instructions similar to those issued in other counties and a list of twenty-five deputy lieutenants for the county and seven for the Inshire to execute them. Throckmorton was removed, as he was already in the king's camp, and the Inshire group were parliamentarian, but the main list comprised one neuter, eleven Parliamentarians and thirteen Royalists – including two who had ridden with Chandos. By contrast, only one of the commissioners of array became a Parliamentarian.[43] Was the king's information that much better, or, more likely, did waverers find his personal appeal to their loyalty that much harder to resist?

The Instructions aimed to integrate local defence initiatives such as this with the cause of Parliament; the deputy lieutenants were to execute the Militia Ordinance and that of 8 August for the suppression of Hertford's 'rebellion', prevent any other forces arising in the county, levy and lead forces according to the directions of the earl of Essex and disarm suspects. The active deputy lieutenants and militia commissioners of 1642, indeed, the active committeemen in the early days of 1643, were the same small group: Cooke, Nathaniel Stephens, Pury and Thomas Hodges, plus Sir John Seymour of Bitton, John Fettiplace of Coln St Aldwyns and Sir Giles Overbury of Bourton-on-the-Hill – a man with a family grudge against the Stuarts. The king's proclamation in February 1643, a fair guide to activism, exempted only five of the local MPs from a general pardon to those who laid down arms, as well as Cooke's son, William, and Jeremy Buck of Minchinhampton. Leslie Zweigman stresses the role of Say and Sele, but there is no clear evidence of his presence in the county at any time.[44]

Cooke and the Stephenses organised a meeting on 25 August which made sixteen propositions for the county's safety. These did more than echo the Instructions (as Harrison says) but neither does this scheme fall into Fletcher's category of 'defensive arrangements that were agreed by a broad spectrum of the gentry and put into effect under nominal allegiance to one side or the other'. It was a partisan move, applying the principles of the Instructions to suit local needs, with particular stress on the role of the gentry in each division. There is no evidence of consensus gentry support for it. Those present agreed to submit to the Militia Ordinance, entertain three commanders and raise 240 horse per division, plus more volunteer foot and dragoons.[45]

The magazine was placed at Cirencester and everything was co-ordinated by large divisional meetings and fortnightly general meetings at Gloucester.

[42] GRO, GBR B3/2, fo. 221; J. K. G. Taylor, 'The civil government of Gloucester, 1640–1646', *TBGAS* lxvii (1968), 75–6.

[43] *CJ* ii. 719–21. Washbourne, *Historical introduction*, 22, mistakenly dates the commission to 25 July.

[44] *LJ* v. 291–3; *Stuart royal proclamations*, II: *Royal proclamations of King Charles I, 1625–1646*, ed. J. F. Larkin, Oxford 1983, 812–13; Zweigman, 'County government', 687–704.

[45] BL, E116 (15), *A Relation from Portsmouth*; Fletcher, *Outbreak*, 387; *LJ* v. 291–3.

This was a scheme designed to bring the uncommitted in on their side, and it had some initial success. The militia finally began to exercise under the regular captains at Gloucester and Chipping Sodbury on 5 September and troops were raised. By then Gloucestershire was becoming a frontier region coveted by both sides. Sir Ralph Dutton, to whom responsiblity for the Array had been transferred, was apprehended trying to recruit for the king around Painswick in late August. On 30 August it was reported that some of Rupert's troops and then Hertford himself had shown up at Tewkesbury and sent out array warrants. The county defence scheme failed, simply because a majority of the gentry put loyalty to Charles I above any desire to keep the war out of Gloucestershire. On 27 September, it was alleged, 500 of the local 'malignant party' and some Cavaliers were roaming the county plundering at will.[46]

Because Parliament controlled Gloucester, to join the king openly still meant leaving the county. Not many would, as yet, but some did. Chandos, Throckmorton, Sir Ralph Dutton – who took many from his area to the raising of the standard – and Richard Atkyns of Tuffley all received recruiting commissions.[47] One might go so far as to say that the royalist party pre-dated the parliamentarian, since the MPs took on the work of raising forces alone. By 18 November 1642 Sir Richard Ducie, Sir Henry Frederick Thynne, Sir Robert Poyntz, Humphrey Hooke of Bristol and Thomas Veel of Symondshall were habitually hindering the execution of the Militia Ordinance. On 29 November Charles Cocks of Bishop's Cleeve wrote from Oxford to his father-in-law, the parson Timothy Gates, asking Gates to send the horse he had promised for Chandos's regiment, in which Cocks was a cornet, and saying that he hoped to see action with them in Gloucestershire soon.[48] Not everyone was squeamish about fighting in his home area.

Hemmed in, the Parliamentarians at last began to exert themselves locally and regionally. The propositions were implemented rapidly from October, and £15,000 was raised by 21 November. When, in October, the Royalists confederated with their Herefordshire and Monmouthshire counterparts, the Parliamentarians joined a defence agreement with those of Worcestershire, Herefordshire and Shropshire. At their request, the earl of Stamford was made commander on 13 December. Gloucester became a garrison when some partisans admitted Colonel Essex's troops, despite the citizens' misgivings, but the deputy lieutenants remained partially in control, agreeing with Essex to raise dragoons. Indeed, the local gentlemen were not unable to look beyond county borders; Cooke and Pury were restrained only by red tape (they needed a

---

[46] Washbourne, *Historical introduction*, 22–3; CJ ii. 731; BL, E202 (42), *An exact and true diurnall*, 29 Aug.–5 Sept. 1642; E202 (45), *A perfect diurnall*, 26 Sept.–3 Oct. 1642.

[47] BL, MS Add. 18, 980, fo. 20; Bodl. Lib., MS Dugdale 19, fos 2, 3v; W. St C. Baddeley, *A Cotteswold manor . . . Painswick*, Gloucester 1929, 188.

[48] Corbet, *Military government*, 6–8; CJ ii. 27; Cocks to Gates, 29 Nov. 1642, BL MS Add. 18,980, fo. 10.

commission to leave the county) from going to the relief of Lady Harley at Brampton Bryan in Herefordshire.[49]

In November some gentlemen of Wiltshire, Somerset and Gloucestershire signed a militia association for mutual defence at Bath, which was approved by the Commons. This association was powerful enough to bully the equivocal aldermen of Bristol into admitting a garrison and to raise money in London for their own forces, and was so feared by the Royalists that *Mercurius Aulicus* later gloated that the taking of Cirencester and Malmesbury had wrecked it.[50]

But the association had already been superseded before then because, in December, Stamford passed through, retreating from Hereford, and left his regiment behind. This effectively determined that Gloucestershire should be formally associated with Herefordshire and four South Welsh counties. The same ordinance established the County Committee. Before leaving, Stamford ordered the deputy lieutenants to add the subscribed horse to his own, which Edward Cooke, Sir Robert's second son, did with some embarrassment.[51] One suspects that the gentry would not have been very happy about this.

The documentary evidence largely supports Corbet's contention that support for Parliament came from a very few gentlemen, the yeomen, clothiers and the 'whole middle ranke'. Certainly, most of the foot captains were of mercantile and professional backgrounds, though volunteers came from all over the county, particularly from the centre and south-east. Even now, only the same few deputy lieutenants were active, and their policies reflected personal issues as much as security. William Guise, whose family had recently quarrelled with Cooke and Stephens, later said that Cooke prevented him from taking forces to oppose Rupert in Worcestershire.[52]

With Smyth they were rather lax, though their letters to him grew more strident: on 16 September they were talking vaguely of 'storms' from Wales and the poor turnout of gentlemen at the last Gloucester meeting, and asking him to appear next time. By October there were blunter hints about subscribing more and the need to speed the raising of horse. By 25 November 'The dangers are neare approaching uppon us' and they demanded that 100 dragoons be at Chipping Sodbury next Saturday. All they could get was a promise from a leading Puritan, Anthony Kingscote of Kingscote, to 'do my best for the uphill vilages'.[53] Although Smyth was manifestly more concerned about defending Lord Berkeley's possessions than the county, they did not seek a more energetic secretary for Berkeley Division, and although they sent Captain Yate to

[49] *Guise memoirs*, 168; HMC, 14th Report, appendix, part ii (MSS Portland, iii), 98–102; *CJ* ii. 886; Corbet, *Military government*, 14–16; GRO, D2510/26.
[50] *CJ* ii. 868–9; BL, E83 (13), *A declaration from the city of Bristol*, Dec. 1643; *LJ* v. 543; BL, E246 (26), *Mercurius Aulicus*, 30 Jan.–6 Feb 1643.
[51] *A&O* i. 47–9, 53–8; Corbet, *Military government*, 14–16; Edward Cooke to Smyth, 26 Dec. 1642, GRO, D2510/28.
[52] Corbet, *Military government*, 16; *Guise memoirs*, 119–20, 168.
[53] Deputy lieutenants to Smyth, 16 Sept., 3 Oct., 25 Nov. 1642, GRO, D2510/21, 22, 27.

garrison Berkeley Castle, they left him at Smyth's mercy as far as supplies were concerned over the winter.[54]

The six months between the outbreak of war and its arrival in Gloucestershire marked the high point of popular Parliamentarianism in the county. Cooke rejoiced that the county 'stands so right for King and Parliament'. Richard Atkyns grumbled that 'the parts about Gloucester . . . happened to be most unanimous for the Parliament'.[55] Corbet believed this was because

> there was no excessive number of powerfull gentry, who . . . care not to render themselves the slaves of princes, that they might rule over their neighbours as vassalls: but the inhabitants consisted of yeomen, farmers, and such as use manafactures that enrich the country, and passe through the hands of a multitude, a generation of men truely laborious, jealous of their properties, whose principall ayme is liberty and plenty.[56]

The Royalist version was that the gentry and clothiers forced their dependants into arms through economic pressure.[57]

This popular support persisted. Even in July 1643, says Clarendon, the zeal of the yeomanry 'so alarmed all other parts that none of the gentry who for the most part were well affected durst stay at their own homes'. The king himself concurred on both points, praising the loyal gentry but adding that no other county had been so rebellious.[58] This was not confined to the areas under Gloucester's control, although, naturally, such areas had more opportunity to express it. A party of Oxford students going to join the king at Worcester were ambushed and imprisoned by local vigilantes at Stow-on-the-Wold on 10 September 1642.[59] By contrast, there are no firm examples of spontaneous popular Royalism, even when the king's troops entered the county.

Particularly after Rupert's sack of Marlborough, Cirencester became the focus of the county's defences and of royalist attention because of the need to expand their quarters as the army grew. But it was the Cirencester garrison, a mixture of regulars and volunteers, who took the initiative, raiding Burford on New Year's Day and worsting Sir John Byron's Cavaliers.[60]

Rupert's first attempt on the town on 6 January failed, partly because of the

---

54 Smyth of Nibley papers, xi. 9, 11. A scribbled note on a parliamentary diary, 'Put out John Smith and put in E[dward] F[ust] Gloucestershire' (Two diaries, p. xvii) probably refers to this, but it was not done.
55 Cooke to Sir Robert Harley, 13 Sept. 1642, HMC, MSS Portland, iii. 98; The vindication of Richard Atkyns, in Military memoirs of the Civil War, ed. P. Young, London 1967, 7.
56 Corbet, Military government, 9.
57 A particular relation of the action before Cyrencester, in Bibliotheca Gloucestrensis, 173. For a detailed study as a source and the role of the 'middle ranke' in the war, see Rollison, Local origins, ch. vi.
58 Clarendon, Rebellion, vii. 157; Stuart royal proclamations, ii. 864.
59 The life and times of Anthony Wood, antiquary, of Oxford, 1632–1695, ed. A. Clark, Oxford 1891, iii. 60.
60 BL, E84 (29), The kingdomes weekly intelligencer, 3–10 Jan. 1643; E84 (30), Speciall passages, no. 22, 3–10 Jan. 1643.

large numbers coming to its relief – so fast, said one news-sheet, that Rupert feared being overwhelmed. All men of military age came out, we are told, 'with Bills and Forks and the like to assist their neighbours against the Cavaleers', when the garrisons of Gloucester, Tewkesbury and Cirencester joined to reduce Sudeley Castle after a five-hour cannonade. Cirencester was mistakenly boosted by some of Stamford's regulars and by the Berkeley garrison. Elsewhere, the foresters of Dean and Tewkesbury guarded against invasion from Wales and Worcestershire. Even when Rupert's 7,000 troops sat down before Cirencester, men came in in such numbers that it was reckoned 'that they have now got an invincible army'.[61] This was all propaganda, of course, but royalist news-sheets said much the same.

Cirencester was stormed by Rupert on 2 February in the face of brave but disorganised defence. Too much had been staked on one sprawling town, and relief from Sudeley was unaccountably delayed. Some blamed 'The treachery of our Malignant gentry'; indeed, a royalist newsletter praised the 'gallant gentry' who turned out, and Rupert's instructions mention consultation with some unnamed gentlemen to co-ordinate operations – Master and Poole were very probably among them. The Royalists also made much of the dying cries of some 'that Sir Robert Cooke, Mr. Stevens, Mr. George and their preachers had undone them', but perhaps this should be seen as another protest at bad leadership. Even so, thousands flocked together soon after, resolving to fight on under 'a grave and well-minded patriot'. He denounced the idea as fool-hardy, whereupon 'the people . . . curst him as a traitor to his country'.[62]

The sack soon entered the general litany of Cavalier cruelty. Up to 200 cartloads of plundered goods were taken, beside 1,200 muskets, five cannons and fourteen colours. Some 1,100 prisoners were locked up in the church and then, chained and stripped to their shirts, were 'driven along by three troopes as you do swine to London or as their brethren the Spaniards use to drive the Indians' to prisons in Oxford 'where never men indured more misery'.[63]

The sack of Cirencester forced Gloucestershire into the war, brought the royalist party into the open and shattered the subscribed forces, demonstrating their inadequacy against regulars. Several prominent Parliamentarians were captured, including George, Colonel John Fettiplace, two Pleydells of Ampney Crucis and a son of John Stephens. Fortuitously, it also defined the nature of the war for three years: a garrison at Gloucester attempting to maintain itself in the face of a changing array of royalist commands, whose aim was to take the city or at least neutralise the garrison. The war was often self-contained; it was at once a crucial flashpoint in a disputed region and a sideshow, for the

<hr/>

61 BL, E246 (7), *Perfect diurnall*, 30 Jan.–6 Feb. 1643; E86 (31), *Speciall passages*, no. 25, 24–31 Jan. 1643; E89 (1), *A continuation of certain speciall and remarkable passages*, no. 31, 6–9 Feb. 1643.
62 BL, E90 (7), *A relation of the taking of Cicester*; GRO, TRS 130; Corbet, *Military government*, 22.
63 BL, E90 (7), *A relation of the taking of Cicester*; E93 (23), *The prisoners report*, 23 Mar. 1643; E92 (2), *The petition of the inhabitants of Cyrencester*, 28 Feb. 1643.

presence of Bristol inevitably meant that resources were diverted there by both sides. Another important development was that the focus of resistance to the Royalists was no longer the subscribed forces but the regulars imported by Stamford, under the remarkable man he left in charge, Edward Massey.

From Cirencester to Newbury: the emergence of rival organisations, February to October 1643

As the allegiance of most of the gentry was out in the open after the sack of Cirencester, this is the time to examine the question in detail. The information shown in Map 3 is based on the (half complete) Victoria County History, supplemented by the older county histories, the heralds' visitations of 1623 and 1682–3, Leslie Zweigman's statistics and other sources where noted. The Royalists are those listed in any commission, who compounded or who were assessed by the Committee for Advance of Money, unless there is mitigating evidence. Accounted Parliamentarian are those named to more than one committee, who voluntarily lent or donated money to the Gloucester garrison or who were otherwise active, unless, again, there is conflicting evidence. Neutrals are mostly those not known to be active and the few divided families (some, no doubt, were not resident), but also such people as the Guises who were very much involved but cannot be categorised in any other way.

Inevitably, there are pitfalls. The most glaring is the absence of any satisfactory basis on which to define the gentry, a difficult enough task even where the evidence is abundant. Zwiegman's group of 325 families reflects a liberal definition of who constituted gentlemen as opposed to well-off yeomen. As a result, he may overstate the degree of neutralism among the gentry, for, as in any county, the less well-off found it easier to avoid committing themsleves. However, his definition of a gentleman – as one who was considered by others to be one – is as good as any.

The sources are often unsatisfactory; the incomplete garrison records, for instance, do not always distinguish between gifts, loans, levies and fines. Thus Thomas Cox of Forthampton is reckoned a Parliamentarian, as he appears making a loan in late 1642 among known Parliamentarians, but Thomas Lloyds of Wheatenhurst, who did likewise, is classified as a neutral because he later bought a royalist safe-conduct.[64] Of course, until the fall of Cirencester, token support for the Gloucester garrison was clearly the line of least resistance. Circumstances dictated that neutralism more often took the form of opting out after initial commitment, rather than keeping out indefinitely. Many appear on either side only a couple of times. Still, with these reservations in mind, it is possible to make some observations.

[64] SP 28/154, fos 1–17; GRO, CG46.

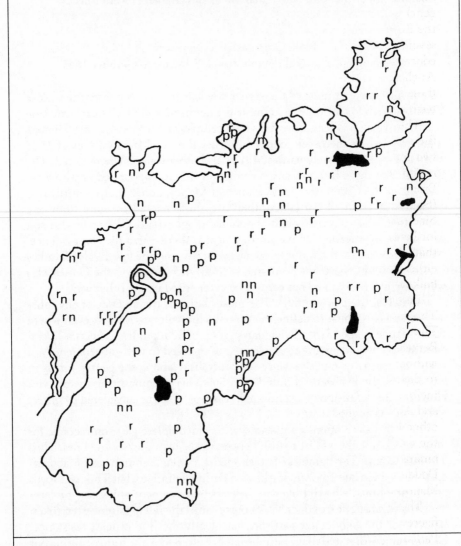

Map 3
The allegiance of the gentry in the Civil War

Key:

r – Royalist

p – Parliamentarian

n – neutral, sidechanger, divided family or no known allegiance

Within the full group of 325, there are some trends worthy of note. Of the Royalists, 31 per cent were of medieval stock compared to only 21 per cent of the Parliamentarians, and, moreover, within this group cadet branches were a higher proportion of the latter. More Parliamentarians (27 per cent to 19 per cent) were of post-Tudor origins. Of Caroline office-holders and their heirs, the Royalists were dominant; eight deputy lieutenants to four, ten sheriffs to seven, twenty-six JPs to fifteen. The Royalists tended to be richer and better educated, but, although there were many Puritans on the one side and strong Anglicans on the other, there were no uniform determining factors. None of these trends are decisive; compared with what was happening in, say, Leicestershire, they are not very pronounced at all.[65]

The geographic pattern of allegiance, however, is plain. Parliament drew the vast majority of her landed support from the Vales, and most lay within two imaginary vertical lines drawn nine miles either side of Gloucester. A vital region was Whitstone Hundred, whence came Nathaniel Stephens, Isaac Bromwich of Frampton, and the many branches of Fowlers and Clutterbucks. (So too, however, did two of the most ardent Royalists, Sir Ralph Dutton and Sir Richard Ducie of Frocester.) To some extent, the depth of gentry support for Parliament here only shows that there were far more gentry in the Vale than anywhere else. Within the seventy-one of 132 families committed to either side in the Vales, Royalists were still in a two to one majority, but the bulk of the wealth and influence in the Vales was for Parliament.

Bisley and Longtree Hundreds were largely parliamentarian, though only Thomas Hodges, MP for Wootton Bassett in Wiltshire, and the county feodary, Thomas Estcourt, both of Shipton Moyne, were of much consequence. Berkeley Hundred was a special case, almost wholly owned by Lord Berkeley, without whom its unity fragmented. Those families with a tradition of service to the Berkeleys – Smyth of Nibley, Veel of Symondshall, Bassett of Uley – inclined to the Royalists, whilst a few Puritans, such as the Daunts of Owlpen and Anthony Kingscote, many of whom were also Berkeley tenants, went the other way. Lord Berkeley himself continued to attend the House of Lords. To the south, the division was even and the two groups clustered, the Parliamentarians around Edward Stephens, Sir John Seymour and the Codringtons of Doddington and Didmarton, the Royalists around Sir Robert Poyntz, Sir Maurice Berkeley and Thomas Chester of Almondsbury.

The Inshire was sharply divided, but unlike in Berkeley Hundred, the major figures – Sir Robert Cooke and William Sheppard of Hempstead – were Parliamentarians and slightly more of the lesser figures were Royalists. Gloucester's control of the Inshire was of course irksome to many gentlemen, but this did not necessarily drive them headlong into the king's camp. Gloucester itself showed a solid front to the world, but even so the besieging

---

65 Zweigman, 'County government', 739–49; A. M. Everitt, *The local community and the Great Rebellion* (Historical Association Pamphlet G70, 1969), 18–19.

Royalists drew up a list of 104 sympathisers to be spared at the sack.[66] The Vale of Evesham was dominated by parliamentarian parish gentry and absentees, many of them Worcestershire Royalists. A key figure on the king's side was the royalist sheriff of 1643–4, Sir William Morton of Winchcombe, a zealous, if not very substantial, gentleman.

There is a sharp contrast between this varied picture and that in the Forest of Dean. Hardly any Parliamentarians lived west of Awre, where John Berrow had recruited for Parliament. The area was dominated by Wintour, his steward, brother-in-law and co-religionist, Benedict Hall of Highmeadow, and his rival, Throckmorton. Of all five divisions, Forest had both the highest ratio of Royalists to Parliamentarians, three to one, and the fewest non-committed, just a third of the total. To a large extent, this reflects the fact that there were fewer and richer gentry here than in the county as a whole.

Eastward, the Parliamentarians peter out as the Cotswold escarpment rises. The only two of any significance, John Keyt of Ebrington and Willam Leigh of Adlestrop, both had near relatives in the king's camp. The areas of Cirencester and Tewkesbury were more ambivalent, and in the Seven Hundreds there were several leading Royalists whose early sympathies had been with the deputy lieutenants, and who may have come into the king's camp more out of fear for their estates than support for his cause, notably Sir William Master and Sir Henry Poole. In the Seven Hundreds as a whole, the Parliamentarians were in a slight majority.

The Cotswolds were akin to a series of large fiefdoms: Lord Chandos's estate had seen better days, but he was still an influential figure. With the Tracys, who owned a total of seventeen manors and estates strung across the Vale of Tewkesbury, he dominated the north. John Dutton, known as 'Crump Dutton' because of his hunchback, was reputed the richest commoner in England, and owned nine manors. Others such as Sir William Whitmore of Lower Slaughter, John Chamberlain of Maugersbury, Edmund Bray and Sir Edward Bathurst were not in this league but they were still men of great wealth and influence and certainly on a par with all the Parliamentarians bar Cooke, Leigh and the Stephenses.

Many of the local Cavaliers were chronically indebted and harsh, unpopular landlords, but in February 1643 they looked formidable indeed. The highest concentration of lands owned by absentees was in Royalist-dominated parts; most of these men were Royalists too, notably Lords Craven and Coventry, the several branches of Somersets and Richard Dowdeswell. Catholics were a negligible force.

Undoubtedly there was much bandwagon-jumping in the upsurges of royalist support after the fall of Cirencester and again after the storm of Bristol, but the evidence shows that many had already made their sympathies clear and put their loyalty to the king above any desire to keep the war out of Gloucestershire. No-one welcomed war but active neutralism was a non-starter for the

[66] BL, MS Harleian 6,804, fo. 69.

greater gentry. Unlike in some counties, a choice usually had to be made. The experiences of John Smyth, who tried, in his slow way, to obey both sides, and William Guise, who tried to avoid any commitment, show how difficult any form of neutrality was. The county was isolated from the developing conflict until 1643, by which time 'militant neutralist' movements in other counties had been decisively crushed.[67]

Conversely, although a choice had to be made, it was there to be made. No-one was far from garrisons of either side. There were few side-changers, other than among the MPs who began to defect in 1643. John George probably did so in sheer terror, after being roughly handled on the way to Oxford and threatened with execution if the Parliamentarians hanged those who had plotted to betray Bristol.[68] There is reason to think that the split of 1643 corresponded to a real difference in attitudes that pre-dated the Civil War.

In February both sides began to organise more thoroughly. Rupert organised musters, which brought an impressive turnout of gentlemen, and he summoned the leading inhabitants of the Cotswolds, who agreed to raise £3,000 now and £4,000 per month thereafter to garrison Cirencester and maintain troops. Although an earlier and a later agreement specified £6,000 per month, it is doubtful whether this was ever enforced. The £4,000 assessment remained the basis of royalist finance, supplemented by special levies, loans, sequestration and Excise revenue. The warrants to the high constables of each hundred specified how much was to be raised from twenty-one townships and laid down prices for a wide variety of goods, with rather optimistic schedules for payment. That to the constable of Westminster Hundred was signed by an impressive list of fifteen major figures, although the expectation that they would be able to collect and deliver the tax in full within ten days was unrealistic.[69]

The Cavaliers seemed poised for victory, however, for on the 7 February Lord Herbert's forces invaded Dean, swept aside Berrow's outpost at Coleford and dug in at Highnam Court, Cooke's house, to await Rupert. With brief interruptions, the Royalists held Dean for the rest of the war, and they exploited its resources to the utmost for the casting of guns and shot, so much so that on some occasions they could not press enough draught animals to carry it all.[70]

Threatened from three sides, Massey had to act ruthlessly, withdrawing the Berkeley, Sudeley and Tewkesbury garrisons. Tewkesbury surrendered not to Chandos but to Sir William Russell, the semi-independent Worcestershire commander 'a neare neighbour and a sworne burgess formerlie'. This did not save them from the hazards of wartime. Russell imposed a £500 fine, to equal

---

[67] Hutton, *Royalist war effort*, 44–8; Morrill, *Revolt of the provinces*, 36–42.

[68] BL, E93 (23), *The prisoners report*, 23 Mar. 1643; E104 (4), *The severall examinations and confessions of the treacherous conspirators against . . . Bristoll*, 25 May 1643.

[69] Morrill, *Revolt*, 71n.; Zweigman, 'County government', 683, 800; SP 23/114, fo. 987.

[70] *The Royalist ordnance papers*, ed. I. Roy (Oxfordshire Historical Record Society xliii, 1964), passim.

the town's donation to Parliament's cause, and allegedly organised a cattle-rustling racket, despite the best attempts of his steward, Richard Dowdeswell, to protect the town. Some inhabitants complained to the commissioners of array, to little apparent effect. The experience much cooled their former zeal, according to Corbet.[71]

Such arbitrary actions reflected the fact that the Royalists had no integrated financial system as yet, but then Gloucester's finances were equally chaotic, and the garrison troops were scarcely any better behaved. Captain Yate's forces having perished at Cirencester, Colonel Forbes and Captain Matthews were sent to secure Berkeley Castle. They ignored protests of goodwill from the group of Berkeley dependents under Smyth who had occupied the castle to protect Lord Berkeley's possessions, and forced them out. Promises of no plunder were broken and Smyth was imprisoned until Berrow let him escape to Oxford. Forbes's behaviour turned the Berkeley connection, hitherto slow but amenable, decisively against Gloucester. Within months, Smyth was sitting in judgement on the Cirencester prisoners, Thomas Veel was signing royalist warrants and others were in the king's army.[72]

Other Royalists or suspects were more overtly victimised. Matthews and another captain, with Forbes's blessing, had caused trouble before. They plundered William Guise's house at Elmore on the way to Berkeley, then got him sequestered by invading his house posing as Rupert's troops and scaring him into making pro-royalist remarks; apparently they had pulled this particular trick elsewhere too. In January the troops had defiled Sudeley, and there was also plunder on the properties of Sir Ralph Dutton, Benedict Hall and Lady Scudamore at Llanthony.[73]

Random plunder could not continue indefinitely if the land was to support armies. The story of the rest of the war is about how both sides tried to create administrations to regularise the burden. On the Parliamentarian side, the deputy lieutenancy had outlived its uses. In the spring, as in all other counties, committees were created, for the assessment, the association and sequestration. Whether the County Committee emerged out of the lieutenancy, as in some counties, or was created by ordinance, as in others, was a moot point here, since the personnel of the lieutenancy and the committees was much the same. From the outset, an all-purpose County Committee was in charge and the members described it as such.[74]

Meanwhile, Parliament improvised other means to integrate the area into a regional strategy. On 11 February Sir William Waller, the closest it yet had to a victorious general, was appointed sergeant-major-general of all forces in

---

[71] SP 19/116, fos 102–38; SP 23/156, fos 361–3; BL, MS Harleian 6,851, fo. 133; Corbet, *Military government*, 23–5.
[72] Smyth of Nibley papers, xi. 9–12; i, 36–7; SP 23/196, fos 539–47; SP 23/114, fo. 989.
[73] GRO, D128/2–21; *Mercurius Rusticus*, vi. 46–7; SP 28/154; Washbourne, 'Historical introduction', 52–3.
[74] A&O i. 91, 113, 139–40, 148; SP 28/129 v, 154, 228, passim.

this and four other counties with wide-ranging powers to levy money from delinquents' estates and by taxation to raise up to ten regiments. Nathaniel Fiennes, governor of Bristol, was commissioned to raise a horse regiment in the area, and £5,285 was hastily subscribed in London for the relief of Wiltshire and Gloucestershire.[75]

Before Massey was formally consituted governor of Gloucester in June, only nine different gentlemen were appointed to various county committees (the Inshire usually had separate committees): Nathaniel, John and Edward Stephens, Cooke, George, Pury, Hodges, John Codrington and Sir John Seymour. Six of them were MPs, away more often than not. The cause depended heavily on the Stephens connection. With sixteen manors along the length of the Vale, they were the vital glue keeping a disparate party together.

Seven of them served Parliament. Nathaniel, despite his opposition to regicide, was nominated to almost every committee until 1660. His first son, Henry, was colonel of the city foot regiment until his death in captivity in June 1643; his second son, Richard, became active in 1644 when he had barely attained his majority. Edward and John Stephens were the MPs for Tewkesbury and were both active locally and in London. Edward's son, Colonel Thomas Stephens, rose to prominence in 1644 as sheriff and an enemy of Massey. Alderman James Stephens of Gloucester may have been a distant relative. From June, though, it became clear that more were needed to fill committees, and new men were nominated, some known supporters, others more in hope than expectation. For the Inshire, there was no shortage of reliable gentry, and the committees proved very stable.[76]

The royalist system grafted the Commission of Array on to pre-war administration, producing a flurry of orders, often mutually contradictory and expressing ideals that could not be lived up to because only the Cotswolds were under military control. Desperate need for supplies forced Rupert to send cavalry around the clothing towns of Stroud, Dursley and Tetbury to seize cloth to make uniforms.[77] In the hope of reducing the tax burden on the loyal, Sheriff Throckmorton, with two JPs, was expected to get money by calling freeholder meetings to ask for contributions, with predictable results. Simply taking the names of refusers was inadequate compulsion in a hostile area.

£5,000 was needed to support the royal army. The whole county could afford this, but the commissioners had only two divisions, as Dean was allotted to Herbert's forces and Berkeley Castle was reoccupied by Forbes. The result was the use of arbitrary free quarter, which only led to the area being less able to make up the shortfall that necessitated it in the first place. Without a proper revenue settlement 'our Garrisons are both disappointed of their subsistence and our good Subjects more grievously pressed upon'.[78] To remedy this, the

---

[75] A&O i. 79–80, 84–5; CJ ii. 960–1; CCAM i. 13.
[76] A&O i. 169, 225, 230 and passim.
[77] BL, E92 (1), *Certaine informations from severall parts of the kingdom*, 20 Feb.–6 Mar. 1643.
[78] Ibid. MS Harleian 6,804, fos 68, 72.

commission was remodelled, as in Worcestershire, as a council of commissioners 'for the guarding of the county'. The twenty-three members, seven of whom were new, took over the sheriff's role. In theory, this was to be a civilian administration, with semi-independent powers of raising and receiving money. What little survives of their records shows them making assessments, settling rating disputes and paying the troops. No soldier was to issue warrants or collect taxes, except in cases of obdurate resistance.[79]

All the king's good intentions failed because the land controlled could not support so many men, however well regulated. By April Maurice's men had received just over half of their wages, but others were two-thirds in arrears, and Sir Matthew Carew's men in Tewkesbury had not even had a quarter. The 1,500-strong Cirencester garrison proved a useless burden to everyone, plundering so many horses that some villages could not sow spring crops that year. On 19 April, after the loss of Tewkesbury and Sudeley, they levelled the fortifications and marched to Abingdon. The commissioners' powers reverted to Throckmorton, as sheriff.[80]

Thus collapsed the second attempt in as many months to settle an administration, partly because the troops were needed at Reading, partly because of overestimating how much could freely be raised to support them, and partly because of poor co-ordination between commands. A little earlier, while Viscount Grandison had sat still at Cirencester, lamenting his inability to move, Sir Jerome Brett had been waiting at Highnam for Rupert, who in turn had been waiting outside Bristol for the Yeomans–Bowcher plot to betray the city to him.[81] Nemesis soon caught up. Waller marched in from Malmesbury, briefly recaptured Cirencester and joined Massey. On 25 March, they fell on Highnam Court from all sides. More than 100 Monmouthshire gentry, 1,300 soldiers and 500 horses were captured. So ended Lord Herbert's 'mush-rump' army, at a personal cost of some £60,000.[82]

Waller continued into Monmouthshire, skirmished with Prince Maurice's forces in Dean and retreated safely to Gloucester. Further sallies followed; the first ended in defeat at Ripple Field, but in May he emerged, left a garrison of 1,000 at Tewkesbury under Cooke, took Hereford with absurd ease and proceeded to milk that rich, royalist county. Another move found Worcester better prepared, and Waller left in July to pursue Maurice south. He took with

[79] Harrison, 'Royalist organisation in Gloucestershire', 71; Bodl. Lib., MS Tanner 303, fos 112–15.
[80] Zweigman, 'County government', 875–6; Bodl. Lib., MS Dugdale 19, fos 6–7; Harrison, 'Royalist organisation in Gloucestershire', 80–1.
[81] BL, MS Add. 1,8981, fo. 98; E97 (6), *A full declaration of all particlers concerning Colonel Fiennes*. . . .
[82] BL, E94 (14), *The kingdoms weekly intelligencer*, no. 13, 21–8 Mar. 1643; E95 (4), *A continuation of certaine speciall and remarkable passages*, no. 39, 30 Mar.–6 Apr. 1643; Clarendon, *Rebellion*, vii. 290–2.

him some of the Gloucester troops, and all of those from Tewkesbury to their doom at Roundway Down.[83]

The Parliamentarians had almost cleared the county, but their resources were dwindling rapidly. The flow of donations that produced £3,756 7s. 9d. between September and December 1642 in cash and plate, amongst total receipts of around £15,000, was almost spent by June, and no relief was in sight. The war was an expensive business. Berrow's ill-fated Dean regiment cost over £1,000 to recruit, Colonel Essex's men about £400 per week during their brief stay. Much had to be loaned by common councillors of Gloucester on the strength of money held in London.[84]

The Parliamentarians were no more willing than the Royalists to face the true costs of war, and good-will dried up once county defence and Parliament's cause were no longer necessarily the same. Only £821 9s. 11d. was raised in March and April, largely thanks to one donation of £276 in plate, plus negligible sums from fines, assessments and malignants' estates. Finance was entirely hand-to-mouth, the garrison in a permanent state of crisis. In March and April only last-minute cash injections saved the companies of Captain Ganner and Captain Evans from disbanding.[85]

It seems that as well as procuring the raising of the city regiment, Waller's presence galvanised the financial administration into life. Control of the Vale meant that collection could resume in safety. (He also instituted a clean-up against corruption, forcing the two captains who robbed William Guise to make restitution.) In what looks like a genuine gesture of support, money poured in from almost every accessible parish, from Tirley in the north to Iron Acton in the south – a total of £3,160 10s. 2d. between 23 May and 17 June, plus a little more later and in gifts and fines. Most of it went straight on to pay off soldiers' arrears, which were substantial and causing problems. Cooke's men at Tewkesbury were close to mutiny for want of pay, despite receiving £340 during May and June.[86]

As the Royalists knew, it was easier to secure towns like Tewkesbury and Cirencester than to make any effective use of them. Massey later said that all the money raised barely covered the burden of Waller's presence, and it is clear that the garrison could not long carry on spending at the rate it did – £1,297 1s. 11d. in April alone.[87] But Waller had revitalised the county administration and may have helped prepare it for the siege brought on the city. After his defeats at Lansdown and Roundway Down, Bristol was stormed on 26 July by Rupert's army. Colonel Sir Ralph Dutton distinguished himself, and amongst

83 BL, E96 (7), *The victorious and fortunate proceedings of Sir William Waller*, 15 Apr. 1643; E101 (2), *Certaine informations*, no. 16, 1–8 May 1643.
84 SP 28/154 (unfol.); HMC, 14th Report, appendix, part i (MSS Portland, i), 78; GRO, GBR B3/2, fos 235–7.
85 SP 28/129 v, fos 52–3v.
86 GRO, D128/4, fo. 2; SP 28/129 v, fos 19–20v and passim; SP 28/228, passim; HMC, MSS Portland, i. 712.
87 SP 28/129 v, fos 3–5v.

those captured, but soon released, were Edward Stephens and Sir John Seymour.[88]

Not the least of the charges later laid against Governor Nathaniel Fiennes was the misuse of the provisions brought in so freely from Gloucestershire and Somerset. With advances to retake Tewkesbury and in the Forest, Gloucester was ringed on all sides and the king decided to rid himself of that last thorn in his side. One consideration in making the fateful decision to besiege Gloucester may have been the assurance of the Royalists of Gloucestershire and the 'Welsh side' of the Severn, that they could recruit an army for him there.[89]

Gloucester's resistance to Charles I's army, crucial though it undoubtedly was in the course of the war, was probably neither as heroic nor as fortuitous as the two sides thought at the time. Morton wrote on 3 August that 'if it were not for Massey Singleton Pury & Nelmes a Townesman the City would be delivered up w[i]thout a stroke'. He held high hopes of Sergeant-Major Ferrars deserting, and had also written of Massey himself returning to the command he had abandoned in the early days of the war. There were reasons for optimism, for the citizens were leaving in droves.[90]

Massey added to the confusion by covering every possibility. While publicly roaring defiance, which convinced Sir Samuel Luke's spies, he sent private messages to assure the Royalists that he would not fight the king in person. Clarendon for one could not fathom his intentions.[91] To Parliament Massey wrote 'our wants are so greate & this Citty so averce to us [tha]t our power cannot enforce men beyond their wills . . . what with the generall discontent of both [th]e City souldiers & our owne (and the Treachery of [th]e City) we stand at p[re]sent betrayed'. He had barely 1,500 men in two depleted regiments and no money. A few were still loyal 'but I feare 10 for one to enclyne [th]e other way'. Thus if the city stood, it was through his courage alone, if it fell, it was not his fault, and his options would be open. As a result of this letter, £1,700 was immediately diverted to Gloucester.[92]

The citizens of Gloucester resisted Charles for severely practical reasons. They had no cause to be reassured by fine words, for Bristol had been sacked for two days, contrary to Rupert's express orders, and in any case many of the king's troops had been present at Cirencester. The booty-laden royal army had swollen and become uncontrollable. As Clarendon said 'A very great licence broke into the army, both among officers and soldiers; the malignity of those

[88] *Memoirs of Prince Rupert and the Cavaliers*, ed. E. Warburton, London 1849, ii. 244, 260.
[89] BL, E67 (36), *An answer to Col. Nathaniel Fiennes relation*, London 1643; Clarendon, *Rebellion*, vii. 201.
[90] BL, MS Add. 18,980, fo. 100; Morton to Rupert, 3, 4 Aug. 1643, in Warburton, *Memoirs*, ii. 273–4; Clarendon, *Rebellion*, vii. 158.
[91] *Journal of Sir Samuel Luke*, ed. I. G. Philip (Oxfordshire Record Society xxix, xxxi, xxxiii, 1950–3), 133–8; Clarendon, *Rebellion*, vii. 158–9.
[92] Massey to Lenthall, 29 July 1643, Bodl. Lib., MS Tanner 62, fo. 197; *CJ* iii. 190.

parts being thought the excuse for the exercise of any rapine or severity amongst the Inhabitants.' [93]

Certain groups, particularly clothiers, were presumed disaffected and plundered as a matter of course, despite vague promises of redress in answer to a petition presented by Throckmorton in August 1643. This was no more than Parliament gave to the same petition.[94] Had the plunder been systematic, it might have dissuaded some. But protections were sold for money alone. Amongst the buyers was Samuel Webb, a rich clothier, who, Sir Arthur Aston said, 'hath and doth assist the Parliament against the King, yet, by what means I know not, he has obtained lately a protection'. In point of fact he obtained two, both of which said he had given ample testimony of his loyalty, but Aston was right – Webb often contributed plate to the garrison.[95]

At least five proclamations against every crime from plunder to racketeering to desertion were issued by the king in August, to no great effect. As a result of all this, the country people, who, at the outset, fearing the consequences of a prolonged siege, 'forsook us and employed some to represent their desires . . . and to befool and excuse our perseverence', now turned on the Cavaliers. Using their superior knowledge of the area, the farmers began to hit back either in guerilla raids, or by simply refusing supplies and information. One band near Berkeley ambushed a cavalry troop, killing six; the miners of Dean ran away rather than give their labour to the Royalists. They agreed to serve Parliament, however, even though they were not paid until December.[96]

The situation deteriorated rapidly. Even the Gloucester Royalists asked no more than exemption from a general sack and the king's Articles of Inquisition, published on 17 August, could, in theory, have led to the punishment of anyone who had so much as withheld rents on Parliament's orders or fled to a garrison town.[97] The aldermen were probably right to calculate that the slim hope of relief was preferable to capitulation on terms that the king could not or would not enforce on his followers.

The second important fact about the siege was its epic quality. It ended the bickering in London, and focused all eyes on the beleaguered city. Every detail in Essex's uneventful relief march was lovingly recorded, until, on 5 September, he arrived to find the Royalists gone. Many news-sheets covered the relief, but the most enduring picture was created by Corbet, whose account was published in 1646, and more immediately by the town clerk, John Dorney, whose *Briefe*

---

[93] Clarendon, *Rebellion*, vii. 201.

[94] *A petition presented unto his maiestie at his court at Bristol on the 7 day of August 1643 by Sir Baynham Throkmorton baronet*, Oxford 1643; CJ iii. 214.

[95] I. Roy, 'The English Civil War and English society', in B. Bond and I. Roy (eds), *War and society: a yearbook of military history*, London 1975, 39; Aston to Rupert, 7 Aug. 1643, in Warburton, *Memoirs*, ii. 277; GRO, CG46; SP 28 /154; SP 28/129 v, fos 68–72v.

[96] *Stuart royal proclamations*, ii. 864–9; Roy, 'Civil War', 38–41; Corbet, *Military government*, 41.

[97] GRO, TRS 186; SP 28/154; GRO, D2510/30.

and exact relation came out in September 1644.[98] Both, in stirring prose, played up the heroism and unity of citizens and soldiers, the apparent hopelessness of the defence, the king's might and the miraculous appearance of Essex when hope was fading.

Above all, they heaped praise on Massey. 'Not one gentleman of the countrey durst be seen to assist us, no member of Parliament did reside here. . . . All things rested on the governour's sole care' writes Corbet – falsely, for Pury and many others were present.[99] Corbet was, of course, Massey's personal chaplain, but Dorney's prose was equally hagiographical. This may have affected general perceptions at the time. Massey had always been a favourite of the London mercuries, but from now on he was their idol. It may also have had its effects on historians, for the third main source on the same side was another adept propagandist – Massey himself.

Massey and Vavasour, September 1643–July 1644

Soon after the relief, Essex withdrew, while supplies came in from the very areas in which the Royalists had quartered, 'so solicitous were the people to conceal what they had and to reserve it for them'. With a neat sense of symmetry, Essex imposed a subsidy equal to Russell's on Tewkesbury. Anxious to avoid a general engagement, he concealed his forces among the lanes and hedges of the Tewkesbury area, then slipped out, made a bold night march on Cirencester and surprised Sir Nicholas Crispe's two horse regiments, taking 400 prisoners and thirty wagon-loads of provisions. He then marched home to London via a drawn battle at Newbury, where Chandos 'bore a principall part in the action it selfe'.[100]

The siege had been a grand social gathering as the gentry turned out to cheer the winning side; Richard Colchester of Westbury-on-Severn got out his old sword and pistol, went down for the day, paid an attorney £10 to do what he could for his brother at the sack, and left, having created ten years of problems for his widow when he died in December.[101] Mostly, though, the local Royalists remained powerless, for the court's attitude was as peremptory to them as to everyone else. Apart from the tireless Throckmorton and Morton, few civilians were much in evidence, although large numbers of warrants were issued. The quartering of the army had been a failure. Even had no relief come, the besieging forces might have begun to starve before the city.

To remedy the situation, the commissioners drew up seventeen propositions

---

[98]   BL, E67 (31), John Dorney, *A briefe and exact relation of the most materiall and remarkable passages* . . ., 1644.

[99]   Corbet, *Military government*, 59–60. John Morrill justly describes Corbet as 'a man whose bigotry made him see everything in terms of black and white': *Revolt*, 100.

[100] Clarendon, *Rebellion*, vii. 206; I. Roy, 'England turned Germany? The aftermath of the Civil War in its European context', *TRHS* 5th ser. xxviii (1978), 137.

[101] SP 19/103, fo. 161ff.; SP 20/2, fos 165, 175v, 197; GRO, D36/A2.

in August, to restructure the war effort. The aim was to settle garrisons of 600 foot and two horse troops each at Painswick, Cheltenham and Newent out of regular forces, the rest of whom were to leave. They were to be paid £500 out of the monthly contribution of the Kiftsgate, Forest and Seven Hundreds Divisions. Berkeley's and part of the Seven Hundreds', by the king's express order, were still diverted to Bristol. In principle, the commissioners should have authority to issue warrants, press men and commission officers. When enough locals had been raised, they would replace the regulars and were not to be removed except for a general battle. The king assented to most details, though he refused to empower the commissioners to compound with surrendering Parliamentarians. This flawed but realistic plan was never followed in every detail, but it did for a time succeed in squeezing Massey, especially as Wintour was entering the war.[102]

Wintour had been slow to join in – he received a commission to fortify his house on 27 September. He may have been waiting until Throckmorton ceased to be sheriff. As a Catholic, a creditor of the crown and a conspicuous beneficiary of the Personal Rule of Charles I, his allegiance was predetermined. Parliament had taken away his bargain of 1640, but there had not been enough time to enforce it, and several attempts had been made to secure his house and goods. However, he had not lifted a finger even to prevent Berrow recruiting for Parliament in Dean.[103]

Meanwhile, Sir William Vavasour became colonel-general of Herbert's shattered command, and led the task of containing Massey over the winter. The scope of Wintour's command was vague. As governor of Lydney, he was to work with the JPs and commissioners of Gloucestershire and Monmouthshire, and, indirectly, was responsible for liaising with Bristol and guarding the Aust to Beachley crossing. From November he was more closely subordinated, as Dean was included in Vavasour's command, but as yet they were allies. Vavasour, Wintour and Sir Ralph Dutton made up the Council of War at Tewkesbury. Dutton seems to have been the only commissioner active near the fray; John Dutton was at the Oxford Parliament and involved in the Irish Cessation negotiations, the Tracys rarely strayed from home, Smyth and Colonel Thomas Veel were active around Berkeley and most of the rest preferred the relative comfort of Bristol and Oxford.[104]

From October £1,500 out of each month's contribution was directed to Sir Humphrey Tracy to sustain Vavasour's forces at the new base of Tewkesbury. The Forest Division's revenue, however, was still reserved for Wintour who, with Hall, set up a number of garrisons to hold down Dean. No more than Massey could they prevent all enemy raids, but by December, Vavasour could

102 Ibid. D115/3; *Stuart royal proclamations*, ii. 990–2.
103 GRO, D421 A1/6; Glos. Pub. Lib., Doc. JF 2.3, *The true relation how Sir John Wintour . . . made a wicket attack on certain soldiers*; SP 20/1, fo. 10; SP 28/228 ii, fo. 319.
104 BL, E31 (14) *Mercurius Britannicus*, no. 21, 29 Jan.– 6 Feb. 1644; Warburton, *Memoirs*, i. 508–9; BL, MS Add. 18,980, fos 87, 101; 18,981, fo. 16; GRO, D2510/32–5.

maintain 1,500 horse and foot in Tewkesbury. From January 1644, the expanding commission was permitted to sequester at will the estates of those in rebellion for over a year, although in the long run sequestration revenues did not yield enough to reduce the assessment burden.[105] But at last the means were there for a county-based assault on Gloucester.

There was a major shortcoming in that Captain Maxwell at Berkeley was not part of Vavasour's command; indeed, Maxwell had major problems of his own in sustaining the garrison against popular pressure, not to mention the demands of the Bristol garrison on the same area.[106] This allowed Massey to control the resources of Whitstone Hundred and much of Berkeley as well. Between September and January there were some fifteen skirmishes around Gloucester. Massey had the better of them, and managed to keep Colonel Mynne's Irishmen at arm's length, but he could not prevent Wintour's brutal clearance of the Forest market towns or break the web growing around him, and he could barely maintain a few tiny out-garrisons.

The fake 'plot' by Captain Backhouse to betray the city wasted Vavasour's time and added to his humiliations after he had been demoted, but it was of no more than propaganda value at the time. The London mercuries were reduced to ominous silence and feeble jokes about Wintour, and disaffection grew.[107] The reason was simple; it had been estimated that Massey would need £8,000 and 1,000 men to sustain him throughout the winter. Spring came, and neither had arrived.

Ironically, the nadir of the Gloucester garrison's fortune came after the relief. During the siege, the troops could not possibly expect to be paid, but now they wanted both pay and their arrears, which totalled £19,000. Hard cash was urgently needed. More was raised in gifts, loans and fines – over £1,600 between October and December, compared to only £417 4s. 6d. between July and September – and a start was made on collecting malignants' rents in nearby parishes. But most of this went straight away in lump sums to Massey and seventeen other officers to pay off arrears. As late as May 1644, Backhouse was receiving arrears dating from the siege. Only about as much was paid out between September 1643 and June 1644 (of what can be computed from incomplete accounts) as between April and July 1643, when most contributions were collectable, which very few were now. From January to March 1644, Sir Samuel Luke's spies constantly reported the imminent collapse of the garrison.[108]

Conversely, the crisis also showed parliamentarian administration at its

[105] HMC, MSS Portland, i. 134; BL, MS Add. 18,980, fo. 116; Bodl. Lib., MS Dugdale 19, fo. 50; Stuart royal proclamations, ii. 995–6.
[106] Maxwell to Smyth, 16 Sept., 4 Nov. 1643, GRO, D2510/32, 33.
[107] Corbet, Military government, 70–5; BL, E71 (11), Mercurius Civicus, no. 21, 12–19 Oct. 1643; E45 (17), A true relation of a wicked plot . . . against the city of Gloucester discovered by Captain Backhouse, 4 May 1644.
[108] SP 28/129 v, fos 3v–5v, 24v–7, 42; Luke journal, iii. 234–5, 238, 245–6, 266.

plodding best. A series of desperate expedients kept the garrison afloat. On 15 September the Commons voted £4,000 of the arrears and a £1,000 reward for Massey himself and further assignments were made for the garrison, including the estates of Sir Richard Ducie and Sir Edward Hales, together worth £6,000, and, in February 1644, that of Sir Francis Willoughby, worth £600. Of course, the value of such grants depended on Massey's ability to enforce them. The Commons were aware of the need to organise outside help. In January they heard unspecified proposals from certain inhabitants to raise £3,000.[109] As a result, the county excise money was diverted there while propositions to raise a further £5,000 were considered. Massey actually imposed an excise on malt, beer and meat and a primitive poll tax on Gloucester, to the great derision of *Mercurius Aulicus*, although he could not enforce them on the county at large.[110]

In March, import duties on currants were also assigned to the garrison. Slowly, and with the advice of the county's MPs, the Committee of Both Kingdoms and some local gentlemen scraped together money and equipment, with 1,700 men from many commands to convey it. Even after this convoy had arrived, the Commons remained concerned with ordinances for the relief of Gloucester. In May an amendment to remove the County Committee's sequestration powers was rejected and discussion of a 'wine project' eventually resulted in the assignment of £3,000 from the London vintners and further investigation into wine duties as a souce of supply.[111]

In the chaos Massey had to make some concessions to civilian rule, and it soon led to disputes. At some stage after the siege (Corbet's chronology is particularly vague at this point), two committees were set up, both comprising officers and civilians, one by the Council of War to hear and adjudge rating disputes, the other by Massey to oversee rating and the disbursement of money, so as to relieve the burden of petitions on him. At some unspecified point, the latter began discussing matters outside its terms of reference, and Massey sent a prohibition at once. We also know of a committee of grievances on which William Bell of Sandhurst and Alderman Thomas Hill sat, and a committee appointed by the council of war to investigate plundering by garrison troops.[112] Neither of these can be positively identified with those mentioned by Corbet.

Around September a parliamentary committee was set up at Massey's request and under Pury's chairmanship, to remove the burden of excess petitions from him.[113] Pury and John Stephens duly came down in person to sort things out. Pury later said that he heard complaints that arbitrary courts had been erected and over £50,000 illegally levied in the six months after the

---

[109] CJ iii. 241, 251, 258, 276, 292, 355, 400.
[110] Ibid. 364; BL, E29 (61), *Mercurius Aulicus*, 30 Dec. 1643– 6 Jan. 1644; Corbet, *Military government*, 70.
[111] A&O i. 396–7; CJ iii. 336, 453, 455, 457–8, 473, 480–1, 539; CSPD 1644, 23–4. The earliest mention of the convoy was on 7 Dec. 1643: BL, MS Add. 18,980, fo. 156.
[112] Corbet, *Military government*, 60–2; SP 23/116, fo. 103; SP 28/228 ii, fo. 331.
[113] Taylor, 'Civil government', 77–8; CJ iii. 247; CSPD 1641–3, 491.

siege; even Corbet admits that there was a flood of complaints against unfair rating. Pury and Stephens decided to accept all accounts of rates and free quarter taken or a composition for all rate arrears, and to negotiate a new contribution, based on the ordinance for £4,000 per month on the county and £400 on the Inshire.

This was necessary, they said, as virtually everything had hitherto been taken in free quarter and the arrears could not possibly be paid in cash. The settlement was the first blow in a long battle, for it allegedly satisfied everyone 'excepting the chiefe commander there', who found any civilian veto on his governorship intolerable. This was the first skirmish in what was to become an undeclared war between Massey and the County Committee.[114]

The process of tracking down the abuses of war is reflected in the work of the Grand Committee, which was in existence by 23 January 1644, and lasted until May at least. This may simply have been the County Committee, which was often referred to thus, acting under another name. However, the personnel of the main committee and this one in 1644 were very different. (The early work of the County Committee is shadowy, as few papers survive from before 1645, though it is known that they took decisions by simple majority votes. In September 1644, William Guise of Elmore was voted a delinquent by a majority of one out of eleven sitting.)[115]

What was most important was the actual work of the Grand Committee, rate arrears. Eleven men signed orders, but the bulk of the work was done by three: Edward Broughton, a Herefordshire refugee, Alderman Thomas Hill and the famous legal author, William Sheppard of Hempstead, who each signed almost all of the 174 known acquittances. Most of the other members were Gloucester men, such as James Wood, William Parry and James Woodward; none was of 'county' status. By their decision, £199 16s. 1d. out of arrears totalling £271 15s. 8d. was remitted and reductions worth £20 9s. 7d. per month were granted, in return for the residue, plus a grand total of twelve loads of hay, sixty-seven bushels of beans and twenty-six of oats. These all relate to Inshire parishes; we cannot know if their authority extended elsewhere or how many slips have been lost.

Certainly, though, they were generous and meticulous. Nearly half of the slips referred to Hartpury, Sandhurst and Maisemore, three parishes north-west of Gloucester. Here poverty and plundering were often specified as reasons for the remittance. On one occasion they journeyed to Down Hatherley to verify a complaint. Clearly, too, Massey was not enamoured of their activities; in this case he simply wrote 'Reffused' on their favourable report.

On 29 February the Grand Committee made five propositions about the money raised by the new 'great rate' forced on Massey by Pury: that it was to be used, with his permission, to pay soldiers according to a muster roll at the

---

[114] Pury to Accounts Committee, 22 June 1646, SP 28/256 (unfol.); Corbet, *Military government*, 60.

[115] *Guise memoirs*, 125, 166.

rates agreed on and not for arrears, which hints at a wide range of familiar military abuses. 'Hic ipse Gubernator nil Fecit', ran the terse postscript. After May, no more is heard of them. Their motives were rational; they were using the institution of a new rate to write off bad debts and make a fresh start. But there were many unpaid soldiers with no reason to love the Grand Committee.[116]

The picture appears even more complex when we remember that the city and Inshire had their own forms of government. The leet, tolsey, hundred, county, inquest and piepowder courts all functioned almost as normal. The Common Council continued to govern, and set up a committee of defence to co-ordinate the defence of the city from August 1642 until after the siege. Corbet says the deputy lieutenants' authority 'was quite fallen' but it was to resurface.[117] In practice, many of these overlapping authorities may have tended to merge into one; Gloucester did not always have separate parliamentary committees and, when she did, aldermen, such as Pury, and local gentlemen, like Silvanus Wood of Brookthorpe, were often named to both.

Finance was an enduring headache and the system remained crude, though flexible. In theory, all moneys passed through the treasurer, Major Blayney, on Massey's orders alone. In practice many others gave orders for payments to be made. Nearly 1,000 acquittances, requests, orders and so forth survive, almost all from 1643–4, giving an interesting if incomplete sidelight on the administration's daily routine. Officers could usually get small debts paid off, but arrears mounted. For example, on 19 December 1643, Captain Mallory asked for £5 to keep his men, his own cash and credit being exhausted. Massey ordered Blayney to pay him at least £4, Blayney found £2 and Mallory struggled on.

Many civilian contractors served the garrison; in January 1644 alone payments for services rendered were made to eighteen individuals or groups, ranging from surgeons to saltpetremen, blacksmiths, woodcutters, coopers and a stocking-maker. In 1644 most of these services were regularised. For instance, Augustine Loggins appears repeatedly for haulage, while other jobs were in the charge of aldermen: Jasper Clutterbuck received £5 per week for poor prisoners and Dennis Wise supervised the rebuilding of the fortifications.[118] These activities were probably more onerous than profitable to the aldermen.

The city's finances were kept separate, under the familiar institutions, and although they faced increasing costs on fortification, fuel and the watch, prudent planning made this not too difficult a burden to bear. There were severe problems at the height of the fighting, with accumulated arrears on the rent roll of £189 6s. 10d. in 1643–4, and an equally swift recovery was made by 1646 by careful husbandry and the slashing of useless expenditure.[119] But

[116] SP 28/228 iii, fos 534, 545 and passim; iv, passim.
[117] Taylor, 'Civil government', 96–109; GRO, GBR B3/2, fos 221, 264, 415; Corbet, *Military government*, 25.
[118] SP 28/228 ii, fo. 346 and passim; SP 28/129 v, fos 28–30v.
[119] Taylor, 'Civil government', 89–96.

the garrison could not support itself indefinitely on such limited resources. It was vital for the relief convoy to get through.

The turn-around came in April 1644. Military failure did not lead to Vavasour's dismissal; rather, it was the other way round. Having long sought an independent command, he had ingratiated himself with Rupert, who was intriguing against Herbert for the presidency of South Wales, within which a commander-in-chief in Gloucestershire would be named. The issue split the local Royalists as Vavasour, Lord Conway 'upon the alliance he hath with the Tracys of that country', and Chandos, who was backed by Throckmorton, Morton, Master and the bulk of the county gentry, each wanted it. By 31 January Sir Humphrey Tracy, 'one very powerfull in this countrie' had agreed to back Vavasour, although the other two 'stood for it and had made several partyes'.[120]

There were knives out for Vavasour at court, and he also argued with Wintour before January. Henceforth, Wintour ceased to co-operate with Vavasour and went his own way along the Wye frontier, safe in the knowledge of the queen's blessing. Colonel Maxwell, then Veel at Berkeley and Colonel Oglethorpe at Beverstone did likewise. Many other commanders lost patience with Vavasour over his secretive behaviour during the Backhouse 'plot'. In February Colonel Mynne began to ignore his orders and appeal directly to Rupert.[121]

To sort out the confusion, the structure was first remodelled, with the whole county placed under Vavasour's command. Wintour was constituted commander-in-chief in Dean under Vavasour. The Lords Commissioners reports of 7 and 12 April put forward ten propositions to perpetuate the blockade by garrisoning Tewkesbury and Sudeley out of the contributions of the Kiftsgate and Seven Hundreds Divisions respectively, the former with 1,900 foot to be raised by Vavasour and Sir Humphrey Tracy, the latter with 800 horse out of Chandos's regiment. All were supposed to be supported by the two divisions' tax and sequestration revenues, to free Vavasour's forces for the field. This sounds optimistic, and the £6,000 per month to be raised even more so. Waller had only imposed the same amount on an area he considered 'totally malignant'.[122]

Indeed, the evidence of royalist warrants suggests that their chance had already come and gone, as receipts had declined steadily since late 1643, probably through sheer exhaustion. By now, there may have been several months' arrears accumulated and a shortage of coin forced the commissioners to take more and more in provisions. In these circumstances, the Gloucester troops, who had been living under a system of assignations by which units were

[120] BL, MS Carte 1, fo. 24; MS Add. 18,981, fos 144, 150.
[121] Bodl. Lib., MS Clarendon 27, fos 73–6; Harrison, 'Royalist organisation in Gloucestershire', 196–9.
[122] BL, MS Harleian 6,852, fos 54–62; CSPD 1644, 341.

tied to a group of parishes for supplies since, if not before, the siege, were at an advantage in coping with the dislocation.[123] More immediately, much of Vavasour's force was recalled into the field army or reassigned to garrisons. This allowed the convoy, hitherto bottled up around Warwick, to slip into Gloucester in several trips, carrying £8,000, two hundred weight of sulphur, five of match and thirty barrels of powder.[124]

The effect was dramatic, as the populace deserted 'Master Dutton and the rest of the Commissioners', and many gentlemen also sought to come in. Among these was Chandos. When Rupert finally got his presidency, Herbert secured the dismissal of Vavasour, whom he hated, as the price of his own resignation, and Rupert chose Mynne as his new colonel-general, despite the court's preference for Chandos. Chandos had reason for bitterness; he had been the first Gloucestershire Cavalier, had seen his home defiled by troops, had raised many men and had often been in the thick of the fighting, barely escaping alive from one ambush. In June, 'out of pure weariness of the fatigue' he left for London; Sir Robert Tracy also sought to come in at around the same time.[125] Dean became little more than Wintour's personal fiefdom within Rupert's vast command, and he spent the rest of the year concentrating on Chepstow and Beachley.

The relief convoy had been a delicate operation in regional strategy, involving not only the Committee of Both Kingdoms but many county and association administrations. Commissary-General Behre had to fight hard to win Parliament's support to detail the Warwickshire forces to the convoy, against the wishes of the earl of Manchester and the earl of Denbigh, and to concentrate on Newark, while keeping two of Colonel Purefoy's troops in Gloucester after the end of April contributed to the wrecking of Denbigh's intricate regional policy.[126]

At last Massey could go on the offensive. He garrisoned Westbury, saw off Mynne, then took Newnham to break Wintour's blockade. He was preparing to move on Hereford when news came that Colonel Oglethorpe, having been left in limbo by the other garrisons and being earmarked for replacement with Throckmorton, was ready to surrender Beverstone Castle. It fell on 23 May. Malmesbury followed, after a twelve-hour battery and an assault courageously led by Captain Richard Ayleworth, and they were garrisoned under Colonel

[123] Zweigman, 'County government', 819–21, 863–5.
[124] *CSPD* 1644, 57, 62–3, 97, 138; BL, MS Add. 18,981, fo. 150; E42 (10), *The Parliament scout*, 4–11 Apr. 1644. It is not clear why Vavasour's troops were moved, but this could not have been connected to Sir Ralph Hopton's defeat at Cheriton (Harrison, 'Royalist organisation in Gloucestershire', 201–2), which was not known of until after the convoy's arrival.
[125] Corbet, *Military government*, 69; Clarendon, *Rebellion*, viii. 53; BL, E47 (75), *Chief heads of each dayes proceedings in Parliament*, 8–15 May 1644; *LJ* vi. 577, 579, 583; x. 36.
[126] *CSPD* 1644, 67–8, 81, 88, 98, 104, 138, 181, 184, 197.

Thomas Stephens and Colonel Devereux respectively. Now the cloth routes were open again. Tewkesbury was retaken and garrisoned.[127]

In June, Waller arrived, pursuing the king via Cirencester and Stow to Evesham. He beat up the royalist quarters at Stow-on-the-Wold, and forced Sudeley Castle to surrender after a three-hour battery, an overnight wait and a few defiant words. Over 300 men were taken, including Morton, the governor. Morton was probably tired of the war; a lawyer of limited estates and vast debts, he had been highly active throughout the war and his brusqueness had made him the local Parliamentarians' pet hate. Corbet calls him 'active and violent . . . of a high spirit and bold . . . most obnoxious to the justice of Parliament'.[128]

Although about two-thirds of the Royalists were still in arms at this point, coherent administration under the commissioners ended, for the efforts in Forest and Berkeley Divisions were no longer connected and there was no further attempt to use the county's resources to reduce Gloucester. Gloucestershire was henceforth treated as a source of supply for Oxford and Bristol. Soon few of the leading figures were left. Throckmorton is last heard of as a cavalry officer in Wales and Somerset in August. At the same time, Viscount Tracy was begging the Harleys to intercede for him and Sir Humphrey Tracy was captured near Worcester. Richard Berkeley of Rendcomb came in by September. Most of the rest had done likewise before the taking of Bristol in August 1645 signalled the end of the royalist cause in Gloucestershire.[129]

For the Gloucestershire gentry, Civil War allegiance was anything but arbitrary. The county lacked 'natural' peer leadership, whether based on ideology, like the split beteen Northampton and Lord Brooke in Warwickshire, or ancient rivalries, as between the Hastings and Grey factions in Leicestershire, but there was a cultural and religious gulf between the two sides, pitching Anglican Cotswolds and Catholic Forest against Puritan Vale. Of course it was not unbridgeable, and no doubt there would have been some sort of active neutralism had it ever been feasible, but there was continuity at leadership level on both sides from well before 1642.

A 'county community' never emerged, and, as often in Midland counties, the gentry had a far wider perspective than just one county. Neither side put concern for Gloucestershire ahead of the cause. But circumstances determined that it would remain peripheral to the royalist war effort. After the Array was botched, no Gloucestershire man was commissioned locally, and the county was abandoned until 1643. The royalist administration never developed any

[127] Corbet, *Military government*, 91–9; BL, E50 (26), E51 (13), *The kingdomes weekly intelligencer*, nos 58–9, 4–11, 12–19 June 1644.
[128] BL, E50 (34), *Mercurius Civicus*, no. 55, 6–13 June 1644; Corbet, *Military government*, 90, 104; Clarendon, *Rebellion*, viii. 53
[129] *CSPD* 1644, 446; HMC, MSS Portland, iii. 123–7; Corbet, *Military government*, 108; SP 23/177, fo. 375; SP 23/195, fo. 633; SP 23/ 197, 193, 213–14.

coherence outside the central command, civilians remained in the background, divided among many places, and a confusing welter of semi-independent commands were never co-ordinated well enough to keep Massey quiet.

The parliamentarian administration was almost as slow to develop, but it had the priceless advantage, until the quarrels of 1644–5, of a unified command and a permanent base. Even so, this should not be overstressed. All the disputes which rent Massey's governorship in its final year were presaged well before they erupted, and they were no less bitter than those which destroyed their enemies. There were overlaps and confusions in the command structure on both sides. Both financial systems were a series of expedients, and depended on the ability to collect through military force. The Parliamentarians were more successful in this and may have collected as much as £100,000 between February 1643 and August 1646, but the fact that an ever increasing proportion came from sequestration and compositions (the latter instituted even before they began nationally) was a bad omen.

The essential differences were ones of framework and attitude, which gave those fighting on either side a vision of what they were fighting for and their own place within the cause. The flexible nature of parliamentarian leadership was crucial; the role of the MPs on the ground, in the Commons and in the parliamentary Committee of Gloucester ensured that local needs were always represented eventually. The system was cumbersome, but often at its best in times of crisis. Rule by county committees established a basis for the integration of local, regional and national strategy. The Royalists also created committees, but then issued too many commissions to individuals, which undermined the whole principle.[130]

On the king's side, too much depended on goodwill between touchy individuals, and, with the chronic squabbling and patronage-seeking at court, there was no adequate means to resolve disputes. Vavasour's command was destroyed because he lacked the personal authority to knit it together; Mynne and Wintour were then rewarded for their parts in destroying it. Loyalism could be intense. Throckmorton was one of the first to answer the call, despite his enmity with Wintour, his belief in Pym's papist conspiracy and his readiness to see the bishops turned out if necessary. The other side of the coin, however, was Wintour's refusal to join in until his rival, who almost single-handedly organised the war effort in Dean until the siege, ceased to be at the helm.

The same few names – Chandos, the Tracys, the two sheriffs and Sir Ralph Dutton – feature in almost all the royalist commissions and other documents, even down to minor rating problems. The rewards of Royalism were only for the elite: John Tracy became Viscount Rathcoole and Bathurst bought a baronetcy. Neither had been notably active.[131] No niche was found for the little men and some, notably Veel, in the way he was later dismissed as governor

130 Bodl. Lib., MS Dugdale 19, passim.
131 HMC, 9th Report, MSS Salisbury, part xxii, 375–9; CCAM i. 64.

of Berkeley Castle, were treated disgracefully. When the leaders defected, the whole party crumbled. Parliament's success owed much to the integration of local defence initiatives with the cause. The MPs were sent to co-ordinate local defence, while Royalists packed into court.

Massey's ability to exploit this reflects the advantage of interior lines and popular sympathy, but simply having popular support was not enough. He also had an ability to marshal the people's desire to defend themselves when necessary. At the lowest ebb, in early 1644, he armed the people of Whitstone Hundred who were 'wholly ours' as a result. He also 'associated' with the Corse area in mutual defence and encouraged Major Banaster's self-defence initiatives round Churchdown, while excusing Bushley from such service because of the royalist strength in the area. Even in February 1645 he could 'raise the country' around Cirencester on his way to Rawden House.[132]

Parliament, inadvertently perhaps, managed to sift through her supporters until the talented and committed rose to the top, and her innovatory procedures also accorded best with localism. This is no paradox. The Royalists relied heavily on existing officers and offices – Chandos as lord lieutenant and Throckmorton then Morton as sheriffs – but such concessions to conservative feeling were useless when they left troops unpaid. By contrast, Parliament's lord lieutenant and sheriffs were not important through those positions alone. Statute and ordinance defined a man's place; the Royalists had no framework within which to view their own allegiance. In times of trouble, they had only personal appeals and bemused assurances of loyalty on which to rely. Their leaders' decision-making process was a mystery to them, as indeed it was meant to be, and in stark contrast to the very public processes of Parliament.

Just as in Wiltshire, another county where the war effort did not feel the benefits of the restructuring of the winter of 1643–4, the royalist party collapsed in the summer of 1644 after some squabbles over authority and a few reverses.[133] The collapse of such apparently enthusiastic support is almost as surprising as the level of support that had existed for so worthless a king as Charles I, but both were part and parcel of the nature of Royalism.

---

[132] Corbet, *Military government*, 87; SP 23/157, fos 103–13; SP 19/16, fo. 123; SP 19/116, fos 103–19; *CSPD 1644–5*, 301–2.

[133] G. A. Harrison, 'Royalist organisation in Wiltshire, 1642–1646', unpubl. Ph.D. diss. London 1973, 486–7; Hutton, *Royalist war effort*, 112–42.

3

Civilians and Soldiers, 1644–1649

Massey and the civilians, 1644–5

Trouble had been brewing among the Parliamentarians before their victories in June 1644. On 31 May two new association regiments were commissioned by ordinance, one of horse under Sheriff Thomas Stephens and one of foot under Colonel Edward Harley. Both were to be subordinate to Massey, whose own regiment was to be brought up to strength first. Massey insisted that they be recruited locally, in the hope that good wages might attract deserters from the royalist forces. But the county was already overburdened by troops. Colonel Purefoy's officers seized horses at random, and Waller's 'plunder malignants, do what we can and embezzle their goods'. Indeed, from April onwards, there had been a notable increase in accusations of casual brutality on both sides.[1]

No sooner were these problems resolved and Sudeley taken than Massey fell out with Waller, who was pursuing the king via Cirencester and Stow to Evesham. On 11 July Waller complained that when he laid a £2,000 rate on Kiftsgate Division, Massey, styling himself commander-in-chief of Gloucestershire (which hardly superseded Waller's own commission as sergeant-major-general), countermanded his warrants and refused to let him take provisions. Both claimed the contribution, and little was raised. Massey, unmoved by the suggestion that he could not have raised anything there before Waller's arrival, retorted that he needed these resources, money raised by the excise and sequestration being already assigned elsewhere, and added that Waller's withdrawal of some garrison troops had allowed the Royalists free rein.[2] This echoed the ongoing quarrel between Waller and Essex, whose 'creature' Clarendon said Massey was. Meanwhile, Waller's pursuit was held up, both sets of troops were in distress for want of pay, and Waller had to depart well before the Committee of Both Kingdoms ruled for Massey.[3]

In July Lieutenant-Colonel White, Major Gray and other officers petitioned the Committee of Both Kingdoms, making unspecified allegations against Massey, who was successfully defended by the faithful Captain Backhouse.

---

[1] *CJ* iii. 511; Corbet, *Military government*, 106; Waller to Committee of Both Kingdoms, 7 June 1644, *CSPD* 1644, 184, 214.

[2] Waller to Committee of Both Kingdoms, 15 June 1644, ibid. 239; Massey to Committee, 6 July, 336, ibid. 321–2; Committee to Waller and reply, 10–11 July, ibid. 341–2; *HMC*, MSS Salisbury, xxii. 375–9.

[3] *The memoirs of Edward Ludlow . . .*, 1625–1672, ed. C. H. Firth, Oxford 1894, ii. 458–9; Clarendon, *Rebellion*, viii. 63; *CSPD* 1644, 239, 336, 341–2; *CJ* iii. 549.

Within a month, Gray had been shot dead in a duel by Major Hammond after a dispute at the Council table.[4] The roots of this quarrel were deep. Hammond was major of horse to the city regiment, Gray to Stamford's, and there was much ill-feeling between the two regiments. By this time these comprised almost all the garrison troops, as few of Berrow's or Cooke's forces remained. During the siege, Massey had written of his inability to enforce civilian obedience 'w[hi]ch I had done & would doe if [Stamford's] regiment had equalled [th]e Citty in strength'. Since the capture of the original colonel of the city regiment, Henry Stephens, he had made himself colonel and insisted on his right to choose the officers.[5]

The two regiments were clearly differentiated. The city's, which was raised at the behest of Waller and the aldermen in 1643, was officered largely by aldermen and common councillors, Stamford's wholly by outsiders. The city's had larger companies and was better and more regularly paid. In September 1643 the arrears of Stamford's regiment stood at just under £13,000, the city's at just under £6,000, although Massey was endeavouring to redress the imbalance. After Gray's death, his troops were ready to avenge him, so that 'all the city and garrison were not far from an uproar . . . helped forward by some of the officers of [Stamford's] regiment'. Somehow Massey cobbled together a force without the mutinous elements and, on 2 August, defeated and killed Mynne at Redmarley, taking 300 prisoners. August was spent driving away Sir Marmaduke Langdale's northern horse from Corse Lawn, and recruiting the new regiments.[6]

Corbet reckoned this barely made up for the men lost through desertion to other garrisons of either side – perhaps 1,000 since the siege. This was an enduring problem, simply because other garrisons would willingly hire such men, pay them better and offer an easier life. Parliament tried to help by voting the garrison £4,000 from the estates of John Dutton and Viscount Camden, nudging the Wiltshire Committee to provide for Devereux at Malmesbury and incorporating Ayleworth's horse troop into the city regiment. Massey was in London on 14 August, for reasons unknown, but evidently the Commons were none too pleased with him, for they ordered that henceforth no commander was to leave his post without permission.[7] Then, having argued with just about every soldier available, Massey fell into a vicious battle with his civilian allies.

Corbet says nothing at all about this, but it is notable that the battle lines drawn up in July in a previous dispute between Corbet himself and an antinomian preacher, Roger Bacon, were quite different. Most of the

4 CSPD 1644, 343–4; Massey to Lentall, Bodl. Lib., MS Tanner 61, fo. 106. The Commons acquitted Hammond as he had acted in self-defence, though the Lords were hostile: CJ iii. 712; LJ vii. 30.
5 Bodl. Lib., MS Tanner 62, fo. 197; Luke journal, ii. 104; Taylor, 'Civil government', 75–6.
6 GRO, GBR B3/2, fo. 254; BL, E309 (39), The kingdom's weekly intelligencer, no. 127, 18–25 Nov. 1645; SP 28/129 v, fos 46–50, 100–2, 228; iii, fo. 549; iv, fos 841–52; Massey to Committee of Both Kingdoms, 4 Aug. 1644, CSPD 1644, 396–8.
7 Ibid. 410; Corbet, Military government, 105–15; Washbourne, Historical introduction, 95.

Committee and the ministers wanted Bacon thrown out of Gloucester, but Bacon asserted (and Corbet did not deny) that Massey and his future enemy, Isaac Bromwich of Bromsberrow, joined in protecting him. Two exiles from Herefordshire, Christopher Catchmay and Henry Jones, were also supportive; Sheppard and the mayor, Nicholas Webb, however, thought Bacon should be expelled, and he duly was. Corbet's riposte contained some jibes against Bromwich and Sheppard, but this cannot be taken as firm evidence of their allegiance, as it was not published until 1646.[8]

The root of the new quarrel was a simple dispute over authority, occasioned by the recruiting of the new regiments, in the context of growing shortages of money and men. Almost all the soldiers sent with the convoy had drifted off on the way. The assessment had to be increased by a special ordinance, from £750 per week in the county and £62 10s. in the Inshire to £1,000 and £100 for five months from August, as sequestration was not bringing in enough.[9] It is not easy to assess the committeemen's motives in the quarrel, as most of the evidence comes from Massey and his allies. But he clearly thought that certain men were trying to seize control of the garrison by using their power to build up Stephens's new regiment and run down the others.

On 1 September Massey complained that his authority was being undermined by civilians raising taxes to recruit Stephens's regiment 'some by virtue of a committee, others by a posse comitatis, lastly by virtue of a deputy lieutenant's authority', which was contrary to orders that Harley's regiment should be recruited first. He also implied that they were deliberately creating discontent by raising soldiers' wages, while not tackling the officers' arrears, and removing the provision for the cavalry's pay, which led to more desertion. As he said, no other county was 'so slenderly provided for', and troops would continue to abandon such notoriously hard duty. As late as April 1645, they were still deserting, 'now they see the Warwicke Troopes soe well cloathed, horsed and armed & soe well payed'.[10]

It is unclear whether or not the mass desertion was actually encouraged by the Committee, but if so they did the task well. Massey's own troop shrank from eighty to fifty-five by 17 September, others even more. They were probably just as short of cash as Massey, who chafed at being dependent on them and spent every penny of the £500 sent by the Commons in October on his own forces. But it may be true. Thomas Pury explicitly called many of Massey's soldiers supernumeraries, and the Committee did obstruct the

---

8   BL, E334 (5), R. Bacon, *The spirit of prelacie yet working, or truth from under a cloud*, London 1646, 5–8; E337 (15), J. Corbet, A *vindication of the magistrates and ministers of the city of Gloucester*, London 1646, 19–22.
9   A&O i. 518–20.
10 Massey to Committee of Both Kingdoms, 1, 5 Sept., 18 Nov. 1644, CSPD 1644, 466, 474–5, 1644–5, 132; Massey to Committee of Safety, 20 Apr. 1645, Bodl. Lib., MS Tanner 60, fo. 127.

attempts of Major Robert Harley and Major Throckmorton to recruit around Gloucester and Dean in October.[11]

Meanwhile Massey had successfully driven away the plundering northern horse and stormed the works Wintour was building to command the mouth of the Wye at Beachley. He then took Monmouth thanks to the treachery of Major Robert Kyrle, who had already changed sides twice before. Every time he left Gloucester, Massey had to raise forces from other commands; at Beachley he needed Denbigh's horse and the Malmesbury foot. Before long he was grumbling that the Committee's behaviour and the shortage of money were jeopardising Colonel Harley's governorship of Monmouth by making it impossible for him to raise his regiment. There were still 1,500 too few men to follow up these successes by blockading Bristol.[12]

By then Massey's conflict with Stephens was getting out of hand. When Massey marched on Monmouth, Major Duit, one of three horse officers sent from Wiltshire to join him, refused to march and went off to London to question Massey's authority. Stephens also withheld three of his four troops. He claimed that they were not Massey's to command, by virtue of the Instructions of August 1642 to the deputy lieutenants – 'few of whom are ... in favour of the Parliament and of which number he never was one', carped Massey, who furiously demanded to know which deputy lieutenants (in the Commons, presumably) were protecting Stephens.[13]

Some of Stephens's officers, he added, were slow to obey orders, and Stephens himself assumed the right to assess the county for horse 'without relation to the command and by virtue of his own warrants'. But Stephens was in a strong position and must have had Parliament's trust, for he was made sheriff indefinitely by special ordinance in June 1644 and was not replaced until November 1645.[14]

This quibble was the crux of the matter. Stephens was in the right, technically, for the deputy lieutenants were established by ordinance of Parliament, Massey by Essex's military *fiat*, which could not supersede it. Of course, there were many overlaps and inconsistencies in the powers created by Parliament, and this was the occasion, not the cause, of the quarrel. Pedantic observation of ordinances at one stage gave the Committee the excuse to deny Massey an allowance and the 'entertainment' promised him, as there was no ordinance providing for either. Massey understood these tactics and demanded to be established governor by ordinance, with full control over finance and the

---

[11] Massey to Committee of Both Kingdoms, 17 Sept., 11 Oct., 11 Nov. 1644, 21 Jan. 1645, *CSPD* 1644, 511–13; 1644–5, 31, 112–13, 266–9; Massey and Major Robert Harley to Edward Harley, 23 Oct., 15 Nov. 1644, HMC, MSS Portland, iii. 130.

[12] BL, E9 (4), *The weekly account*, no. 5, 11–18 Sept. 1644; E10 (22), *The kingdomes weekly intelligencer*, 24 Sept.– 1 Oct. 1644; *CSPD* 1644–5, 113; BL, E10 (23), *The London post*, no. 7, 1 Oct. 1644; *CJ* iii 671.

[13] Massey to Committee of Both Kingdoms, 21 Sept. 1644, *CSPD* 1644, 488–90, 524–5; Robert Harley to Edward Harley, 21 Sept. 1644, HMC, MSS Portland, iii. 127–8.

[14] *CSPD* 1644, 524–5; *CJ* iv. 264, 329.

militia, arguing that it was quite impossible for the garrison to function if these powers were split. The Committee also took their case to Westminster, with the support of most of the county's MPs.[15]

In similar disputes elsewhere, the Committee of Both Kingdoms might support one side against the other, but this one did not really mirror national politics and it was only a rather hapless arbiter. In December, together with the parliamentary Committee of Gloucester, it discussed Massey's nine-point petition. He demanded that he be vindicated from all 'false and scandalous aspersions' and confirmed as governor and commander of all forces in the Association by ordinance, that the Committee should be obliged to deliver him money 'as he shall moderately require' for any enterprise, for which he would give an account and so forth. Most of this received bland answers, referring all either to future deliberations or existing ordinances, to the satisfaction of no-one, and the Committee of Both Kingdoms simply asked both sides to bury the hatchet.[16] Parliament could not legislate for personality conflict.

Massey was a true professional soldier, with enough sense to be aware of civilians' views, but no empathy for them. He was ruthless in subordinating all to the cause; when Sir Robert Cooke died in October 1643, Massey ejected his widow from Highnam Court to make way for a garrison.[17] It is perhaps surprising that he took so long to fall out with everyone, for, if what he wrote to the Committee of Both Kingdoms, Sir Samuel Luke and the Harleys is anything to go by, he must have been a perfectly insufferable man. His letters show a deeply paranoid capacity to find links between unconnected events, combining epic accounts of his victories and plaintive reminders of past services and present woes with gratuitous sniping and warnings of imminent doom. He invariably contrived to give himself the credit for every success and blame others for every setback.

Massey must have had a peculiar talent for alienating people, for his opponents were a very mixed bag. The initial encounter was with Colonel Stephens and Pury, with whom he had previously clashed over the assessment arrears in 1643. Massey detested Pury, of whom he wrote in November 'The Poll Clerk, Mr Pury, having for his own pleasure taken a journey some way to London . . . if the Parliament desire him, I shall desire they would be pleased to keep him, for Gloucester finds little need of him.'[18]

Pury, Stephens and another enemy, the Cromwellian legal reformer William Sheppard, had very little in common with Isaac Bromwich, with whom Massey first argued when he chose Colonel Harley as governor of Monmouth rather

---

[15] Massey to Committee of Both Kingdoms, 18 Oct. 1644, 21 Jan. 1645, *CSPD 1644–5*, 53, 266–9.
[16] Ibid. 186–7, 190–1.
[17] Washbourne, *Historical introduction*, 89.
[18] *The letter books of Sir Samuel Luke*, ed. H.G. Tibbutt (Bedfordshire Historical Records Society xlii, 1963), 382.

than the renegade, Kyrle, whom Bromwich preferred. Bromwich was a syco-phantic crypto-Royalist, usually drunk, who fancied himself as honest broker to the Cavaliers. But he was consistent in his opposition to military abuses and pursued Stephens's major, Ingoldsby, who had embezzled recruitment funds and fled the county in October 1644, as fiercely as he pursued any of Massey's men.

Bromwich also accused Massey of selling off cattle for his own profit ('when I disposed not of a hoof', grumbled the governor) and helped Viscount Tracy and Viscount Scudamore make their peace, for which the former rewarded him handsomely. Pury, by contrast, was well-known to bear 'no good will to gentlemen'.[19] The followers of Charles II with whom Massey was to share his exile in the 1650s did not rate him either. Sir Walter Strickland thought that he cut a comically poor figure in political intrigue and Clarendon called him 'a wonderfully vain and weak man'.[20]

The Committee may have been irresponsible in withholding their troops and money, but Massey was no less so in deserting his command in October, when he had refused to return from Monmouth until cleared of the 'bitter articles' against him. His absence seems to have increased the Committee's taste for formulating strategy themselves. (They had already written to the Committee for Both Kingdoms questioning the wisdom of Massey's slighting of the Beachley works, and events had to some extent vindicated them when the Royalists reoccupied the works, though Massey soon righted this.)[21] But in November Massey was ordered away to relieve Banbury. In his absence, Major Throckmorton's rash attempt on Chepstow exposed Monmouth, and the Royalists retook it. As a result, the new regiments filtered away.[22]

This triggered another row as Throckmorton and others unnamed laid charges against Bromwich for his conduct in Gloucester during Massey's absence and at a Council of War in Monmouth at some time before 2 December. We can only reconstruct the charges through Bromwich's replies, but matters evidently centred on whether or not Throckmorton could attempt a 'design' – presumably the attack on Chepstow – without Massey's express approval. Bromwich thought that he could, because Massey had made him commander-in-chief in his absence, and most of those present agreed. Throck-morton remained unsure, but was confident that the plan was feasible. After-wards he blamed the disaster on Bromwich, alleging that the decision to march was made at an improperly constituted Council of War out of Bromwich's

19 Massey to Committee of Both Kingdoms, 8 Jan. 1645, CSPD 1644–5, 238, 272; Viscount Tracy and Thomas Tracy to Edward Harley, 14, 24 Aug. 1644, HMC, MSS Portland, iii. 125–6; Bromwich to Scudamore, 5 Oct. 1646, BL, MS Add. 11,044, fo. 215.
20 Memorials of the Great Civil War in England from 1646 to 1652, ed. H. Cary, London 1842, ii. 203–10; CSP iii. 144.
21 Luke letter book, 30–2; Committee to Committee of Both Kingdoms, 22 Sept. 1644, CSPD 1644, 528.
22 Corbet, Military government, 125–6; HMC, MSS Portland, iii. 131.

desire to 'entrench' on Massey's honour, which Bromwich vehemently re-futed.[23]

Thus a disagreement over procedure escalated into implications that a committeeman pursued a vendetta with Massey into treason. No more was heard of the charges, but these two men were not finished yet. Matters inevitably worsened as the run of success fizzled out. On 11 November Massey had complained that he had but 2,000 foot and sixty dragoons for six garrisons, and that only four of nine of Harley's companies were being recruited. This he blamed on the 'passions, envy and malice' of the Committee.[24] Lashing out blindly, he also argued with the parliamentary committee for the Association. They sent him a letter dated 26 November in response to one of his, which apparently accused John Stephens of slighting him by removing Captain Ayleworth to London without his permission. With the restrained bemuse-ment with which one treats the slightly deranged, they suggested that his 'somewhat high and harsh' words were caused by his 'understanding things in a worse sense than we intended'. They denied any intention of meddling in military matters, and declined his challenge to say why they should quarrel with him, as they 'neither know nor owne any quarrell'.[25]

Massey's petulance was getting out of hand. On 27 November Walter Powell, vicar of Standish, preached a sermon in the cathedral, with the approval of Massey, who probably knew the contents beforehand. It was an ill-disguised attack on the Committee, full of phrases like 'The injustice, oppression, tyranny and unreformation of Countrey Committees'. One un-identified member – 'a New Committee man, an old Hangman, and a posted Malignant and a professed Newter' – pointedly walked out before Powell started. Indeed, so far as can be deciphered through Powell's dreadful prose, the Committee may even have sponsored an alternative sermon in the city at the same time.

In backing Powell, Massey was making new enemies. The Committee were seriously divided as some began moves to sequester Powell from his living. Whoever did this, they did not include 'that quick-sighted much-knowing justice', Bromwich, who prevailed on the rest not to deny Powell the chance to defend himself, nor Anthony Clifford of Frampton, who opposed the ejection, nor Pury 'one of the first that . . . broke the Ice for me on my return', nor Edward Stephens, who procured his temporary restoration.[26] Massey had a case against some of the committeemen, but his behaviour and that of his allies could only make matters worse.

In the king's heartlands, meanwhile, all resources were devoted to putting

23 HMC, 13th Report, appendix, part ii (MSS Portland, viii), 4; BL, MS Loan 206, fos 16–17.
24 Massey to Committee of Both Kingdoms, 11 Nov. 1644, CSPD 1644–5, 112–13.
25 Parliamentary Committee to Massey, 26 Nov. 1644, BL, MS Loan 29, fo. 174.
26 W. Powell, Newes for newters, London 1648, 28, A3–6. Massey later supported Powell's application for relief: HMC, MSS Portland, i. 256.

down neutralist risings, reorganising the war effort and raising the army that was to perish at Naseby. Wintour was sick of the war and after the men Maurice sent him in January mutinied and broke up, he began to shut himself up in his mansion and made only the occasional, if destructive, sally. The Bristol Establishment, which came into being in late 1644, abandoned any pretence of using the Vale's wealth to suppport a force against Gloucester. The idea was to maintain Bristol from the adjacent parts of Gloucestershire, Somerset and Wiltshire. It cost Berkeley Division £300 per week. There were also plans, possibly never implemented, for an Oxford Establishment with payment schedules guaranteed to bleed the Cotswolds white, which was happening anyway.[27]

A more direct threat was Sir Jacob Astley's arrival at Cirencester in January 1645 with 1,500 foot. From there warrants were sent 'even to the gates of Gloucester for contribution with great threats' and Lypiatt House, John Stephens's home, was burned down. Meanwhile, Sir Henry Bard's garrison was exercising its 'illimited tyranny' over the Chipping Campden area before leaving, burning Campden House as it went. To deny Massey's supplies, the king sent his army into the Cotswolds in December and the rate of desertion rose again.[28] Gloucester was again exposed, with alarums on all sides, but there was no longer any pretence of co-ordination among the Royalists.

The feud continued into January, and, while the issues were being discussed, Stephens continued to deny Massey his troops. Massey grew isolated, with no allies but the Harleys and his brothers, whom he had made captains in Stamford's regiment to stiffen its loyalty. He grudgingly accepted the Committee of Both Kingdoms' rather meaningless findings, but soon the quarrels with Bromwich and Pury intensified. Massey claimed that Pury had accused him of not answering propositions which had not even been put to him, and was making unfair aspersions about his failing to ensure the double-locking of the gates of Gloucester as agreed in December.

Within weeks this had become full-blown treason and Pury stood accused of having 'engaged certain soldiers of the garrison, intending to have formed a party with them', and making promises of pay that could not possibly be fulfilled, so that many came to Massey to lay down their commissions. This situation was – of course! – rescued by Massey's personal appeal to their patriotism. He went on to accuse the Committee of taking away various assignations to deprive some men of winter quarters, so that the officers feared mutiny more than the Cavaliers. He had received only £50 from them since last June and none of the £1,000 sent from London, which left him in desperate straits. He was also being pressed to find men to move on Evesham and

---

[27] Hutton, *Royalist war effort*, 145–75; Harrison, 'Royalist organisation in Gloucestershire', 162–6, 232–3, 237; BL, E23 (12), *The London post*, no. 18, 7 Jan. 1645.
[28] *CSPD 1644–5*, 237–8; Corbet, *Military government*, 130–2; Clarendon, *Rebellion*, ix. 32; Hutton, *Royalist war effort*, 167.

Campden House when he had so few that he could barely stir from Gloucester.[29]

The Committee fought back too. On 5 February Major Throckmorton complained that although Massey had vindicated him of any blame for the loss of Monmouth and placed him in a garrison at Highmeadow to command the whole Forest Division, the Committee, led by James Kyrle and 'that unworthy man Mr Bromwitch and his adherents', had deprived him of sustenance so thoroughly that he had had to beg Massey to remove them to Stroud. They were also still preventing the recruitment of the Harleys' regiment.[30] The exoneration of Throckmorton implied the guilt of Bromwich himself. Now that the Committee were openly driving their enemies out of the county, Massey's accusations were finally turning into a self-fulfilling prophecy.

Massey became increasingly bitter and vindictive. In February he barely hid his gloating when Stephens, marching from Beverstone to join Devereux's Malmesbury force at the relief of Rawden House, was boxed in by the Cirencester, Fairford and Lechlade Royalists. Massey was prevented by foul weather and Astley's greater numbers from reaching him, and Stephens surrendered. He was later exchanged and came back to Gloucester without the forces that were to have ended Massey's governorship. Publicly, Massey stated that this was the result of 'his owne act and pleasure without my approbation or knowledge thereof', and he made some trenchant comments on the danger of 'Independent Colonels' and the need for his own command to be established.[31] Privately, he commented to Colonel Harley that 'Collonell Stephens as high sheriff may doe anythinge, and as collonell, is but subservient to Thomas Stevens, vice-comes, and not at all bound to give me an accompte.' He then reported a victory over Wintour at Lancaut, adding, smugly, 'Thus hath God beene good unto us, giveing us some victorys by such as wilbe comanded by me.' He repeated much the same to Sir Samuel Luke, and such was his venom that a similar ill fortune to another garrison veteran, Colonel Hopton, at Castleditch House, brought only more sniping in the same vein.[32]

Stephens's defeat drew the sting out of the battle. Parliament replaced his forces with three of Essex's horse regiments, plus five assorted troops out of other garrisons under Colonel Edward Cooke (though not all showed up), and asked Essex to make Massey commander of all the Association forces.[33]

[29] Massey to Committee of Both Kingdoms, 21, 22 Jan. 1645, CSPD 1644–5, 186–7, 190–1, 238, 250, 266–71.
[30] Throckmorton to Edward Harley, 8 Feb. 1645, HMC, MSS Portland, iii. 135; Major Robert Harley to Edward Harley, 13 Feb., ibid. 136.
[31] B. Whitelocke, Memorials of English affairs, London 1682, 132; Massey to Committee of Both Kingdoms, 12, 16 Feb. 1645, CSPD 1644–5, 301–2, 308; Massey to Luke, 23 Feb., Luke letter books, 458.
[32] Massey to Edward Harley, 23 Feb. 1645, HMC, MSS Portland, iii. 136; Massey to Luke, 10, 23 Feb. 1645, Luke letter books, 448, 458.
[33] Committee of Both Kingdoms to Waller and Massey, 10 Apr. 1645, CSPD 1644–5, 322, 345–7, 398; Massey to Commons, 19 Apr. 1645, Bodl. Lib., MS Tanner 60, fo. 103.

Massey's problems did not end there, but his last, unintentionally funny, letter was written on 17 March to Edward Harley. Speaking of the need for new men on the Herefordshire Committee ('Ours must be all transplanted or cut off') he said that it was to Colonel Stephens and Lieutenant-Colonel Kyrle that

> the eyes of old choleric Mr Kyrle and high strained Mr Sheppard exceedingly look . . . they have 'out studdyed' themselves in the things and ordinances of Parliament that they have quite cast them aside and now have found a rule of their own by which they resolved to walk. And Mr Pury and Mr Bromwich, their guides at a distance, have new tricks to show to the world . . . Mr Kyrle and Mr Sheppard have refused to come and sit at the [Committee] these two or three days. Mr Bromwich has doubtless 'principled' them, and hopes to erect some new structure of his own fancy.[34]

It scarcely mattered at that moment, for the royalist cause was quietly collapsing in Gloucestershire. The fall of Shrewsbury led to Astley's withdrawal from Cirencester, and Massey began to spend much of his time in Herefordshire. The latest governor of Berkeley, Charles Lucas, like others before him, was reduced to despair by his inability to collect contributions due to enemy garrisons and popular hatred. He was also hampered by others' demands on the area as the Bristol Establishment collapsed under the weight of its own ambiguities.[35]

Massey was reinforced by the Warwickshire and Northamptonshire horse and found allies in the Herefordshire Clubmen brutally suppressed by Rupert. Although worsted in an engagement at Ledbury where Backhouse was mortally wounded, he withdrew in good order to Dean and flushed out Wintour, who burned his house as he left. Massey remained inactive, apart from a diversion towards Bristol, until on 26 May, with most of the king's forces gone, he stormed Evesham.[36] This was the concluding honour of the military government of Gloucester, as Massey now left to join Sir Thomas Fairfax's army in the west.

This dispute was not the only one to affect local parliamentarian commands, but it was distinct in many ways. The parties did not correspond to 'peace' and 'war', 'moderate' and 'radical' parties, nor did they truly reflect Westminster politics, in contrast to other similar disputes. For instance, Sir John Gell intervened, from Derbyshire, in Nottinghamshire and, as the ally of Sir William Brereton, the radical Cheshire leader, helped to purge the 'moderates' on the Staffordshire Committee allied to the earl of Denbigh, who in turn was trying to force a 'radical' Warwickshire Committee into line in his West Midland Association, in a convoluted feud fought both locally and at Westminster.[37] Massey's argument was confined to two counties and had scant

---

[34] Massey to Edward Harley, 17 Mar. 1645, HMC, MSS Portland, iii. 137.
[35] Harrison, 'Royalist organisation in Gloucestershire', 216–51.
[36] Corbet, *Military government*, 140–52; BL, E277 (14), E281 (5), *The moderate intelligencer*, 3–10 Apr., 24 Apr.–1 May 1645.
[37] Beats, 'Derbyshire', 146–7; Morrill, *Cheshire*, 76–81; *The committee at Stafford: the order*

central dimension. Neither side was less committed to winning the war; both were guilty of corruption and pettiness. It was in the main a personality clash.

Massey was not like Sir William Brereton in Cheshire, or Sir John Gell in Derbyshire. Although he was a 'county' commander like them, he was also a soldier of dubious origins and even more dubious character, trying to command a touchy set of gentlemen. He could inspire great loyalty and he always had his supporters; an implacable foe who long nursed his grudge against Thomas Stephens, he was also a faithful friend to Backhouse, taking great concern for his widow's welfare, as he did for the 'well affected' in general. He enjoyed much greater popularity among the rulers of Gloucester than he did among the gentry.[38]

The issues raised between Massey and his enemies on the Committee also split the civilians, including the Stephens clan. On 16 May three petitions arrived in London, one from the Gloucester corporation for his retention in the city, which was delivered by Nathaniel Stephens, and two against him from the Committees of Gloucestershire and Herefordshire, which were delivered by Edward Stephens.[39] Now and throughout his eventful career, Massey was above all a man who provoked division and trouble.

Taking accounts and the end of the war

As in many counties with a strong but disputed parliamentarian presence, the Committee – or to be precise that part of it acting as the Committee of Sequestration (which formed the bulk of the work anyway) – soon fell out with its sub-committee of accounts. Resentment of such bodies of men of relatively low origin, who inspected the accounts of soldiers and officials alike and reported directly to London, is not surprising, but the resulting conflicts varied greatly in their nature and intensity. A sub-committee might be a mere pawn of the main committee or of one of its factions, or might attack it autonomously. Much depended on who, on the main committee, approved or nominated the sub-commitee; in this case it was Pury. Most sub-committees were 'moderate' bodies seeking to root out unjustifiable actions, as in the most spectacular example in Warwickshire, where the two sub-committees aligned themselves with Denbigh in the wider general feud. But the essential problem was the same everywhere; what extra-legal activity was justifiable in order to win the war and who was to make that judgement?[40]

book of the Staffordshire County Committee, 1643–1645, ed. D. H. Pennington and I. A. Roots, Manchester 1956, p. lxx; Hughes, *Warwickshire*, 220–8.
38 *CJ* iii. 476, 497–8; iv. 165; HMC, MSS Portland, i. 262; Massey to Accounts Committee, [Feb?] 1647, *CSPD 1645–7*, 527.
39 *CJ* iii. 145; Massey to Lenthall, undated, *HMC*, MSS Portland, i. 223.
40 D. H. Pennington, 'The accounts of the kingdom', in F. J. Fisher (ed.), *Essays in the economic and social history of Tudor and Stuart England*, Cambridge 1961, 182–203; Morrill, *Revolt*, 69–70; Beats, 'Derbyshire', 268–70; Hughes, *Warwickshire*, 220–54.

In Gloucestershire, the sub-committee, which was in being by January 1645, was unusual in confronting the County Committee from a 'radical' standpoint. The Committee was as touchy over its authority with the sub-committee as it was with Massey, and responded to preliminary enquiries with a sardonically over-friendly letter, refusing to delay matters or question the sub-committee's right to call committeemen and their officers to account, well though it might, even though the sub-committee wanted the accounts handed in within ten days when its own clerks were struggling to get them done every quarter. Thus encouraged, many soldiers failed to give in their accounts. From the outset, the sub-committee found itself 'slighted' and found it hard to get more than a small core to sit, though it often asked for more to be named.[41]

In September 1645 conflict erupted as the sub-committee imprisoned Giles Birt, a sequestration official, for his refusal to bring in his accounts for over a year or to pay fines imposed for it. The Sequestration Committee immediately released Birt and compounded the insult by ordering his arrears and losses to be paid, so that his account should add up. Soon after, in Gloucester market place, Anthony Clifford publicly called a sub-committeeman 'peremtorie rogue' for daring to summon him to explain his actions, and threatened to release Birt again if they rearrested him.[42]

There was a social dimension to this. The Committee was still dominated by 'county' gentlemen like Clifford, Bromwich and Sheppard (who most encouraged Birt), whilst the leading sub-committeeman, William Mayo, was an obscure figure, so poor that his estate was said to be ruined by the plundering of five oxen. Conversely, the sub-committee also castigated Birt as a 'pore Cobler', unfit to handle large sums of money and lead a group of officials.[43] Perhaps more significantly, in view of the Inshire dispute, the sub-committee came to be dominated by Gloucester men like Anthony Edwards and Robert Payne.

Some measure of disagreement was inevitable given the *ad hoc* nature of the wartime administration, but it does seem that the sub-committee uncovered a web of partiality and petty corruption, possibly involving Sheppard and Blayney.[44] It accused the Sequestration Committee of letting out estates to delinquents and its own agents at undervalues and pressed for wider powers to convict delinquents. Probably in August 1645, it asked for many additions to both committees and power to enforce the prescribed oaths on Royalists 'for

41 Committee to Sub-Committee, 4 Apr. 1645, Sub-Committee to Accounts Committee, 4 Apr., 18 Oct. 1645, William Mayo to Accounts Committee, 26 July 1645, SP 28/255; Sub-Committee to Accounts Committee, 15 June 1647, SP 28/257; SP 28/253, fos 46, 55v.
42 SP 28/228, fos 761–3; Mayo to Accounts Committee, 22 Sept. 1645, Sub-Committee to Accounts Committee, 18 Oct, SP 28/255; Morrill, *Revolt*, 185. The fine was paid by 1649: SP 28/154.
43 Thomas Morse to Accounts Committee, 9 Aug. 1645, Sub-committee to Accounts Committee, 9 Sept., SP 28/255,
44 SP 28/252 i, fos 24v–5.

there have beene formerlie to much favour to Malignantes'.[45] It was not within the central Committee's remit to grant this, but the sub-committee continued to protest about 'some fewe [of the Committee] that medle most with the Treasurie' over the irregularities in the Tewkesbury garrison accounts and fought a long battle to force the treasurer, Theophilus Alye, to give proper accounts. With many delays, this dragged on into 1648.[46]

Personal quarrels may have been involved, but there is no doubting the zeal of some sub-committeemen like the Gloucester aldermen and the ferocious old Puritan, Anthony Kingscote, who later disinherited his eldest son for Royalism. The sub-committee also publicised the fact that Alderman Powell had been voted no delinquent by the 'Graund Committee', despite fleeing to the king's army in 1643, and this may have helped to bring him to book. It was patently the Committee that courted the conflict, whilst the sub-committee refused 'to make comparisons of power, all are derived from one Roote'.[47] There were many soldiers and officials with something to hide from interfering outsiders.

There was also an element of shadow-boxing in all of this, for the two committees had members in common, namely Kingscote and Alderman Webb (contrary to the letter of the Act establishing sub-committees of accounts) and shared a treasurer, Alderman Clutterbuck, while Edwards was also clerk to the main Committee. Moreover, the accounting process was also useful to the Committee as it harrassed Massey for fifteen months, even tipping off the central Committee when he was in London, to a predictably shrill response. In July 1646 Pury actually berated the sub-committee for not being active enough in one particular case.[48]

Taking accounts could both twist old battles and create new ones. After demobilisation began in the summer of 1646, more and more accounts came in and the sub-committee spent most of the time worrying about being evicted from its makeshift offices for not paying the rent as all but the diehards gave up.[49] By then the personnel of the County Commitee was changing too.

[45] Mayo to Accounts Committee, 26 July 1645, Sub-Committee to Accounts Committee, 9 Sept. 1645, SP 28/255; SP28/252 ii, fo. 4; 253A vi, fo. 25.
[46] SP 28/252 ii, fos 4, 24v–5; SP 28/253 v, fos 5v; Sub-committee to Accounts Committee, 30 May 1646, SP 28/256; Sub-committee to Accounts Committee, 9 Apr. 1646, SP 28/257.
[47] H. R. P. Finberg, 'Three studies in family history', in Gloucestershire studies, Leicester 1957; Sub-Committee to Accounts Committee, 18 Oct. 1645, Sub-Committee to Committee, 4 Apr. 1645, SP 28/255; CCAM ii. 824–6.
[48] Edward and John Stephens and Pury to Accounts Committee, 19 Dec. 1645, SP 28/255; Pury to Accounts Committee, 22 June 1646, Mayo to Accounts Committee, 18 July 1646 SP 28/256; Pury, Hodges and Nathaniel Stephens to Accounts Committee, 26 Feb. 1647, SP 28/257; CSPD 1645–7, 527.
[49] Sub-committee to Accounts Committee, 16 Aug. 1647, 9 Apr., 13 June, 3 July 1648, SP 28/257; SP 28/252 passim.

After an interim period during which Nathaniel Stephens and Hodges were sent to take charge and Colonel Walter Lloyd was appointed governor, Colonel Thomas Morgan succeeded Massey on 18 June 1645. He seems to have been on better terms with the Committee, but in other ways military–civilian relations were deteriorating. This was not a decline from the excellent spirit that prevailed during the siege; rather different troops reacted to different circumstances. New forces came and went throughout 1644 and 1645. Massey took Stamford's regiment, much of the city regiment and Major Buller's newly arrived horse away to the west, where they earned an appalling reputation and his wounded vanity became even worse. Those left behind were a curious ragbag from many forces, including the Northampton, Newport Pagnell and Aylesbury horse. The lists of officers for 1645–8 bear no resemblance to those of 1643–4; Morgan himself referred to his men as 'soldiers of fortune'.[50]

Although Parliament had always been generous to the garrison, Massey also left behind a dire financial situation. Between August 1643, when the impending siege sparked off a flurry of activity, and June 1646, grants and loans totalling £33,780, plus arms, ammunition and clothing, were made, and none of Gloucestershire's revenue was sent up to London as it was supposed to be. But much had to be assigned out of the excise and advanced by the MPs. Some never reached Gloucester, where the garrison's wages alone cost £7,000 per month in May 1644.[51]

We cannot know how much was raised or simply taken locally, but by April 1645 the Committee painted a bleak picture, saying that by taxation, free quarter and plunder 'our countrey was soe extreamely exhausted and miserably destroyed that it was quite ready to give up the ghost. . . . It must not be expected that a destroyed country shall maintaine this garrison.' As long as the royalist presence persisted the only way to get money was to 'wander up & downe after Contribution'. This was a circular problem when the sole horse regiment was shrinking for want of pay.[52]

Reinforcements were a mixed blessing too. In July the Committee was totally unable to pay the horse it had borrowed, and the Committee of Both Kingdoms had to offload the problem elsewhere, referring Colonel Edward Cooke's regiment to Massey and that of Captain Andrewes, who 'extreamely complain for want of pay', to the Newport Pagnell Committee, lest they desert completely.[53] In August, as a result, Morgan could not prevent Rupert's *chevauchées* around Berkeley. There were added problems as the ill-equipped

---

[50] *CSPD* 1644–5, 599, 602; *HMC*, 7th Report, part i, appendix (MSS House of Lords 1648–65), 68–9.
[51] *CJ* iii. 480 and passim; v, passim.
[52] County Committee and Massey to Committee of Safety, 8, 25 Apr. 1645, Bodl. Lib., MS Tanner 60, fos 75, 127.
[53] *CSPD* 1645–7, 18, 22, 38, 41, 63; Luke to William Love, 1 May 1645, *Luke letter book*.

New Model Army straggled to Bristol, and the Scots quite impoverished the Herefordshire border area.[54]

Fairfax's siege of Bristol saw the zenith of popular wartime activity, as large numbers of men rose to help him in both Gloucestershire and Somerset, whipped up by Hugh Peter's sermons. They are referred to as Clubmen or 'Sir John Seymour's Clubbers', though this was not a typical Clubman rising. The local gentry led them, notably a Mr Stephens, Seymour, Philip Langley of Mangotsfield, Matthew Huntley of Boxwell and John Codrington. The miners of Dean, who had fled rather than help the king besiege Gloucester, also helped as pioneers.[55] Berkeley Castle was stormed two weeks later on 23 September. If it is true that supplies were found there 'in so much that it was thought there was victuals for 300 men for five months', the burden of this garrison on the country must have been staggering.[56]

In some ways the fall of Bristol worsened the whole situation. Gloucester was permanently reduced to, and regarded as, a lesser consideration. A Bristol garrison had to be supported, and the town could not manage it alone. While the Commons debated a new establishment for Bristol, including Berkeley Division and the Bath area, the officers of the New Model sent out warrants into Gloucestershire and Somerset for provisions, giving debentures for repayment.[57] But the`Clubmen' and the Gloucester troops, after they had returned from South Wales in October, needed these same resources. With the support of the militia and the rest of the garrisons, the foot petitioned Parliament. Quite apart from the injustice of taking away what had been the main incentive for the troops to fight on, they claimed that they were already living on 12d. per week and the officers on nothing. If Berkeley Division's £600 per week (out of the whole county's total of £1,100, which was still £400 short of the wages bill) were removed, then all bar one foot regiment and two horse troops must disband, the county would be open to plunder, and the assignation system, which the County Committee had laboured to perfect, would be irreparably disrupted.[58]

The Committee supported them by demanding two years' assessment arrears 'to the very walls of [Bristol] . . . and inforce it by driving the country, imprisoning persons, beating and wounding such as resist them in this violence'. The Bristol commissioners asked them to stop, pointing out that the inhabitants could barely pay their present assessments, much less arrears, but the Committee retorted that they had no business freeing the inhabitants from

54 LJ viii. 513; CSPD 1645–7, 56; Zweigman, 'County government', 889.
55 BL, E302(2), The moderate intelligencer, no. 29, 11–18 Sept. 1645; E302 (14), Mercurius Aulicus, 31 Aug.–7 Sept. 1645.
56 BL, E305 (5), E304 (8), Mercurius Civicus, 9–16 Sept., 1–8 Oct. 1645; E307 (14), Two letters from Colonell Morgan.
57 Bristol Commissioners to Lenthall, 8 Oct. 1645, HMC, MSS Portland, i. 283; CJ iv, 300–1, 311.
58 BL, E309 (39), The kingdom's weekly intelligencer, no. 127, 18–25 Nov. 1645; HMC, MSS House of Lords, 1644–7, 77–8.

these arrears in the first place. Both sides were right. There were simply not enough resources to maintain so many troops, troops moreover who were becoming unruly and even clashing with each other. The Bristol commissioners begged Parliament to send money lest 'it may exasperate the Clubmen and begett a new contest'.[59]

Fortunately, the New Model marched away and the Clubmen dispersed, but when Morgan's men returned from Wales in November, the problem returned. Meanwhile, other parts suffered continuing warfare as the Scots besieged Hereford and Devereux fought the Cavaliers at Lechlade. There was more gruelling duty for the Gloucester garrison in December, with another Welsh campaign and the taking of Hereford. The tension between soldier and civilian was such that the Committee of Both Kingdoms drafted a letter warning Morgan to take care that no violence erupt when his men marched through Gloucester.[60] Having almost won the war, the Parliamentarians were already beginning to throw away the peace.

Any attempt to quantify the 'effects' of the Civil War is difficult when so much of the evidence is subjective and anecdotal, but some details are very revealing, showing how the war was often fought determinedly at all levels of society. One of the earliest Parliamentarians, Jeremy Buck, personally beat up the royalist rector of his home parish, Minchinhampton, and twice ransacked his house. And when some local troops seized another royalist rector, Robert Rowden, at a Nympsfield inn, they not only made no distinction between local Royalists and others but intended to carry out a symbolic revenge for the treatment of the Cirencester prisoners by making this obscure, harmless man 'goe to our garrison w[ith] us as the souldiers did from Cirencester to Oxford, that is naked'.[61]

Those after-effects of the war which seemed to loom largest at the time are worth highlighting. John Morrill reckons that in Cheshire the costs of warfare, in plunder, free quarter and so forth, were heavier than taxation. This may also have been true of Gloucestershire, where experience of the war was in some ways similar. Here, Parliament assessed £188,000 between February 1643 and October 1647, but there are few clues as to how much was actually raised. Of four assessments, all after June 1644, where the amounts demanded of and paid by the stewards of Pebworth and Marston in the north-eastern corner are recorded, about 80 per cent was paid each time.[62]

The evidence on the war's immediate costs is clearer. Nathaniel Stephens's rent roll in Eastington and Frampton fell by only a fifth during the war.

---

[59] Bristol Commissioners to County Committee and reply, 27, 29 Sept. 1645, Bristol Commissioners to Lenthall, 8 Oct., HMC, MSS Portland, i. 283–6.
[60] Committee of Both Kingdoms to Morgan, 29 Nov. 1645, CSPD 1645–7, 242. This letter was never sent.
[61] *Mercurius Rusticus*, xvii. 129–32; GRO, TRS 128.
[62] Morrill, *Cheshire*, 108–9; A&O, passim; HMC, MSS Salisbury, xxii. 375–9.

Although both villages were garrisoned on and off, they were under Gloucester's immediate control so the burden of assessments and quartering was minimised. But the military situation meant that very few were that lucky. The Grand Committee found almost every Inshire village plundered at some stage before 1644, and some suffered again when Astley governed Cirencester. Accusations of plunder by Royalists, sometimes by policy, sometimes because the troops could not be controlled, were legion. Massey too habitually pillaged enemy-controlled territory. Trade links along the Severn were disrupted, and the cloth industry suffered heavily because the war prevented the products from reaching London.[63]

Some areas suffered repeatedly. The Tewkesbury region was plundered by Massey in October 1643, again by Mynne and Wintour in July 1644 and had to quarter part of the Scots army in 1645.[64] The earl of Middlesex's estates at nearby Forthampton were mulcted, and William Hill, his steward, imprisoned, by both sides in turn; in 1645, with affairs more settled, £80 out of their annual value of £600 went in taxes. This in itself was bearable, but the addition of free quarter crippled the estate. As a result, the land's value declined so far that tenants refused to pay rents, abandoned their leases or dictated their own terms to renew them. There is more reliable evidence for the north-eastern corner of the county. Here Middlesex suffered even more, paying out according to the fluctuating fortunes of the Cotswold and Oxford Royalists and the garrisons of Gloucester, Coventry and Warwick. This meant £600 per year from Seizincote, Welford-on-Avon and Weston-on-Avon in 1643 (25 per cent of their value) and twice as much under Bard's tyranny. Even more tenants quit than at Forthampton. Seizincote was allegedly depopulated as a result of the war.[65]

There is a striking similarity between different estate accounts in this area. John Chamberlain of Maugersbury, near Stow, a vulnerable crossroads town, lost £446 10s. 4d. in quartering, contributions and spoiling of crops, besides pilfered stock, bribes to soldiers to go away and other charges, in fifty-six separate entries. The stewards of Pebworth and Marston paid much the same, £452 2s. 4d., between March 1643 and November 1645 in eighty-three items. Chamberlain paid out at different times to Vavasour, Morton and the garrisons of Gloucester, Oxford and Beverstone, while the Pebworth and Marston accounts name eight garrisons, most often Evesham, Sudeley and later Chipping Campden, and no less than thirty-three commissioners, soldiers or groups of soldiers and others unspecified. Chamberlain's revenue from fairs in Stow fell from £77 in 1641 and £62 in 1642 to £1 0s. 6d. in 1643, nil in 1644 when plague, spread by soldiers, forced the cancellation of the fairs and £5 10s. 7d. in 1645, recovering only in 1647 to their pre-war level.[66]

---

63 GRO, D547A/F2; SP 28/228 iv, v; *CSPD* 1644–5, 237–8; Roy, 'England turned Germany?', 134, 137–9.
64 Harrison, 'Royalist organisation in Gloucestershire', 185; *CSPD* 1644, 321; *CJ* iv. 265.
65 Prestwich, *Cranfield*, 568–70, 573; Hughes, *Warwickshire*, 218; S. Rudder, *A new history of Gloucestershire*, Cirencester 1777, 645.
66 GRO, D621/E2 M18, loose fos; D45/T5; HMC, MSS Salisbury, xxii. 375–9.

What is most striking is the sheer fluidity of the war. More often than not, Chamberlain and the Pebworth and Marston stewards were paying out to both sides. Similarly, Minchinhampton, Avening and Uley, parliamentarian by military circumstance as well as inclination, paid similar sums to the Royalists at Malmesbury and to the parliamentarian garrison at nearby Stroud. Many parishes in the north were continually mulcted by Worcestershire Royalists. Those under exclusive royalist control were no better off – Eastleach Turville had to compound for large arrears dating from when it had been controlled by Malmesbury. Only large garrisons were of any use in protecting the surrounding areas.[67]

Cirencester and Tewkesbury saw fighting several times. The former suffered because she was defensible. The latter was not, and was thus forced to co-operate with both sides, as a result of which she was then fined by both for half-heartedness. Gloucester alone remained under one side's control throughout, and the siege was reckoned not particularly destructive, yet a 1646 investigation found 241 houses and other buildings to the value of £22,400 destroyed, as well as goods worth £4,500, a heavy burden for a 'declining' city. Some 1,250 people were left homeless – one family was lodged in a pigeon house – and the suburbs were not rebuilt until the eighteenth century. Plague was another well-known effect of war and recorded plague deaths in Gloucester rose by 50 per cent in 1643 and another 100 per cent in 1644. Post-war apprenticeship registration patterns were similar in Gloucester, Worcester and Shrewsbury, hinting at a trade slump followed by a short-lived revival in the late 1640s.[68]

Not all destruction was accidental. At Chipping Campden 'neere half the houses in the Towne' were pulled down when Campden House was fortified. Rupert burned the villages of Clifton (Gloucestershire) and Bedminster (Somerset) to deny cover to the besiegers of Bristol; likewise, Massey fired Beachley.[69] Perhaps most striking to contemporaries, many of the county's grandest houses were ruined. The White Cross, Lypiatt House, Yate Court, Campden House and others all went up in flames; Highmeadow Hall, Beverstone Castle and Highnam Court were badly damaged. Sudeley Castle was defiled by troops in 1642; in 1646, 'by the breaking down and burning of fair and costly wainscoting and other utensils that house ... is very much defaced', and in 1650, after much argument, it was slighted lest an invading army garrison it.[70]

Berkeley Castle was hit particularly severely. Colonel Forbes broke the 1643 surrender articles by pulling down the walls, bridges and houses and ransacking

---

[67] GRO, D621/E2; HMC, MSS Salisbury, xxii. 375–9; SP 28/154; Zweigman, 'County government', 887–8.

[68] S. Porter, 'The destruction of urban property in the English Civil Wars, 1642–1651', unpubl. Ph.D. diss. London 1983, 61, 64, 107–8, 190, 210; Roy, 'England turned Germany?', 142–4.

[69] LJ vii. 584; CSPD 1644–5, 43.

[70] Mercurius Rusticus, vi. 46–7; CSPD 1645–7, 298; 1649, 73, 106; 1650, 53–4, 194.

the estate to his own profit. With successive governors' misbehaviour and constant warfare in the area, Smyth reckoned that by June 1645, £3,000 worth of furniture had been 'imbeaseled and spoyled', £300 worth of wood cut and so much lost that soon the ancient estate would be worth less 'then [Lord Berkeley's] great grandfather yearly expended in livery cotes and badges'.

When Lucas surrendered the castle, Morgan allowed his hungry troops 'free bowte' and five shillings apiece. The plunder went on for another year. None other than Captain Matthews was appointed governor, and he presided over the sale of much lead, the castle bells and gates, the destruction of hundreds of ancient charters for their silk strings, and the removal of some 700 moveables to Gloucester for auction; in September 1646 Charles Jay tipped off Smyth that Matthews himself intended to buy most.[71]

Eleven other officers were involved, mostly recent arrivals, but including locals like Lieutenant-Colonel Silcocks and Captain Raymond. And it is only because Lord Berkeley was not a sequestered Royalist and could complain in the Lords that we know about this. Not for the last time, the Committees of Gloucester and Bristol, faced with the troops' pressing needs, were harsher than the Commons. Some Bristol men wanted the castle demolished so that the contributions of Berkeley and Pucklechurch Hundreds could be diverted to Bristol; the move found support on the County Committee and Smyth had to pull strings with his friends there, Richard Stephens and Stephen Fowler, to prevent further slighting when the castle was disgarrisoned. Lord Berkeley was lucky to have friends in London as well, and at length his nominee, Colonel Berrow, was made governor.[72]

Civilians and soldiers, 1645–48

Parliament had originally intended to include Gloucestershire in the new Western Association of 1644, but when the ordinance passed the county was instead kept in a less formal association with Herefordshire and the four Welsh counties. The terms of this were always vague as the Lords rejected the Commons' instructions, though they agreed to the continuation of sequestration ordinances.[73] Like the Western Association, it was run by a parliamentary committee. Local gentry nominated to one provincial committee were to have full control of the taking of goods and free quarter. In practice, these acted separately in each county, although both the Gloucester and Hereford groups styled themselves 'the Committee of Parliament for Glouc[ester], Heref[ord] &c', or vice-versa.[74]

71 LJ vi. 68–9; vii, 507–8; Smyth to George Berkeley, 15 June 1645, Smyth of Nibley papers, xi. 36; Jay to Smyth, 9 Sept. 1646, ibid. 44; HMC, 5th Report, MSS Cholmondely, 356–7.
72 Ibid.; HMC, MSS House of Lords, 1644–7, 81.
73 CJ iii. 532, 582–6; LJ vi. 663, 670, 676–7, 683; vii 35.
74 SP 28/229 passim; G. E. McParlin, 'The Herefordshire gentry in county society and government, 1625–1661', unpubl. Ph.D. diss. Aberystwyth 1981, 113.

The aim was to provide for the forces in those parts, which were all put under Morgan's command. Although the parliamentary Committee was dominated by Gloucestershire MPs, the burden was also heaviest here, as the other counties were still under royalist control. The £1,100 per week charged on the county and Inshire was barely less than on the other five counties put together. It became plain that sequestration and the excise (which was in force by April 1645) would not provide as much as had been envisaged. By ordinance, the Association was entitled to the proceeds of undiscovered estates of papists and delinquents in the region worth less than £6,000 per year. None were worth more. In an impoverished county, these were powerful incentives against leniency to the Royalists.

Moreover, no-one could yet solve the problem of supporting Bristol. The Bristol garrison was to be supported by a monthly assessment of £3,000 for the next six months out of the city and adjacent counties, including £800 per month out of Berkeley Division. This would have left the Gloucester garrison vulnerable, reliant on sequestration and other revenues for support, as almost half of the remaining assessment also came from this rich but exhausted division. In February 1646 Governor Skippon complained that the last contributions were three months in arrears. He had had little from Wiltshire or Somerset, but there was 'not one penny as yet so much as settled as far as I can understand by the Committee of Gloucester'.[75]

Soon after, possibly in response, the parliamentary Western Committee formally annexed £194 per week from Berkeley Division's assessment to Bristol. On 13 April 1646 the Gloucestershire Committee complained to the Speaker that they could barely maintain two foot regiments and one of horse anyway, as the rest of the contribution was assigned elsewhere and the repair of Gloucester's fortifications was a heavy commitment.[76] By May, three of Morgan's best troops were said to be close to disbanding and the Committee was at a loss for what to do. The assignation system was collapsing. It is not clear how this was resolved, but Morgan continued to lament the 'Miserable Condic[i]ons' of his forces at Raglan Castle, forced to pay for everything on site, and short of powder and equipment. He blamed this squarely on the removal of their assignations for the maintenance of Bristol. The siege was in jeopardy for want of money and powder, until the Commons came to the rescue. As a result, the assessment on the Association had to be extended for a month.[77]

The Bristol ordinance remained and the Bristol troops resisted the Committee's attempts to get them out, even skirmishing with those of Gloucester when the latter tried to secure the division's contribution for themselves. Finally, in August, both were ordered to cease collecting and to withdraw to

[75] J. Latimer, *The annals of Bristol in the seventeenth century*, Bristol 1900, 209; *LJ* viii. 153.
[76] Committee to Lenthall, 13 Apr. 1646, Bodl. Lib., MS Tanner 59, fo. 52.
[77] Corporation to John Lenthall, 19 May, Committee to Lenthall, 25 May, Morgan to Lenthall, 23 July 1646, ibid. 62, fos 220, 247, 420; *CJ* iv. 628.

their garrisons, while a new establishment for Bristol was debated; 'they are friends, why should they fall out?' went the rather unhelpful official line.[78] After the defeat of the king's last field army at Stow-on-the-Wold on 21 March 1646, every garrison except Gloucester and Bristol was slighted and most of their troops were earmarked for Ireland. The assignments issue, however, was still being discussed in October, and disbandment dragged on for years, as it made the troops even more determined to have their arrears.[79]

At this point, some comments are needed about who was actually ruling Gloucestershire in the aftermath of the war. As we have seen, few of the pre-war elite supported Parliament but there were no *parvenus* in power as yet. Attendances at quarter sessions can be reconstructed from the Exchequer Pipe Rolls, which, though not an accurate guide to activism, give an idea of who was present at some of the sessions in each twelve-month period from the resumption of sessions in October 1645.

In the three years to July 1648, only four of sixteen identifiable JPs in attendance – Sheppard, Richard Ayleworth, Matthew Huntley of Boxwell and Walter Nurse of Longhope – had not been JPs before 1643, and, of these, only Sheppard was active every year. The other leading figures were respectable county gentry: Seymour, Bromwich, Wood, Clifford, Estcourt, Leigh, John and Samuel Codrington and William Stafford of Thornbury, who was also known as a controversial pamphleteer.[80]

As yet, the Committee, in its various guises, was also composed of county gentry. There is no evidence whether or not a separate Inshire Committee ever functioned. A number of gentlemen had been nominated to different committees during the war and others were added piecemeal. Most of the signatories of letters in 1645–6 were of pre-war county gentry families, such as Bromwich, Fettiplace and Leigh, although the social composition of the Committee was somewhat lower than that of the bench. In April 1646 they complained that they were 'soe fewe that wee can hardly get enough to sitt our sitting dayes', but they could still ask for eight esquires and two gentlemen to be added. Eight promptly were. Indeed, the Daunt letters mention as committeemen in January 1646 Bromwich, Carew Raleigh (another man with a family grudge against the Stuarts), Sir Giles and Sir Thomas Overbury and Mr [Matthew] Herbert, two of whom had not yet been nominated to any committees. It was an eminently respectable ruling group and remained so until 1649.[81]

---

[78] Ibid. iv. 649, 692; *LJ* viii. 373, 450–1; BL, E351 (14), *The moderate intelligencer*, no. 77, 20–7 Aug. 1646; Latimer, *Annals of Bristol*, 213.

[79] *CJ* iv. 628–9; BL, E513 (14), *A perfect diurnall*, no. 168, 12–19 Oct. 1646; E513 (7), *Perfect occurrences*, no. 35, 30 Aug. 1646.

[80] PRO, E372/490–3; C231/5, fos 30, 51, 97; *DNB, s.v.* William Stafford. For the limitations of this source see VCH, *Wiltshire*, v. 90–1. I am indebted to Paul Gladwish for this reference.

[81] *CJ* iii. 537; iv. 238, 321, 583; Bodl. Lib., MS Tanner 59, fo. 52; Thomas Daunt jr to Thomas Daunt sen., 2 Jan. 1646, GRO, D979A F3/2.

Table 1
The assessments of 1644 and 1645

Division	Kiftsgate	Seven Hundreds	Berkeley	Forest
Sept. 1644–Sept. 1645				
Assessed	£2,061 4 6	£1,412 3 4	£1,941 10 0	£929 19 4
Received	£454 10 2	£633 18 6	£958 16 7	£124 15 3
% Received	22.05	44.90	46.40	13.41
Nov. 1645–Nov. 1646				
Assessed	£2,045 3 8	£1,402 3 8	£1,941 10 0	£927 19 4
Received	£1,058 6 11	£782 1 5	£914 15 6	£425 11 7
% Received	51.75	51.90	44.30	45.86

Source: SP 28/197, part 1, fos 111–14. GRO, D149/X2, a collector's assessment book for 1645–6, gives broadly similar figures for those parishes it covers, but is not full enough to be used statistically.

None the less, finance was an enduring problem that did not disappear with the war. It is interesting to compare the receipts of the almost identical assessments of September 1644 and November 1645 (see Table 1). In 1645-6, with peace restored, the amounts coming out of the newly liberated Kiftsgate and Forest Divisions rose from only 22.05 and 13.41 per cent respectively of the sums assessed to around half, but the rise in the Seven Hundreds was negligible, and in troubled Berkeley Division receipts actually decreased. The overall increase was from only 34.31 per cent of the total assessed in the 'war' year to 50.35 per cent in the 'peace' year. Or was it? These are centrally audited accounts and when we read that a total of £5,357 15s. 11d. out of £12,661 12s. 10d. assessed reached London, the assertion of a satirical pamphlet that all bar about £400 of a total of £13,000 assessed in 1644 and 1645 was collected, but that £5,000 stuck to local hands seems highly plausible.[82] In either case, these figures reflect badly on the administration.

Whether this document is an accurate record of receipts or a cover-up for a massive fraud, the effect was that the unreliability of the assessment reinforced the need to maximise sequestration revenue and made the distasteful business of sequestration unusually important to the Committee. Indeed, this form of revenue may have accounted for two-thirds of the total coming in.[83] The local problem mirrored the national; to satisfy a large, unpaid and

[82] SP 28/197 i, fos 111–14; Harry Hangman's honour, 14.
[83] SP 28/109B, 129 v; 228 iv, fos 721–8.

articulate army, it was necessary either to keep to wartime levels of taxation and thus alienate society from Parliament, or further to fleece the vanquished and end hopes of a rapid reconciliation.

The latter option had its attractions to the troops as the Royalists owned so much of the county's wealth. Some tried to recoup themselves directly. Many joined the spoil of the Berkeley estates, Captain Clifford spent much of 1646 harrassing William Archard for Smyth's rents and Cornet Castle chased William Batson of Bourton-on-the-Hill through all the parliamentary committees.[84] The Colchester estate attracted speculating soldiers like vultures. While trying to keep the family estate intact, Elizabeth Colchester saw her stepson, Duncombe, made a ward of Captain Lovell of the Gloucester garrison, who forbade the tenants to pay rents. In September 1646 she was arrested and menaced, not for the last time, and from 1648 she had to cope with two colonels who were seeking to make up their arrears out of a sequestered annuity payable to the recusant widow of the man from whom Richard Colchester had purchased the estate. Two more officers were involved in the 'discovery' of this annuity and then in distraining her rents.[85]

This was not just greed, for arrears were a critical problem. Of six officers whose accounts were audited and who served wholly in Gloucestershire, none had received more than 30 per cent of his pay and, even when some was 'respited on the public faith', all had between 60 and 90 per cent owing. Those who had also served outside the county, such as Devereux, fared significantly better.[86]

The Committee were not soft on those they considered delinquent; the Colchester and Guise families among others found them harsher than the parliamentary Sequestration Committee in deciding who was or was not a delinquent, and in the cases of Richard Atkyns and Giles Carter, they even defied orders to discharge lands and remit a fine.[87] But they took a careful line, and, as individuals, often intervened to help a friend. Richard Stephens and Fowler prevented the demolition of Berkeley Castle, though Wood, Fettiplace and Seymour favoured it.

Smyth himself was helped by Fowler, who had, in 1644, tipped him off about Massey's intention to plunder the area, and by Nathaniel Stephens, who urged the Committee to give him good terms to induce others to compound 'which now stand of'. In turn, Sir Maurice Berkeley asked Smyth for Lord Berkeley's help in prosecuting his composition.[88] Fettiplace promised to speak for William Guise at a parliamentary hearing, and John Stephens was a 'constant faithful

---

84 Archard to Smyth, 9 Mar. 1646, Smyth of Nibley papers, xi. 42; SP 20, ii–iv passim; CCAM ii. 840; CCC iii. 1800–1.
85 GRO, D36/A3, fos 10, 26, 42, 51–7, 81.
86 SP 28/252, fos 190v, 193, 283, 289; SP 28/253, fos 9v, 13, 51, 74, 77.
87 SP 20/1, fos 537–8; CCC ii. 1308.
88 HMC, MSS Cholmondely, 356; Stephens to Smyth, undated, Smyth of Nibley Papers, xvi. 28; anonymous to Smyth, 11 Apr. 1644, ibid. xvi. 43, xi. 26; Smyth to Stephens, 1 July 1645, ibid. xi. 37; Berkeley to Smyth, 10 Jan. 1646, ibid. ii. 92.

friend' to the family, as was Silvanus Wood. The whole Committee put in a plea for Richard Berkeley as 'the most innocent and best affected' of all those under sequestration.[89]

The process of demobilisation itself could cause problems, as an outbreak of disorder around Berkeley in August 1646 showed. In response to a county petition, they ordered a £4,400 levy to disband supernumeraries or enlist them for Ireland, and the pressing of men for Ireland in February 1646. This was an attractive proposition for some. Thomas Daunt intrigued at Gloucester in March to secure a commission for a brother and a cousin, at the same time as men were being recruited in the Quedgeley area. The existing troops, however, were less keen. After the levy, all assignations of assessments to pay troops were to be removed, and free quarter prohibited. But not until 19 September were orders given to constables to make the levy and return the names of refusers so that the soldiers could distrain on them. Nothing came of this potential solution, presumably because not enough could be raised, and the problem worsened.[90]

Matters came to a head at the Cirencester by-election in January 1647. (Sir John Seymour was returned for the shire at the same time without incident, as was Massey for Wootton Bassett in Wiltshire.) Cirencester was contested by two slates, Fairfax and the future Fifth Monarchist, Colonel Nathaniel Rich, against John Gifford of Bream and Bromwich. This was not a straightforward civilians against soldiers contest. Gifford and Bromwich had been in arms too, and they were to clash with each other later over the spoiling of the Forest of Dean. However, they clearly drew their support from anti-military sentiment.

Bromwich, the veteran troublemaker who had antagonised Massey and his officers, had also served on the Warwickshire and Herefordshire Committees and had recently been imprisoned and sent to London by Colonel Birch under sentence of death, having publicly associated with Royalists and challenged Birch to a duel at a Council of War. His Harley connections saved him from punishment. An unidentified 'libell' later accused him of 'debauch't' behaviour at the election, to which he retorted by calling on Fairfax to vindicate him, though he admitted opposing Rich as 'a meer stranger to the relations and severall interests of this County'.[91]

The poll was taken on 3 January 1647. According to a pro-Army source, Fairfax and Rich had a clear majority of voices, but the town was packed out by rowdy ex-Cavalier soldiers and the influential Lady Poole bribed the bailiff to adjourn until Monday. Then, amidst threats and drawn swords, Gifford and Bromwich were returned. The sheriff, William Browne of Hasfield, was also

[89] William Guise to Thomas Syms, 15 Apr. 1645, Syms to Guise, undated, GRO, D128/6, 12, 18; Committee to Committee for Compounding, 23 Jan. 1647, SP 23/197, fo. 253.
[90] Smyth of Nibley papers, i. 39; GRO, D2510/41; Thomas Daunt jr to Thomas Daunt sen., 25 Jan., 6 Mar. 1646, ibid. D979A F3/3–4; LJ viii. 426.
[91] *Military Memoir of Colonel John Birch, written by Roe, his secretary*, ed. J. and T. W. Webb (Camden ns vii, 1873), 140–2; Hughes, *Warwickshire*, 179, 360–3; I. Bromwich, *The spoiles of the Forrest of Deane asserted*, London 1650, 9.

implicated and shrugged off the threat of a petition, saying 'do it when you will we have as strong a party in the House as ye'. This double return became locked in the Committee of Privileges until February 1649, when Fairfax and Rich were declared elected. It was a lot of fuss over an honour Fairfax was said to have 'little desired'.[92]

One might be suspicious of the assertion that the inhabitants were for the 'military' candidates, but we should remember the dreadful experience that the town had been through at the Cavaliers' hands. Any royalist support for Bromwich and Gifford might well incline substantial numbers of the freemen the other way. Another source mentions that in October, when the New Model passed through Cirencester on the way to disband Massey's forces at Devizes 'the Mayor and Officers did ring the bells and made great preparations for us desiring our stay'. Popular attitudes were very different here from, say, Berkeley Division, where people were sick of all soldiers. At any rate, the voters seemed to have had a freer rein here than in most other 'recruiter' elections held in many other seats at this time.[93]

1647 was a year of confrontation between Parliament and the Army, and also between angry civilians and soldiers in almost every English county.[94] In March, Morgan was voted to continue as governor with 600 foot. This was a heavy burden considering that Hereford and Oxford were reduced to 130 and Coventry, among others, was disgarrisoned altogether, though the county was at least spared the presence of the unpaid and brutal troops that plagued her neighbours. On the surface, the Committee and the troops were all-powerful, and this Committee had wider power than most, for ordinances had empowered them to sequester estates at will and to use the rents and profits, furnishing accounts to the Committee of Accounts. But in reality one man's determined resistance almost brought the whole system down, and the tale also shows how strongly a formerly parliamentarian area had turned against military rule.

Sir Richard Ducie had first been captured defending his house against Waller in 1643, and he had already escaped imprisonment at Gloucester when he was recaptured at the fall of Bristol. Ducie had a grievance in that he was within the Bristol Articles and thus, according to some interpretations, exempt from composition. Moreover, a letter to him from John Driver suggests that he may have been convicted on false information from Sergeant-Major Ferrars, although there was no doubting his Royalism. He soon learned how easy it was to reduce the Committee to desperation by not co-operating with the

92 BL, E371 (5), *Perfect occurrences of every dayes iournall in Parliament*, no. 2, 8–15 Jan. 1647; E513 (34), *A perfect diurnall of some of the passages in Parliament*, no. 180, 11–18 Jan. 1647; CJ iv. 714.
93 BL, E358 (17), *Perfect occurrences*, no. 43, 16–23 Oct. 1646; CJ vi. 136, 142, 145–5; D. Underdown, 'Party management in the recruiter elections, 1645–1648', EHR lxxxiii (1968), 235–264.
94 J. S. Morrill, 'Mutiny and discontent in English provincial armies 1645–1647', P&P lvi (1972), 49–74.

sequestration process; in October 1646 we find John Clifford virtually begging Ducie to pay his rent lest the soldiers take it themselves.[95]

Ducie was leased half of his land, and later compounded with the Committee for his Tortworth lands at £100 per quarter. The arrears situation forced the Committee to allow such terms, to get hard cash in quickly. When they threatened not to let him continue for not prosecuting his composition fully, he produced an order of the Committee for Compounding. This was accepted and the rest of his land was leased to him at £400 per year, before they discovered that the order was out of date.

In July 1647 Ducie flatly refused to pay anything and Captain Godfrey Ellis of Elmore was sent to levy the rent by distraining his cattle at Tortworth. After a brief argument at the roadside, Ducie rode off and returned with some forty armed men, who squared up to Ellis and, 'cocking their peeces, said come lets charge them to the Divell'. Ellis retreated to Gloucester and charged Ducie with riot. At the next attempt, Ducie got out 300 locals, but Ellis's men were mounted and he got the cattle safely through, whereupon Ducie came in and paid his £100 to redeem them. Then came a message from Goldsmith's Hall to secure him. A special Council of War and two attempts were needed. First, Ducie's servants kept the soldiers by a bolted door until 'there came greate Store of Countrymen, with armes' to force another retreat. Finally, it took a commando-style night-time raid by 240 musketeers to seize him, and he was led away to spend a year and a half in prison.

Unfortunately, this was no help to the Committee or the soldiers, both of whom wrote to Goldsmith's Hall in November to explain the situation; the Committee also asked the county's MPs for help. So strapped for cash were they that it was not worth seizing Ducie's estate, 'for thereby his whole half yeares rent will be lost'. They could only beg higher authorities to intervene for 'more this Committee cannot doe then they have done against him already'. If Ducie did not rent back his lands, no-one else would. Ellis added that Ducie had turned out a minister sent by the Assembly of Divines to Cromhall parish, who was thus ruined. All the Committee could think of was to get Sheppard to 'desire Sir Richard to send him some releefe for the present'. Sir Richard's reply has not been recorded. So much for 'parliamentarian tyranny'.[96]

Ominously, the Committee added that one captain of the county troop had disobeyed orders to arrest Ducie, and, by his example, other Royalists were withholding rents or even re-entering their land. One troublemaker may have been Benedict Hall who, before November 1647, took part of his sequestered estate and started receiving the profits, even though Major Wildman had taken a lease of them.[97] Another, undoubtedly, was Smyth who, on 11 November 1647, received a letter from Sheppard in reply to a request for money to quarter

95 SP 23/213, fo. 410; Ducie to . . . , undated, GRO, D340A/F13; Driver to Ducie, 25 Oct. 1645, ibid. C1/7; Clifford to Ducie, 11 Oct. 1646, ibid. C1/11.
96 SP 23/213, fos 391–5; Morrill, Revolt, 53.
97 SP 23/213, fo. 395; SP 23/110, fos 929–30.

troops. Sheppard said that by now only sequestered rents were assigned to pay troops. If Smyth's neighbours wanted allowance made for free quarter, they should have paid their contributions, 'w[hi]ch they have not done by many skore pounds'. All he could suggest was that Smyth should draw up their expenses, and this much would be taken off their tax arrears, which they would soon have to pay. In fact, his and others' assessments were written off because of this burden. It was a vicious circle; troops impoverished the land in a vain attempt to secure their arrears, thereby making it even more difficult for the people to pay them.[98]

Disorder in the west continued. In August 1647 the Gloucester Common Council drew all the garrison back in for safety's sake. In December some troops kidnapped an alderman of Bristol, demanding a month's pay and full indemnity. Excise rioters at Chippenham confessed they had been expecting help from Gloucestershire and Hampshire.[99] There was more talk of mutiny, much of it in Colonel Edward Cooke's and Colonel Kempson's regiments, which had already overburdened the Cotswolds. The treasury was nearly empty. It was said that Lord General Fairfax had to promise what little there was in it to the Gloucester garrison before they would admit him to the city.[100]

Civilians or soldiers, something had to give, and in the event it was the soldiers. In December 1647 the Commons, with the backing of the Army grandees, voted through a disbandment of supernumerary forces and an end to free quarter, with strict provision for dealing with resisters. At this time, Gloucestershire still supported Morgan's and Kempson's foot and a horse troop. The troops of Captain Roberts, Captain Wells and Captain Castle were disbanded in January, with pious hopes for their arrears, which were still unpaid in June 1649. Some troops were still causing headaches in February 1648, when the Committee were complaining of the problem of quartering of troops bound for Ireland, and two captains had to be reprimanded for taking free quarter near Cirencester.[101]

Most of the soldiers, however, went quietly enough. With the support of Fairfax, who suggested enlisting them for Ireland, Morgan petitioned the Lords for half of their arrears and for the rest to be assigned out of the excise. Some of the officers also asked for the benefit of discoveries of concealed estates, but they did not get it. Inevitably, a large number, including Hammond and Massey's brothers, drifted into the London reformado rabble.[102]

---

98 Sheppard to Smyth, 11 Nov. 1647, BL, MS Add. 38,588, fo. 61; CCAM ii. 826.
99 GRO, GBR B3/2, fo. 424; BL, E418 (2), *The perfect weekly account*, 24 Nov.–1 Dec. 1647; E421 (6), *A declaration concerning his majesties royall person*.
100 CJ v. 441; BL, E423 (20), *Two letters read in the House of Commons on Munday 24 Jan: 1647 of a great bloody plot discovered at Broadway in Worcestershire*; E411 (25), *The perfect weekly account*, no. 48, 20–6 Oct. 1647.
101 BL, E429 (10), *A true relation of disbanding the supernumarary forces*, 28 Jan. 1648; CCC i. 81, 144; CJ v. 471–2; vi. 59; CSPD 1648–9, 21.
102 Fairfax to Lenthall, HMC, MSS House of Lords, 1645–8, 68–9; BL, E405 (24), *Mercurius Melancholicus*, 4 Sept. 1647.

The collapse of the Committee

With taxation revenues so unreliable, sequestration was particularly important in Gloucestershire, but many Royalists were in no hurry to compound
and Ducie's example did not lead to a flood of compositions, to say the least.
Sir Maurice Berkeley, Sir Henry Frederick Thynne, Sir Humphrey Tracy
and Sir Edward Bathurst did compound shortly after Ducie's capture, but
some others preferred to sit tight. For the Committee it was vital to maximise
its income from this source, but it had already had one hand tied behind its
back. A large number were within the Oxford and Bristol Articles, and the
parliamentary Sequestration Committee made several decisions which were
financially damaging to the Committee – indeed, in July 1647, the latter's
order to revoke leases made of Ducie's estate and to let him take his harvest
may have been the occasion of the argument.[103]

We are fortunate to have a schedule of lands under the Committee's
control in March 1648, with their 'late' (pre-war) and 'present' values.
Theoretically, they disposed of land worth £11,170 2s. 7s. per year, about a
third owned by papists, the rest by delinquents, plus about £1,500 more (where
only 'present' values are given). But the 'present' value was only £5,281 4s.
4d., plus maybe £200 more (where only 'late' values are given). Where we have
both values, this represents a near 55 per cent fall. Of the Royalists, twenty-
eight were compounding, but fourteen voted delinquent at Gloucester were
discharged by the Sequestration Committee, which is suggestive. Nine, including Wintour, Throckmorton and Sir Ralph Dutton had such heavy debts that
their estates had to be discharged to pay them, thirteen had died, thirteen more
were not rich enough to be worth prosecuting or had no real estate, and
nineteen, including Morton, had no estate discovered at all.[104]

Moreover, wartime conditions had forced the Committee to make hasty
deals for cash. In some cases the Committee was helpless. Sir William Master's
house was sold back to him as soon as he came in 'least he should have deserted
it & p[ai]d noe Contribution w[hi]ch was that [th]e Garison was maintained
by'. Attempts to get tougher after the war were doomed by the law, the
continuing military burden, and the financial woes of many Royalists. Master's
estate was 'greatly overburdened by free quarter and Contribution', Thomas
Jeynes's houses in Tewkesbury were decayed and his lands 'unserviceable'
because of the garrison there. In 1647 the Committee justified one previous
agreement by explaining that the county was in a very bad way and 'the
Com[m]ittee were glad then to doe and take what they could'. Shortage of cash

---

103 *CJ* v. 381, 395, 431, 487; SP 20/3, fo. 187 and passim.
104 CCAM i. 85–7. BL, MS Add. 5,494 contains a similar schedule, which varies marginally
in detail.

Table 2
Indemnity cases in Gloucestershire, 1647–55: the causes

Number of cases

21 Plaintiff paid rents/debts/bonds to County Committee by order

13 Plaintiff took arms/goods/provisions/money by authority for the service of Parliament

12 Plaintiff distrained animals/goods for tax/contribution/ arrears by authority of Parliament

10 Plaintiff arrested/assaulted/imprisoned/slandered/damaged property of defendant while on the service of Parliament

5 Defendant refused to deduct taxation from rents/allow for rents distrained by the Royalists, or sued plaintiff for doing so

5 Defendant suing plaintiff for unpaid quartering costs

5 Defendant interrupted plaintiff's lease/seized his estate for serving Parliament

5 Defendant a delinquent illegally in office

4 Defendant suing plaintiff on bonds extorted under duress

3 Defendant harrassing plaintiff with frivolous suits

Source: SP 24

also partly explained their re-sequestration of William Batson in January 1648.[105]

Efforts had been made to stamp out corruption and not to lease to delinquents without a pre-war rent roll, but even when lands were auctioned, it was difficult to lease them to any but the owners or committee agents, and at low rates. The Committee took pride in relating that they had raised the receipts from the lands in the schedule from £1,020 to £1,622 per year, despite free quarter. Much, however, was unlet as tenants could not be found, and soldiers would not take them in lieu of arrears.[106] Moreover, the disbanding of troops took away the Committee's means of coercing the Royalists, who had seen how easy and successful resistance might be.

Indemnity proceedings, by means of which troops and officials could secure protection against lawsuits for actions taken in Parliament's cause, can also throw some light on the state of affairs. Their evidence is anecdotal and not representative, for only disputes that had gone to law could be taken to the Indemnity Committee, but they can help deepen our general understanding of events. Eighty-nine cases were generated in Gloucestershire, of which sixty-one were commenced before 1650. The origins of the disputes taken to the Indemnity Committee are shown in Table 2.

[105] SP 23/245, fo. 76ff.; SP 19/83, fo. 17v; Committee to Committee for Advance of Money, 3 Jan. 1648, SP 19/204, fo. 71.
[106] CCC i, 81, 119; MS Add. 5,494, fos 109–10, 123–5; SP 28/154.

The way the same names keep cropping up indicates the vulnerability of some Parliamentarians. Colonel Richard Ayleworth, one of very few in the Cotswolds, was hounded from all sides and was constantly seeking indemnity. A Royalist who had once been outlawed for murder, Giles Carter, had successfully sued him for paying a debt into the Committee in 1647, and then he was prosecuted for assault by a renegade soldier whom he had tried to arrest. He was later harassed by the parliamentarian Selwyns of Matson for the grass eaten by his sheep as they were driven into Gloucester to feed the garrison.[107]

More important still was the battle waged against him and his family by the Tracys of Stanway. Sir Humphrey sued Ayleworth to outlawry in 1647 for three colts he had distrained for tax arrears, and then sued his mother over some jewels bequeathed to him by a relative, which she handed in to the Committee as executrix of the estate.[108] Tracy also kept himself busy persecuting a tenant in Middlesex for deducting taxes from his rent, defrauding some nephews and nieces of part of their inheritance and fighting an action through the Lords against Lady Anne Cromwell. Meanwhile, his cousin, Sir Robert, was hauled up before the Lords for fraud, and his equally formidable mother and her steward wore down with frivolous suits a soldier who had entered her estate to retrieve his impounded cattle and another who had recovered damages against her.[109]

We should not overstate the case. Most Royalists were quiescent, most Parliamentarians unmolested, but, although many of the protagonists were humble, a large number of prominent men felt sufficiently threatened to seek indemnity. Morgan's deputy, Major Dobson, was arrested for quartering debts by Gloucester householders twice in a month in 1647, and, in 1649, Fettiplace, George, Seymour and Edward Stephens had to account for moneys levied for the defence of Cirencester in 1643.[110]

The issues were not always party-based: a Royalist, John Chamberlain, appears as a plaintiff when sued for rent arrears in Prestbury, whilst the committeeman Anthony Clifford appears as a defendant when he sued for damages the tenant of his manor house, which was partially demolished to house a garrison. The plundering behaviour of Captain George Raymond and Lieutenant-Colonel Guy Silcocks is put in context by their cases. Silcocks claimed that during the war he was arrested as a felon and imprisoned in Bristol

---

[107] VCH, *Glos.*, xi. 167; SP 24/31 (unfol.); SP 24/1, fos 7v, 91v, 106v (Ayleworth v Carter); SP 24/1, fo. 146; SP 24/5, fos 80, 89, 101v; SP 24/ 6, fo. 44v (Ayleworth v Collins); SP 24/1, fo. 132v (Ayleworth v Selwyn).

[108] SP 24/31; SP 24/1, fos 100v, 106v (Ayleworth v Tracy); SP 24/3, fos 76, 79v (Mrs Ayleworth v Tracy). The feud may have begun with the Commons' assignment, in January 1644, of a £200 legacy to Tracy for Ayleworth's pay: CJ iii. 366.

[109] SP 24/2, 4, 6–7, 13–14 passim (Bloome v Tracy); SP 24/3, fos 95, 122; SP 24/4, fo. 95; SP 24/5, fo. 47v (Collins v Tracy), fos 44, 53, 56, 61; SP 24/6, fo. 102 (Freeman v Willis), 73v, 176 (Freeman v Tracy); PRO, C3/461/10; LJ vii. 658; viii passim.

[110] SP 24/1, fos 5v (Dobson v Robins), 9–9v, 12v (Dobson v Isaac); SP 24/5, fos 95, 98, 144; SP/8, fo. 118 (Fettiplace and others *v.* Clutterbuck and others).

for seizing the goods of Sir Maurice Berkeley, who then extorted bonds worth £200 from Silcocks's aged father on which he prosecuted later. This is made all the more credible by a similar case against Berkeley.[111]

Raymond featured in two more of many ugly little quarrels in the south, being sued on a mortgage he claimed to have entered into under duress, and for malt he had taken for the Slimbridge garrison.[112] Not all plaintiffs were helpless victims, of course. When the JP, William Stafford, tried to secure indemnity against a suit for wrongful arrest, it emerged that he was abusing his office to pursue a private grudge, aided by Raymond, who intimidated witnesses. The case was dismissed.[113]

Most plaintiffs did secure indemnity and the very fact that Stafford was caught tells us something positive about the process. Then again, most of them had already had verdicts against them in the courts. That a Royalist stood a fair chance of getting court orders in his favour was suggested as early as September 1645, when Thomas Morse of the sub-committee of accounts complained that at least £1,000 had already been lost by legal motions on behalf of delinquents.[114] Many more potential plaintiffs probably could not or dared not take their cases to the Committee for Indemnity. This evidence, then, must cast further doubt on the security of the Committee's grip on Gloucestershire in the late 1640s.

Meanwhile, the work of the Committee was becoming increasingly onerous and unpopular. In April 1646 nine men were added at the Committee's request, and thirty-five were nominated to one or more committees between June 1647 and December 1648. These were mostly second-rank gentlemen with a proven track record, such as Berrow, Clifford and Huntley, together with a sprinkling of soldiers and unknowns. (However, we should remember that simple name-counting is not necessarily a guide to activism. In Warwickshire, some men only sat for certain committee functions and signed some but not others of the orders on any one day.)[115]

Certain facts are clear enough from the attendance figures (see Table 3). After 1645 most of the major figures ceased to appear. The Stephenses, Pury, Seymour and Hodges were at Westminster; the Herefordshire refugees – Broughton, Robert Kyrle, and Henry Jones – had mostly gone home, and James Kyrle died in 1646. Others, such as Leigh, Clifford and Fettiplace, were falling

---

111 SP 24/75 (unfol.); SP 24/5, fo. 94v (Chamberlain v Paul); SP 24/4, fos 70, 97 (Morse v Clifford); SP 24/5, fos 67, 145v (Silcocks v Berkeley); SP 24/5, fos 70, 145v; SP 24/6, fo. 89 (Packer v Berkeley).

112 SP 24/3, fo. 136v; SP 24/4, fos 9, 64, 105; SP 24/5, fos 40–v, 65v (Raymond v Butcher); SP 24/2, fo. 93v; SP 24/4, fos 21, 63v, 105v (Raymond v Perratt).

113 Ibid. SP 24/77 (unfol.); SP 24/10, fos 29, 51, 115, 150v; SP 24/11, fos 11, 117; SP 24/12, fo. 32; SP 24/15, fos 161, 208v–9 (Stafford v Edwards).

114 Morse to Accounts Committee, 9 Sept. 1645, SP 28/255; SP 28/252 ii, fo. 4v.

115 CJ iv. 230, 265, 321, 383; Bodl. Lib., MS Tanner 59, fo. 52; A&O i, passim; Hughes, *Warwickshire*, 182.

Table 3
The County Committee: signatures to orders, 1644–9

Year	1644	1645	1646	1647	1648	1649
Total Documents	4	11	15	17	13	7
Gentry						
Isaac Bromwich	2	4	5	3	4	1
William Leigh	1	3	5		1	
John Fettiplace	1	4	4			
William Sheppard	2	11	9	14	12	6
Sylvanus Wood	1	2	8	7		
Richard Stephens		3				
Anthony Clifford		4	2	5		
Stephen Fowler		5	6	4	2	
Christopher Catchmay		3	1			
Sir John Seymour				4		
Gabriel Beck				5		
Outsiders						
Henry Jones		2	8	1		
James Kyrle		1	3			
Colonel Thomas Morgan				2	2	
Gloucester Men						
Nicholas Webb	2*	1	2	13		
Thomas Hill	1			1	1	
Lawrence Singleton	1*	3*				
Jasper Clutterbuck	1	1	3*	14*	1	1
John Dorney			3	11	13	6
John Maddocks				1*	8*	
Henry Cugley					2*	6*

Signed two or less

Gentry
Thomas Stephens (1644), Nathaniel Stephens, Thomas Hodges (1645), John and Samuel Codrington (1646), Edward Rich (1646–7), George Ken (1647).

Outsiders
Robert Kyrle (1648).

Gloucester Men
Luke Nurse (1646–7), Thomas Pury (1647), William Singleton (1648), John Hanbury (1649).

* mayor of Gloucester when a signatory

Sources: SP 19, SP 23, SP 28 passim; HMC, 8th Report, part i (MSS Duke of Marlborough), 11b; HMC, MSS Portland, i. 286; BL, MS Add. 1,1044, fos 213, 215; Bodl. Lib., MSS Tanner 60, fo. 75; 59, fos 52, 247, 401, 403; GRO, D128/2, D340

by the wayside at an alarming rate. On 13 March 1647 Morgan, Dorney and Aldermen Webb and Clutterbuck complained that the schedule of delin-quents' estates required of them should more properly have been done by 'the original Committeemen, who are now dead removed or absent then by us who have been inserted into the Committee of late and therefore being but strangers to the worke'.[116] It took a year to produce the schedule.

In December 1647 eighteen more men were added to the Assessment Commission, an expedient used in only one other county. Most were minor gentlemen. But sequestration still constituted the bulk of the work, and it was made an even more unpleasant prospect by an order of January 1648, repeated in August, that revenues should in future be sent to London (as, in theory, they always should have been). Few new men became involved and, as the burden of work grew, more dropped out until almost the entire load fell on Sheppard, Dorney and successive mayors of Gloucester, with occasional help from others. Perhaps not coincidentally, the Commons and Lords argued over the choice of sheriff for Gloucestershire in December 1647 and again in December 1648.[117]

When the Second Civil War broke out in 1648, the Commons had to look for whatever support they could find. A foot company was raised under Captain John Crofts and the 'Well-affected' of Gloucester petitioned to put themselves in a posture of defence against 'the desperate and menacing Carriage of Malignants and Delinquents'. The Commons ordered the seizure of all undis-charged delinquents in Gloucestershire and Monmouthshire and passed an ordinance to put certain unspecified men in charge of the militia for six months in some of the associated counties.[118] The royalist press had no doubts as to who these men were – 'the Saints rampant'. They were not far wrong. One commission survives, signed by Say, several MPs and Wood, constituting the reliable Ayleworth, a committed Independent, commander of 600 horse and dragoons to be raised in Kiftsgate Division to quell revolts.[119]

Gloucester's role in the Second Civil War was as little more than a supply depot at the beginning and a prison at the end. The garrison's presence forestalled any risings, but there are hints of growing polarisation in the shire at the time. The New Model passed by in May to quell the Pembrokeshire rebels, and some 100 citizens, sporting their blue ribbons, joined up as volun-teers. But when a printed libel against Pury turned up in Gloucester, the corporation felt so insecure that they commissioned a riposte defending him.[120]

The Gloucestershire gentry in 1648 were considered thoroughly malignant,

[116] Committee to Committee for Advance of Money, 13 Mar. 1647, SP 19/83, fos 17–v.
[117] CJ iv. 733; v. 361, 372, 401; vi. 84–5, 89; LJ viii. 590; x. 610; Zweigman, 'County government', 892.
[118] CJ v. 553, 555–7; LJ x. 253, 255–6; A&O ii. 1136–7; BL, E436 (10), The perfect weekly account, no. 6, 12–19 Apr. 1648.
[119] BL, E442 (15), Mercurius Pragmaticus, no. 7, 9–16 May 1648; GRO, D1867.
[120] BL, E441 (16), The declaration of Lieutenant Generall Cromwell, 9 May 1648; E465 (35), Packets of letters, no. 29, 3 Oct. 1648.

and a royalist newssheet reckoned that 600 horsemen rose in Gloucestershire and Shropshire. 'You hear in what a flame these western parts are', wrote Cromwell as he left Gloucester, and he commissioned an indigent captain, Thomas Roberts, to hunt down seditious meetings in the county.[121] As ever, the Royalists tended to look beyond county boundaries: Morton, unchastened by three years in the Tower of London, was involved in intrigue, Sir William Poole was in touch with Lord Byron, Duncombe Colchester was allegedly active in Surrey and Sir Humphrey Tracy was in arms in the Kentish rebellion.[122]

The Bristol area was a hive of activity. Some feared an insurrection at Bath: it was reported that meetings of the 'disaffected' of Somerset and neighbouring counties were being held at bull-baitings there in May. But in December Bristol and the adjacent areas also produced a pro-Army petition, which claimed 4,000 signatures. In October, it was asserted that 'Gloucestershire and Sommersetshire are acting against the grand Treachery' (the Treaty of Newport), although in the end, Somerset, under the close control of John Pyne, did manage to send up a petition against it, whereas Gloucestershire did not.[123] Perhaps one reason the county remained an oasis of (relative) calm was the great storm of mid-August which ruined the harvest. Reaping had barely begun in the Vale in any case before 22 August, 'soe colde and wett' was the summer, and this pushed grain prices to record local levels, which might have been even worse but for the sudden arrival of 'infinite quantitie of outlandish corne' at Bristol.[124] The weather must have made it almost impossible to raise forces for anything other than a food riot.

In the end, nothing lasting came of the new militia proposals and the same committeemen struggled on. On 20 November 1648 Sheppard, Dorney and Henry Cugley, mayor of Gloucester, complained bitterly that hardly any of the other thirty-odd members ever showed up and that the burden was too heavy when they also had to exercise other public offices. Sheppard, one of the greatest legal experts of his day, was particularly overworked, and his opinion was often sought in the many cases arising out of the situation.[125] The king's execution, not surprisingly, did not improve matters, and only those same three were notably active after January 1649.

One reason why some men were ceasing to work on the Committee was because they were busy feathering their own nests. The way some managed to

121 BL, E452 (18), *Mercurius Elenthicus*, no. 33, 5–12 July 1648; Cromwell to Fairfax, 8 May 1648, in *The writings and speeches of Oliver Cromwell*, ed. W. C. Abbot, Harvard 1937, i. 606–7; CSPD 1655, 331.
122 Ibid. 1648–9, 227–8, 231; CCAM i. 430; GRO, D36/F18; SP 19/104, fos 90–1.
123 BL, E441 (22), *The perfect weekly account*, no. 9, 3–10 May 1648; E477 (4), *The moderate*, no. 23, 12–19 Dec. 1648; CJ vi. 102; Underdown, *Somerset*, 139–53.
124 BL, E458 (23), *The kingdomes weekly intelligencer*, no. 178, 8–15 Aug.; GRO, D2688, 1648.
125 Committee to Committee for Compounding, 20 Nov. 1648, CCC i. 133–4; Sheppard to 'Mr Slaughter', 22 Dec. 1647, GRO, D149/E13, fo. 1.

enrich themselves from the spoils of war caused embarrassing divisions. In 1645 Parliament rewarded some officers out of Wintour's concession: Captain Thomas Pury junior, who had seen service in the city regiment and then became recruiter MP for Monmouth, Colonel Robert Kyrle, the renegade Royalist from a Herefordshire gentry family, Captain Griffantius Phillips, a Welshman, and Colonel John Braine, who owned land at Little Dean. From 1645 they operated an informal cartel to run those furnaces and forges, and bought out others, previously Wintour's, which had been granted to Massey. But their lowly origins, the already depleted state of timber stocks in the Forest and the fact that, after the *de facto* 'freedom' of the 1640s, any ordered rule would seem oppressive, all conspired to raise local opposition.[126]

Charges of prodigious corruption and waste were made, which ranged Bromwich, Berrow and a Bristol-based Commission of Enquiry against the concessionaries. The four were accused of massive destruction of ship timber – 4,000 trees in one year in Ruardean alone, according to the radical Captain George Bishop of Bristol. Allegedly, the Committee was either too feeble or too corrupt to act against them. Whenever 'any Spirit of Justice' appeared there, the Committee broke up, then those in the concessionaries' pockets returned later to complete the business. Any JPs who tried to act against them were menaced with indemnity actions or worse. Their own men were put into forest offices and committed major depredations, and they derided the Commission as 'a hedge Commission, bragging they could make men sweare and unsweare what they pleased'.[127]

The redoutable Bromwich also implied corruption against unspecified committeemen in making the grant in the first place and weighed in with some colourful abuse of Phillips, Pury and Kyrle, his former protegé. Their retorts made the most of Bromwich's chequered career. Alleging that the rest of the Committee had refused to act with him, they accused Berrow of 'irreligion, scandall and disaffection', and observed, not unfairly, that plenty of Bristol men had a stake in the matter too. The upshot, in 1650, after a long enquiry, was the destruction of all iron works, amidst reports that the four, with Gifford, had defrauded the state of £20,000, and great damage to the morale and prestige of the county's rulers.[128]

Earlier on, the MPs had played a vital role in mediating between centre and locality, but they now grew preoccupied with parliamentary business and their visits became rarer. In 1648 they began commissioning militia officers from London without reference to what was left of the Committee. All the MPs bar Hodges and Seymour were active. The Stephenses were named to many Committees and Nathaniel often acted as a teller. Pury was a hard-working chairman of the Commitee for Irish Affairs, while John Stephens, a lawyer,

---

[126] Hammersley, 'Iron industry', 206–33.
[127] *CSPD* 1649–50, 443–4; G. Bishop, *A modest check to part of a scandalous libell*, London [1650].
[128] Bromwich, *Spoiles*, 5–6, 9–11; *CSPD* 1649–50, 443–4; 1650 passim.

often managed conferences with the Lords and was also appointed to the Committee for Compounding.[129]

Some MPs profited from their places. Pury became Clerk of the Petty Bag, worth £400 per year, and was given £3,000 (his defenders made this £100 per year and £1,000, less than his expenses in Parliament's service), and he and Hodges were granted £1,000 each out of the earl of Worcester's estate. His son, a more obvious profiteer, was made clerk of the peace and receiver of the king's rents in Gloucestershire and Wiltshire. John Stephens had an ordinance granting him £1,000 out of Astley's estate for the burning of Lypiatt House and was accused of conspiring to defraud the Commonwealth. Edward Stephens's dealings with another MP also came under scrutiny. The speaker's son, John Lenthall, the 'recruiter' MP for Gloucester, was notoriously corrupt.[130]

Most remained active until Pride's Purge. Indeed one royalist newspaper included Nathaniel Stephens ('who hath one foot in the Grave but his whole Body in the Junto'), Pury and Hodges in the radical group that met on 28 September to try to co-ordinate a motion quite contrary to all precedent, to reverse a previous vote that nothing concluded in the negotiations with the king should be binding until full agreement was reached. Stephens, apparently, botched his speech and was shouted down, whereupon others took over and 'Pury forgot himselfe so far as to forfeit the Reputation of a Brother, and tell a Lie' in a vain bid to rescue the situation.[131]

Be that as it may, Pride's Purge on 6 December 1648 received little support from Gloucestershire MPs. According to Underdown's classification, none were actively revolutionary (that is to say, gave any support to the regicide). Only Pury conformed to it, but it was later said that his son 'blessed God that his father and he had no hand in that —— Action of Killing the King', and neither was active in the Rump.[132] John Lenthall and Nathaniel and John Stephens all showed their opposition by staying away. Nathaniel said explicitly that cutting off the head was as unlikely a cure in the political as the physical body, and called on the House to vindicate its privileges, saying that if they did not he could not in conscience remain there. John Stephens continued to work at the Committee for Compounding, but was not readmitted to the House until 1651.[133] Seymour and Hodges were secluded. Edward Stephens was reckoned one of '4 Asserters who ... will stand out to the utmost'. From prison, he called

---

[129] CJ iv, v, vi passim; A&O i. 914–15.

[130] BL, E458 (12), A list of the names of the members; CJ iv. 536, 550; v. 39, 366; LJ ix. 617; BL, E442 (3), Tertia pars de comparatis comparandis.

[131] BL, E465 (19), Mercurius Pragmaticus, no. 27, 26 Sept.–3 Oct. 1648.

[132] D. Underdown, Pride's purge: politics in the Puritan revolution, Oxford 1971, ch. viii; Bishop, A modest check, 5; A. B. Worden, The Rump Parliament, Cambridge 1974, 65, 99.

[133] BL, E477 (19), The second part of the narrative; Worden, Rump, 72, 390. The false legend that Nathaniel was a regicide (Zweigman, 'County government', 846; Rollison, 'Bourgeois soul', 309) was born out of a nineteenth-century poem. See W. H. Davies, 'Some notes on Chavenage and the Stephens family', TBGAS xxii (1899), 128–37.

on Fairfax to save the king, calling the regicide 'the most execrable villainy that ever tainted any Christian Kingdom'. [134]

There is no evidence of any general reaction in Gloucestershire to the execution of Charles I on 30 January 1649, or to the establishment of a republic under a Council of State and the remaining 'Rump' of the Commons. Most people had enough worries nearer to home, and it was not long before many who were otherwise sympathetic became disillusioned by the new regime's inability to relieve the burdens of taxation and quartering on the 'well-affected'.

In March a Tewkesbury correspondent of a radical newspaper, *The moderate*, lamented the decision to impose new taxes in order to take off free quarter rather than raise money by selling off confiscated land and thereby ease the burdens on the well-affected. He painted a picture of utter misery: 'How many thousand families, besides my own, are like to starve, when a company of Pettifoggers and caterpillars drink the sweat and eat the fat of our daily hard labours, heap up thousands for their children, though scarce worth six pence before the war began . . . ?'[135] The evidence shows that this was not all hyperbole. The omens for the republic in the localities were not exactly promising.

Gloucestershire's experiences at the end of the war and after illustrate the strengths and weaknesses of government by committee. The legislation of the early 1640s threw together a series of administrative institutions which ultimately proved far more durable than their royalist counterparts, but in truth they were better at winning the war than the peace. The real source of their durability was the very nature of parliamentarian allegiance. The grey areas in between the authority of governor, committee and sub-committee – not to mention between the Committees of Gloucester and of Bristol – provided endless occasions for quarrels. But although the ruling group might bend, it did not break. Feuds were often quite vicious, but not until peace was restored did anyone defect. The supreme irony was that Massey went over to the Stuarts before his arch-enemy Bromwich, who had been lukewarm to the cause all along.

Leadership was based on the greater gentry until 1649, although some of the men who were to form the ruling clique of the 1650s were already climbing the greasy pole through service in arms and in administration. But in the late 1640s disillusion set in as Parliament failed to find solutions to the pressing problems of pay and quarter for the troops, and Gloucestershire had a heavy burden by comparison with most other counties. Far from lording it over the county through the soldiers, the Committee could not control them and was quite often working against them, as individuals. Because most gentlemen were

---

[134] BL, E477 (30), *Mercurius Pragmaticus*, no. 39, 19–26 Dec. 1648; E536 (38), 'E.S.', *A letter of advice from a secluded member*.
[135] BL, E548 (2), *The moderate*, no. 36, 13–30 Mar. 1649.

Royalists and the financial administration was so chaotic, the distasteful business of sequestration assumed a peculiar importance here. And partly because of this, the Royalists, if they were game for a fight, found it easy to defy the Committee (though not to profit by it personally), and so drive more and more of them into abandoning the work.

Centre and locality drifted apart in two ways. Just as so many former supporters lost patience with Parliament's endless delays, so did the county MPs grow further apart from the county as they became absorbed in Westminster politics. If the Civil War was the overthrow of provincial England, the aftermath was something akin to a posthumous revenge. All the twists and turns in politics up to Pride's Purge reflect the inability of committees and troops to overcome the inertia of society at large. After the regicide, many of the men prominent in the 1640s abandoned public life altogether. The fledgeling republic had to cast very low down the social scale for support. As in many counties, the 'revolution' of 1649 was the watershed in the gradual transformation of local government and society. Whether the new rulers could hold down an alienated and impoverished countryside remained to be seen.

4

Politics and Religion, 1649–1659

The early 1650s and the city of Gloucester

The Interregnum saw some men rise to heights to which they could never normally have aspired, particularly the minor gentry and others of lower origins who dominated County Committees and commissions of the peace. This did not mean that the minor gentry as a whole were more republican than their social superiors, merely that with most 'county' gentlemen proscribed for Royalism, the authorities had to dig deeper. This was generally a shift of power within a class. Only in Westmorland were there not enough gentry left with some experience of county government to fill the bench.[1]

Every county's experience of this process was different. In most counties held by the king during the war, Parliamentarians of all sorts were more committed and less likely to quarrel later. By contrast, the Second Civil War of 1648 occurred in Parliament's heartland partly because those areas contained so many gentlemen swept into nominal allegiance in 1642 by the local situation, who had been alienated by harsh committees, the military and radicals. But perhaps personality was the key factor. In Dorset, the same knot of major gentry families dominated the county from Civil War to Protectorate, faithful to each new regime, whereas in Sussex, Herbert Morley and his allies remained to the fore in county affairs, though implacably opposed to the Protectorate.[2]

Service was not necessarily a guide to allegiance. Most of those active in every county in the 1650s were not committed republicans. However, Gloucestershire does fit into a broad pattern in that moderate 'county' gentry diverged from radicals, mostly of lower origin, after the regicide. Many of the former were either removed from the bench and Committee or refused to serve. The 'Good Old Cause' did not disintegrate entirely, however. Alienated Parliamentarians rarely favoured an unconditional Stuart Restoration, and the Civil War had left a big wedge between the two parties. But for a while Gloucestershire, like most counties, experienced 'a minor social revolution in government'.[3]

---

[1] C. B. Phillips, 'County committees and local government in Cumberland and Westmorland, 1642–1660', Northern History v (1970), 34–66.

[2] Everitt, Kent, 231–70; J. A. Casada, 'Dorset politics in the Puritan Revolution', Southern History iv (1982), 13–18; Fletcher, Sussex, 290–343.

[3] Hughes, Warwickshire, 291–341; B. G. Blackwood, The Lancashire gentry and the Great Rebellion, 1640–1660, Manchester 1978, 101.

Without many of the usual sources, our knowledge of who ruled Gloucestershire in the 1650s is patchy, but lists of JPs and committeemen in the period
1650 to 1653 can at least tell us whose compliance was hoped for. Minus a
thick cluster of Royalists in the north-east, the geographical distribution of JPs
in the 1650s was similar to that of the 1630s, considering how regionalised
Parliament's support was. There the comparison ends, for the 1650 bench
contained only five pre-war JPs, plus nine sons or relatives of pre-war JPs who
would have acceded anyway. This was inevitable since so many county gentlemen had been Royalists, but there were many newcomers even so. Only
thirty-one of sixty-five had served on the Committee before Pride's Purge, even
when we omit fourteen new committeemen who were not JPs.

After 1648, sixteen men ceased to serve on the Committee, some – like
Massey, Bromwich and Edward Stephens – for obvious reasons, others not. Five
of these were clearly not out of favour as they now became JPs. The barrel was
scraped hard. Of forty-six new JPs, only thirteen belonged to families of
sufficient standing to be summoned to either or both of the heralds' visitations
of 1623 and 1682–3. Another twelve were so obscure that nothing else is
known of them. By contrast, twenty-three of twenty-nine of those named to
Committees before and after 1649 were summoned to at least one visitation.
The Rump threw together a large bench and Committee, nominating anyone
who might conceivably serve the regime. Many never did.[4]

Constant emergencies and the Third Civil War of 1650–1 meant that the
governor of Gloucester, Sir William Constable, remained an important figure.
The government's prior concern was with Bristol, the port for Cromwell's
descent on Ireland, but Gloucester, being 'on so considerable a pass', could not
be entirely overlooked. In 1649, the Council of State even considered razing
the walls or building a citadel, though in the end only a rather obtrusive
guardhouse was erected.[5] Constable was not just a soldier, for he was named to
the bench and all committees, took an interest in administration, to the extent
of reporting individual misdemeanours to parliamentary committees, and was
later praised by the local gathered churches 'for his tendernesse to God's
people'.[6]

Despite this, religious radicalism hardly touched the Gloucester garrison,
none of whose 'foreign' officers are known to have joined sects – in marked
contrast to Bristol, where their support for Quakers led to an explosive conflict
in 1654–5. A garrison petition of October 1648 implicitly backed the Vote of
No Addresses and the London petition for annual elections, religious toleration and for the king to be subject to the law. However, this was made in the

---

4   PRO, C193/13/2–4; SP 16/212, fo. 405; BL, MS Harleian 2121, fo. 111v; 2097, fos 76–8v;
MS Stowe 577; *The names of the justices of the peace . . . this Michaelmas Terme*, 1650; A&O
i. 24–57, 265–318, 450–90, 653–88.
5   *CSPD* 1649, 232; H. M. Reece, 'The military presence in England, 1649–1660', unpubl.
D.Phil. diss. Oxford 1981, 148.
6   *CSPD* 1651–2, 267–8; *Originall letters and papers of state, addressed to Oliver Cromwell*,
ed. J. Nickolls jr, London 1743, 126.

interests of Army unity, by men who avowed that they 'desire not to lead but to follow', as they were far away from the Army and ill-informed of its deliberations.[7] One wit wrote that after tobacco was planted in the Vale of Evesham, 'Bridewel marched away in discontent to Gloucester, thinking to find some idle persons among the souldiers; but when it came there, it found none of the souldiers idle, some slept on their Beds, others slept on the Guard, some playing at Ball, others playing at Skittles.'[8]

The garrison was a heavy burden on Gloucester, which housed 640 men in 1651, compared to only 280 at Bristol. With the Royalists defeated, the annoying aspects of it – such as the way the guardhouse blocked access to the market and caused a conduit to decay – were felt as grievances. In 1652, the Corporation petitioned for its withdrawal, saying that its presence and 'the miscarriages of the souldiery' had greatly damaged the city's trade. At Tewkesbury, quartering charges may have been an issue in the strife which later divided the burgesses.[9]

Though Gloucester preferred to raise its own militia as and when required, the city remained on generally good terms with the military. Many officers profited from their time there: Captain Russell and Captain Evans both became freemen, while Evans and Captain Hatch also took leases of land; Major Wildman and Major Bannister and Captains Phillips, Woodward and Ellis all at various times became agents for the recovery of war losses. Ellis rose to become a common councillor even though he was not a Gloucester man by birth, and the employment of Phillips, a Welshman, would have been unthinkable before the Civil War.[10]

Gloucester was disgarrisoned in January 1653, but the garrison's long-term presence and Constable's interest had thrust to the fore several talented men. All were minor local gentlemen, rose through military service and remained prominent throughout the 1650s. Major John Wade of Little Dean surfaced in 1650 as a conservator of the Forest and a JP, then, in 1651, as Constable's deputy. He was added to the assessment committee in 1652, and stayed on after the disgarrisoning to head a state ironworks project.[11] William Neast of Twining first appears as a collector for, and captain of foot in, the Tewkesbury garrison, and as a captain of horse in 1651. He progressed rapidly to the bench and Committee after 1650. Neast was an active member of an Independent

[7] BL, E462 (17), The moderate, no. 3, 30 Aug.–6 Sep. 1648; E526 (8), The true informer, no. 1, 7 Oct.–2 Nov. 1648.
[8] Harry Hangman's honour, 8. The Gloucester bridewell was repaired in 1650: GRO, GBR B3/2, fo. 534.
[9] Ibid. fos 722–3; GRO, D2688 (unfol.), 1649; HMC, corporation of Gloucester, 508.
[10] GRO, GBR B3/2, B3/3, passim. Corbet (Military government, 27) spoke of 'an inveterate hatred derived by fabulous tradition' between Gloucester men and the Welsh.
[11] CSPD 1649–50, 482; 1651, 100; 1651–2, 501; 1652–3, 156, 292, 584; 1653–4, 107; CJ vii. 541.

Table 4
Nominations to government commissions, 1650–3

Total

11 Richard Ayleworth

9 William Sheppard

8 Sylvanus Wood, Giles Hancock, Thomas Hill (A)

6 John Geering

5 Andrew Solace, Jeremy Buck

4 Samuel Codrington, John Howe sr, William Leigh, John Wade, Dennis Wise (A), James Stephens (A)

3 Matthew Huntley, Laurence Singleton (A), George Raymond, William Neast, William Stafford, William Bourchier.

2 William Singleton (A), Anthony Edwards (A), Thomas Walter, Robert Holmes, Walter Raleigh

1 24 other men

(A) = alderman of Gloucester

Sources: SP 24; *CSPD* 1649–50, 1650, 1651; *A&O*

congregation, as was John Crofts of Lower Swell, who fought under Morgan, took much royalist land in 1648 and came to prominence in 1653.[12] So too was Colonel Richard Ayleworth, who had been 'the first gentleman in the county in arms for the Parliament', served with distinction at the siege of Gloucester, raised his own horse troop and was made governor of Sudeley Castle after the war. He became a JP and was added to all committees in 1647.[13] A less savoury character was Captain, later Lieutenant-Colonel, George Raymond of Thornbury, who led the spoiling of Berkeley Castle, commanded the firelocks at the siege of Hereford and arrested Bromwich there in November 1646. Becoming a committeeman and JP in 1650 launched a chequered career.[14]

With the same reservations in mind as before, the Exchequer Pipe Rolls can give us some idea of which JPs attended quarter sessions between October 1648 and July 1653. It was not a very socially distinguished group. Of those active before 1649, only Bromwich, Fettiplace and Seymour (who were all removed) ceased to appear immediately, but more drifted away over the next year. Only Wood, Leigh, Estcourt, Sheppard and Stafford remained regular attenders. Of the thirty-two who appeared at least once in these five years, twenty had been nominated to the bench since December 1647, a remarkable figure when we

[12] SP 28/129, fo. 58; SP 28/228, fos 759–60; BL, E113/5/1A (unfol.); Bodl. Lib., MS Rawlinson A39, fo. 528.
[13] PRO, C231/6, fo. 51; *CSPD* 1644, 11, 446; 1645–7, 25; 1656–7, 11.
[14] *LJ* viii. 157; *Birch Memoir*, 29–30, 140–2.

remember that many of them were not nominated until 1650 or later. They included the sequestration commissioners, William Selwyn, Jeremy Buck, Giles Hancock and Andrew Solace. Among the soldiers, Ayleworth did not attend and Crofts was not nominated until March 1653, but Neast, Wade, Raymond and Captain Mark Grime all served alongside a host of obscure minor gentlemen of whom little else is known.[15]

The same types of men, minor gentry and Gloucester aldermen, also predominated among the forty-six JPs appointed at various times up to 1653 in groups of two to four by the Council of State and various committees to examine matters varying from enclosure riots at Slimbridge to heretical preachers and indemnity cases.[16] The number of nominations of the leading figures (see Table 4) gives some idea of who was most active in the years 1650–4. The prominence of Ayleworth, who accumulated eleven nominations, is intriguing, for he was also the county's most active litigant at the Indemnity Committee. Sheppard, the second most active with nine, was an enthusiastic supporter of the Rump, to which he wrote in 1649, 'you are engaged in as acceptable a service to God and man as ever any assembly was'.[17]

Contemporaries would certainly not have been impressed by the 'quality' of the men ruling over them. Of the forty-six nominees, only John Howe and William Leigh were of pre-war 'county' status. According to an anonymous paper, Crofts was 'of very small meanes', Ayleworth was 'farr indebted & many executions in the Glouster hands ag[ains]t him', Neast was in debt, worth barely £100 per year and burdened with many children (which is true; he was often absent from Parliaments because of sick children) and John Batch of Tewkesbury was committed for acting as a JP when not worth £20 per year.[18]

Gloucester deserves separate treatment from the rest of the county for its experience was wholly different. Where the county saw a ruling class overthrown, Gloucester continued to be governed by the same men. No member of the corporation was ejected for Royalism. The only royalist alderman, James Powell, died before sequestration, although there were some suspicions against William Capel. Seven aldermen – William and Laurence Singleton, Pury, Dennis Wise, Capel and Jasper Clutterbuck – lasted from before 1646 until 1659 or later, and they provided great stability. Neither rigidly dictatorial, nor subject to popular pressure, the aldermen were able to rule as normal, delegating to others where appropriate and grooming their 'natural' successors in the process.[19]

The war gave Gloucester serious economic problems but it also gave the

15 PRO, E372/493–7; C231/6, fos 154, 253 and passim.
16 CSPD 1650, 53–4, 218, 426, 433; 1650–1, 501; 1653–4, 380; SP 24 passim.
17 N. L. Matthews, *William Sheppard, Cromwell's law reformer*, Cambridge 1984, 25.
18 Bodl. Lib., MS Rawlinson A27, fo. 293; *The diary of Thomas Burton, esquire*, ed. J. T. Rutt, London 1828, i. 284.
19 CCC i. 86–7; iv. 2810; BL, MS Harleian 6,804, fo. 69; VCH, *Glos.*, iv. 377.

corporation a regime to their taste. No member is known to have been wholly alienated from any of the pre-1659 expedients. Other than William Singleton, who effectively went into retirement after his second mayoralty, no member of the Corporation suddenly or permanently changed his habits in attending meetings. Most had every incentive to serve the Commonwealth. Successive windfalls gave some the chance to acquire land, and maybe gentle status, cheaply; by far the largest regular items of corporation business were surveys and leases of civic property, most of which were taken by members. 'Oliver's Survey' of former chapter properties in the city found that most had been leased or sold to councillors and their friends, including Sheppard and Thomas Pury junior.[20] As a separate county, Gloucester had her own committees, staffed almost entirely by Gloucester men. Some aldermen also served on county commissions, acquiring powers normally beyond mere merchants.

In religious matters, too, their zeal had free rein. Under a long-sought ordinance in May 1648, eleven tiny parishes were united into four and staffed, each at the parishioners' recommendation, by conservative Puritans – Samuel Kenrick at St Mary de Crypt, John Nelme at St Michael's, Thomas Jennings at St John's and Helpe-on-High Fox at St Nicholas. They were lodged in the prebends' old houses and took turns to deliver a new weekly lecture at the cathedral.[21]

A move to unite two others into the close and to make the cathedral a parish church was unsuccessful, but, after much lobbying, the Corporation did obtain jurisdiction over the cathedral in 1657. They showed they were in earnest by demolishing most of the other churches and the cross on College Green in order to reuse the materials in the surviving churches and for the repair of the market house and tolsey court; Trinity became first a school then a shelter for the fire engine. They even ordered the removal of the signpost of an inn called the Saracen's Head on religious grounds.[22]

All these gains were achieved through Parliament and bound Gloucester closely to the new regime. One might not expect the 'old Puritan' aldermen of Gloucester to see eye to eye with the Independents prominent in the county, but in fact they acted together easily enough. The godliness promoted in Gloucester was not of any pronounced hue. The ministers appointed in 1648 were conservative, but later appointments included the Independent James Forbes as cathedral preacher and the Anglican Clement Barksdale to St Mary's in 1657. Town Clerk Dorney opposed excessive zeal against those who agreed on fundamentals, and although Alderman Edwards tried to dissuade men from Quakerism, he refused to persecute them.[23]

[20] GRO, GBR B3/2, passim; B3/3, fos 126–7 and passim; S. Eward, *No fine but a glass of wine: cathedral life at Gloucester in Stuart times*, Salisbury 1975, 90–7.
[21] GRO, GBR B3/2, fos 172, 208, 211, 455, 465–6, 496, 503–4; Eward, *No fine*, 92–3, 97.
[22] GRO, GBR B3/2, fos 397, 453, 583–4, 653, 700–1, 711, 775, 795, 799, 801, 859, 863–4; Eward, *No fine*, 90–1.
[23] VCH, *Glos.*, iv. 100; GRO, GBR B3/3, fo. 53; J. Dorney, *Certain speeches made upon the*

However, more time and energy was given to pursuing reparations for Civil War damage (estimated at more than £26,000) through various Parliaments and committees. Much effort was spent on attempting to recover lands worth £4,335 16s. sequestered from Sir Humphrey Tracy (to whose father the debt-ridden Sir Henry Poole of Sapperton had mortgaged them), which had been assigned to the garrison in 1647. This took years because Poole's son, Sir William, had also attempted to sell them to pay his own composition fine. Despite careful attention, they could not be managed profitably, and the corporation decided to sell. Even then, Tracy wore them down from £2,200 to £1,800 in November 1650, once Poole had abandoned his bid.[24]

In May 1642 the Corporation, fourteen of its members, the Mercers' Company and others had invested £1,125 in Irish lands, sealing their commitment to Parliament. This too had to be pursued through Parliament. Agents were retained in London, and Dr Clarges argued in Dublin and in Parliament for a grant of land, yet the business dragged on. All Croft's endeavours on this matter in the 'Barebones' Parliament of 1653 were ruined by its sudden dissolution. In July 1656 they were ready to sell out for £300. Finally, an Act settling £10,000 in Irish land on certain citizens in consideration of their wartime losses finally passed the Commons in May 1657, but they never acquired more than a fraction of what was due.[25]

As the Commons' debates of 1657 showed, there was immense respect for Gloucester's past heroism. This, and her present, genuine loyalty, were the corporation's trump cards, stressed constantly in petitions. Three times during the Interregnum, in August 1651, March 1655 and December 1657 (and again during a Spanish invasion scare in March 1658) the city militia was raised promptly and efficiently in response to the threat of armed royalist uprisings. On each occasion the corporation chronicled their actions in exhaustive detail with tentative hints about repayment, which was not forthcoming.[26]

Patronage was relentlessly pursued. Cromwell was made Lord High Steward in 1652, and this office was later conferred on his son Henry, Lord Deputy of Ireland. It was hoped he might expedite the business, but all he gave was a £50 gift, for which profuse thanks were returned. The traditional New Year gift of lamprey pies to the king were redirected to Cromwell, the county's MPs and other dignitaries. In January 1657 Secretary of State Thurloe too was given a reminder in the form of two salmon pies.[27]

day of the yearly election of officers in the city of Gloucester, London 1653, 36, 56; 'The first publishers of truth', ed. N. H. Penney, London 1907, 109–11.

24 SP 28/128, fos 443–5, 456–62; CCC ii. 1050; CCAM i. 430–1; GRO, GBR B3/2, fos 515, 591, 698–9.

25 Ibid. fos 211–14, 786, 821–3; B3/3, fos 33, 37; HMC, corporation of Gloucester, 511, 514–15; *Burton diary*, i. 203–4; ii. 207–11; CJ vii. 322–3; A&O ii. 737–8.

26 Corporation to Speaker, 23 Aug. 1651, Cromwell to Corporation, 24 Mar. 1655, Corporation to Cromwell, 9 Dec. 1657, City Militia Commissioners to Cromwell, 15 Mar. 1658, HMC, corporation of Gloucester, 502–4, 509–10, 515–16.

27 Ibid. 505, 507, 514–15; GRO, GBR B3/2, fos 443, 494, 594; Corporation to Henry

Firing off fish in all directions could not secure redress of all Gloucester's grievances. There were many other deserving cases and the process of sifting through them was painfully slow. In any case, there was no urgent reason for the government to act. The city's rulers, its reformed churches and any hope of compensation depended entirely on the regime's survival. The Interregnum governments did not, at least, strip Gloucester of its independence as they did many towns, and it retained its authority over the Inshire, to the chagrin of some of the gentry. The dispute was to flare up again in the 1650s, with the massive general increase in taxation and Gloucester's impoverishment. By 1652 Dorney's fear of the 'adverse party' was replaced by the worry that 'many of the Gentry are much cooled in their affections to this City'.[28] Since it was the gentry who conducted the attack once again in the 1650s, this was yet another factor tying Gloucester to the government and to the radical group in the county.

The sequestration commissioners

The three main elements in county government – taxation, sequestration and the militia – became largely separated after the Revolution, as the county committees' powers were removed. The militia commissioners began to sign themselves as such, and when the sequestrators appear in their roles as JPs, it is usually in connection with sequestration business. In March 1651 we find John Driver warning Smyth of 'Mr Justice Handcox' intending to distrain his goods for tax arrears. Sequestration had been firmly separated when this business was handed over to four commissioners accountable directly to the parliamentary committees in February 1650.[29]

The sole gentleman of any standing among them was William Selwyn of Matson, the king's reluctant host during the siege of Gloucester. He appears never to have served, though it took until February 1651 to replace him with Alderman Anthony Edwards, a noted 'ranke Puritan' and protegé of Pury, who had risen via the sub-committee of accounts and serving as clerk to the former Committee. Of Thomas Rogers of Badgworth almost nothing else is recorded. Giles Hancock or Hancocks was a burgess of Cirencester as was the sub-commissioner, Andrew Solace. Hancock had been a captain of foot, then secretary to the Committee and was made a JP in December 1647. According to one hostile source, 'Giles the Mercer' was a leading member of a sect variously described as Brownist or Anabaptist and firmly in support of the regicide.[30]

Cromwell, 24 July, 17 Nov. 1658, BL, MS Lansdowne 822, fo. 158; 823, fo. 155; Corporation to Thurloe, 5 Jan. 1657, Bodl. Lib., MS Rawlinson A34, fo. 195.
[28] Dorney, *Certain speeches*, 55, 80.
[29] SP 28/229, fo. 80; Driver to Smyth, 16 Mar. 1651, Smyth of Nibley papers, xi. 68.
[30] CCC i. 201, 403; CJ v. 400–1; vi. 239; SP 28/129, fo. 56v; C231/6, fo. 130; T[homas] T[hatch], *The gainsayer convinced*, London 1649.

Table 5
The sequestration commissioners: letters and orders signed, 1650–4

Year	1650	1651	1652	1653	1654
Name					
Giles Hancock	9	17	17	13	6
Thomas Rogers	8	17	14	5	–
Jeremy Buck	4	12	2	–	–
Anthony Edwards	–	13	18	17	1

Source: SP 19, SP 23.

Jeremy Buck of Minchinhampton was the only man from outside the county elite to be exempted from pardon in Charles's proclamation of 1642. Derided as 'a busie mercer' and accused of slipping out of Cirencester the night before the storm, he showed courage enough later when he arrested the Bristol conspirators. As well as beating up the royalist rector of his own parish, Buck exhibited a gruesome sense of humour in threatening to hang Humphrey Jasper, vicar of South Cerney, from the sign of the King's Head in Cirencester for preaching against Parliament, and he had to be restrained by Fettiplace and George from actually doing so. He was also accused of taking profits from sequestered estates for his own use and stealing lead from church roofs.[31]

The commissioners were chosen as administrators rather than partisans. They undertook their heavy burden at a difficult time. In March their expected half year's revenue of £1,698 fell short by £418, although this was far from the worst return.[32] Of one hundred cases in Gloucestershire up before the two Committees of Parliament, only eighteen had been completed by 1650. All delinquents were now compounding directly with London, although the commissioners were still involved in administration, surveys, correspondence and depositions. The impression of an increasing workload is largely the result of the loss of pre-1649 papers, but Gloucestershire still had its fair share of long-drawn-out and complex composition cases (see Table 5 for a rough guide to the activism of the commissioners, in terms of the number of orders each signed between 1650 and 1654).

In May 1650 two simultaneous arguments blew up, one especially damaging as it involved two dedicated servants of the Commonwealth, Sheppard and Dorney. When the London committees nominated Dorney to replace him as steward, Sheppard refused to hand over many of the papers, notably bonds

---

31 *Stuart royal proclamations*, ii. 812–13; *A particular relation of the action before Cyrencester*, in *Bibliotheca Gloucestrensis*, 164; BL, E104 (4), *The severall examinations and confessions of the treacherous conspirators*, 1643; *Mercurius Rusticus* xvii. 129–31; Bodl. Lib., MS Walker C3, fo. 374.
32 CCC i. 312.

worth £800 relating to the earl of Newcastle's Tormarton estate, and questioned the order 'by virtue of an ordinance of Parliament'. Despite repeated orders confirming Dorney and requiring him to deliver the papers, Sheppard continued to hold out until faced with a large fine in December 1651. This did not stop the two men acting in consort elsewhere, nor did it halt Sheppard's rise to national prominence, but it did hinder local business considerably.[33]

In August, and again in November, the commissioners tartly observed that they still had no steward, and thus could not proceed with the case of Lady Elizabeth Somerset, whose estate they had re-sequestered in the (correct) belief that a deed of 1644, allowed by their predecessors, assigning her estate to Sir Robert Poyntz and others to settle a debt was merely a device to allow her to retain control of it. In the event, the case dragged on into 1654.[34]

Also in May 1650, Joseph Collett accused Edward Rogers, the commissioners' agent, of taking seven bribes, mostly to persuade him not to prosecute or to let lands at knock-down prices. He had also tipped off Sir Henry Frederick Thynne, one of the most troublesome individuals, of an impending distraint of his cattle so that he could hide them. The process of depositions and petitions continued until Rogers was finally proved guilty and sacked in February 1651. Almost comically, Hancock once wrote to Buck in London, asking him to expedite Rogers's return from answering these charges.[35] Hancock still did not know then that Buck was an even more corrupt rogue than Rogers.

Rogers was replaced by Hancock's brother, Richard, and the commissioners reluctantly obeyed orders to engage an indigent officer, Captain John Smith, as their assistant. Smith was prosecuting Benedict Hall of Highmeadow, seemingly a plum case, for Hall's Catholicism and activity in arms were well known. However, with multiple claimants on the estate, it became bogged down. Most of Smith's accusations were discounted, having already been dismissed by the Sequestration Committee. Then when he proved that Hall's servants had given false evidence, and that Hall had conspired to conceal much of the estate, Smith was given the added burden of prosecuting the servants and making new allegations. Matters came to a head in April, when Smith alleged that depositions taken in January had been tampered with, which the commissioners denied.[36]

On 30 May, goaded by frustration at his lack of pay or recognition, he confronted the commissioners. Their report shows just how isolated they felt amidst a hostile populace; Smith, they said, 'did very much abuse & affronte

[33] Ibid. i. 224, Commissioners to Committee for Compounding, 15 May 1650, 245, 262, 275, 516; C. R. Elrington, 'The survey of church livings in Gloucestershire, 1650', *TBGAS* lxxxiv (1963), 85–98; SP 28/229 fo. 80.
[34] Commissioners to Committee for Compounding, 23 July, 2 Nov. 1650, SP 19/96, fo. 97; SP 23/118, fos 847–53; CCC i. 279; iii. 2247–9.
[35] Ibid. i. 234, 279, 290, 317, 347, 393; Hancock to Committee for Compounding, 13 Jan. 1651, ibid. i. 403–4, 407.
[36] SP 20/1–5, passim; CCAM i. 451–6; SP 19/96, fos 123–4; CCC iii. 2000–3.

us in the face of the cuntry beyond what any person ever did to us', accused Buck of altering the depositions and would not be persuaded otherwise. 'The Abuse was soe high and purposely & sawselly & openly & our Authority soe disputed . . . that unless you take some extraordinary Course . . . y[our] Authoritie & our power here will be rendered contemptible.'[37]

All four commissioners and two clerks swore that the depositions had not been touched. The truth only emerged in November (after the case against Hall was temporarily dropped, and consideration had been given to prosecuting Smith), when Hancock went to London and examined the depositions. He found one note, on which Buck had forged his signature as well as signing in his own name. Hancock realised the truth at once. Forgery may also have been involved, without ever being noticed at the time, in two other cases. Meanwhile, no money was received from Hall's estate between November 1650 and February 1652.[38]

Also on 30 May 1651 William Newarke, a Cranham yeoman, deposed that after he had brought deponents to spend a whole day testifying, a clerk 'told them they might goe home and said the order was false and of noe authority and that this dep[onent] had very much abused the witnesses in bringing them thither', whereupon one angry man assaulted him. Newarke later observed 'the said clerk witnesses & delinquent [illegible] & did accompany and drink together'.[39]

Buck and an unnamed clerk – probably Hancock's own clerk, Devereux Poole – were also in the pay of another suspect, William Chapman of Tetbury. Another man saw Buck deliberately twist the evidence of a couple who came to depose against Chapman and badger them into signing certain documents, with the threat that otherwise they would not be compensated for their lost corn. Hancock later told this man that Buck 'was not Sworne'. But the commissioners still denied that anything untoward had occurred and plaintively asked the London Committees not to let them be abused in this way. Buck continued to act until next April, though only in Hancock's absence. Chapman spun matters out until 1652, when the Act of Oblivion pardoned all but the most recent delinquencies.[40]

This all held up business. Of the major cases, only those of Sir Robert Tracy and Sir Ralph Dutton, neither of which involved the commissioners, were completed between May 1650 and May 1651. Some accusations were made in this period and never heard again, many so insubstantial as to suggest that oppportunist prosecutors were taking advantage of the chaos in the hope of a quick payoff. Scarcely any further progress was made. Ten Gloucestershire Royalists, including Sir Humphrey Tracy, were discharged, and five more cases,

37 Commissioners to Committee for Advance of Money, 30 May 1651, SP 19/96, fo. 125.
38 SP 19/96, fo. 98; SP 19/134, fo. 138; SP 23/116, fo. 229; CCC i. 337.
39 SP 19/141, fo. 101.
40 Ibid. fo. 104; SP 19/96, fo. 125; SP 23/118, fos 787–90; CCAM ii. 1243–4.

including those of Richard and Sir Maurice Berkeley, were wound up around the time when the Act of Oblivion was passed.[41]

Multiplied across the country, this act represented an admission of failure and a forlorn attempt to reconcile the irreconcilable. It also slashed the workload of the local commissioners, who now spent most of their time administering the few estates still under sequestration – mostly Catholic recusants and those who could not or would not compound. It is striking how the same cases continued to cause most concern year after year: the Catholic Sheldons of Stratton, Lady Somerset, Benedict Hall, the Pooles and Thynnes and the earls of Newcastle and Worcester. In John Chamberlain's case, the commissioners were mere bystanders in a feud between one man and the borough of Stow-on-the-Wold. All of these dragged on into 1653, some as late as 1655.

It was difficult to run the estates at a profit to the state without ruining them. Sir Henry Frederick Thynne, a Shropshire man with estates at Buckland and Laverton, had fought every detail of his composition and continually evaded orders to settle his impropriate rectories to maintain preaching ministers at Cirencester and Kempsford.[42] The commissioners had gone to great lengths to survey the estates and let them to the tenants at an improved rent, only for the Committee for Compounding to order, in March 1651, that Thynne be admitted tenant. Now none of the tenants, who were on bad terms with Thynne and had worked together to secure the estate, dared put in a bid. The commissioners feared losing £300 out of this and they demanded immediate orders. None were forthcoming and Thynne was confirmed in October, though the London Commmittees, their wires thoroughly crossed, had apparently not got around to telling the commissioners this by December. Thus encouraged, Thynne continued to chip away at the settlements imposed on him until he was resequestered for non-payment. Meanwhile the estate was of no value to anyone.[43]

Also in December 1651, the commissioners realised that a profit might be made from the woods on the estate of Sir William Poole of Sapperton, whose newly-inherited estate was likewise secured because his father, Sir Henry, burdened by mortgages and settlements of almost £9,000, had not only under-valued his estate in his composition but had also sold off much to pay his fine when it was already mortgaged to Sir Humphrey Tracy, from whom it had been sequestered to pay the Gloucester garrison. In December Hancock asked for directions in this case without delay. Delayed they duly were; then, when the commissioners had taken the initiative and started to fell Oakleigh Wood, orders came to stop them. It was not until April 1652 that this was reversed, by which time, they feared, the timber would rot or be pilfered where it lay and

[41] CCC ii. 1273; iii. 1675–6; CCAM ii. 702, 727, 741, 794–5, 824–6, 830–1, 1108, 1138–9, 1174–5; iii. 1242–5, 1277, 2079–80.
[42] Ibid. i. 415–16; ii. 910–13.
[43] CCC i. 415–16; ii. 910–13; SP 23/156, fo. 161; CCAM i. 98.

the prospective chapmen were taking their custom elsewhere. Meanwhile, the purchasers were confirmed in the estate.[44]

It would be dangerous to speculate when we do not have enough figures to assess the commissioners' performance, but the general impression is that they made a conscientious effort to make the best of a bad job with one hand tied behind their backs. Technically, this system was more centralised than that of the all-in Committee of the 1640s, and certainly communications with London were more thorough and regular. But it was often the worst kind of centralism, where local men were given extensive powers then hamstrung by the delays, orders, petitions and counter-petitions endemic to the system. This and the scrupulous legalism of the two central Committees encouraged those who hoped to get off lightly or who sought to profit from malicious prosecutions. Often frustration creeps into the commissioners' letters; in Lady Somerset's case they smelt a rat at once and were barely polite in dismissing the Committee's queries.[45]

We should not assume that the new commissioners were necessarily harsher than the old county committeemen simply because they were of lower social origin. They were certainly less likely to act for personal reasons, but considering how faction-ridden the gentry were, close acquaintance could cut both ways. Like their predecessors, they viewed each case differently. When, in November 1651 after a two-year lapse, Thomas Deaves reopened the Dowdeswell case, which had already caused a mountain of paperwork, they did not conceal their irritation and spun out the time of his commission to examine with impossible conditions. Conversely, Thomas Haines, vicar of Sapperton, took Buck, Hancock and Rogers to court, alleging that they sent some hired toughs to intimidate him into entering a bond for his estate, on which they later prosecuted him, though he claimed that he qualified for the Act of Pardon. Hancock put a stop to this through the Committee for Indemnity.[46]

Hancock became the key figure. He had acted as treasurer from the outset, and, as early as February 1651, he intervened with a personal plea for Thomas Remington. He also helped to end the proceedings against Henry Chapman with an informal letter saying that he thought the prosecution 'very uniustly begun and p[ro]secuted w[i]th much malice'.[47] Despite his opposition to Buck, Hancock may not have been incorruptible himself. In 1652 Constable was writing to the Great Seal Commissioners about an unspecified 'miscarriage' of his, and after the Restoration he had to disgorge £500 from sequestered estates 'above the moneys paid to him'.[48]

---

44 CCC i. 573; ii. 1050; SP 23/95, fo. 223A; CCAM i. 430–1; Hancock to Committee for Advance of Money, 13 Dec. 1651, SP 19/86, fo. 63.
45 CCC i. 279; SP 23/118, fos 847–9.
46 SP 19/116, fos 134–5; CCC iv. 2838; PRO, C3 446/155; SP 24/13, fo. 40v (Haines v Hancock, Rogers and Buck).
47 Attorney General v Rogers and Hancock, PRO, E113/5/1A; CCC i. 618; Hancock to Committee for Compounding, 26 Nov. 1651, SP 19/141, fo. 110.
48 CSPD 1651–2, 267–8; 1661–2, 348; CTB i. 396.

But with Buck's sudden death in 1653 and Thomas Rogers fading from the scene, Hancock and Edwards did most of the work. They spent much of 1653 investigating a quarrel between their Herefordshire counterparts. From March 1654, as business wound down, one man per county was appointed to manage the few remaining estates sequestered. In Gloucestershire this was Hancock, with his brother as his agent and his friend, Andrew Solace, as his assistant. With full power of distraint he duly dealt with the Sheldons in no uncertain terms.[49]

He was still running twenty-seven estates in August 1655, twenty of papists, but some belonging to figures like Lord Craven and Lord Stafford. He might even be seen as a 'county boss', except that his power was restricted to sequestration alone. He was never a militia commissioner, and in July 1652, near the height of his influence, he was dropped as a JP, along with Solace, who was later restored.[50] Still, for an Anabaptist mercer this was power enough to make a mockery of any fond hopes of reconciling the Cotswold gentry to the Commonwealth.

One must wonder if other historians have been right to dismiss other sequestration commissioners as timid menial servants of the central Committees. Central appointment and their low origins did not necessarily make them so. In practice, though bombarded with orders, the Gloucestershire commissioners enjoyed a degree of initiative. The lead-footed system of petitions, counter-petitions and orders within which they had to operate prevented them making much of a success of it as surely as it eventually rooted out corruption from among them; left to their own devices, they could be very efficient. Admittedly, though, the autonomy they had from other local agencies was exceptional. Their Herefordshire and Somerset counterparts argued just as spectacularly, but only within the context of other ongoing wrangles.[51]

What was truly remarkable was the resilience of the Royalists to a potentially ruinous process. Many had huge debts before the war, almost in inverse proportion to their enthusiasm during it. Morton owed £2,150 and had virtually no estate. Throckmorton's lands had been mortgaged to pay debts nearly ten times their value, a mortgage upon which he had already once defaulted, and he was included in the second Act of Sale. Chandos, Master, Ducie and Sir Ralph Dutton all had serious problems even before composition added more.[52] Yet only the Pooles were pushed over the brink. Even then, the eventual buyer was another Royalist, Sir Robert Atkyns, and their ruin was

49 SP 23/187, fos 87–92.
50 SP 19/259, fos 64–64i; PRO, C231/6, fos 241, 267.
51 Everitt, Kent, 292; Fletcher, Sussex, 321; McParlin, 'Herefordshire gentry', 166–8; Underdown, Somerset, 164–7.
52 SP 23/123, fos 15–45; SP 23/156, fos 373–405; SP 23/188, fo. 95; SP 23/207, fo. 1; SP 23/213, fo. 391; SP 19/95, fo. 195; SP 19/104, fo. 73a; A&O ii. 523–32.

due more to the maladministration of the lands by yet another Royalist, Sir Humphrey Tracy, than to the commissioners. Despite everything, Gloucester-shire in the 1650s was still very much a gentry society.

The rule of the Independents

The revolution in government was matched by another in the Church. No definite religious settlement ever emerged out of the 1650s, but it was clear at the very least that there would be an extensive reformation, beginning with the removal of Arminian and inadequate clerics. Twenty-two men were ejected from their livings in Gloucestershire by various committees before 1650. Of these, Walter Powell of Standish and Thomas Whynnell of Cranham, the former Gloucester lecturer, were victimised by the County Committee and were no Royalists; Powell was later restored and Whynnell resurfaced at Bishop's Cleeve. Twenty-two was not very many in a county of 237 parishes, many of which were very poor.

A survey of 1650 returned details of the livings and their current occupants. In most parishes throughout the county there was a sufficient, resident, preaching minister (see Table 6). Only three were specified as inadequate. Most old or incapable men employed a preaching curate. Firm theological considerations were not involved in these assessments. Among those passed fit were many who had signed the rigidly presbyterian 1648 Testimony and such overt Anglicans as Clement Barksdale at Sudeley and Humphrey Jasper at South Cerney. The County Committee had also presented Richard Harrison, an Anabaptist, to Charlton Kings.[53]

The whole system of presentation was confused. For instance, Thomas Audley was ejected from Cromhall by the Committee in 1646, for 'being ill affected' according to them, 'for differing in judgement' according to him. Later however, the county commissioners licensed him to preach at Nibley, and he was presented to Woodchester by Sir Richard Ducie, then to a Leicestershire living by Lord Berkeley, with four Gloucestershire committeemen vouching for him.[54]

Despite the parliamentary Committees' involvement, the presentation process remained decentralised and informal, so that, in the absence of church discipline above parish level, authority devolved by default on the congregation, whatever its theological inclination. Thus, the ministers 'intruded' into parishes where an Anglican minister had been removed could be influential out of all proportion to their numbers, especially if, like Carnslew Helme at Winchcombe, they were instituted at the behest of parishioners dissatisfied

53 A. G. Matthews, Walker revised, Oxford 1948; Elrington, 'Survey of church livings'; Powell, Newes for newters; Thatch, Gainsayer convinced, 54; Bodl. Lib., MS Walker C7, fo. 141.
54 SP 18/183, fos 120i–vi.

Table 6
The survey of church livings, 1650

quality of minister	Kiftsgate	Seven Hundreds	Berkeley	Forest	Total
able/preaching/ constant/godly/ painful minister	54	72	30	22	178
minister, quality not specified	13	8	6	8	35
non-preaching minister	3	–	–	–	3
vacant	7	3	9	2	21
Total	77	83	45	32	237

Three pluralists are recorded as constant preachers twice, though in each case their quality is not specified in one of their two cures (Lower Swell, Miserden and Hewelsfield respectively). I have assumed that they were preachers at both. Two chapelries (Aust and Northwick) shared one preaching minister.

Source: C. R. Elrington, 'The survey of church livings in Gloucestershire in 1650', *TBGAS* lxxxiii (1964) 85–98.

with the existing minister. Because conservative Puritanism was entrenched in the Vale, the new radicals were mostly to be found in the Cotswolds and the north. Independent congregations were not unknown in the Vale, but there were also more able Presbyterian ministers and established discipline in place there to challenge them.

The leading 'Independent' ministers, notably Helme, Anthony Palmer at Bourton-on-the-Water, William Tray at Oddington, John Wells at Tewkesbury, William Beale at Stow-on-the-Wold, Francis Harris at Deerhurst, James Forbes, the Gloucester Cathedral preacher, and a few others were closely connected to each other and to sympathetic JPs. In 1654 Helme, Palmer, Tray and Beale were assistants to the commissioners for the ejection of scandalous ministers. They also appear frequently in petitions of the gathered churches. Tray and Beale were also joined by nine other ministers all over the north-east of the county, in testifying for Thomas Yarneton of Winchcombe, who had been falsely accused of delinquency. Wells was so famous a radical that, in 1655, dissident Anabaptists sent him anti-Cromwell pamphlets, hoping he would distribute them among his allies.[55]

[55] B. S. Capp, *The Fifth Monarchy men*, London 1972; *Originall letters and papers*, 123–4, 125–6, 139–40, 145–6; Bodl. Lib., MS Rawlinson A39, fo. 528; A&O ii. 980; SP 19/129, fo. 103; BL, E491 (7), *Mercurius Politicus* no. 288, 13–20 Dec. 1655.

These men were 'Independents' in that they believed that church member-ship belonged only to the visibly godly and began with 'the minor part voluntarily uniting with their own Minister to submit to Discipline'. The book which expressed this view, written by Palmer, emerged out of the 'private weekly seeking the Lord together' of the ministers around Stow, and bitterly attacked one Mr Humphreys for advocating 'that soul-damning practice of mixed communion'.[56] In theory they denied the civil magistrate any role in reformation, but in practice they were very dependent on their allies on the bench. They did, after all, choose to be a godly minority among the unregen-erate masses. The idea of the congregation electing their minister added only a specious tinge of democracy to a very authoritarian creed.

That said, they were highly influential in county affairs, as two episodes show. Helme invited the ministers of the Winchcombe area to give weekly lectures. Inevitably, disagreements arose, 'brotherly admonition' turned to hatred, and hatred to smears and abusive letters. This argument carried on between 1651 and 1653, and ranged Helme, Palmer, Tray and Wells against Clement Barksdale, then at Sudeley, William Towers at Toddington and one Mede. Finally, Barksdale answered Helme's challenge to meet them in a disputation at Winchcombe church on 9 November 1653.

The debate, as portrayed by Barksdale, was rather sterile, as the two sides were arguing on different levels. The obvious gulf between them was that Helme and Tray demanded proof of godliness before they would admit anyone to the sacrament, whilst Barksdale, an unashamed episcopalian, stood by the principles of Jewell and Hooker in admitting any of whom he knew no harm. Wells, perhaps the most radical of all, held that the saints, not the building, constituted the church.

This was no mere academic dispute. The views put into practice by the Independent ministers had profound implications for society at large, and laymen were involved at all stages of the quarrel. Helme had many 'disciples', but some from Winchcombe had abandoned him in favour of Barksdale's more comforting message at Sudeley. Others were 'bringing home their ears tingling with the strange doctrines . . . others absenting themselves from the church . . . others looking about where they might find a more conformable ministry'.[57]

Before June 1653, Helme had complained of his 'malignant neighbours' to the JPs at Winchcombe. Possibly as a result, Richard Ayleworth sat in on the disputation making learned interventions. Both sides played to the large, vociferous audience present; Barksdale's retort to Wells, that ministers of Independent congregations allowing of no appeal were like a horde of little popes, provoked a burst of ironic laughter. The bailiffs of Winchcombe itself were among many joining Barksdale and Towers in an alehouse afterwards.

---

[56] BL, E1496 (2), A. Palmer, A scripture-rale to the Lord's table, London 1654, pp. A1–A6, 1–6.
[57] Bodl. Lib., Wood 835 (1); C. Barksdale, The disputation at Winchcombe, London 1654, 21.

Laymen were involved again later as witnesses when Helme went to the JPs to demand Barksdale's removal with bizarre accusations, which, he said, exposed the JPs 'to much contempt among the People'.[58]

The Independents were no more tolerant of wayward enthusiasts than of stubborn Anglicans, as the 'Ranter' Richard Coppin found. Coming to Stow-on-the-Wold in March 1654 at the request of some in the area, he heard Helme preach a sermon containing what he viewed as a 'gross . . . error'. With Helme's grudging consent he began an impromptu lecture, but it was overheard by Crofts and Ayleworth who 'were much moved and enraged in their spirits against me', and had him hauled to Beale's house to grill him on his belief in basic Christian tenets, to which he gave evasive answers. They then accused him of blasphemy, and locked him up. Nothing daunted, Coppin began to speak from his window to a large crowd.

Unable to silence him, Crofts, Helme and Palmer finally had to arrest him themselves. He was indicted at the July assizes for preaching antinomianism, disturbing the peace and slighting the JPs' authority by telling the people 'to stand to their liberty and not to suffer the Justices to entrench upon it'. However, none of the charges could be made to stick. Indeed, Sergeant Glyn reproved Crofts and Ayleworth for bringing the case and unscrupulously taking phrases out of context to pursue the blasphemy charge.[59]

Thus, with the support of some JPs and committeemen, the Independents managed to keep the lid on dissent from both left and right. Nevertheless, they remained a small and unrepresentative group. Neither they nor the more conservative gentlemen and ministers had any time for the Quakers who appeared in Gloucestershire from the mid-1650s. Harris noted with concern their multiplying numbers, while John Stephens, Estcourt and Raymond, as sheriffs, were all responsible for acts of oppression. However, the scale of 'sufferings' was quite small compared with most other counties.[60] Quakers were always unpopular. As early as 1655, the Grand Jury complained 'that Ranters, Levellers and atheists, under the name of Quakers, made a disturbance, and petitioned some course might be taken'.[61]

The Quakers were not the only active sectarians. An extreme group existed by 1649 in Cirencester to which Hancock belonged; the other known members were all artisans and traders. Their particular enemies were local Presbyterian ministers, notably Alexander Gregory at Cirencester itself and Thomas Thatch, then at Kemble in Wiltshire, with whom they came to blows over a

---

[58] Ibid. passim; Bodl. Lib., Vet A3 f1732 (2); C. Barksdale, *The Winchcomb papers revived*, London 1658, passim.

[59] BL, E829 (2), R. Coppin, *Truth's testimony; and a testimony of truth's appearing in power, life, light and glory*, London 1654, 78–86.

[60] F. Harris, *Some queries proposed to the . . . Quakers*, London 1655; D. Roberts, *Some memoirs of the life of John Roberts*, 2nd edn, Bristol 1747, 6–10; J. Besse, *A collection of the sufferings of the people called the . . . Quakers*, London 1753, i. 208–10.

[61] *Early Quaker Letters from the Swarthmore MSS to 1660*, ed. G. F. Nuttall, London 1952, no. 174.

sermon he preached at Gregory's invitation. Whether they were actually Anabaptists is unclear; they were certainly republican, as exclusionist as the Independents and violently averse to established church ceremony. The Baptists had spread rapidly in the early 1640s, but never became a major force. By 1655 there were congregations of Particular Baptists at Tewkesbury, Moreton-in-Marsh and Bourton-on-the-Water in the Midland Association, which received into it a Gloucester meeting in 1658.[62]

But the Quakers outnumbered all other sectarians by far. Like the gathered churches, they tended to cluster in areas of scarce pre-war Puritanism. Their rise was initially due to the proximity of Bristol, where Quakerism spread like wildfire, with the garrison's support, until it erupted into violence. The Frenchay Monthly Meeting in the far south was the largest in the county and began when two Bristol men, John Camm and John Audland, held meetings at Filton (where the Broadmead Baptists had long been proselytising) in 1654. The word spread quickly in the immediate area, particularly in the parishes of Olveston, Elberton and Winterbourne. Individual conversions and a regular meeting place played a similar role in founding meetings in south-eastern towns like Nailsworth, Painswick, Tetbury and Minchinhampton, and the pattern was reinforced by George Fox's tours, which drew new converts to the established meetings.[63]

Despite standing apart from the masses, the sects always had a political role. In 1653 Helme, Palmer, Tray and Beale, with others of their churches signed a petition to Cromwell and the Council of Officers recommending twenty-one candidates for the nominated 'Barebones' Parliament, which was convened after Cromwell's dissolution of the Rump that April. It was a predictable list, containing ten JPs and nine soldiers, among them Raymond, Buck and Ayleworth; Crofts, Neast and Wade were singled out for 'godlynesse, self-denyall, zeale, faithfulnesse, wisdome, justice and tendernesse'.

It was presumably much the same group that, in the name of 'several Churches of christ and others well affected', petitioned the Barebones itself to encourage the godly in the pursuit of Christ's kingdom by acting against the 'carnal, prophane and ungifted ministry' still prevalent. This group had already, they said, sent a representation in support of the Army Petition of August 1652, 'but unsuccessfully to say no more'. Only in one other county, Devon, were the churches well-organised enough to frame such a petition.[64]

This recommendation was enough to secure Neast and Crofts their seats in the Barebones, along with another minor gentleman, Robert Holmes of

62 Thatch, *Gainsayer convinced*; W. T. Whitley, *A history of British Baptists*, London 1923, 68–70; B. R. White, 'The organisation of the Particular Baptists 1644–1660', *JEH* xvii (1966), 209–26.
63 'First publishers', 104–9; *The records of a church of Christ meeting in Broadmead, Bristol, 1640–1687*, ed. E. B. Underhill, London 1847, 19–22; GRO, D1340 A1/R1–3.
64 *Originall letters and papers*, 125–6; *Several proceedings of Parliament*, no. 6, 23–30 Aug. 1653; A. Woolrych, *Commonwealth to Protectorate*, Oxford 1972, 244.

Dymock. There was a gathered church at Dymock, which joined those of Cirencester, Oxenton, Weston and Herefordshire in another petition, probably of 1653, to Cromwell, asking him to destroy the influence of 'a prophane prelaticall ministry' and provide support for ministers through means other than tithes. None of the three was notably active in the Barebones, though Crofts was named to several committees concerned with Gloucestershire issues, such as tobacco-growing.[65]

Austin Woolrych's work has questioned the long-held assumption that the institution of the Protectorate after the dissolution of the Barebones was the victory of resurgent conservatism over the radicals, however much some thought or feared that it was.[66] Some moderate gentlemen could stomach a quasi-monarchical regime better than a republic, and Cromwell was keen to win over such men by restoring them to office. In Somerset, for example, John Pyne's crew were reduced to merely a few among many. The Protectorate was – perhaps it was meant to be – all things to all men. In many counties, some ventured to challenge the radicals at the polls in 1654.[67]

But one suspects that the change was superficial. As Cromwell's religious faith almost always got the better of his social conservatism, there was little reason for conservatives to support him except as the least of many evils. Certainly, no Gloucestershire supporters split from him at this time. With no committed Rumpers, Gloucestershire never developed any anti-Cromwellian republicanism. Locally, the most notable result was that Sheppard was lost to county administration, as he was taken on as an adviser on legal reform.[68]

In terms of appointments, nothing changed. Thurloe's list of potential militia officers in 1655 consisted of familiar names in Ayleworth, Crofts, Raymond, Wade, Neast, and others of the same hue. The assessment commissioners appointed by the ordinances of 24 June 1654 and 8 February 1655 were entirely unchanged from before. Indeed, the Pipe Roll evidence suggests that the bench became, if anything, more dominated by minor figures. As the veterans died off, only Wood and Hodges remained active; John Stephens returned, but not, as it will appear, out of love for the regime. Meanwhile, Raymond, Solace, Grime, Wade and the Purys were joined by more newly-nominated obscurities, including such radicals as Thomas Wells, Thomas Surman and, most controversially, the leading Quaker, Nathaniel Cripps.[69]

It is probably no coincidence that the Inshire gentry, led by Christopher Guise, now resumed the battle against Gloucester, with allegations of unfair rating in the new assessment. Personal feuds were no doubt also involved, for

[65] *Originall letters and papers*, 123–4; GRO, D2688 (unfol.), *1653*; CJ vii. 301, 322, 337, 340.
[66] Woolrych, *Commonwealth to Protectorate*, 391–8. Barksdale for one (*Winchcomb papers revived*, 64–5) was much heartened by the dissolution.
[67] Underdown, *Somerset*, 175–7; Beats, 'Derbyshire', 301–5; Fletcher, *Sussex*, 301.
[68] Matthews, *Sheppard*, 21–6.
[69] Bodl. Lib., MS Rawlinson A23, fo. 197; A27, fo. 293; A&O ii. 904–5, 1029–35; BL, E372/498–502.

by 1655 Guise was being prosecuted in Chancery by the older Pury in a dispute over fishing rights in Pury's recently acquired manor of Rodley, opposite Elmore. The corporation viewed the move as 'a designe ... to oppresse the City and to ease themselves', appointed agents and permitted the mayor, Pury himself, to go to London about it. Business was seriously hampered for a year until matters were temporarily cooled by a parliamentary order that county and Inshire should pay for the next three months in a thirteen to four ratio.[70] Such disputes between the committed and the gentry made the government reflect on alternative forms of taxation.

The most dangerous royalist conspiracy of the Interregnum was hatched by Colonel Penruddock in Wiltshire in February 1655. It found no support in Gloucestershire where there was no leader, Chandos having just died of smallpox, and none of Major-General Disbrowe's prisoners were from the county.[71] Royalist plotting in Gloucestershire had hitherto been ineffective, because it relied entirely on over-optimistic expectations of Chandos. He showed willing in 1651 by corresponding with Charles II, but he had no sooner been arrested and bailed than he was in trouble for slaying a man in a duel and had to flee abroad. Returning to save his estates in 1653, he was convicted of manslaughter and burned in the hand, 'a strange doom for a nobleman', and he shied away from political involvement ever after. After his death, his title and lands were separated and his widow's second husband, George Pit, acquired Sudeley.[72] It took years of work by Thomas Veel and later John Howe to reconstruct any basis for a royalist rising in the county.

The Royalists' failure to appear did not dampen the zeal of the familiar combination of Gloucester and the gathered churches. A newsletter named ten JPs, 'most of them of the Congregational way or such as wish well to the same' who joined the godly 'under divers dispensations ... Independent, and Anabaptist and Presbyterian' in raising troops and pulling down bridges – which can hardly have increased their local popularity. They included Ayleworth, Crofts, Wade, Neast, Batch and Surman. A letter from Oddington, presumably from Tray's congregation, praised 'that experimentally faithfull City Glocester' (which again had to pay the troops), and the four volunteer companies raised under Major Creed and Captain Ellis, for their loyalty to the 'honest interest'. There was a propaganda point in this, naturally, for the writer wanted to show that these men, who some would have turned out of county government, were still Cromwell's truest friends.[73] None the less, there is no reason to think that this account is not true.

The predominance of minor gentlemen who had risen through military

[70] GRO, D326/L3, fos 1–42; GBR B3/3, fos 760, 769, 798; VCH, Glos., iv. 99; HMC, corporation of Gloucester, 509.
[71] TSP iii. 305–8. There is a later reference to some Gloucestershire prisoners (ibid. 557).
[72] CSPD 1651, 147, 417; 1651–2, 123, 240; CSP iii. 172; The Clarke papers, ed. C. H. Firth (Camden ns il, liv, lxi, lxii, 1894–1901), iii. 7; The Nicholas papers, ed. G. F. Warner (Camden ns xl, l, lvii; 3rd ser iv, 1886–1920), ii. 206.
[73] BL, E381 (6), Perfect proceedings of state affairs, no. 288, 29 Mar.–5 Apr. 1655; GRO,

service to Parliament is clear enough, but what of the more substantial old Parliamentarians? The little evidence there is suggests that few were heavily involved in county administration and none were enthusiastic. More often they acted to restrain their colleagues. Nathaniel Stephens continued to be named to bench and committees, and he, John Stephens and Hodges were made commissioners for the ejection of scandalous ministers in August 1654. But Nathaniel's only extant papers of the period are purely personal. It may be significant that in the early 1650s he was fighting a legal battle against the Cliffords and other old Parliamentarians over his lordship of Whitstone Hundred. Guise and William Cooke also had government commissions addressed to them.[74]

John Stephens appears again, as do Hodges and Wood, at the December 1658 sessions, and he was at another in 1655, imprisoning Quakers because 'I fear to sleep in my Bed, lest such Fanaticks should come and cut my throat.' Hancock's ally, Andrew Solace, who was also brother-in-law to the famous Quaker, John Roberts of Siddington, released them on his own authority the same evening.[75] The JPs could work together on mundane issues, but, of all the leading men of the 1640s, only John Stephens, William Cooke, Hodges, Howe, Leigh, Guise, Estcourt and the Codringtons definitely served the Interregnum regime. Several showed a distinct lack of enthusiasm. Indeed, Leigh's loyalty had always been questionable, and Cooke had actually been under sequestration for four years in the 1640s.[76]

The split between moderate county gentry and the Independents may have surfaced in the election to the First Protectorate Parliament in 1654. Under the Instrument of Government, which created the Protectorate, the county was allocated five seats in Parliament, Gloucester kept two and the other boroughs were reduced to one. This meant more candidates and a wider scramble for places and precedence. The county result came in late and it was reported that 'Some from Glocestershire . . . have made addresses to his Highnes to complain of some Elections of persons to sit in Parliament.' As the eventual winning candidates were eminently respectable – George Berkeley, Matthew Hale, the famous jurist who lived at Alderley, Howe, Guise and Wood – it may be that it was the Independents who lost out and complained.[77] If so, they were to have their revenge in spectacular fashion.

There may have been slates contesting the election. Hale was said to have avowed that he stood reluctantly 'more out of a design to hinder mischief than to do good'. Gloucester followed tradition in returning Pury and Recorder Lenthall. Tewkesbury and Cirencester again chose outsiders; the former

GBR B3/2, fo. 817; T. Liu, *Discord in Zion: the Puritan divines and the Puritan Revolution*, The Hague 1973, 168.

[74] CSPD 1654, 403; 1655, 100; A&O ii. 971; BL, MS Loan 29/176, fos 285, 289; GRO, D149/M10.

[75] SP 18/184, fo. 81; Roberts, *Life of John Roberts*, 6–7.

[76] CCC iii. 2307; CJ iii. 300; v. 120.

[77] BL, E231 (29), *Severall proceedings of state affairs*, 27 July–3 Aug. 1654.

elected Francis St John, after Sir Anthony Ashley Cooper had been returned but chose to sit for Wiltshire instead, the latter John Stone, a Londoner with no local connections.[78]

Cromwell's decision, in the wake of the Penruddock rebellion, to divide the country into eleven military districts under the major-generals has been seen as the zenith of Puritan military dictatorship and the end of his attempts to reconcile moderate gentlemen to his rule. But, as H. M. Reece has shown, this was not entirely correct. Soldiers were already involved at all levels of local adminstration in the 1650s, working alongside civilians, commissioners and JPs, without necessarily provoking resentment; most of the major-generals were already working in the areas allotted to them, so that the move, which in fact evoked little comment at the time, was essentially a formalisation of their roles. Nor was this the creation of a military dictatorship. Andrew Coleby considers it as decentralised and inefficient as every other Interregnum expedient. Much depended on the major-generals themselves. Goffe, who hardly touched the administration of Hampshire while he vainly tried to build up alliances among the local gentry, was no more typical than the ferociously energetic Worsley in Cheshire.[79]

The genuinely resented aspect of the major-generals' rule was that they came to enforce the decimation, a punitive tax on all sequestered Royalists with estates worth over £100 per year. This seemed unjust to many when these men had already paid heavily for their allegiance and few had been involved in the plotting that occasioned the tax, but, since the assessment had proved so unpopular, the only way to appease the nation and satisfy the Army was to mulct the 'enemy' still further on the (correct) assumption that most were irreconcilable anyway. In any case, seventeenth-century Englishmen were wholly averse to realistic taxation levels. Those who protested against the decimation did not necessarily like the assessment any better.

Gloucestershire's experience confirms both old and new views of the major-generals. Disbrowe's intervention in local politics was detrimental to relations between centre and locality, precisely because it was brief and ill-informed. He had one of the largest bailiwicks and Gloucestershire, the least royalist of his counties, came low among his priorities. Affairs there usually appear as an afterthought in his early letters, from June 1655, as he settled the militia in the other five. He came twice and stayed only briefly. On the first occasion he arrived at Bristol on 29 December 1655, met the county commissioners and shortlisted Estcourt and Wood for sheriff. He was in Gloucester on 4 January 1656, when 'the worke goes pleasantly on', and returned to Bath the same day, having summarily ejected, on information locally gathered, four

78 Williams, *Parliamentary history*, 56–7, 194–5, 239.
79 Reece, 'Military presence', 177–210; Coleby, *Hampshire*, 32–82; Morrill, *Cheshire*, 276–87.

common councillors of Gloucester for 'adheringe to the Scotts king's interest' and nine Tewkesbury burgesses for unspecified delinquency.[80]

Having been on the road for six months and become weary of the job, Disbrowe must have been relieved to find a zealous group of commissioners in Gloucester. They wrote to Cromwell in December 1655, thanking God for directing him to a work so conducive to peace and security, against 'the inveterate and implacable malice of the late King's party, seeking upon all occasions to involve the nation in a continual deluge of blood, notwithstanding those many acts of mercy and favour extended to them'.[81]

Disbrowe was content to rubberstamp their suggestions and accept the rather uneven list of suspects they produced. On their certificate, he recommended, with weary cynicism, the rejection of petitions from Sir Edmund Bray and Richard Berkeley against decimation. He relied on familiar men, like Crofts and Neast (who were both considered as militia commanders, Crofts being chosen), and especially Wade, who he thought 'a faithfull person and exceedingly useful'. It was with Wade, Crofts and Captain Wallington, as Disbrowe's deputies, that decimated men had to enter bonds for their good behaviour and register before they were allowed to travel.[82]

The Gloucester 'delinquents' were presumably (it can only be deduced from their absence from the list of councillors in 1656) Richard Massinger, William Scudamore, Toby Langford and Thomas Yate. As all four became aldermen after the Restoration, the accusation may be true, but the corporation quietly restored them before October 1657. None were senior figures, as they had been named to the Common Council between 1645 and 1651. All bar Massinger had good attendance records. This did not affect business or relations with Disbrowe, who was made a freeman in August 1656 'for his noble favours to this Corporation'.[83]

The Tewkesbury purge was on a larger scale: nine of forty-eight principal and assistant burgessses were removed. Eight of the nine had been attacked in 1649, in a petition of twenty-one citizens headed by the new recorder, Thomas Bulstrode and the low bailiff, Christopher Atkinson, who alleged that a faction headed by John Man, a former Royalist, had plotted to elect disaffected bailiffs, settle a disaffected minister and exclude loyal men from places of trust. William Hill, the town clerk and another victim, blamed Bulstrode, a very recent arrival, for his chagrin at not being exempt from quartering charges and a counter-petition blamed 'turbulent spirits'. The truth never emerged, for the case was not pursued after it was referred to the Committee of Indemnity and then a local commission of six JPs, though it is notable that Atkinson's group

---

[80] Disbrowe to Thurloe. 29 Dec. 1655, 1, 4 Jan. 1656, TSP iv. 360, 391, 396.
[81] Commissioners to Cromwell, 27 Dec. 1655, ibid. iii. 94.
[82] Ibid. iii. 308–9, 439, 557; iv. 360; Bodl. Lib., MS Rawlinson A40, fo. 301; BL, MS Add. 34,014; CSPD 1655–6, 102; Smyth of Nibley papers, v. 53–4.
[83] GRO, GBR B3/2, fo. 876 and passim; B3/3, fos 1, 45.

nominated as their JPs Constable, Hancock and Holmes, the other side Leigh, Wood and Sheppard.[84]

Tewkesbury was a faction-ridden town, and the council chamber had seen serious division and disorder over the years. This was not, however, simply the purge of a royalist rump. Of the nine, Man and Hale had refused to contribute to the Royalists in 1644, and in 1643 Hill was chosen by Morton specifically as a reputed Puritan, to persuade the defenders of Gloucester to surrender, and his entries in the feoffees' book were conventionally parliamentarian in tone.[85]

No doubt the quarrel was at the root of the many frivolous denunciations of Tewkesbury men to parliamentary committees. Conway Whithorne and Thomas Jeynes senior were genuine Royalists, but one list of 1648 also included several who were not, and in December 1649, five of the eight plus – oddly – Batch, William Croft and Atkinson were also denounced. No action was taken in any of these cases. If Disbrowe's aim was to improve order, he did not achieve it for long; in 1658, there was further conflict about a new 'malignant lecturer', who was supported by some of the burgesses and fiercely resisted by John Wells, the minister.[86]

With the assessment commission in eclipse, new blood might have entered the ruling circle in 1655 and 1656 via the decimation commission, but the commissioners' three extant letters show that it did not. None of the twenty signatories bar the two outsiders, Disbrowe himself and Wallington, were new to county government; nine were local soldiers, four were of the Gloucester corporation and only three were substantial gentry; Hancock was another of them.[87] The influence of such men greatly increased as they held the information necessary when the major-general could not do the groundwork himself. If the views they expressed to Cromwell in December 1655 are representative of their general outlook, the Cavaliers might have welcomed a centralising military dictatorship taking power from zealots such as these.

Three county gentlemen were also decimators, but they clearly did not share this enthusiasm. When Disbrowe came to enforce the decimation, Hodges asked for time to consider, then cried off claiming toothache, as did Howe (whose son was already deeply embroiled in royalist plots) with gout. Christopher Guise incurred the wrath of the others by trying to protect Royalists; this is surely the purport of his memoirs, which resume in 1655 after a seven-year gap, when referring to 'theyr indemnification which I did sometimes, but found my power soe litle there that they could nott receave an assistance from mee proportionable to theyr expectations'.[88]

Matters between the two parties, if we can call them that, came to a head

[84] Ibid. TBR A1/3, fo. 6; D2688, 1649; Disbrowe to Cromwell, 7 Jan. 1656, TSP iv. 396; SP 24/5, fos 115, 129.
[85] Bennett, Tewkesbury, 186–7; GRO, D2688 1642, 1644.
[86] CCC i. 86–7; iii. 1949; iv. 2908; CCAM ii. 1170; CSPD 1658–9, 117.
[87] TSP iv. 394; Smyth of Nibley papers, iii. 71; Bodl. Lib., MS Rawlinson A40, fo. 301.
[88] TSP iv. 360; Guise memoirs, 129–30.

at the elections in August 1656 to the Second Protectorate Parliament. George Berkeley and Howe were unopposed for the first two places. Guise says that there was strong support for him, but that the rest of the commissioners 'prevayled with Desbrowe to come from Salisbury to hinder our election, which by very foule meanes he did', so much so that Guise feared for his life.[89]

This agrees in essentials with a petition from Guise and the other defeated candidates, Robert Atkyns and Sir Thomas Overbury. Both were of the second rank of county gentry and of royalist and parliamentarian backgrounds respectively – an indication, perhaps, that the gentry were uniting against the Independents. The three claimed that the sheriff, Raymond, deliberately hindered them by twice adjourning the election meeting, refusing a poll and then reconvening at seven o'clock next morning with only twenty voters present to elect Berkeley and Howe with Neast, Crofts and Baynham Throckmorton junior 'who had few or no voyces'.[90]

Presumably Raymond acted at Disbrowe's request. Disbrowe was certainly in Gloucester at the time to secure his own election for the borough (though he later waived it in favour of Somerset), and released from the gaol a Quaker, Walter Clement, who reported that 'at the election here for Parliament men stood very fast to [Disbrowe] and his party'. Raymond was also active at Tewkesbury, where as sheriff he formulated a tripartite indenture with the bailiffs and ninety-four inhabitants, including Neast and Batch, to return Disbrowe's son, Valentine, with the proviso that he should not have power to alter the government as settled. This was a common proviso used against those who had attacked the Instrument of Government in the last Parliament. However, in the end Lieutenant-Colonel White, not Valentine, was elected.[91]

There was a general campaign by the major-generals to 'pack' Parliament with suitable men. Disbrowe did so in Gloucester with some success and local support, in marked contrast to some other counties where no amount of browbeating could overcome the hostility to 'Swordsmen and Decimators'.[92] The decimation had proved an unqualified disaster. Everywhere people had managed to avoid it by undervaluing their estates or through the help of influential men. Cromwell himself wrote to secure exemption for John Dutton, a personal friend. The Gloucestershire commissioners decimated only twenty-four men and made some surprising omissions.[93]

As Cromwell reverted to the assessment and flirted with Parliament's offer of the crown, the saints everywhere grew alarmed. None were better organised than those of Gloucestershire. A petition signed by the ministers and churches of Stow-on-the-Wold, Winchcombe, Bourton-on-the-Water and Tewkesbury

[89] Ibid.
[90] GRO, D2768 1/1.
[91] Williams, *Parliamentary history*, 196–8, 238–9; Clement to Margaret Fell, 4 Oct. 1656, *Early Quaker letters*, no. 321; GRO, TBR A14/2.
[92] Morrill, *Cheshire*, 287–92; Fletcher, *Sussex*, 310–11; Beats, 'Derbyshire', 333–6.
[93] GRO, TRS 144; *Historical and genealogical memoirs of the Dutton family of Sherborne*, privately printed, 1899, 116–17; Smyth of Nibley papers, iii. 71.

continued to hammer the same themes – the dangers of backsliding from the incomplete work of godly reformation, the continued malice of 'the prophane party' and his duty to remember 'the rock which has hitherto preserved you'. It also bewailed the continued pollutions in worship, scandalous ministers, corruption, the oppression of the saints, and the resurgence of the ungodly. Even before the crown was formally offered, Forbes, Helme, Palmer, Tray, Harris, Beale and other ministers of the region begged Cromwell to refuse, calling it a trick of those who 'openly boast of laying levell the Lord's work' once the major-generals were voted down.[94]

Their most impressive effort, probably in June 1656, was subscribed by four congregations, nine ministers (including all of the above), and 102 of the county's godly, mostly quite humble, but also including eight JPs. They asked Cromwell to 'maintain the distinction of the cause of Christ' and keep His enemies – 'dis-affected persons or politick & flattering neutrals' – out of power, end the oppression of the well-affected, act against corrupt ministers (for there were too few able or willing to do so locally), reform the law and regulate corporations.[95]

Thus, although they were often worried about his intentions, the gathered churches always looked to Cromwell, whatever his title. And although he did want to broaden his regime's support among the gentry, and accepted the bulk of the Humble Petition and Advice while refusing the crown, he did not let them down. The maintenance of godly religion was always his first priority.

In 1656–7, new commissions of the peace and assessment commissions were issued. These have been viewed as the confirmation either of a gradual acceptance of Cromwell's regime by the gentry, or of a conservative resurgence. Either view is hard to sustain. In most counties, the government pitched for support by simply nominating more of every group.[96] In Gloucestershire some returned to one or both who had been in and out before, and some radicals were indeed dropped, but little was new. Of the restored county gentry, only Guise and George are known to have attended quarter sessions. Indeed, in February 1656, the government took up Disbrowe's suggestion to add some reliable Bristol men to the benches of Gloucestershire and Somerset 'in respect ther is not one Justice in Either of these Counties neare the Citty of Bristoll and yet much Vice raigneinge', and confirmed them in 1657.[97] This could hardly have been more calculated to annoy the gentry, who were invariably touchy about old boundaries.

A few men of royalist family background came onto the assessment commission, but not one of those excluded since 1648, let alone an ex-Royalist,

94 *Originall letters and papers*, 139–40, 145–6.
95 Bodl. Lib., MS Rawlinson A39, fo. 528.
96 Underdown, *Somerset*, 185–7; Hughes, *Warwickshire*, 295–7; Beats, 'Derbyshire', 360–1; McParlin, 'Herefordshire gentry', 195.
97 PRO, E372/401; C231/6, fos 307, 326, 340; C193/13/6; Bodl. Lib., MS Rawlinson A33, fo. 74.

was chosen. Moreover, this commission was in any case much expanded, with seventy-five men compared to forty-seven, forty-eight and sixty-six on the previous three assessment commissions. The few who were wholly new to committees were utterly obscure.[98]

The limited evidence for the 1657–9 period suggests that the same group remained to the fore. Indeed, from the Pipe Roll evidence, 1658 was the year in which the bench was most completely dominated by the radicals. In October 1657 the two Purys, Wade, Crofts, Neast, Hodges and Raymond were chosen as commissioners of the Public Faith. Those definitely present at quarter sessions in December 1658 were John Stephens, Hodges, Wood, William Oldisworth, Crofts, Wade, Mark Grime, Batch and Thomas Pury junior.[99] Not all of the active men of the 1650s in Gloucestershire were sectarians, nor were they all socially obscure but most of those consistently at the heart of affairs were both.

Cromwell died on 3 September 1658, to profound general indifference. At Tewkesbury, the town clerk noted that this was the anniversary of his two greatest victories and wrote 'Death Conquers him who had beene so eminent in Armes. And if . . . '. But he stopped short of reflection and simply added 'Sic transit gloria mundi'. The Gloucester corporation received the news with sadness and ordered appropriate mourning. It is notable, though, that after some debate a draft address to his son and successor Richard was amended to omit a reference to the 'well deserving souldiery', and to emphasise Richard's providential accession as much as Oliver's courage, prudence and vigilance. Most significantly, the new version spoke of 'the cause & church of Christ' instead of different 'churches of Jesus'.[100]

Does this reflect a struggle between men of differing outlooks? Richard was an unknown quantity; hardly anyone could be sure of, or despair of, his support. Thus all raced to assure him of their loyalty and tried to win him over to their views. In these circumstances, it is definitely no coincidence that the Inshire controversy was renewed in March 1659, with petitions (which are not extant) from the gentry of the county and the Inshire itself, to which Gloucester responded by appointing a committee to peruse the records and prepare an answer.[101] County unity was completely out of the question, in Gloucestershire and everywhere else. It was a troubled inheritance for an inexperienced young man.

Richard did not have time to alter local benches and committees, but his summoning of a Parliament under the old franchise gave men another chance to air their views. The bench had become even more radical, as two of the JPs

98   A&O ii. 299, 467, 664–5, 1069–70.
99   PRO, E372/402; BL, E505 (35), Mercurius Politicus, no. 383, 22 Sept.–9 Oct. 1657; SP 18/184, fo. 81.
100 GRO, D2688, 1658; GBR B3/3, fos 87–8, 90–1.
101 Ibid. GBR B3/3, fos 95–6.

were converted to Quakerism. Colonel Mark Grime, who had been at the heart of affairs in the Army's greatest days in 1647, bought an estate at Corse Lawn in 1648 and was nominated to various committees between 1651 and 1659.[102] Nathaniel Cripps ('a serviceable man in his day') lived at Upton near Tetbury. George Fox visited both in 1656 and Cripps again in 1660.[103] It was no doubt with one of these two in mind that the county MP, John Stephens, complained in April 1659 that 'Many Quakers are made Justices. There is one in my county that could lead out three or four hundred with him at any time. The Judges have complained, but could not get him out. I know not what hinders.'[104]

Stephens had been returned with John Grubham Howe, John Howe's second son. There is no evidence as to whether they had to struggle to defeat radical opponents. However, the younger Howe was at the centre of royalist plotting in the county and had stood, with Charles II's permission, to avoid suspicion of his recent behaviour. Cirencester again returned John Stone with Robert Southby, another Londoner. Tewkesbury pursued a patron more desperately than ever, writing to Thurloe to offer him one seat and the right to nominate to the other. He let Disbrowe choose Colonel Edward Cooke and Robert Long.[105]

Gloucester's previously rock-solid unity finally cracked. The two successful candidates, James Stephens and Laurence Singleton, apparently stood together on a moderate ticket against the older Pury. Some 500 voters turned out, and chaos ensued. Pury's supporters complained that one of the sheriffs wrongly took both votes at once so that his opponents picked up each other's second preferences and each enough of his to beat him into third place, even though he had 280 first votes. Possibly, though, this simply reflects the fact that the city was not accustomed to polls. Such was the expense involved that the sheriff, Massinger, was later excused serving another term because of it.[106]

The first signs of a crack in the ranks could hardly have appeared at a worse time for Gloucester or the godly. But the events of the next year were to demonstrate the enduring strength of the Good Old Cause. That the Independent party had held together is shown by the petition raised in the name of the JPs, gentlemen and others in Gloucestershire 'well-affected to the peace and settlement of this Commonwealth' when the Army overthrew Richard and recalled the Rump. The petitioners welcomed the Rump and opposed the return of the MPs secluded in 1648, regretting that the lack of a firm basis of government had led to the local revival of 'the old Cavalier party and the rigid presbyterian'. They hoped to see the 1649 version of the Agreement of the People as the basis of settlement, the franchise restricted to those expressly

102 *Clarke papers*, iv. 69–70; VCH, *Glos.*, x. 276; CJ vi. 562, 604.
103 '*First publishers*', 108; *Early Quaker letters*, nos 529, 175; *The journal of George Fox*, ed. N. H. Penney, Cambridge 1911, i. 258, 262, 352.
104 *Burton diary*, iv. 337.
105 Williams, *Parliamentary history*, 58–9, 163, 199, 239–40; TSP vii. 572.
106 *Reasons inducing the justice in equity of Mr Pury's petition in Parliament*, London 1659; GRO, GBR B3/3, fo. 270.

opposed to the monarchy and a 'civil sword' in religion, and wanted some of the godly to sit in future Parliaments as observers to ensure that these fundamentals were not breached. Clearly they were not shaken by recent events and saw no reason to believe that the nation could not remain a godly oligarchic republic. Indeed, the petition only survives because it was reprinted by another author who regretted that the Gloucestershire men had delivered their petition too hastily, rather than wait and join like-minded men from other regions.[107] The slide towards a Stuart Restoration was far from inevitable in mid-1659.

Tobacco and timber: relations with central government

It was on two seemingly trivial matters that the county had most regular contact with Whitehall. The Commonwealth took only until April 1652 to follow the Caroline lead and prohibit tobacco-growing in England. Joan Thirsk has suggested that the regime's motive was concern for customs revenue on Virginian tobacco, and pressure from the merchants themselves.[108] The evidence agrees to some extent, but there may have been better arguments against the noxious weed than she allows. One memorandum of 1655 mentions eight reasons of which the hindrance of navigation and colonial cultivation was only one. There was also the poor taste and consistency of native tobacco when compared with American.

More substantially, it caused thousands of 'disolute p[er]sons' to converge on the Winchcombe area, where, because of the crop's seasonal nature, they were begging or pilfering for nine months a year. By consuming vast quantities of manure, it inflated the price and rendered otherwise good land elsewhere uneconomic to cultivate, and thus impoverished farmers, setting off rating disputes. So many workers were occupied by the crop that worthier trades like clothing were in decline for want of labour. It had ruined the county's once thriving trade in sending imported tobacco up to London and Gloucester's Common Council had resolved against it. This last statement was indeed true. The corporation of Bristol was equally hostile, and had instructed its MPs in 1654 to act against the crop, vast amounts of which were being brought into Bristol to the detriment of trade.[109]

In suppressing tobacco, the government was not acting against a united county community, but intervening in a local dispute that would not realistically admit of any compromise. Equivocation made the problem worse. The ban was rescinded by Barebones in 1653 when the growers' agreed to pay Excise, only for the Virginia merchants to secure a new ban and the appointment of commissioners to enforce it in April 1654. Orders were sent in June

[107] Glos. Pub. Lib. (H) B1.4, *Panarmonia: or, the agreement of the people*, n.p. [1659].
[108] A&O ii. 580, 718–19; Thirsk, 'New crops', 280.
[109] SP 18/98, fo. 16; GRO, GBR B3/2, fo. 761; Latimer, *Annals of Bristol*, 251.

to the commissioners and the governor of Gloucester (the Council of State apparently forgot that there was no governor at Gloucester any more) to act against those who had rioted to defend the crop at Winchcombe after it had been destroyed elsewhere.

Governor Scroope of Bristol vainly tried to root out ringleaders. 110 Winchcombe men, most poor and illiterate, but some more substantial, promptly petitioned for, and were allowed, this year's crop, on condition that they promised not to plant without licence again. Of course, they had no intention of doing any such thing for 'it is the Trade and Occupac[i]on wherein yo[ur] Petitioners have for well near ffortie years been trayned up in. And many have served Apprenticeships in it'.[110]

Planting was already in progress next March, and it was not halted by the Council of State writing to the county JPs, the town authorities of Gloucester, Tewkesbury and Winchcombe, and nine other counties to publicise the ban, or by renewed orders to destroy it. The next two years were quiet, but in 1658 an armed raid on Cheltenham ended in farce when a crowd of up to 600 defied orders to disperse and forced the troops to return to Gloucester.[111]

Destroying tobacco was not an easy task. In 1658 John Beaman found his efforts to do so hindered because many JPs with a personal interest refused to issue warrants and many of the county troop were also dealers and planters. The riots were well-disciplined and organised. In 1654 eighty turned out when the bells were rung, and, in 1658, some 200 came from Winchcombe to Cheltenham to help. In any case there was simply too much growing for a small company to uproot. But the government was not without local support. The soldiers who said 'if this be suffered, farewell all levies and taxes, and farewell the Virginia trade for tobacco' were both regulars and locals.[112] On such matters was the government's ability to rule tested, and they neither satisfied their loyalists nor cowed a 'disaffected' interest group.

Committed to the Navigation Act and the First Dutch War and faced with shortages of naval iron, the government soon reversed the decision taken in 1650 to demolish the ironworks of the Forest of Dean. Ostensibly this had been done to conserve ship timber in England's largest woodland reserve, though in reality Dean had hardly ever contributed to the navy. On 27 August 1653 Major Wade was appointed to head a state-run experiment with instructions to erect or repair two furnaces, cut dotard trees to make charcoal for fuel, while

110 SP 25/75, fos 12, 374–5; SP 25/76a, fos 43–4; BL, E743 (13), *Mercurius Politicus*, no. 212, 29 June–6 July 1654; SP 18/72, fo. 65.

111 CSPD 1655, 100–1, 201; BL, E831 (6), *Perfect proceedings of state affairs*, no. 28, 29 Mar.–5 Apr. 1655; SP 18/182, fo. 50; BL, E756 (5), *Mercurius Politicus*, no. 427, 29 July–5 Aug. 1658.

112 SP 18/182, fo. 50; BL, E743 (13), *Mercurius Politicus*, no. 212, 29 June–6 July 1654.

reserving good timber for naval and other uses, and liaise with local woodwards and the Council of State.[113]

Wade himself pushed the idea of combining timber and iron. As he later wrote 'To make iron without building ships or vice versa is a loss, as what is to become of the offal timber? . . . Both building and making of Iron togeather is as agreeable the one with the other as health to the body.'[114] With the large amounts of decaying wood in the Forest and her coal and iron ore deposits, the project made good economic sense.

There were teething troubles, naturally. Furnaces required a heavy initial outlay and continuous investment – Wade estimated £50 per week to make fifteen tons of shot and five of sow iron. Both he and Augustine Aldridge, a surveyor sent to work under him dealing with timber, were perennially short of money, writing begging letters to the Navy and Admiralty Commissioners. A forge had to be added as Wade soon learned the hazards of dealing with ironmasters, as well as the legacy of many conflicting claims over the land, some of which threatened to jeopardise the project. Finance was rudimentary and organised through Bristol where the naval commissioner, Thomas Shewell, had his hands full with a large shipbuilding and fitting programme. As late as June 1656, Aldridge could not get money because Wade's clerk, who handled it, was away in Bristol – more than two years after Wade had asked to be supplied by the county receiver-general.[115]

Moreover, it was a complex business. To make a ton of iron involved fifteen batches of ore, sixteen horseloads of cinders, even larger amounts of coal, eight short cords of wood, and labour, skilled and unskilled, at all stages; raw materials had to be dug and transported between furnace and forge, timber had to be sorted, surveyed and accounted for. Wade was not operating in a free labour market, for men born in St Briavel's Hundred had the sole right to mine there. Labour was plentiful, but it was seasonal and not always reliable. Wade was delayed at the outset for lack of chapmen to sell the product locally and, in the spring of 1657, Aldridge lacked transport 'by reason the Carriers are sowin of Theare corne'. At other times, bad weather held Aldridge up for months on end.[116]

Above all it was lack of money that kept down productivity. It took until March 1655 before the forge could become operative and September before 100 tons of timber reached Chatham. Once the supply became more regular, matters slowly improved with Wade, who virtually ceased to write. However Aldridge still spent much of 1655 and 1656 short of money for himself and his

[113] SP 18/39, fo. 107. The episode is also covered in Hammersley, 'Iron industry', and C. E. Hart, *Royal forest: a history of Dean's woods as producers of timber*, Oxford 1960.
[114] Wade to Admiralty Commissioners, 25 Nov. 1656, SP 18/40, fos 61, 73, 103; SP 18/182, fo. 32ii.
[115] SP 18/141, fo. 32.
[116] Aldridge to Navy Comissioners, 30 Mar. 1657, SP 18/68, fo. 13; SP 18/80, fo. 53; SP 18/89, fo. 64; SP 18/163, fo. 94; *CSPD* 1655–6, 529, 533, 535.

workmen and complaining. His mood was not improved by several misunderstandings with Bristol, when two ships in turn arrived which were too large to dock at Lydney, and Aldridge was involved in arguments over procedure with the captains for several months.[117]

In August 1656, the navy commissioners sent a shipwright, Daniel Furzer, to build a fifth-rate frigate at Lydney. Possibly this was to oust Aldridge, the admiralty commissioners' protégé, whose last shipment of treenails had been sub-standard. There was not really enough work for both a surveyor and a shipwright, and by next spring the two were at odds, competing for workmen at spiralling wages, a spectacle which Wade found 'uggly to behold'. Wade had to sort out the dispute. He thought both honest and careful, but he effectively damned Aldridge with faint praise for obeying orders to the letter in bringing timber to the yard rather than the frigate. Aldridge was recalled in June 1657.[118]

Building ships on site reinforced the project's dependence on Bristol, where master, crew, sails, anchor and other materials had to be found. This could cause further bureaucratic delays – for instance, when Shewell was ordered to find a pilot to take the frigate down to King's Road, to his annoyance, as he was busy, and Furzer's, as Wade had already found one. None the less, the *Forester*, a ship of 306 tons gross, carrying twenty-two guns and one hundred men, was launched and taken down in September 1657, and timber continued to be shipped out at intervals.[119]

However, enthusiasm was fading in Whitehall. Furzer's new first-rater ('for w[hi]ch there hath beene never A tree felled', he announced proudly) had to be abandoned for lack of money, despite having squared 500 tons of timber in December. In April 1658 Furzer's unpaid carriers downed tools in protest.[120] Wade managed to pack off a large cargo of timber and ironwork on the *Friendship*, but only hard lobbying about 'the greate losse the state did sustaine in not continuinge the buildinge' persuaded the Admiralty Commissioners to commission another frigate before 1,500 tons of timber on the waterside and countless decaying trees were wasted. The work progressed more smoothly for nine months, despite continuing money problems and disagreements between Wade and Shewell. While building this ship, Wade also repaired the *Grantham*.[121]

Wade's accounts were audited three times, in 1656, 1657 and 1660. Though deficient in many ways, they illustrate the wide variety of the project's work and its undoubted success. 3,750 tons of pig iron, over 720 tons of bar and 700

117 SP 18/118, fo. 36; SP 18/112, fo. 49; SP 18/135, fo. 101; *CSPD* 1655–6, 533, 553, 557, 577.
118 Wade to Admiralty Commissioners, 9 May 1656, SP 18/145, fo. 65; SP 18/166, fo. 70; SP 18/167, fo. 6; *CSPD* 1657–8, 376, 390.
119 SP 18/170, fo. 117; SP 18/171, fos 52, 71, 74, 95; Hart, *Royal forest*, 144–5.
120 Furzer to Admiralty Commissioners, 6 Feb. 1658, SP 18/188, fos 25–8; SP 18/190, fo. 50; *CSPD* 1657–8, 525, 537, 555.
121 SP 18/188, fos 27–8; SP 18/182, fos 32 i–ii; Hart, *Royal forest*, 145; *CSPD* 1658–9, 214, 298, 516, 537, 540.

of shot plus other forgings had generated £41,000 income and a £12,000 profit. Between September 1656 and March 1659, more than 50,000 treenails had been made while 300 tons of timber had been shipped to naval stores, 643 had gone into the *Forester*, 200 into the new ship, 173 to other uses and up to 800 still awaited carriage.[122] The potential, given steady supplies and peace, was enormous.

Ironically, the letter recording this also made the first mention of the riots that would eventually cause the collapse of the venture. But we should beware of labelling this the inevitable 'localist' backlash to unwarranted central interference. After all, the project had kept many in work and provided owners with a buyer for their wood. Wade was not an outsider, and he was well aware of Dean's unique situation. From the outset, he had pressed 'that the ancient government be settled'. He combined his post with an array of traditional offices, and he brought in local JPs to combat waste in the forest.[123] Conflict was not inevitable. On the contrary, a petition of 1655 in the name of the gentry, freeholders and inhabitants, and signed by 113, including many local gentlemen, agreed with him in essentials. While asking for a constable to be appointed to protect timber and hold courts to try all differences between them and uphold their rights, it positively eulogised the usefulness of Dean's resources for naval timber.[124]

The real disasters ensued after the Act to Mitigate Forest Law in 1657, under which the Protector could enclose and coppice a third of it. 18,000 acres were set aside for timber and common rights temporarily extinguished there. This was vital to ensure the regeneration of the woods to supply fuel to the ironworks and for naval timber trees which needed twelve years unhindered growth. Just as in Charles I's grants to various projectors in the 1630s, the Act made generous provision for the freeholders and tenants who gained wider rights over their property.

But it ignored the fact that Forest Law actually suited these people more often than not, and it ignored the squatters and cottagers, who had no rights there and whose livelihoods depended on extensive exploitation of the wastes. As Disbrowe said in answers to objections in the Commons that all this went against the liberties Parliament had fought for, the object was 'to make wild men tame men'. Wade, sure that the gentry and freeholders would accept the 1657 Act in the long run, had set about the problem at source by expelling hundreds of squatters.[125] It was most probably these people, encouraged by a few landholders and royalist agents, who initiated the riots that brought him down.

---

[122] SP 18/130, fo. 102; SP 18/157, fo. 175; SP 18/202, fo. 70 i; Hammersley, 'Iron industry', 236–7.
[123] SP 18/40, fo. 61; A&O ii. 811; Hart, *Royal forest*, 142, 147; Hammersley, 'Iron industry', 220.
[124] SP 18/102, fo. 85.
[125] Hart, *Royal forest*, 151; A&O ii. 1114; *Burton diary*, i. 228–9.

The eventual decline and fall of the project mirrored that of the Protector-ate regime which had created it and upon which it relied. Given more time it might have succeeded. In many ways the episode typified Interregnum govern-ment. A bold, imaginative plan, it was hampered by the regime's chronic lack of credit. Heavy outlays were made but cash shortages threatened to scupper the plan before it could pay off. To set up the stocks and then call a halt after one frigate, for instance, would have been pure folly.

A cumbersome structure, unreliable funding and the perpetual need to wait for orders all caused delay, yet, in terms of what it set out to achieve, the project was a success. This was a tribute to Wade's vision and exemplified how local enthusiasm, the right contacts and judicious string-pulling could generate activity in Whitehall. Charles II's decision to keep Furzer on in Dean showed that it had been recognised as useful. But even though it was the men on the spot rather than the government who had the will to see it through, in the final analysis it collapsed because they were wholly dependent on the regime for money and support.

About the quality of government during the Interregnum little can be said, but in addition to the Tewkesbury man who raged against 'Committee-men, Sequestrators, Treasurers &c (the common cheats of the Nation)' in 1649, another local put his thoughts into print. The pamphlet *Harry Hangman's honour* has been quoted by Joan Thirsk on the subject of tobacco-growing, but it is also a satirical skit on the rulers of England in general and of Gloucester-shire in particular, not unlike Humphrey Willis's attack on John Pyne's crew in Somerset in *Times Whirligig*.[126] Indeed, though less specific than Willis, 'Harry Hangman' may have been more accurate, as he had no political axe to grind. The author may not have been the county hangman as he claimed to be, but his intimate knowledge of local scenery, recent assizes and the 'old clothes, lice and shitten stiles' of Deerhurst Fair mark him out as a true Gloucestershire man.

After a long discourse on tobacco-growing, the hangman laments the decline in his trade that it has caused. His wife then berates him for not finding a better job. As a sequestrator, she says, he might have procured false witnesses to inform on men of great estates, taken their goods to force them to redeem the estates with a £20 bribe, or let the estates to neighbours and terrified others with the threat of false accusation. (It is not hard to imagine this of Edward Rogers and Jeremy Buck.) As a committeeman – people thought 'that you had as good a face and as honest a face as some of them' – he could have taken bribes to let estates worth £2,000 to £3,000 at £200 to £300 'and so cheated on both sides'. As a captain, he might have profited from the vast booty of

126 BL, E548 (2), *The moderate*, no. 36, 13–20 Mar. 1649; J. Thirsk, 'Projects for gentlemen, jobs for the poor: mutual aid in the Vale of Tewkesbury 1600–30', in *The rural economy of England*, London 1984, 287–307; Underdown, *Somerset*, chs vi–vii.

Hereford and Worcester. As a collector, he could have joined in the massive fraud of 1644 and 1645.

More explicit pointers follow, about a 'neighbour' who had been soliciting causes with the Commissioners for Approbation, getting 'very able Dunces' presented to rich livings and even duping the Gloucester Corporation. This man could speak 'Hebrew Greek Latin Italian Syriack Arabick Chaldee and all other Tongues and Languages exprest in Weem's book of Antiquities', but his English was not so good. This is surely a reference to Matthew Herbert, a committeeman of the 1640s, identified by Thomas Daunt of Owlpen as the author of a travel book who spoke Arabic and Persian.[127]

The hangman worries that he is not learned enough for these jobs, but his wife advises him to learn the army officers' religious jargon, ingratiate himself and bribe 'Mr. Marston' with a good living lest he 'print you for a Bribe-taker, Broker and Forger of hands'. John Marston, vicar of Henbury, was indeed an arch-opportunist, who obtained the living despite having been ejected at Canterbury for hostility to Parliament. He had gone to join the king in Oxford in 1643, then later bought his restitution by revealing the whereabouts of a royal jewel. In 1653 he petitioned the Council of State not only for his removal by the Committee for Plundered Ministers to be rescinded, but also to be allowed to prosecute a delinquent and have his witnesses examined by someone other than the county commissioners.[128]

Harry Hangman's account is inherently credible and agrees with some known details. And who knows better than the hangman that little thieves hang while great ones prosper? In fairness, much of this may relate to the 1640s when the chaos was far worse. Only Buck and Raymond were guilty of constant partiality and corruption throughout their careers. Harry Hangman was picking on outrageous examples to pour scorn on a regime that executed the king but did nothing for the poor.

The Independent ruling group would probably have retorted that this was not the point. Their prime interest was in bringing about godly reformation from above, and they proved a very cohesive group in pursuit of that aim throughout the decade. Most of those who rose to prominence in the early 1650s were still there in 1659. They were, of course, a minority among the JPs and committeemen, a minority among the lesser gentry and a minority ruling on behalf of their own kind. But then so was every other local ruling group in seventeenth-century England. Strength and unity of purpose counted for far more than their numbers. These men had come into power by similar means and were closely bonded through service to one cause and mutual membership of gathered churches.

After Andrew Coleby's work, no-one will portray the Interregnum governments as ruthlessly efficient military dictatorships. Relations between centre

---

[127] *Harry Hangman's honour*, 10–15; Thomas Daunt jr to Thomas Daunt sen., 2 Jan. 1646, GRO, D979A F3/2.
[128] *Harry Hangman's honour*, 15–16; *CSPD* 1653–4, 170; Matthews, *Walker revised*, 272.

and locality were often marked by confusion and misunderstanding. Some of the men who ruled Gloucestershire were corrupt, vicious, incompetent or all three. This may mean only a few bad apples among them; Buck and Raymond were both praised by the gathered churches as worthy men. The sequestration commissioners struggled through a morass of papers but never achieved any appreciable result. Neither did the decimation commissioners produce much, for all their feral zeal. That said, one doubts very much whether government by these men was any worse than that of the pre-war gentry whose sons swept back into power in 1660.

The sheer scale and complexity of the new structures created in the period meant that decentralisation in government was both inevitable and desirable. It would scarcely have been possible for the major-generals to do their job without dedicated and efficient men on the spot. The problem with the central governments of the 1650s was that they did not know how and when to delegate. Quite often, the state's servants managed best when they were left to do as they saw fittest. Instead, they were perpetually bombarded with orders which could be changed or abandoned without notice. The ironworks project was slowed down because of the short-sighted policy of a government that started such projects but could not fund them properly. Tobacco continued to grow, despite considerable local opposition, partly because the Council of State allowed the planters a year's grace and thus encouraged them to persist.

Centralisation and efficiency are not the same thing. The decentralisation of the Interregnum could have been its greatest asset, as long as there were enough dedicated men on hand in the counties to carry through policy – and there were in Gloucestershire. Although the power of the gentry was not entirely broken, it was demonstrated that county government could continue well enough without a Tracy or a Stephens at the heart of it. The ruling clique carried out jobs meant for more substantial men than they were. But for the chronic lack of credit and the bureaucratic confusion of successive regimes, they might have done their jobs very well.

Apart from godly reformation, the major preoccupation of the county's rulers was security. The county's forces, be they garrison regulars or volunteers from Gloucester and the gathered churches turned out promptly on every alarum, although they were never really tested. But the strength of resistance to the slide towards the Restoration, to be examined in the next chapter, tells us something. A regime should be judged according to its own aims. The gathered churches had sought to purify themselves away from the unregenerate multitude. Their leading civilian members, who were presiding over a cauldron of alienated gentlemen and potentially riotous poor, had perhaps succeeded only too well in this. The contrast between spiritual ideals and the realities of the political world in which they had been thrust into power was something with which they never quite came to terms.

5

'Cotteswold Shephards and the Vale Weavers'

Popular culture and politics before the Civil War

Chapter one introduced the recent upsurge in interest in popular culture and allegiance during the Civil War and after. This interest was largely sparked by David Underdown's study of Somerset, Wiltshire and Dorset in *Revel, riot and rebellion*, which argues that the main difference between areas of opposing outlooks was cultural: the actively parliamentarian 'cheese' wood-pasture regions and the more royalist 'chalk' arable downlands. Chapters two and three have already covered some of this same ground, revealing a consistent and active support for Parliament among the common people in certain areas of the county.

Without repeating material from these chapters at length, it is clear that there were major economic differences between the various regions of Gloucestershire. The Vales of Gloucester and Berkeley were very much 'cheese' countries; indeed, many yeomens' inventories of the 1640s mention up to 500 cheeses in store, and Chipping Sodbury was famous for the greatest cheese market in the region.[1] These were areas of pastoral 'open' villages, with many rural artisans, where enclosure was common and manorialism generally weak, and there were large numbers of migrant poor. Dean, Kingswood and the Vale of Evesham fit this category too, albeit that their societies and economies were very different from those of the Vales. And although the soil of the Cotswolds was limestone, this was a typical 'chalk' country, with a predominance of sheep-corn husbandry, open fields, nucleated settlements and tight manorial control. Perhaps the one important difference from Underdown's 'chalk' region of the neighbouring counties was that the Cotswolds lacked small resident gentlemen.

Inevitably, in the absence of good local records, the evidence for popular culture and festivity in Gloucestershire is impressionistic. However, many of Underdown's definitions fit well in this respect too. Stoolball, the game of the 'cheese' country, is found in the cloth-making parishes of Tetbury and Rodmarton in 1609 and 1610. John Smyth, in 1639, wrote of 'the inbred delight that both gentry, yeomanry, rascallity, boyes and children doe take in a game called stoball' in various parts of Berkeley Hundred, and, he adds, 'not a son of mine but at 7 was furnished with his double stoball staves and a gamster thereafter'.[2]

---

1 Thirsk, *Agrarian history*, v. 189; Defoe, *Tour*, ii. 60.
2 GRO, GDR 108, fos 5v, 19v, 33, 111; Smyth, *Description*, 10.

Stoolball was indeed a game of the 'cheese' country; it was also a game fit for gentlemen which cut across class lines. The only local references to football, the archetypal game of the downlands, both come from Gloucester. In 1593 a man was killed 'with a blowe one the heade at football' and, in 1660, a match between two streets was to be the pretext for a riot.[3] This rough sport could act as the focal point for community rivalries both rural and urban.

While there was some pressure against popular culture in the wood-pasture regions in particular, we should not presume that the issue is between popular culture either surviving or being suppressed. Often it simply died of its own accord or was artificially preserved. Most reformers objected to the drunkenness and disorder of such events more than the customs themselves and hindsight often gave them a golden glow they scarcely deserved.

The Cotswold Games were a case of traditional festivities preserved in aspic. Held annually in Whit week in Weston-sub-Edge, these were a revival of the long-decayed Cotswold Whitsun Ales by Robert Dover, a London attorney with local land and connections. They combined the Olympic spirit with a conscious protest against the Puritanism of the age. In 1636 they were celebrated in some atrocious poems, mostly by local gentlemen. John Trussell lamented that

> Carnivalls
> Palme and Rush-bearing, harmlesse Whitson-Ales
> Running at Quintain, May-games, generall Playes
> By some more nice, than wise, of later dayes
> Have in their Standings, Lectures, Exercises
> Beene so reprov'd, traduc'd, condemn'd for vices

The verses compared the Games (favourably) to the ancient Olympics, eulogising them for bringing together men of all ranks and reaffirming their common identity. Ritual inversion was a part of it, for the young elected a lord and lady for the duration of the games, with stewards to attend them. The sports involved were both gentle (hunting and coursing) and plebeian (football, skittles, cudgels, wrestling and so forth), but the verses reek of highly paternalist, even patronising, attitudes which remind us that this was a festival for the entertainment of the gentry. William Denny thought the games would turn the idle poor into soldiers, and Thomas Randall exhibits a particular contempt for the participants:

> What Clod-Pates, Thenot, are our Brittish Swaines!
> How lubber-like they loll upon the Plaines
> No life, nor spirit in 'um . . .

---

[3] GRO, P154/15 IN1/1; Bodl. Lib., Wood 593 (7), *Mercurius Publicus*, no. 7, 9–16 Feb. 1660.

Dover rode about the proceedings wearing the king's cast-off clothes – Endymion Porter, a courtier and lord of nearby Aston-sub-Edge, was a keen patron – and distributed his ribbons to the winners while the gentry watched from their pavilions.[4] It was because of this elite support that the games were so widely known and celebrated.

Alas, churchwardens' accounts and other parish sources say little about the survival of popular culture in Gloucestershire. Of all the Cotswold villages, only Welford-on-Avon has left pre-war accounts, and these are not very useful, though there is an interesting reference to 'glovers shredds, eggs and cheese curds to mend the steeple' in 1638. At nearby Buckland, a minister was ejected in 1647 for, amongst other things, countenancing Sunday games.[5] Customs could easily survive in one parish but die in another for purely local reasons. Within Berkeley Hundred in 1639, the young of Alkington, a tithing of Berkeley, still met at Riam Mead on the Sunday after Whitsun for 'dancinge, leapinges, wrastling and the like exercises' and Sunday games survived in Cowley, whilst similar revels, including stoolball, on Blue Mead in nearby Stinchcombe were lately 'by some severe and rigid Catoes exclaiminge against such recreations, quite discontinued'.[6]

However, other evidence supports Underdown's view of a long-term decline in festivities in the Vale and clothing region. In Minchinhampton, a sprawling market town at the foot of the Cotswold escarpment, a profitable church ale and the collection of 'hoggling money' (an informal levy on new lambs) vanished in the 1590s. Soon after, church rates and payments to visiting preachers were instituted. In the 1630s the churchwardens began the profitable but unpopular practice of selling life interests in pews, and the first taker was that archetypal rising Puritan gentleman, Jeremy Buck.

The Puritan influence was even stronger in Dursley, where seat-payments began in 1579. Both hoggling money and 'Hoke-days' (when the young men and women on alternate days put out ropes across the street and made a levy on passers-by to raise money for the church) were discontinued by 1625. Nibley had a church-rate by 1615 and was selling pews by 1625; religious zeal among the rate-payers is plain – in 1634, they raised £24 to pay their aged curate to resign and still more to give a godly replacement a decent stipend.[7]

It is probably no coincidence that such records survive best in the areas where there was most disorder and poverty and the parochial means to do something about it. Those which do survive from outside the Vale and cloth region are of no interest. It was in the Vale that detailed accounting of income

---

4 R. Dover and others, *Annalia Dubriensa*, London 1636, passim; Whitfield, *Chipping Campden*, 95–101.
5 GRO, P353 CW2/1 (now transferred to Warwickshire Record Office); Matthews, *Walker revised*, 173.
6 Smyth, *Description*, 35, 152–3, 349.
7 J. Bruce, 'Extracts from the accounts of the churchwardens of Minchinhampton', *Archaeologica* xxv (1883), 413–20, 443; J. H. Blunt, *Dursley and its neighbourhood*, Gloucester 1975, 38–44, 49–60; GRO, P230 CW2/1.

and expenses was so necessary; some Cotswold villages lacked the incentive, others the means to do so. But despite the never-ending burden of poor relief in the Vale, the wealth clearly was there. Nibley, for example, managed to raise a quadruple rate in 1632 for church repairs on top of all the usual outgoings.[8]

Where the records say nothing of popular festivities, it is because their existence or demise was taken for granted. Only where there was something worth arguing about are the details full. The one dispute captured in the diocesan records occurred at Bisley, another large parish at the foot of the Cotswolds. In 1610 the vicar, Christopher Windle, was presented by his churchwardens for encouraging Whitsun revels and setting up a maypole. He retorted to the reproofs of 'the well Desposed people' that 'pipeinge & Daunce-inge at a Maye Poule & keepinge of Somerale' was just as lawful as hearing sermons. Windle later dedicated a book defending sports to James I. His assertion that maypoles had recently been pulled down in Gloucester and Berkeley suggests that there were potential revellers everywhere, but, as Anthony Wood later observed, those who set up maypoles in 1660 to annoy the godly soon got tired of them and went back to the alehouse.[9] Their main use was symbolic, as Windle realised when he made one the focus of an ongoing feud in a divided parish.

The county's main towns were also experiencing economic dislocation, and the increasing aldermanic oligarchy and civic Puritanism of the corporation of Gloucester which resulted showed itself in a clampdown on idleness, drinking and popular culture. The people were reduced to being spectators at civic parades. In the 1630s travelling players, hitherto popular, were increas-ingly refused permission to perform whilst the corporation retained its own musicians and actually increased the number of civic waits. In 1641 the corporation led the onslaught on episcopacy, denouncing Bishop Goodman for (amongst other things) encouraging May games and morris dancing and 'maintaining fidlers in his howse on the sunday and dancing in the cittie'.[10]

One reason for the aldermen's concern for preaching and order was the poverty and ignorance of the city clergy, only one out of eleven of whom was a preacher in 1641. Only in two parishes in 'puritan' Gloucester did the custom survive of dressing the church in 'Rosemary Bayes & holly' at Christmas.[11] None the less, it seems that the corporation's drive on public morality bore some fruit. Fleeing from Puritan-bashing mobs in Worcester in 1640, Richard Baxter was surprised to find at Gloucester 'a civil courteous and religious

---

8 Ibid. P230 CW2/1.
9 Ibid. GDR 114, fos 4–v, 8–v; *Records of early English drama: Cumberland, Westmorland, Gloucestershire*, ed. A. Douglas and P. Greenfield, Toronto 1986, 284–8, 365, 402–19; *Life of Wood*, iv. 317.
10 VCH, *Glos.*, iv. 75–92; Soden, *Goodman*, 197–8, 327; Willcox, *Gloucestershire*, 291–3.
11 *LJ* x. 173–5; GRO, P154/14 CW2/2 (St Michael's Gloucester). St Aldate's (P154/6 CW2/1) records 'hollye at Christide' in 1631.

people, as different from Worcester as if they had lived under another government'.[12]

Tewkesbury, likewise, was experiencing new tensions through the great numbers of indigent poor settling in the town. There was a drive for sobriety and church attendance; town ordinances constantly reiterated the need for the burgesses to do their jobs properly and wear those robes commensurate with their status, which in itself suggests an uphill struggle. The Cirencester vestry book likewise shows the increasing concern of the wealthy for the moral welfare of the poor, with constant watchfulness against 'idleness, drunckenes and thefte'. [13]

The concept of 'riot and rebellion' presupposes something to riot about, the ability to do so without much fear of retribution and the lack of better means of redress. Each area of the county affords examples of good and bad relations between lords and tenants, but such quarrels were conducted in many different ways. After Mickleton, in the north-east, was enclosed by agreement, the tenants fought a running battle through several courts against the lord, Sir Edward Fisher, alleging that he was defrauding the poor of their due and wearing down resistance by intimidation. There was resistance to attempted enclosures nearby, by the Whitmores at Slaughter and Endymion Porter at Aston-sub-Edge (despite what *Annalia Dubriensa* said of 'bad owners of enclosed fields / That have your soules as narrow as your bounds').[14]

One factor most common in the Cotswolds and the north was the legacy on the market towns of oppressive monastic landlords. Cirencester and Winchcombe in particular still suffered from a historic lack of a borough government commensurate with their size, and in Winchcombe this was exploited by the new lords, the Whitmore family.[15] Likewise, ever since its incorporation in 1604, Stow-on-the-Wold had fought to shake off the Chamberlain family's manorial authority, refusing to attend their stewards' courts and commencing various legal actions. A jurisdictional dispute at Tetbury between the feoffees and the town representatives, the 'Thirteen', simmered for a century.[16] Few of these quarrels were forgotten in the 1650s, but none ended in violence.

Historically, the areas of riotous unrest were the open country, particularly the banks of the Severn, the Forest of Dean and the Stroudwater clothing district. All experienced turmoil in the pre-war period. Violence was also seen in the Vale of Evesham as, from 1627 onwards, the Privy Council tried to stamp out tobacco-growing. Their warrants were openly torn up by the town authorities at Winchcombe in 1631, and there was violence against the messengers both there and at Cheltenham in 1635 and riots in subsequent years. The

[12] *The autobiography of Richard Baxter*, ed. N. H. Keeble, London 1974, 39.

[13] GRO, TBR A1/2, fos 5–8v, 13; S. E. Harrison, *The Cirencester vestry book in the seventeenth century*, Gloucester 1914, 12–14.

[14] GRO, TRS 31; Johnson, *Stow-on-the-Wold*, 69; Whitfield, *Chipping Camden*, 100.

[15] Hilton, *A medieval society*, 170, 176, 296; Moreton-Jackson, 'Dissolution', 48.

[16] VCH, *Glos.*, vi. 157–8; xi. 275; M. C. Hill, 'The borough of Stow-on-the-Wold', *TBGAS* lxv (1944), 175–86; E. Hodgson, *A history of Tetbury*, Dursley 1976, 43–52.

people of Winchcombe may have learnt from this, for, in 1637, when Thomas Whitmore toured his father's estates to raise rents and end the lax system of tenure, he found 'a Charme of Scoulds raysinge their voyces to God save the Kinge and his Lawes and they and there Ancestors had lived there and they would live there and w[i]thout the danger of hott spitts, scaldinge water and firye tonges there is noe gaineinge of poss[ess]ion'.[17]

Many combined to intimidate the compliant few, so that only ten would agree terms – defiance on a scale far beyond that found in the family's Cotswold estates. It was followed by a lawsuit of 1638–9, in which the vagueness of the customs is clear. The defendants denied that they were tenants at will, and stood by established practice of 'tenantright' – that tenancies were freeholds, which could be exchanged simply by handing over the key without reference to the lord or revision of the rent. Clearly, though, the defiance was not unanimous, as there was intimidation on both sides.[18]

The many pre-war troubles in Dean have been studied at length elsewhere. Those between 1628 and 1631 have been labelled, with those in other forest areas, as a 'Western Rising'. This is misleading, for Dean differed from the other forests in her size and largely untapped resources of naval timber, coal and iron ore. Pressure on these, from crown and inhabitants alike, was increasing, especially under Charles I. Buchanan Sharp argues that those involved in successive waves of enclosure riots were not the established smallholders, whose rights were scrupulously regarded in successive disafforestations, but the multitudes of rural artisans whose precarious independence depended on extensive exploitation of the Forest's resources. They had no legal title to the ground they occupied and their 'rights' were wholly irreconcilable with any attempt to enclose nurseries for ship-timber or cordwood for ironworks. It was their resistance, Sharp contends, that ruined every concession until Charles in desperation threw the problem into Sir John Wintour's lap.

The biggest enclosure riots in Dean occurred in 1631. These were characterised, as so often, by a well-organised destruction of the concessionaries' enclosures, the filling-in of pits and the beating-up of imported labourers. The year 1631 also saw the appearance of 'Skimmington', a figure of communal outrage that could be directed against anyone from cuckolds to the government, and was most often seen in wood-pasture parishes. News of the coming of 'Skymingtons leiutenante' also inspired separate disturbances in Frampton-on-Severn the same year, and set the government off on a wild goose chase after one man they identified as Skimmington.[19]

Slimbridge and Frampton were perennial trouble-spots due to the Berkeleys' attempts to enclose the reclaimed New Grounds, which 'drawe many poore people from other places, burden the township with beggerly Cottages, Inmates

17 GRO, D45/M1, fos 1–v.
18 Ibid.; Willcox, *Gloucestershire*, 158–62; GRO, L19.
19 Sharp, *In contempt*, 5–8, 82–125, 180–219; Hammersley, 'Iron industry', 134–205; Willcox, *Gloucestershire*, 179–202.

and Alehouses and idle people'. Again, the riots were the work of the very poor, though the issue was doubly complicated by lawsuits over the title to the New Grounds, which Lord Berkeley invariably won, and a dispute between the two townships over their common lands. To some extent, however, John Smyth managed to unite tenants and landless against him by his harsh measures.[20]

The disturbances in the clothing industry resulted from the severe depression of the early 1620s in the aftermath of the Cockayne project. In February 1622 unemployed weavers rioted and banded together to extort food and money from the rich, and the threat of further trouble was seldom far away. Although this was a highly capitalist industry, in which a handful of clothiers made fortunes and many thousands scraped a living by weaving and spinning, there was a fundamental unity of interest among them. The real problem was the decay of the trade itself, and protest was usually against unemployment or the damaging effects of state quality control legislation; when mozing mills were banned in 1633, clothiers, tuckers, weavers and spinners combined to complain.[21]

It is notable that the man who led the industry's united effort to thwart Anthony Wither's mission to reform the trade in white cloth was Nathaniel Stephens, the same man who had led Gloucestershire's resistance to the forced loan (which was especially intense in Cirencester, Whitstone and Bisley Hundreds) and who later helped to lead the county's battle against ship money. Indeed, the insults bandied about after the Short Parliament election about 'Cotteswold Shephards and the Vale Weavers' show that the gentry were also part of the cultural gulf. But whether Stephens was thrust to the head of popular movements or fomented them, it is certain that, in parts of the county similar to Underdown's 'cheese country', ordinary people had learnt to resist the government in quite sophisticated ways, with or without gentry leadership. This lesson had not been forgotten in 1640.

Popular allegiance in the Civil War and after

We have seen how widespread opposition to the court was reflected in the 1640 elections and in sustained support for the Long Parliament's measures. But in 1642 self-defence and Parliamentarianism went hand in hand in Gloucestershire. It is hard to measure 'real' support against apathy or even sullen acquiescence, and much of our evidence is flawed in that it comes from partisan propaganda sheets. However, one cannot accept John Morrill's stricture against Brian Manning's use of this material on the grounds that many also believed propaganda to the effect that Catholics were predominant in the

---

[20] Smyth, *Description*, 328–31; Smyth of Nibley papers, xvi. 4–5.
[21] Perry, 'Woollen industry', 121–33.

king's counsels when they were not.[22] Claiming popular sympathy was merely a feather in the cap in no way analogous to labelling the enemy papists or sectarians. If we cannot call the populace of Dean generally parliamentarian in sympathy when Royalists called them 'those tryed notorious Foresters of Deane' and Parliamentarians called them 'constant friends of the Parliament', then it is difficult to know what evidence we can accept.[23]

Of course, phrases like 'the common people' could refer to anyone or everyone below the gentry, and it is often impossible to be sure to whom reference is being made. We should perhaps remember Corbet's description of the typical poor man in Gloucestershire who 'did not live by the breath of his great landlord but observed those men by whom those manafactures were maintained that kept him alive'.[24] That is to say the elusive 'middle ranke' of yeomen and clothworkers.

Much of what has been said already suggests that the 'wood-pasture' parishes were not as divided and unharmonious as Underdown argues; if they were, surely many of the poor would have at least sympathised with the Royalists against those who had suppressed their meagre amusements and clucked over their morals? There is little evidence that they did. Quite often the poor, for whatever reason, shared the outlook of the godly, notably towards Arminian clerics. Successive vicars of Painswick were removed by a combination of legal action and the mob; the rector of Dursley was sent to prison in Gloucester facing backwards on a horse, a truly plebeian ceremony of ridicule.[25]

Another potential source for the distribution of Civil War allegiance, the names of royalist pensioners in 1662, is lost, as the relevant order book is not extant. We know of parliamentarian recruiting at various stages of the war. That the Royalists did likewise on a large scale can be deduced from an order of 1662 to the high constable of Longtree Hundred, presumably part of a circular, to levy a double rate for wounded soldiers and prisoners, as the usual one would not be enough.[26] Such evidence is unreliable as a guide to popular feeling; men could enlist for many reasons and, as the war progressed, they were more usually conscripted. Underdown says that 'even conscripts were products of communities whose outlook they would naturally have tended to share'. This is debatable, for – even if such men were invariably conscripted by the side their community preferred, which patently was not the case – the evidence shows that parish constables faced with this unpleasant duty would normally pick on the young undesirables the community would miss least.[27]

Both sides were perennially worried about the disaffection of their conscript

---

[22] Morrill, *Revolt*, 50; B. S. Manning, *The English people and the English Revolution, 1640–1649*, London 1976.
[23] *Mercurius Aulicus*, 13–20 Apr. 1645; BL, E277 (14), *The moderate intelligencer*, 3–10 Apr. 1645.
[24] Corbet, *Military government*, 10.
[25] *CJ* ii. 99, 144; Matthews, *Walker revised*, 171, 179; Blunt, *Dursley*, 61.
[26] Cited in Hodgson, *Tetbury*, 92; Smyth of Nibley papers, iii. 73.
[27] Underdown, *Revel, riot and rebellion*, 189–90.

troops. In 1643 many Vale farmers ran away lest Waller press them, whilst, despite their dreadful experiences, only fifty of the Cirencester prisoners refused to take up arms for the king. These were set to dig trenches at Oxford, while Rupert sent 140 volunteers 'without hatts, shooes or almost any clothes' to the garrison at Reading, where the governor took one look at them and sent them straight back.[28] What is perhaps more striking is the extent to which unstable market towns, like Tewkesbury, proved a fertile recruiting ground for both sides. In general, the recruiting and discharging of soldiers seems to have had its own logic, quite divorced from popular opinion.

Every instance of popular activity – or inactivity – could be interpreted in the light of particular circumstances, but certain patterns should be clear without the need to repeat detail from chapter one. Several areas were, by any definition, solidly parliamentarian. The area near the border with Somerset and Wiltshire, which sent help to drive the Royalists out of Somerset, Clarendon considered 'the most absolute disaffected parts of all three'. After Rupert's first failed attempt on Bristol 'the contry rising upon him made him to flee as his own soldiers report'.[29]

The rest of the Vale fought the guerilla war against the king's army during the siege, and later the Berkeley area helped Massey's incursions and harassed successive royalist governors at Berkeley Castle. Whitstone Hundred was better integrated into Massey's self-defence schemes and was always reliable. Naturally, there were limits to this zeal, which flagged when Massey failed to provide support, and when Gloucester's resistance seemed a hopeless folly that would ruin the county. However, desire for a rapid surrender was not a declaration for the king. On the contrary, it did not take very long for the area to turn against the occupying Cavaliers. Even Corbet, never slow to denounce the common man's fickleness, was impressed by the solidarity of the Vale.[30]

To some extent the Royalists' assumption of an area's general disaffection was a self-fulfilling prophecy. They thought Tetbury, for instance, 'a most rebellious Towne' and treated it accordingly; in 1643 a party of horse extorted £300 not to plunder the town after one of them was insulted by a local carrier, and the Berkeley garrison plundered it even more thoroughly in 1645. This may not have brought the citizens to a greater appreciation of their duty.[31]

Similarly, the king and the commander of his northern horse both thought Dean solidly parliamentarian in sympathy. Wintour extended this to 'most of the citizens of the Welsh side of Severn'. The Committee later referred to the foresters as 'that poore willing people who were all in arms for us'. There are many instances of this. Although the foresters fled rather than be conscripted

---

[28] BL, MS Add. 18,980, fo. 86; E90 (3), *Certaine informations from severall parts of the kingdom*, 13–20 Feb. 1643; *Luke journal*, i. 7, 9–10, 42.

[29] Clarendon, *Rebellion*, vii. 10; *Luke journal*, i. 28.

[30] Roy, 'Civil War and English society', 24–43; Corbet, *Military government*, 9–10.

[31] *Mercurius Aulicus*, 25 May–8 June 1645; *Luke journal*, ii. 150–1.

to mine Gloucester, they were willing enough to help against Berkeley Castle in 1645.[32]

Townspeople inclined the same way. Gloucester had raised and maintained troops for Parliament from the outset, and, despite her hesitation before resisting the siege, there is no doubting her loyalty. In April 1643 one of Luke's spies observed (as Corbet had) that some of the poor at Bristol, particularly the watermen, were pro-royalist, but 'though Bristow bee the greater parte malignants . . . Gloucester on the contrary . . . they are all for the Parliament and at unity amongst themselves and both soldiers and townesmen united'. At Tewkesbury, Town Clerk William Hill, who sat through all the comings and goings, considered the town 'forward and active for [th]e p[ar]rliament'.[33]

The fit between the areas of wood-pasture parishes, pre-war Puritanism, declining popular festivity and popular Parliamentarianism is strong. By contrast, the Cotswolds and the north saw virtually no spontaneous plebeian activity in the Civil War. Was this the result of Royalism, indifference or inactivity born out of fear? It is impossible to tell. We should allow for logistics; whilst Whitstone Hundred could rise as one against Mynne's Irishmen, it was hardly feasible for the dispersed hundreds of the Vale of Evesham, and, apart from the Winchcombe and Cheltenham areas, these regions were not accustomed to collective organisation outside the law. For all that, the Cotswolds were quiescent under royalist rule, and we must look at later events to glimpse the mood there.

Of course, popular activity could take many forms and occur for many reasons. It would certainly be wrong to say that the people were mere auxiliaries of the Gloucester garrison or that their risings were unrelated to royalist plundering in their area. Most rose in arms, if at all, to defend their homes from the side that threatened them most, which was usually the Royalists. But perhaps that was no coincidence, and it was precisely because they were denied supplies by the common people that the Royalists plundered as severely as they did.

Not every rising was politically motivated. At Slimbridge, the inhabitants took the opportunity afforded by the war to throw down Lord Berkeley's enclosures yet again. There were riots in 1646 and they continued on and off, despite Lord Berkeley managing to procure orders from both king and Parliament to confirm him in possession.[34] In this case, a group of people accustomed to rioting as a way of expressing their grievances continued to do so in all conditions. When Parliament later threatened the interests of the perennially troublesome commoners of Dean, they reacted in the same way.

The fit between the areas of popular and gentry Parliamentarianism is not

32 BL, MS Harleian 6,852, fo. 222; Committee to Committee of Safety, 8 Apr. 1645, Bodl. Lib., MS Tanner 60, fo. 75; BL, E307 (14), *Two letters from Colonell Morgan*, London 1846.
33 *Luke journal*, i. 29; GRO, D2688, 1644.
34 LJ viii. 200–1, 611; I. H. Jeayes, *Descriptive catalogue of the charters and muniments . . . at Berkeley Castle*, Bristol 1908, 248.

identical. Whereas there were plenty of gentry to give a lead in the Vale and the south, there were hardly any at all in Dean. However, this fact is probably not significant. Most of the major gentry were absent in Gloucester, and popular activity was not visibly more spontaneous in one area than another, whatever the precise social status of the participants.

Gloucestershire saw none of the popular uprisings against the excesses of the war which took place in many southern and western counties in 1644 and 1645, known collectively as the 'Clubman' risings. This is suggestive, for almost every nearby county did experience them. Perhaps the commoners were simply scared of Massey, whose attitude to third forces was unbendingly hostile. Perhaps, too, we have underestimated the element of protest, particularly in Shropshire, Herefordshire and Worcestershire against the failure of the ruling party to protect them from enemy incursions, often those of Massey himself. In Gloucester, muttering began not with the continuing burden of war but when lack of men or money kept Massey in Gloucester too long. In general, though, the way he integrated the county in its own defence was exemplary.[35]

The 'royalist' risings in the west when the New Model Army came and in Berkshire, Sussex and Hampshire all reflect, to some extent, the leadership of royalist minor gentlemen, yeomen and clerics who were rare in Gloucestershire. Since the New Model never passed through, the incentive to rise to support the winning side and put an end to the war was lacking until the siege of Bristol in 1645 when the south turned out again. There was also action born out of sheer war-weariness; in April 1645, when Rupert chased the Herefordshire clubmen into Dean, some of the exasperated populace left their homes and vowed to make the war their livelihood. Several were as good as their word for later that year they 'had made turnpikes in the avenues and passes into the countrey and sufferd none to enter without their leave. The Parliament soldjers cap in hand for a nights quarter'.[36] Soon, however, Morgan removed the troops to Monmouthshire and ended this sideshow.

The rest of this chapter focuses on the evidence for popular politics in the 1650s, particularly in the abortive royalist rising of 1659 and then in the run up to and the immediate aftermath of the Restoration of Charles II. Because of the nature of the sources, attention is focused on elite and populace together when describing the eventful last year of the republic. This method seems preferable to separate analyses of the two at a time when their roles were so intertwined.

It is an obvious but easily forgotten fact that to be a Royalist in the 1650s, when the party was defeated and proscribed, was a very different matter from

[35] Morrill, *Revolt*, 97–111; G. J. Lynch, 'The risings of the Clubmen in the English Civil War', unpubl. MA diss. Manchester 1973; D. Underdown, 'The chalk and the cheese: contrasts among the English Clubmen', *P&P* lxxxv (1979), 25–48.
[36] Lynch, 'Clubmen', 87 and chs iv–v; *Diary of the marches of the royal army*, ed. C. E. Long (Camden os xxiv, 1859).

being a Royalist in the Civil War. One weakness of the 'chalk and cheese' analysis lies in assigning the same labels to the same areas in wholly different contexts. The evidence for the 1650s, when the press was censored and carried little local news, is thinner and very different to the Civil War material. Nevertheless, pertinent questions can be asked: did the arrival of a Puritan regime intensify moral reformation at parish level? If so, where, and how was it received? Did rioting continue to occur when authority was restored? And above all, how did the county respond to the threat of royalist incursion in 1651 and 1655 and to a real revolt in 1659?

After the war, the Vale parishes with established Puritan tendencies exhibited them even more. Dursley removed the stained-glass windows and communion rails from the church. Nibley got rid of the Book of Common Prayer in 1645-6, and both Twining and Eastington rapidly acquired the new Directory of Public Worship. Various ways of disciplining the poor were stepped up. Twining and Minchinhampton bought copies of acts for better observance of the Sabbath; Eastington, Dursley and Minchinhampton all set up houses of correction in 1650, the latter two also contributing to a new bridewell at Gloucester. Nibley went to great lengths to bind poor children apprentices, even forcing them on unwilling masters, and took bonds to ensure that bastards should not be a charge to the parish. St Michael's Gloucester, newly united with run-down Grace Lane, began to levy fines 'for Swearing & drunckenes &c' to repair the church, while Samuel Sheppard, the lord of the manor, was among those fined for Sabbath violations at Minchinhampton. It was also mostly in the Vale that there was the will and organisation to appoint civic marriage registrars.[37]

In August 1651 Charles II's Scottish army reached Worcester. They were to get no further, but Gloucester was directly threatened, and several locals were involved to the extent of sending help to either side. Massey, who was with Charles, 'thought himself now in his own territory' and hoped to raise the area.[38] The Cotswolds and the south were unlikely to act while the threat was so distant, but the north could not be unaware and the reactions there were very varied. Gloucester raised the city militia, strengthened her walls and was commended for her 'good affection and unanimous resolution to defend that place', while 'The Forrest of Deane rise for the Parliament'.[39]

Now as before, self-defence and Parliamentarianism went together, and this action did not, of course, indicate any mass republicanism. Yet the Vale of Evesham, no less threatened, did not rise, though quite capable of raising a crowd to defend their crops. This should all be seen in the context of traditional attitudes towards politics as a concept, rather than of political viewpoints as such. The foresters were accustomed to rising *en masse* and lived in a

37 Blunt, *Dursley*, 60–1; Bruce, 'Extracts', passim; GRO, P124 CW2/1; P127 CW2/1; P230 CW2/1; P154 CW2/1; P343 VE2/1.
38 CCC ii. 1457; iv. 3158–9; Clarendon, *Rebellion*, xii. 73.
39 CSPD 1651, 368; *Mercurius Politicus*, no. 65, 29 Aug.–4 Sept. 1651.

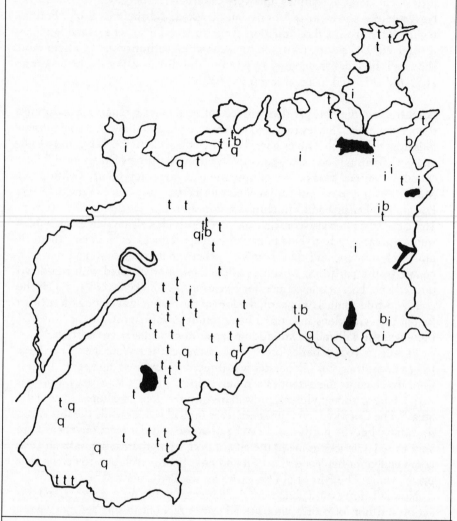

Map 4
The distribution of religious groups, 1648–60

Key:

t – minister signed Gloucestershire ministers' testimony (strongly Presbyterian), 1648

i – Independent congregation

b – Baptist meeting place

q – Quaker meeting place

self-enclosed society where this could easily be organised. The poor of the tobacco country had become equally accustomed to violence, but were less politically conscious and had no hope or fear of a change of policy under a new regime. In any case, it was harvest time, which affected them more than it did the foresters or the citizens of Gloucester, and an invading army, however voracious, was unlikely to eat tobacco! The Vale of Evesham was apolitical rather than pro-royalist. When arrested in 1654, some rioters there admitted they had intended to fight the troops 'but not for Charles Stuart as they declare on oath'. The poor of Slimbridge and Frampton also knew only one way of fighting enclosures. Riots had broken out again in 1650 and were suppressed by quartering troops on both parishes – the action of a regicide government acting on behalf of a neutralist peer with a royalist steward. It is known that a Digger commune existed in Gloucestershire, and although further detail is lacking, it seems likely that it was in the area of these two parishes.[40]

From other evidence, however, there is reason to think that the pre-war division in terms of political attitudes may not have stayed the same during the 1650s and may even have been reversed to some extent. Religion was a major factor in this. Conservative Puritanism was well-entrenched in the Vale, the major towns and the clothing districts. It was this area that supplied the preachers who helped Nathaniel Stephens's 1640 election campaign and from where came the signatories to the rigidly Presbyterian Gloucestershire Ministers' Testimony in 1648.[41]

Because these ministers were never purged from their cures, unlike the Anglicans of the Cotswolds, true religious radicalism struggled to gain a foothold in the Vale against able Presbyterian ministers like Joseph Woodward at Dursley. On the other hand, the Independent congregations of the 1650s blossomed in 'royalist' areas, just as many of the ruling group of the 1650s came from places where they had been isolated Parliamentarians in the Civil War.

These new congregations were found mainly in the market towns, but also in quite a few rural parishes under royalist landlords, in the north and east of the county – notably Tewkesbury, Deerhurst, Winchcombe, Stow, Oddington and Bourton-on-the-Water (see Map 4). A hostile pamphlet of 1660 speaks of Independent congregations at Cirencester, Fairford, Stow, Bourton-on-the-Water, Kempsford and Northleach. Puritan reformation of some colour also struck in the Cotswold village of Barnsley where, in 1652, John Taylor, the water poet, saw two women put in the stocks for taking a stroll after divine service. Baptist meetings were found in the three boroughs, Bourton-on-the-Water, Moreton-in-Marsh and possibly Fairford and King's Stanley.[42]

---

[40] BL, E743 (13), *Mercurius Politicus*, no. 212, 29 June–6 July 1654; *CSPD* 1650, 218; K. V. Thomas, 'Another Digger broadside', *P&P* xlii (1969), 57–68.

[41] BL, E433 (25), *The Gloucester-shire ministers testimony to the truth of Jesus Christ, and to the Solemne League and Covenant*, London 1648.

[42] *Originall letters and papers*, 123–6, 139–40, 145–6; Bodl. Lib., MS Rawlinson A39, fo. 528; *CSPD* 1656–7, 12; BL, E1045 (5), R. Clark, *The lying wonders or rather the wonderful*

In their formative years the Quakers tended to build around prominent individuals in large, dispersed parishes with few gentry, particularly in the south-west of the county at Olveston and Winterbourne, at Corse, Tetbury and Nailsworth, a growing town on the borders of three parishes.[43] It was ministers such as Helme and Palmer who made the running in the 1650s, while a previous generation's radicals, such as Richard Britten at Bisley and Thomas Thatch at Stonehouse, turned away in disgust. It would be wrong to put this distribution down to resentment against Cotswold landlords or to the outlawry of tobacco-planting in the Vale of Evesham, but it is unexpected and intriguing none the less.

There are other indications of non-violent turmoil in hitherto passive regions. Naturally, the downfall of almost an entire ruling class of royalist gentry had most impact where their power had been greatest, but even so plenty of people used the circumstances to pursue other ends. In several market towns, antagonisms were brought to the surface by the prosecution of controversial individuals at the Committees for Compounding and for Advance of Money.

Tewkesbury was divided by successive prosecutions of Richard Dowdeswell of Pull Court in Bushley, a man of great local influence who managed to get many (mostly his clients) out to testify in his favour. At Winchcombe, a large section of the community turned out to defend Thomas Yarneton against malicious accusations by the ejected minister and some allies among the more conspicuously ungodly elements. All sorts of scandal was uncovered when two ne'er-do-well tenants prosecuted William Chapman, a wealthy merchant of Tetbury, who may have been genuinely royalist but had covered his tracks well.[44]

Possibly the most intense friction of all was generated in Slaughter Hundred, an area known for bad relations between landlords and tenants. Here, *Men and armour* recorded twenty-two manors, nine with no resident landlord. The fourteen gentlemen who did live there had many dependent servants, and were closely inter-related; Sir William Morton was the pre-war high steward of the hundred and Edward Slaughter of Upper Slaughter his deputy. They had also been Royalists almost to a man. The resulting composition processes gave their enemies a chance to hit back.[45]

John Chamberlain was of the second rank of county gentry, a gentleman-farmer with seven manors and estates, who did his own accounts and slaughtered his own sheep. Stow-on-the-Wold, Maugersbury and the profits of the markets and fairs of Stow were the heart of his estate. The latter, which rapidly recovered their pre-war profitability to between £57 and £64 per annum in 1647–9, were the real bone of contention in his family's long-running battle

lyes, London 1660; J. Taylor, *A short relation of a journey through Wales*, ed. J. O. Halliwell, London 1859.
[43] Whitley, *Baptists*, 68–70; Braithwaite, *Quakerism*, passim; *Fox journal*, passim.
[44] SP 19/116, fos 105–46; SP 23/156, fos 360–1; SP 19/129, fo. 103; SP 19/141, fos 101–8.
[45] GRO, D45/M19, M20; Tawney and Tawney 'Occupational census', 51–2.

against the burgesses of Stow, which had simmered for many years before the Civil War.[46]

Chamberlain had been trying to compound for four years before 1649, but the process was hampered by vast debts and encumbrances on his Churchdown and Prestbury estates and his own undervaluations, which were reported by Joseph Collett, a London cutler, and Colonel Bosevile, almost as soon as his £316 fine was set. This cost him £1,180 in further fines, but he continued to cause trouble until finally in March 1651, Collett was allowed to take a seven year lease of the fairs, paying £30 per year (Chamberlain's valuation) to Chamberlain and £15 to the state.

Chamberlain's persistence, his friendship with an MP, Samuel Moyer, and the inconsistency of the two central Committees deprived Collett of any profit. First the lease was revised to £70, then, as Collett was unready, Chamberlain was allowed to hold the September 1650 fair, retaining the profits on security, and he spun out time, forcing Collett to spend £60 on hurdles on top of £140 expenses in prosecuting the case. In 1652 he even accused Collett of defrauding the Commonwealth by not paying the £40 due. Collett did his utmost, even taking out an advertisement in the London press to publicise this 'very great Sheep Faire', but by 1654 he was reduced to the point where he again offered £70 for the fairs rather than be stuck with £60-worth of otherwise useless hurdles. Only then did he find that Chamberlain had been allowed to compound for them for £50. The case petered out.[47]

The burgesses of Stow were not ciphers in this struggle. They supported Collett fully and even appointed him their solicitor. In September 1653, with Collett and William Neast, they petitioned Parliament for a new trial of their cause in the name of the impoverished inhabitants of 'a poore and populous Borough and Corporac[i]on'. They alleged that Chamberlain's father, with his friend, Lord Chief Baron Tanfield, had conspired to deprive them of the profits of fairs and markets and view of frankpledge, and that a subsequent retrial had to be abandoned on a technicality.[48]

Collett had many more irons in the fire. He also prosecuted Edward Rogers, the sequestration commissioners' corrupt agent, William Try, Richard Bridges, John Keyt, Lady Leigh and William Poole for delinquency within Gloucestershire alone, as well as acting on behalf of Sir Humphrey Tracy. John Collett, a burgess of Stow, prosecuted Lady Leigh, with Joseph as solicitor, and ran Joseph's errands in Poole's case.[49]

It is highly probable, then, that Joseph was a relative of the Stow Colletts and was tipped off by them to bring the case. Alas, the burgesses were in no shape to pursue the feud. They had had problems ever since the 1630s in

---

[46] GRO, D621/M18; *LJ* iv. 271.
[47] CCAM ii. 1133–5; CCC iii. 1981–4; GRO, D149/E2; BL, E797 (11), *Several proceedings in Parliament*, 9 Sept. 1652.
[48] SP 19/119, fos 523–4.
[49] SP 19/95, fo. 224; SP 19/135, fo. 15 and passim.

keeping up their numbers. Between 1631 and 1641 five burgesses were displaced and one fined for reasons varying from non-residency to contempt at the annual burgess meetings on 29 September to elect bailiffs and officers. From 1648 onwards the situation grew worse still, with further removals and repetitions of the town ordinances about the meeting, and also the need to fine absentees and enforce regulations against engrossing and undersettling. The year of the petition, 1653, was the nadir. When the time came to replace four dead or absent burgesses, the only men available included three who (most unusually) could not sign their names, one of whom had already been ejected for 'Manifold Contempts'.[50] Chamberlain exemplified the enduring strength of the gentry.

The Collett connection merits further examination, for they were a numerous clan in Slaughter Hundred. Colletts lived at Stow (where John and Richard, who signed the petition, were burgesses), and also at Oddington, Naunton, Bourton-on-the-Water, Wick Rissington, Sherborne and Upper and Lower Slaughter. The Colletts were also the bane of the Whitmores of Lower Slaughter. We have seen how Sir William, a London merchant, had attempted to tighten his control throughout his Gloucestershire estates, provoking both violent and legal protest at Winchcombe. In the 1650s his younger son, Richard, inherited the estates, cleared them of his father's delinquency and came to settle at Lower Slaughter.[51] He also began a systematic overhaul of the estates, provoking a flurry of suits and more direct action, which pitted the tenants against him and each other, with violence and damage done on both sides.

In 1649 just as Chamberlain's brother, Edmund, was at odds with the radical new pastor at Stow, William Beale, Whitmore was sued by Thomas Stone, rector of Lower Slaughter, who alleged that Whitmore was refusing to hold a Court Baron to admit him to a tenancy – and he continued to do so, despite Chancery orders to desist. In another Chancery bill, Stone, John Collett and another denied Whitmore's interpretation of various customs and accused him of trying to make entry fines arbitrary at the lord's will. Whitmore said explicitly that they were arbitrary in other cases, in which the same themes cropped up and which also involved Colletts.

In 1655 John Collett of Northleach accused Whitmore of collusion with William Arkill in the latter's reneging on an agreement to transfer lands to him – a case which dragged on into the 1660s. Then, in 1658, John Collett of Notgrove sued Whitmore for refusing to admit him to an inherited tenement despite agreeing terms, accusing him of trying to overthrow all established customs 'for his own private profitt'.[52]

The Colletts were not always on the same side in these disputes, for Joseph Collett of Clement's Lane, Middlesex, possibly the same man as Chamberlain's

---

50 GRO, D621/M18, fos 39–47v, 49, 53–v, loose fos.
51 VCH, Glos., vi. 136; GRO, D45/M19 (index), E1, E17.
52 Ibid. D45/L5–7; PRO, C3/462/80, 467/10, 438/74.

prosecutor, and yet another John appear as co-defendants in the last case, as did Thomas Collett against Stone, but collectively they were very active in litigation throughout this period. After the Restoration they were particular targets for Whitmore. He was indicted three times in July and August 1660 alone for assaults against John and Bridget Collett at Upper Slaughter, and it took several mutual acts of violence to property and a fresh commisssion of examination to disentangle the case against John Collett of Notgrove in 1662.[53]

Such evidence is interesting, but not conclusive unless backed up by solid figures. The only statistical evidence for popular Royalism in the 1650s is the return made by Major-General Disbrowe of those suspects who were required to give security in the western counties in 1655–6. Of 5,115 names in five counties (there were no returns from Cornwall) there are 205 from Gloucestershire and seventy-seven from Bristol and St Philip's (see Table 7).

There are inherent problems with this source, as some commissioners merely listed all the convicted delinquents in the area. However, this is a genuine list of suspects. Of sixty-seven knights, esquires and gentlemen, twenty-five were convicted Royalists, eight were their relatives and four had been accused but not convicted. Twenty-eight had previously gone unrecorded, whilst Philip Langley of Mangotsfield had been an active Parliamentarian. The gentry comprise over a quarter of the suspects whereas the figure in Dorset, Wiltshire and Somerset, which were better documented and witnessed more widespread popular Royalism, was under 10 per cent.

The geographic imbalance of the distribution is plain, for almost exactly half the Gloucestershire suspects, 102, were in Berkeley Division. A further fifty-six were from the Seven Hundreds, and thirty-two from Kiftsgate. The latter were nearly all gentlemen, whereas in Berkeley and the Seven Hundreds barely a quarter were. This and Stephen Roberts's analysis of the Devon returns might suggest that the government's concern was with the security of Bristol and Exeter and that their interest in humbler suspects diminished away from the two major towns of the region. But if so there would have been a heavy concentration in northern Somerset and northern Wiltshire, which is not the case.[54] The distribution of suspects is plainly the result of the relative zeal of divisional commissioners – hence the paucity of names in parts of each county.

The Inshire and Forest commissioners did not do their job well, for the tiny numbers they listed, nine and four respectively, are absurd. For the other three divisions some conclusions, tentative because the sample is small, might be ventured. Roughly equal numbers of gentlemen occur in each. The places with

53 GRO, D45/M20/1–3, L15, L7. One index identifies John Collett of Stow and John Collett of Slaughter as one and the same, but this cannot be confirmed.
54 BL, MS Add. 34,012; S. K. Roberts, *Restoration and recovery in an English county: Devon local administration, 1646–1670*, Exeter 1985, 50; Underdown, *Revel, riot and rebellion*, 201–3.

Table 7
Royalist suspects by division and occupation, 1656

Occupation Division	A	B	C	D	E	F	G	H	J	Total
Gloucester and Inshire	7	1	1							9
Forest	3					1				4
Kiftsgate	21		6		1		4			31
Seven Hundreds	14	2	4	4	8	15		7	2	54
Berkeley	22	3	9	21	16	24	7	1	1	104
Bristol and St Philip's	11	19	8	1	2	4	13	17	2	77
Total	78	25	28	26	27	44	24	25	5	280

A gentry (knights, esquires and gentlemen)
B merchants (merchants, mercers and vintners)
C yeomen
D husbandmen and labourers
E rural artisans (tailors, thatchers, carpenters, coopers, millers, sadlers, blacksmiths)
F cloth trade (clothiers, [broad]weavers, wool and worsted combers, cordwinders, feltmongers)
G victuallers (butchers, bakers, cooks, inholders, brewers, victallers)
H urban artisans (nineteen occupation, for example glazier, soapboiler, plumber)
J miscellaneous and unspecified

Source: BL, MS Add. 34,012

relatively large numbers of ordinary suspects were a broad belt of market and clothing towns and large villages in the south-east fringe: Cirencester, Horsley, Minchinhampton, Berkeley, Cromhall, Wickwarr, Dursley and Thornbury, though not Chipping Sodbury or Tetbury.

Speculating in individual cases or tabulating these as a proportion of the population would be futile. But if the figures are in any way representative, they cast doubts on the durability of the wood-pasture parishes' parliamentarian outlook. The figures for the south may be inflated by local hostility to the Quakers who were so numerous there, yet the figures for those parishes where Quakers were established are not high. Suffice to say that the supporters of the Stuarts in Gloucestershire were mainly unreconciled old Cavalier gentlemen. Those of humbler origin who thought likewise were independent yeomen and artisans who thought so on their own account and not their landlord's. Clearly, too, if the tenants of the Cotswold gentry shared their masters' Royalism, it was not thought worth recording. Probably they did not.

*

There were real differences between different regions. The wood-pasture parishes abandoned their popular festivities earlier than the fielden areas; they were also more prone to rioting and they definitely produced a more sustained support for Parliament. But the Cotswolds were no rural Arcadia, whatever Dover's gentlemen-poets thought. There were no riots in these areas because there were other ways of going about things, not because there was nothing worth rioting about. Nor were the wood-pasture parishes necessarily more divided and unharmonious on the eve of the Civil War; the Cotswolds produced the most visibly oppressive landlords and the bitterest feuds, particularly in boroughs which lacked a framework in which to pursue differences.

Part of the reason for the activism of the Vale and Forest and the passivity of the Wolds may simply be that the former were more used to collective bargaining by riot, the latter to a legal way. Moreover, the conflicts in the Vales and Dean pitched the landless poor, often with elite sympathy, against the government, those in the Cotswolds pitched landlord against tenant. The Royalists were strong enough to hold down the Cotswolds, where the populace was used to oppression, but provoked resistance in those areas which had learned to resist it.

This, rather than a division in allegiance, was the key difference between the regions, for real popular Royalism did not exist. After the war, however, the position may have become reversed as radical religious sects made more rapid headway in the north and east, and the tenants of Royalists seized the chance to fight back. All areas continued their political struggles, if at all, by the means they knew best. This pattern was continued when the county was again divided on national party lines in 1659, when Massey returned to try and raise the area for Charles II.

The people and Massey's Revolt

Despite the strategic importance of Bristol and Gloucester, whose seizure was suggested as the starting point for a royalist rising, Gloucestershire was not at first integrated into the plotting that continued throughout the 1650s. The power-base of the Sealed Knot, the most important co-ordinating group, was in East Anglia. Only with the rise of a new 'Action Party', opposed to the Knot's perennial caution, were local leaders recruited.[55] Colonel Thomas Veel, the wartime governor of Berkeley Castle, engaged with Major Clayton to raise men to surprise Bristol and Gloucester. Veel was not rich, but he had shadowy backers, including one worth £3,000 per year. His rebels included a fifth column in Gloucester, which would open the gates to 600 'malcontented tobacco-planters'. One Mr Ross spoke at various times of raising up to 3,000 men in Gloucestershire and Bristol. Veel, who had been recommended by

55 Idem, *Royalist conspiracy in England, 1649–1660*, New Haven 1960, 35, 143, 203–4 and passim.

Massey, twice received personal letters and blank recruiting commissions from the king.[56]

This plan was never tried, for early in 1658 the rising was called off. In general, regional conspiracies. and this one more than most, were poorly co-ordinated; royalist circles were riddled with divisions, backbiting and Thurloe's spies.

Like many old Cavaliers, Veel faded into the background with the creation of the Great Trust. The brainchild of a rising star at court, Lord Mordaunt, the Trust aimed to revive the Sealed Knot's organisational basis without its aversion to direct action or to allying with Presbyterians. Bristol and Gloucester were to be the focus of a regional rising to be synchronised with others across the country. The leaders, as elsewhere, were former Parliamentarians. John Grubham Howe of Compton Abdale made tentative contact with the court from 9 September 1658, promising to raise 3,000 men at a few days' notice. Howe was the second son of the former county MP, John Howe, who had rarely lived in Gloucestershire before the 1650s. The Somerset end was handled by the rich but diffident Alexander Popham. The third main figure was Massey.[57]

Massey came over to England in February 1659 to co-ordinate the plans, which never went smoothly. This reflected faction-fighting and crossed wires at court. Secretary Nicholas had full confidence in Massey as 'an excellent commander, faithful and loyal', and Clarendon admired him for his courage and integrity, adding that Charles thought him useful 'in spite of his many weaknesses'. It was intended that Massey should have overall control, but orders to this effect came too late. Mordaunt's arrogance made him many enemies, one of whom one was Massey. As a result, Mordaunt trusted all to Howe, whom he thought the richest and most influential man in the county.[58]

This was unwise. Howe was often absent at Richard Cromwell's Parliament – for which he had stood with Charles's permission, to avoid the attention of the authorities – and, after being arrested and detained in May, he inclined to excessive caution. When Henry Cromwell and the Irish army submitted to the Rump early in July, Howe, amongst many others, wanted to postpone the rising, but the Great Trust, with Massey present, decided to go ahead even though the hearts of many were not in it and the government was fully aware of what was planned.[59]

Once again, the personality of Massey was at the root of the problem. Despite the twists and turns of his career, he had clearly not changed a bit. Almost as soon as he arrived back in Gloucestershire, he sank into broody

[56] CSPD 1655–6, 344; CCSP iii. 314–15; Latimer, Annals of Bristol, 266; GRO, D225/F12–13.
[57] Underdown, Royalist conspiracy, 236, 260; CCSP iv. 78, 88, 104, 115, 137.
[58] Latimer, Annals of Bristol, 286, 290; Hyde to Mordaunt, 6 May 1659, in The letter book of John, Viscount Mordaunt, 1658–1660, ed. M. Coate (Camden 3rd ser. lxix, 1945), no. 20; Mordaunt to Hyde, 8 Mar. 1659, CSP iii. 433.
[59] Nicholas papers, iv. 158–9; CCSP iv. 87, 154; Underdown, Royalist conspiracy, 249–51.

pessimism and shrill complaints against Mordaunt for not confiding full details in him and relying exclusively on Howe. The month he spent holed up with the Veels amid delays and indecision before the go-ahead was given skewed his frail sense of proportion more than ever. Almost everyone was false, and Howe's promises were likely to come to nothing; Veel and Clayton were still faithful 'but Mr Popham and Howe have ruyned us'.[60] These divisions, mirrored at all levels of the party, proved fatal. However, a lot had been achieved in terms of preparing large numbers of Gloucestershire men to rebel.

By 1659, very few men anywhere in England were still so in awe of their lord as to follow him blindly into arms. Rising in revolt implied a real, personal commitment to the Stuart cause. There are indications that some elements in Gloucestershire's old ruling elite saw Oliver's death as an opportunity, and that this may have reflected the view of a wider public. Most importantly, the elections to Richard Cromwell's Parliament saw the return, for the shire, of the leading plotter, Howe and John Stephens, a man known for his violent hatred of sectaries, while at Gloucester a moderate slate combined against an old radical, Pury. This was part of a nationwide trend in which some twenty pro-Stuart Presbyterians were elected, who formed an important core of resistance to settlement.[61]

The same process was visible at another level. We cannot assess public opinion in seventeenth-century England in any meaningful way. However, a number of unconnected events – which, it should be stressed, are recounted as anecdotes and not as cumulative evidence – suggest that there was a rise in politically conscious activity in Gloucestershire in 1659. These stories also hint at growing polarisation in some areas. From late 1658 a number of parishioners of Bagendon near Cirencester resisted their 'intruded' minister, Edward Fletcher (allegedly a cutler from Gloucester). Under the leadership of Samuel Broad, who had been ejected from neighbouring Rendcomb, they disrupted Fletcher's services and intimidated others into withholding tithes. Cromwell's death particularly encouraged these men, as they themselves stated.[62]

Criminal disorder was also on the increase. The assizes were not held in January 1659 'by reason of troubles that happened'. By April, as a result, Gloucester gaol was full to overflowing and John Stephens demanded in Parliament that the JPs should be ordered to hold a general gaol delivery. The assizes on 27 July saw an unprecedented bloodbath in which sixteen were hanged, seventeen branded and eight whipped.[63] This contrasts with the two assizes in 1658, at which only three and two respectively were hanged. The only earlier record is of the height of disorder in the summer of 1646, when

[60] Massey to Nicholas, 5 Mar., 4, 22 Apr., 23 June 1659, in *Nicholas papers*, iv. 74, 77–9, 114–18, 158–9.
[61] Underdown, *Royalist conspiracy*, 233.
[62] SP 18/123, fo. 122; Clark, *The lying wonders*, dedication to the reader.
[63] GRO, GBR B3/3, fo. 113; *Burton diary*, iv. 341; PRO, ASSI 2/1, fos 25–8v.

twelve were hanged. Harry Hangman again confirms the impression, relating (in June 1655) that he had hanged four in January, which was more than usual, and that he had sometimes hanged none at all.[64]

Ten of the condemned, including seven of one family, were members of a large gang which had committed a spate of burglaries in the Forest Division. Their victims included many gentlemen, such as Throckmorton, Benedict Hall and Thomas Ayleway. The Grand Jury took the unusual step of petitioning the court to reward the officers who had arrested the gang, 'whereby the county of Glouc[ester] is likely to be free from such dangerous p[er]sons & at securety in their persons and goods'. The JPs present contributed £10 each. Evidently the whole community was relieved to see the disorder ended.[65]

Fear of crime may have alienated some, but others may have reacted by clinging to the regime as the bulwark of any sort of order. The crime wave may also have been distantly related to the most serious disorder of the time. In April 1659 suddenly and unexpectedly, the foresters of Dean rose up against Wade. These disciplined and organised riots followed the pre-war pattern of practical and symbolic action to reclaim common rights. Coppices were burnt, enclosures torn down and animals turned in to graze on the timber nurseries. Furzer was openly abused and his workmen intimidated. Wade's report suggested that many were encouraged by talk in Richard Cromwell's Parliament of abandoning the ironworks, for 'horrid offenders . . . impudently appear with petitions in their hands, calling that to be right which is against all law and justice . . . there are boasts of what great promises some members of the House have made, that all things shall be granted that is desired'.[66]

This was not a royalist rising, although the Royalists did seek to profit from it and the commoners sought to portray it as such after the Restoration, when their common rights again came under threat. A committee attended the restored Rump on behalf of the inhabitants in June, and some of them said that 'the Parliam[en]ts hard usage in supporting Maior Wade will force [the]m to turne Caviliers'. This clearly implied that they were not Cavaliers already. But, when they were refused redress, they 'resolve by force to doe [the]mselves right'.[67]

Who was, or was supposed to be, involved in Massey's rising in July 1659? A fair number of local gentlemen took part. Massey's aspersions about the unreliability of the 'great ones' and the fact that Alan Brodrick drew up a map of the king's friends in the county suggest that many more were loosely

[64] BL, E513 (1), *Perfect occurrences*, no. 32, 7 Aug. 1646; PRO, ASSI 2/1, fos 3–4v, 12v–13; *Harry Hangman's honour*, 7–9.
[65] PRO, ASSI 2/1, fos 25–8v.
[66] Wade to Admiralty Commissioners, 8 Apr. 1659, SP 18/202, fo. 70.
[67] CCSP iv. 210; PRO, E112/565/555; Alan Brodrick to Hyde, 22 July 1659, Bodl. Lib., MS Clarendon 63, fo. 4; *A true narrative concerning the woods and iron-works of the Forrest of Deane*, n.p. [1661?], 7.

involved.[68] It is notable that, just as in the Civil War, the Parliamentarians were active within Gloucestershire, whilst the Royalists dispersed themselves far wider. Of the latter, Sir Hugh Middleton was arrested and plundered by Wade's men while preparing to rise at his house at Pinbury Park; Howe, Sir Robert Poyntz, Thomas Chester and Thomas Buck were plotting with some Somerset and Wiltshire gentry at Bristol.

More old Cavaliers were busy elsewhere. The younger Throckmorton, a friend of Richard Cromwell, was briefly detained in London; Henry Norwood of Leckhampton was employed in correspondence for the king and joined an attempted rising in Shropshire; Francis Finch of Kempley, 'a very honest and discreet person', intrigued to win Fleetwood over; John Prettyman of Driffield led a twenty-man 'rising' in Leicestershire, where the rest of his lands lay.[69] Apart from the Veels, the grass roots organisers had been former Parliamentarians.

The commoners whom Massey hoped to recruit were not the tenants of the old Royalists. One reason for this was geography. The aim was to surprise Bristol and Gloucester, and the Cotswolds were further away and less populous than the Vale or the Forest. Still, the prospective rebels were drawn from precisely those areas which had supported Parliament in the Civil War. Veel's 'malcontented tobacco planters' and the fifth column in Gloucester never had a chance to act, but several hundred were raised in Dean and the Stroudwater district. Although Bristol was held securely by Colonel Okey's regulars, Gloucester was not garrisoned, and the Royalists had some hopes of the mayor, Robert Tyther, a junior alderman with no stake in the regime. There was also a group ready at Cirencester, but the authorities were tipped off by 'a Quaker from Tidbury', presumably Nathaniel Cripps, and their meeting was aborted.[70]

The Rump's supporters acted first. The two Thomas Purys, together with Crofts, quickly raised 300 volunteer foot who 'shewed themselves very ready and resolute, leaving their trades and occupacions to serve upon the occasion'. The militia seized horses as far afield as Lacock in Wiltshire to press into service. They were officered by common councillors and supplemented by the militia horse and Captain Dale's regulars. Intelligence about Massey's movements was gathered slowly. Howe was arrested on 29 July while Okey seized Popham and reinforced Bristol. On 30 July, the Purys pounced before Massey was ready. It was touch and go, for they were desperately short of funds to pay the troops.[71]

Some of the thousands of miners reported to be ready to rise in Dean after Massey's secret meetings with leading local men were trapped at Berrow's house

[68] Brodrick to Hyde, 11 July 1659, Bodl. Lib., MS Clarendon 62, fo. 62.
[69] CSPD 1659–60, 75, 96; 1660–1, 92; CCSP iv. 263, 296, 360, 371; BL, E993 (6), The weekly intelligencer, no. 13, 26 July–2 Aug. 1659; Mordaunt letter book, nos 55n, 86, 91, 148.
[70] CCSP iv. 244, 306–8, 313–14.
[71] CSPD 1659–60, 50, 68, 209; CCSP iv. 296, 307–8; Thomas Pury sen. and Thomas Pury jr to Council of State, 27 July 1659, Clarke papers, iii. 127; iv 34–7.

at Awre by the horse. Berrow had been a Parliamentarian, and with him was one Colonel Browne and John Gaynsford of Awre, a former captain and assessment commissioner. Rather oddly, the Gloucester forces took their word to come in to surrender the next day, which they did not do, and there was some suspicion of collusion.

The action was enough to deter others and to nip the rising in the bud, but even the London press had printed rumours that 'many hundreds are in a Body and a great Concourse of people resorting to them'. This left only Massey and the Veels, who were arrested on 31 July, along with Lord Herbert. Massey escaped by rolling off his horse down Nympsfield Hill during a thunderstorm at dusk as he was being taken to Gloucester, and he later fled to the continent.[72] There was always something faintly comical about Massey's derring-do.

The Stroudwater section was the most dangerous part of the plot. Howe had proved himself a 'man of Dursley' with his wildly optimistic talk of 10,000 men in arms, but even so 1,000 were expected. The rising depended on a network of contacts among the clothing elite. The depositions of those involved on an abortive night march to Symondshall to join Massey on 31 July show that careful plans were laid and arms and horses set aside for their sons or servants.

Most of those involved were from Stroud where they owned small estates, but the web of intrigue stretched to Stonehouse, Bisley, Minchinhampton and possibly further. They included clothier gentlemen like Daniel Fowler, of the Stonehouse parliamentarian family, William Window and Thomas Freame of Lypiatt in Stroud, many Webbs and William and Thomas Warner from Paganhill in Stroud. They counted on widespread local support, and Presbyterian ministers played important roles as recruiters and 'intelligencers', notably Thomas Hodges at King's Stanley, Thomas Thatch, the former scourge of the Cirencester Anabaptists, and Richard Britten, who 'said the Anabaptists and Quakers would pull down the light of the Gospel and the ministry, if a course were not taken with them'.[73] These men had been subversive radicals in 1642.

Massey's plot ended in farce, but he came closer than anyone other than Sir George Booth in Cheshire to achieving insurrection – far closer than any of the nearby county groups whose plans dovetailed into his. These all faded away after his capture. Only Booth put a sizeable force into the field, but for lack of support General Lambert easily crushed it. With the Knot's heartland quiet and a few desultory risings in the Midlands, this was the sum total of an enterprise wrecked by bad timing, divided counsels and mistrust between Royalists and Presbyterians.[74] From August, relative calm returned and Furzer

---

[72] Ibid. v. 35–7; BL, E933 (7), *The weekly post*, 26 July–2 Aug. 1659; Underdown, *Royalist conspiracy*, 263.

[73] VCH, *Glos.*, xi, 112–21; SP 23/262, fos 35–6; CCC i. 748–9.

[74] Underdown, *Royalist conspiracy*, 260–84; CCSP iv. 292–3, 295, 306–10, 313.

managed to resume work on his frigate. But Massey had shown that the manpower for resistance was there, and the unity between the ruling powers did not long survive his defeat.

Gloucestershire and the Restoration, 1659–60

It is already clear that there was a good deal of continuity of personnel among the rulers of Gloucestershire in the 1650s. The events of July 1659 confirmed this trend by reviving the Committee for Compounding and its local commissioners. Most of those nominated in Gloucestershire did not serve, and those who did were a familiar mixture of Gloucester men, the godly and the obscure, including Crofts, William Sheppard junior, Edwards and Philipps.

Even more than their predecessors in the job, these men were entangled in red tape. They had to await a new commission before they could act in the Inshire, and their meetings became irregular and ill-attended. Administering the Veel estates proved impossible when three generations of Thomas Veels each had lands with conflicting claims upon them at Symondshall. In October matters worsened when the Army once again turned out the Rump and began to rule through a Committee of Safety. Encouraged, some Veels returned from hiding and proceeded to turn the commissioners' agents out of their house and taunt them with the prospect of General Monck coming from Scotland to overthow the regime.

It was easy to defy the commissioners. Most of the plotters' neighbours simply did not turn up to give evidence against them and many of those who did, including some of the accused, refused to take the oath. The commissioners were paralysed with uncertainty. Even before events cut short their deliberations in January 1660, the business was moribund. In December 1659, the central Committee told them that the few depositions they had garnered were based entirely on hearsay, and so 'general' and 'interwoven' as to be worthless. Meanwhile Howe had absconded and Middleton was disdaining to acknowledge repeated summonses.[75]

Similar men remained in charge of the militia, but now there was little overlap and less communication between them and the sequestration commisssioners. As the militia captains, the power of Wade and Crofts was redoubled even before the revolt. From May to July they had sole charge of troops and money and were receiving orders directly from the Council of State. It was they who reported the suppression of Massey's revolt to London on 6 August.[76]

Likewise, the Purys' actions confirmed the high profile of the Gloucester

[75] SP 23/59, fos 54, 59, 72–6, 263 passim; SP 23/243, fos 160–1; CCC i. 746, 767, 769, 771; iii. 2020.
[76] CSPD 1658–9, 353, 360, 362; 1659–60, 16, 209; Wade and Crofts to Council of State, 6 Aug. 1659, CCSP iv. 315.

men who commanded the militia and volunteers. They raised a foot regiment and, on the 11th, the Inshire militia officers were confirmed in their positions, with the younger Pury as colonel.[77] A new militia commission, entirely dominated by the faithful minor gentry of the 1650s with a smattering of old moderates, had been issued on 26 July, and the Rump continued to strengthen it during August with military outsiders – first Colonel Bradshaw and Major Fallows, then Disbrowe and Okey. On 15 August the commissioners were authorised to raise up to £35,000 per month to dispose of as they saw fit under the Militia Act, two days later they were ordered to raise four foot regiments out of the volunteers and, on 1 September, Wade and Crofts were confirmed as commanders.[78]

This was the high point of their influence. Before long, power was snatched from the local radicals as the Council of State agreed to proposals from Disbrowe and Fleetwood to pay off the militia and to quarter regulars in several western towns. By mid October, Bristol, Gloucester and Exeter each housed three companies of Sir Bryce Cochrane's battle-hardened Flanders regiment. Gloucester also had some of Colonel Berry's horse.[79] There were problems from the outset. Quartering money was unavailable, and the corporation had to lend money for the soldiers' immediate needs. There were simply too many troops for the city's depleted housing stock. Prevented by an Act of Parliament from forcibly quartering troops on the citizens, the common councillors had to house most of them themselves. In December, as tension rose, they were so alarmed by 'some threatening speeches' of the soldiers that they raised arms as a precaution.[80]

According to a pro-Monck writer who chronicled events at Gloucester for the London press, Cochrane 'exercis'd more cruelty over us then if we were the vilest Rebels and Traytors living'. The older Pury was forced to flee, and the younger lost his militia command to Dun, the city postmaster. Some citizens were imprisoned for their loyalty to Parliament, money was extorted from the mayor, aldermen and excise commissioners, and Captain Philipps was disarmed and locked up. On 27 December Cochrane disbanded the city militia. Soon the troops were out of control, for they raised a riot over billets, marched around town with pike and guns, plundered shops and wounded at least one citizen. Further stories of brutality and extortion emerged later. Although these lost nothing in the telling, the city records do give some corroboration.[81]

The situation was highly complex. Cochrane seems to have been a loyal

---

[77] Bodl. Lib., MS Tanner 51, fo. 155; CJ vi. 755.
[78] A&O ii. 1324–5; BL, E766 (28), Mercurius Politicus, no. 582, 4–11 Aug. 1659; CJ vi. 749, 782; CSPD 1659–60, 111, 117.
[79] Ibid. 1659–60, 176, 195; Reece, 'Military presence', 217–18; Mordaunt letter book, no. 28.
[80] HMC, corporation of Gloucester, 517–18; GRO, GBR B3/3, fos 117, 120–1.
[81] BL, E182 (16), (18), (20), The parliamentary intelligencer, nos 2, 3, 6, 26 Dec. 1659–2 Jan. 1660, 2–9, 23–30 Jan. 1660; CSPD 1659–60, 321; HMC, corporation of Gloucester, 517–18.

Army supporter terrorising Rumpers, yet the Royalists held high hopes of his joining them. Perhaps the Rump, restored to power once again in January 1660, feared so, for one of its first actions was to order the regiment's withdrawal. The confusion of the sources over what ensued probably reflects that of the participants. On 4 January the soldiers were drawn up. The troop of Captain Coates, who had expressed great zeal to fight Lambert, was ready and willing to leave, but many of the rest mutinied, attacked and disarmed Coates's men and ran amok in the county magazine, calling for money. Eventually, they were pacified and left.[82]

However, Major Wood, a Royalist, said that the soldiers were ready to declare for a free Parliament and that many gentry had come to join them. Some were in touch with Wood, who agreed to 'helpe them to Massey', but Howe's friends discouraged this, saying that 'it was not yet the Kings time'. Thereupon, the soldiers left, 'cursinge the gentry for a Company of cowards and fooles'. Whatever the case, the regiment was taken to Gravesend and continued to behave in a similar manner until Cochrane's dismissal.[83]

The royalist effort in Gloucestershire was as divided as ever, but there is evidence that the gentry were uniting in the name of that universal icon, a free Parliament. One petition was raised on 23 January, in the name of the knights, gentlemen and freeholders of Gloucestershire, resolving to join the Common Council of London in declaring that no new laws or taxes could be imposed on the nation without its consent in a free Parliament. Another, undated but soon after, specifically refused to obey new laws or pay new taxes until the MPs secluded in 1648 were restored.[84]

For the moment, the effect of Cochrane's withdrawal was to restore power to local hands. On 5 January the mayor of Bristol and, in Gloucester, the younger Pury were authorised to raise forces to keep the peace. Pury duly ordered the beating of the drum for volunteers until four fully armed companies were raised. A close adherent of General Monck, he was to be a crucial figure in the coming months.

The corporation was divided over tactics and possibly over much more. At the height of the violence, the mayor and some aldermen met with local gentlemen at John Singleton's house, possibly to consider joining London's declaration for a free Parliament, and there was a heated debate on 6 January when a proposal to put the city in a posture of defence – before Pury pre-empted them – was voted down as contrary to the Rump's declaration that no forces be raised without its approval.[85]

---

[82] Mordaunt to king, 9 Oct. 1659, in *Mordaunt letter book*, no. 93; *CSPD* 1659–60, 292; BL, E182 (17), *The parliamentary intelligencer*, no. 3, 2–9 Jan. 1660.

[83] Wood to John Shaw, 20 Jan. 1660, Bodl. Lib., MS Clarendon 68, fo. 175; Wood 593 (6), *Mercurius Publicus*, no. 6, 2–9 Jan. 1660.

[84] BL, 669 f23 (9), *The remonstrance of the knights, gentlemen and freeholders of the county of Gloucester*, 23 Jan. 1660; Glos. Pub. Lib., 506 h 13 (8), *A declaration of the city and county of Gloucester*, London 1659.

[85] BL, E182 (18), *The parliamentary intelligencer*, no. 4, 9–16 Jan. 1660.

The split grew as the men who made this proposal also tried to 'draw in the scattered remnants of the late Rebellion' by spreading rumours of Massey's arrival. Others planned to surprise Gloucester but were foiled by Pury's vigilance. Meanwhile, a petitioning movement for a free Parliament was growing in Stroud in late January. Pury was not only opposed from the right. He also had to be alert in mid-January to avert trouble from a radical group at Cirencester. They too called for a free Parliament, though in this case, the phrase allegedly meant 'the Ammunition Parliament the late Committee of Safety would have set up'.[86]

All over the country, large numbers of humble men were responding to national events within their localities. In the west, as in London, the apprentices took the initiative. At Bristol, the news of Okey's approach led to a major riot on 3 February. The apprentices seized the main gate, some shouting for the king, some for a free Parliament. Some citizens joined them, but most soon lost their nerve and were persuaded to disperse by the mayor. The city was quiet before Major Izod and then Okey himself marched in.

This riot was the cue for the Gloucester apprentices and some citizens to lay plans to follow suit on 8 February, with a football match as the trigger, but an alert captain nipped the riot in the bud, and nothing happened. The Bristol apprentices kept up the pressure. On 5 March they defied orders not to indulge in their usual Shrove Tuesday sports and demonstrated symbolic resistance by beating up the bellman who made the proclamation and hurling geese instead of cocks, cats and bitches instead of dogs. Later, in April, they took the symbolism further by erecting maypoles.[87]

The groundswell for the return of the secluded MPs was growing all over the nation. Gloucestershire's men were all still alive and active; Nathaniel Stephens, despite his great age, had been one of many who vainly tried to assert their right to sit in December 1659. Such men were in the driving seat locally and nationally. Some were among those whom the Bristol apprentices had boasted would join them, including Sir John Seymour, who was imprisoned by Okey.[88]

Massey was also approaching Bristol at the time of the riots, and he had contacts within the city and in the 'forward and well resolved' Colonel Edward Stephens, son of Edward Stephens, the MP. William Cooke came under suspicion in February for spreading rumours of a free Parliament among the 'ruder sort'.[89] His brother, Colonel Edward, was a key figure in London, who held 'great sway' among the Presbyterians and the secluded MPs. He was also

---

[86] BL, E182 (15), *The parliamentary intelligencer*, no. 5, 16–23 Jan. 1660; Bodl. Lib., Wood 593 (6), *Mercurius Publicus*, no. 6, 2–9 Feb. 1660.
[87] Ibid. Wood 593 (6), (7), *Mercurius Publicus*, nos 6–7, 2–9, 9–16 Feb. 1660; Latimer, *Annals of Bristol*, 292–3.
[88] BL, E1011 (4), *A brief narrative*; E755 (10), *Mercurius Politicus*, 23 Feb.–1 Mar. 1660.
[89] Massey to Hyde, 17 Feb. 1660, CCSP iv. 525, 564; CSPD 1659–60, 570.

trusted implicitly by the king, for he had been stationed at Hurst Castle in December 1648 and had been prepared to help Charles I escape.[90]

Such spontaneous reuniting of communities all over the land forced Monck's hand. The secluded MPs were finally readmitted to the Commons on 21 February. One of the first acts of the restored Long Parliament was to wrest control of local militia forces from the radicals. But an unconditional restoration was not envisaged, either of the king or of his father's supporters. In Gloucestershire, twenty-four of the forty-eight new commissioners were old Parliamentarians and their sons, including Seymour, Hodges, both Codringtons and four Stephenses. Ten more were aldermen and common councillors of Gloucester. Only five of the men of the 1650s survived – and of these one was George, Lord Berkeley, who had acceded to the title in 1658. The only Independent was Wade, who was still needed in Dean. The door towards a general reconciliation was left ajar by the inclusion of seven sons of Cavaliers.[91]

This represented a major overhaul in the personnel of county government. Excluding the aldermen of Gloucester nominated to earlier city commissions (Gloucester did not have a separate commission in March 1660), only thirteen of the new commissioners had been nominated to the previous Militia Commission of 1659, or to the Rump's Assessment Commission of January 1660, nine of whom were named to both. More surprisingly, only eighteen and twenty respectively had been nominated to the 'moderate' Commission of the Peace and Assessment Commission of 1657; thirty-eight of those JPs and forty-nine of those Assessment Commissioners were left out in March 1660. Of the Sequestration Commissioners, only Edwards survived in county government until the Restoration. There was some continuity within change, as seven decimators did survive: four were aldermen of Gloucester for whom the reckoning would come later. The others were John Howe senior and Christopher Guise, who had already redeemed themselves, and Wade.[92]

At a stroke the Stephenses were restored to prominence. Early in March, Edward Stephens, aged and nearly blind, made a major speech in the Commons, saying '[tha]t till [th]e sunne, [th]e moone & [th]e starrs were placed in their proper orbs, this nation could never be happy; [tha]t untill the King, Lords & Commons satt in Parliam[en]t England must be unhappy'.[93] This speech and others in the same vein must have made a powerful impression, for they were acclaimed in the Commons and noted by several correspondents, including the Venetian ambassador. Meanwhile Colonel Edward Stephens returned to Gloucestershire to execute the militia commission.[94]

---

90 CCSP iv, passim; *Mordaunt letter book*, no. 240; *Ludlow memoirs*, i. 130n.; Bodl. Lib., MS Tanner, fos 437–41.
91 A&O ii. 1431–2; CJ vi. 863, 866, 870–1.
92 A&O ii. 1069–70, 1324–5, 1369, 1431–2; PRO, C193/13/6.
93 Massey to Hyde, 7 Mar. 1660, Bodl. Lib., MS Clarendon 70, fo. 104.
94 CCSP iv. 584, 592, 603; *Nicholas papers*, iv. 194; *Calendar of state papers Venetian*, xxii. 1659–61, 128.

However, until the new militia emerged in April, the younger Pury, who was reinforced several times in February, remained the key figure. Since 1659 his republican views had changed and he had become a faithful follower of Monck, although Monck's ultimate intentions, even after he had restored the secluded MPs, remained unclear. In March Pury's regiment subscribed a petition vowing to uphold the changes in government effected by Monck, sudden and unexpected though they were. The regiment spent that month stamping out the vestiges of the 'fanatic party' among the troops in the West Midlands. On the 27th Monck ordered them into Herefordshire and Monmouthshire where, with the Harleys' forces, they were able to repress dissent over a wide area.[95]

Thus in the first quarter of 1660, the scene was transformed as the old Roundhead party, in touch with developments elsewhere, put themselves in a seemingly unassailable position. Although a Stuart restoration was growing more likely, it seemed that it would probably be on terms of some sort. The Cavaliers had been conspicuously quiet since July 1659, and the gulf between the Civil War combatants was still wide. Massey was superfluous to the needs of those now in control in Gloucestershire. Most of his letters of 1660 were taken up with complaints of being cold-shouldered by Mordaunt and Howe.[96]

Even in 1660 no-one could polarise opinion quite like Massey. After the Long Parliament dissolved itself and summoned a Convention, Massey was invited by the corporation to stand for Gloucester. Down he went, morose and pessimistic as ever. On 31 March he was leaving a service at St Nicholas's church to dine with the mayor when some of Major Huntingdon's troops began to agitate against him. Scuffling broke out and several were wounded on each side. Massey ludicrously blamed unnamed enemies for making false accusations against him to Monck, but he surrendered, as the soldiers had orders to secure him.[97] Next day the corporation hastily made him a freeman so that he could stand for election. He and Alderman James Stephens, a known enemy of the Rump, were returned in preference to Recorder Lenthall, who was an embarrassment in view of his past career as speaker of the Long Parliament. The Convention duly acquitted Massey of causing the riot.[98]

The issue was not simply civilians against soldiers. According to one pamphlet 'a certain person (you may guess who)' procured the order for Massey's arrest and tried to conceal the election writ, while not all the troops opposed Massey – the cavalry were 'very civil'. Whilst the Royalists reported the incident in terms of 'the towne desiringe to choose him for the towne &

95 Bodl. Lib., Wood 593 (11), *Mercurius Publicus*, no. 11, 8–15 Mar. 1660; CCSP iv. 590; HMC, MSS Cholmondely, 361.
96 Massey to Hyde, 3 Feb. 1660, Bodl. Lib., MS Clarendon 69, fo. 55; 70, 71 passim.
97 CCSP iv. 614, 620–1; Bodl. Lib., Wood 632 (44), *A letter from an eminent person at Gloucester to a friend in London*, London 1660; Massey to Edward Harley, 2 Apr. 1660, HMC, MSS Portland, iii. 220.
98 GRO, GBR B3/3, fo. 13; Williams, *Parliamentary history*, 199–200; CCSP iv. 643, 648, 656; CSPD 1659–60, 570.

the soldiery opposing it', George Fox found Gloucester 'very rude & devided, for one part of [th]e soldyers were for [th]e Kinge & another for [th]e Parlement'; indeed, some pro-Stuart troops were furious at finding that they had let the Quaker leader pass through and swore they would have killed him, had they known.[99]

Gloucester still went her own way, but elsewhere the Royalists reasserted themselves. Despite the parliamentarian hue of the militia commission in March, the officer list which emerged in April and May was more balanced. Most of the colonels and majors were of parliamentarian backgrounds, but a majority of the captains (except, of course, in the separate city and Inshire regiments) were former Royalists like Richard Baugh and Middleton.[100]

This reflects the way the Royalists had moved in to take control of the militia. In February and March Colonels Cooke and Stephens, together with Howe, the younger Throckmorton, Herbert and Guise, none of them old Royalists, had taken the lead in organising the militia. By 15 April Massey found that 'Coll[one]l Stephens hath by some of the wary or prudentiall Commissioners of [th]e Militia in his Absence found hard measure . . .' Within a week the business ground to a halt 'because Ned Cooke is made Collo[ne]ll of the Horse surruptitiously, and most of the gentry oppose him', as Cooke himself had foreseen.[101] Having let the Parliamentarians do the dirty work, the Royalists were not about to share the fruits of victory with them.

Other than in Gloucester, the elections also demonstrated the Royalists' growing confidence. Cirencester returned Thomas Master and Henry Powle, two young scions of Cavalier families, over the veteran John George, who petitioned without success against the return. Richard Dowdeswell and Henry Capel, son of an executed Royalist, were returned for Tewkesbury; George Fox said he had never seen such public drunkenness as at Tewkesbury, Evesham and Worcester at that time 'for they had been chuseinge Parliament men'.[102]

The county election went to a three-day poll before Matthew Hale and Edward Stephens were chosen over an unnamed competitor, possibly Howe, who had allegedly spent over £1,000 campaigning. According to his biographer, Hale was 'brought thither almost by violence by the Lord Berkeley, who bore all the charge of the Entertainments . . . and had engaged all his Friends and Interest for him'.[103] The influence of the young Lord Berkeley was growing. In March he had written to John Smyth, gently warning him not to pursue his

99 Letter from an eminent person, 5; Bodl. Lib., MS Clarendon 71, fo. 167; Fox journal, i. 352.

100 BL, E182 (28), Mercurius Politicus, 5–12 Apr. 1660; E183 (12), The parliamentary intelligencer, no. 12, 30 Apr.–7 May 1660.

101 CCSP iv. 561, 583; Massey to Hyde, 6 Mar., 15, 20 Apr. 1660, Bodl. Lib., MS Clarendon 70, fo. 70; 71, fos 267, 343.

102 Williams, Parliamentary history, 161–2, 242–3; CJ vii. 92; Fox journal, i. 352.

103 G. Burnet, The life and death of Sir Matthew Hale, Kt., London 1682, 30–1; R. P. Robinson, 'The parliamentary representation of Gloucestershire, 1660–1690', unpubl. Ph.D. diss. Yale 1975, 83–4.

support for Sir Thomas Overbury's candidature and declaring his own intention to come down if necessary to secure the election of Hale and Lord Herbert, for 'he must want modesty and policy that opposes either'.[104] In the event, Herbert stood down, but he too was becoming influential.

A Cavalier-controlled militia had other consequences. In April the Baptist minister, Henry Jessey, reported that 'The most eminent Cavaliers, imbittered persecutors in the County, ride about armed with sword and Pistols, pretending to be a Troop.' Former soldiers and members of separating congregations, including Crofts, Helme and Palmer, were disarmed and attacked.[105]

Thus encouraged, people with personal grudges turned violent. At Rendcomb, the ejected minister, Broad, returned 'with a company of rude companions' to drive out Warren, his replacement. At neighbouring Bagendon, Edward Fletcher was again harassed by parishioners, and fled to Gloucester after his house was ransacked. Mr Finch was likewise thrown out by the mob at Lower Lemington to make way for his predecessor. Helme had his house ransacked 'by the New Militia', who allegedly frightened his wife to death, and Palmer was further abused. Some of these vendettas had begun earlier; all reached a peak in April. Meanwhile Quakers were mobbed in Gloucester and harassed by individual opportunists in many more places.[106]

England was not truly 'a democracy' in April 1660, except insofar as the general desire for an immediate, unconditional Restoration coincided with what the gentry wanted.[107] However, the situation did give certain groups a wider than usual freedom of expression. The Cooke–Stephens party, which had seemed so strong, was swept aside by a popular upsurge of emotion, exemplified by these religious revenge attacks and even more so by events in Dean.

The way had been cleared in March when Baynham Throckmorton junior and Sir Trevor Williams, a Monmouthshire gentleman, raised men to disarm the 'Phanatick Party' in the Forest region. Rioting resumed almost at once, and this time a Forest committee was in direct contact with the king. On 13 April, Wade resigned. He spoke bitterly of 'the throwing open of the enclosures and coppices, and of the horrid wastes and spoils committed', against which no action had been taken nor ever seemed likely to be. A group of commissioners relieved him on 25 April and Furzer carried on the unequal struggle to complete his frigate.[108]

It was obvious now where things were heading, but the Good Old Cause refused to lie down and die. Pury had to move quickly to avert trouble among Colonel Alured's men. Some were heard abusing Monck at two inns in

104 Lord Berkeley to Smyth, 13 Mar. 1660, Smyth of Nibley papers, ii. 97.
105 BL, E1038 (8), H[enry] J[essey], The Lord's loud call to England, London 1660, 17–24 and passim.
106 Ibid.; A. G. Matthews, Calamy revised, Oxford 1934, 174; Besse, Sufferings, i. 210.
107 R. E. Hutton, The Restoration: a political and religious history of England and Wales, 1658–1667, Oxford 1985, 113.
108 Bodl. Lib., Wood 593 (11), Mercurius Publicus, no. 11, 8–15 Mar. 1660; CCSP iv. 585; Wade to Admiralty Commissioners, 13 Apr. 1660, CSPD 1659–60, 413.

Tewkesbury, and it was claimed that the senior bailiff, Christopher Smyth, 'would have a troop ready for them'. Some familiar figures were active. In one extraordinary document, Helme was commended for 'spending himselfe & being spirit among the neighbouring Congregac[i]ons' as part of a plan for a general sectarian rising to oppose Monck. This letter may have been fabricated to discredit Disbrowe, one of the purported authors, but it may have been genuine, albeit full of wishful thinking, for it shows an intimate knowledge of the local congregations.[109]

More certainly, the 'disaffected' continued to organise resistance from Crofts's house at Lower Swell until his arrest in late April, and Massey continued to fear that Lambert's supporters would seize Gloucester and Bristol as the general excitement and uncertainty persisted. On 25 April the over-whelmingly royalist Convention assembled. By then there was no going back, but in Gloucestershire, as in the nation as a whole, the republic 'did not die naturally but was murdered with great skill and effort'.[110]

In some ways, events in Gloucestershire responded to those elsewhere more closely in 1659–60 than at any other time. The royalist revolt of 1659 was part of a much larger edifice and its failure in the county caused the collapse of plots elsewhere. Campaigns for a free Parliament were synchronised with those elsewhere. The violence was anything but mindless. Ultimately, though, the provinces did not decide their own destiny. The Independents' regime in Gloucestershire ended quietly, because a Parliament cut the ground from under them by taking away their control of the militia.

By March 1660, in any case, most of the 1650s clique had disappeared. They had remained at the helm throughout 1659, but the demoralising experience of the sequestration commissioners and the eclipse of the militia may have driven a wedge between them. When locals resumed power in 1660, some, like Wade and Crofts, remained faithful to their conception of the Good Old Cause. However, the younger Pury and his officers (including Neast and Phillips) grew hostile to Lambert and the extremist faction in the Army.

Despite spending the 1650s half-in and half-out, the old parliamentarian gentry retained a coherent identity. The early months of 1660 saw the return of the Cooke–Stephens group. Maintaining contact with the king, Monck and the Presbyterians, they exploited every opening to regain power. Such groups led Monck as often as they followed him. In the end, though, they could not dictate terms to the king. The Gloucestershire party were almost all veterans of 1642 and their sons; many were very old. They may have been out of step with a younger generation to whom the issues of 1642 meant less. These issues meant nothing at all to the apprentices of Bristol and Gloucester, who had grown up in the 1650s and knew the Army only as an expensive burden. As

109 HMC, MSS Cholmondeley, 361; SP 18/220, fo. 70.
110 Bodl. Lib., Wood 593 (17)–(18), *Mercurius Publicus*, nos 17–18, 19–26 Apr., 26 Apr.–3 May 1660; CCSP iv, 661; Hutton, *Restoration*, 122.

in London, they provided the brawn in riots for a free Parliament and, by implication, for Charles II.

Even though the activists of these two years did not represent the entire community (and we should not forget that, as ever, most people were uninvolved and uninterested in public affairs), the geographical distribution of allegiances was striking. In July 1659 several hundred Gloucester citizen volunteers foiled a rising based on the Stroudwater clothing region and the Forest of Dean. However, the corporation itself was divided and Cochrane's brutality deepened this split and politicised many citizens.

The moderate 'Presbyterian' campaign for a free Parliament in early 1660 centred on Bristol, the south, Gloucester and Stroud, whilst the Forest, with a specific grievance against the government, grew more overtly royalist. Hatred of sectaries may have played some part in fuelling Royalism, but this is too easily exaggerated by Quaker propaganda. Most assaults on Quakers came after the Restoration and the attacks on individual ministers in Gloucestershire seem to have owed more to old grudges than to theology.[111]

Most of the political activity of all shades originated in the areas where the people had been actively parliamentarian in the Civil War. The tobacco-planters did not riot, despite their grievances and their manifest ability to do so. The Cotswolds were deafeningly quiet. The evidence for these regions is ambivalent. There were attacks on godly ministers at Rendcomb and Bagendon (both near Cirencester) and at Lower Lemington, Chipping Camden and Bourton-on-the-Water in the Cotswolds.[112] But then Cirencester was also the centre of radical resistance in these years.

These are intriguing facts, because they run contrary to David Underdown's conclusions. He argues that the areas which welcomed the Restoration most in Somerset, Wiltshire and Dorset were those which had been most royalist in 1642. Of course, public dissent was not much in evidence in May 1660 but, as he says, there was a world of difference between the token bell-ringing at old Puritan strongholds like Lyme and Dorchester, and the jubilation at royalist Sherborne.[113]

The Gloucestershire evidence of how communities greeted the proclamation of Charles II suggests that Underdown's correlation is too simple. Gloucester responded in character with a sober civic parade at which the populace were mere spectators. On 15 May the Common Council met in full regalia for a sermon and a dinner, then joined some local gentry on a specially erected stage in the wheat market to make a formal proclamation. Popular joy briefly exploded in a burst of fireworks, guns, trumpets and drinking. However, it was not really a people's festival.[114]

---

[111] Besse, *Sufferings*, i. 210–12.
[112] Jessey, *Lord's loud call*, 17–24; Bodl. Lib., Wood 643 (4), *Enaiantos terastios: mirabilis annus or, the year of prodigies and wonders*, London 1661, 67, 79.
[113] Underdown, *Revel, riot and rebellion*, 371–5.
[114] BL, E183 (16), *The parliamentary intelligencer*, no. 21, 14–21 May 1660.

At Tewkesbury, the news arrived just as Overbury and Richard Cocks of Dumbleton were exercising the militia there. They immediately summoned the bailiffs, drew up the troops and proclaimed Charles 'to the great joy of all the spectators'. That they had no business doing this themselves in a chartered borough naturally went unmentioned. Next day they journeyed to Winchcombe and Moreton-in-Marsh, in the heart of the tobacco country and the Cotswolds respectively, to make the proclamation again. Whatever celebrations there were in these towns were evidently not thought worth reporting.[115]

By far the most ecstatic and genuinely plebeian celebrations were at Dursley, the clothing village in the heart of the Vale, which had endured several generations of Puritan reformation. The people, 'almost ravished with joy', put up a decorated scaffold and organised themselves into companies to march around the town under local gentlemen of both parties, amidst drums and shouts. Eight hogsheads of beer were drunk and spiced loaves were handed out as a symbol of future prosperity. Over the next two days the young women and men in turn danced on the scaffold and marched up Stinchcombe Hill to drink the king's health; they even set up a mock court to fine those who presumed to keep their children and servants indoors. This was a rejection of socially divisive Puritanism with a vengeance. The continuator of Jessey's work also records that around this time some who had been denied communion during the Interregnum by the minister, Woodward, began to demand it again and became violent when he refused.[116]

What of the Cotswolds? Evidence is lacking, and reactions to political events had always been less pronounced there than in the Vale. However, the summer of 1660 did see two remarkable events in the Cotswolds. An incident in June put the village of Fairford, in the south-eastern corner of the county, at the centre of pamphlet controversy. It was reported in similar detail by two radical writers, Jessey and a local man writing as 'N.T.', that after Andrew Barker, the lord of the manor, and William Oldisworth, a local JP, had refused to protect a separatist congregation from harassment by mobs, their homes were invaded by a vast army of frogs and toads sent by God, which only disappeared when Oldisworth relented and did his duty.

There was soon a fierce rejoinder to this extraordinary story from Robert Clark, vicar of nearby Northleach, who denounced it as a pack of lies and added plenty of vitriol against separatists for good measure. One would dismiss it all as nonsense but for the fact that another pro-Anglican pamphlet, printing what purported to be a letter from five leading inhabitants, let slip that there really was a plague of frogs in Fairford in June 1660, albeit with a perfectly natural explanation.[117]

---

[115] BL, E183 (17), *Mercurius Publicus*, no. 21, 17–24 May 1660.
[116] BL, E183 (21), *Mercurius Publicus*, no. 22, 24–31 May 1660; *Enaiantos terastios*, 68–9.
[117] BL, E1035 (12), 'N.T.', *Strange and true newes from Gloucester*, 2 Aug. 1660; Jessey, *Lord's loud call*; Clark, *The lying wonders*; E1045 (6), *A perfect wonder of the phanatick wonders seen in the west of England*, n.p. 1660.

171

The implications of the episode are discussed at greater length elsewhere. However, it is clear that the story presented by the dissenter writers was an honest account of local gossip. The people of Fairford and the surrounding area believed that the frogs had been sent by God to punish Barker and Oldisworth for failing in what had been hitherto one of their most sacred duties, to preserve the freedom of worship of separating congregations. Did no-one see the woes of Barker and Oldisworth in terms of the pasts they were carefully leaving behind? They were no Cavaliers; both had been active in county government in the 1650s. Events like this suggest that a sizeable proportion of the people of this area of were not nearly so pro-Anglican as their lords.[118]

The 'Campden wonder' occurred in August 1660 when William Harrison, the aged steward of Viscountess Camden, disappeared near Charringworth while collecting rents. Suspicion fell on a former servant, John Perry, who had been sent to look for Harrison. Perry, who was clearly mentally disturbed in some way, made a number of mutually contradictory statements, confessing that he, his mother and his brother had robbed and murdered Harrison. As a result, all three were hanged, only for Harrison to reappear two years later and present himself to Sir Thomas Overbury with a patently untrue story of being kidnapped and sold into slavery in Turkey. The mystery was never solved. This story is peripheral to general events, yet Overbury's account does give some idea of the panicky mood in the area at the time, in the way in which omens were spoken of and, of course, in the way the community – albeit with the help of a hostile judge – sent three innocent people to the gallows on the basis of a false confession, without a dead body or any material evidence.[119]

Ultimately, the evidence is not good enough to say positively that the Civil War and Interregnum reversed the positions of the Vale and the Cotswolds in 1642. Other, short-term factors that can only be seen dimly may have been at work. It is notable that in the years between 1657 and 1659, the only Gloucestershire village among fourteen in the sample used by Tony Wrigley and Roger Schofield in *The population history of England* to experience a short-term mortality crisis was Fairford, which was also the only Cotswold village in the sample. Before 1642, such crises had been fairly common in the sprawling Vale parishes, but none had been recorded at Fairford in living memory.[120]

Demographic crisis may have added to the tension in 1660. But then a lot had changed since 1642. Not least, the political outlook of the common people had become considerably more complex than simply royalist or parliamentarian, active or passive. The people of Dursley may have felt that the increase in

---

[118] A. R. Warmington, 'Frogs, toads and the Restoration in a Gloucestershire village', *Midland History* xiv (1989), 30–40. See also J. Friedman, *Miracles and the pulp press during the English Revolution*, London 1993, 239–51.

[119] Sir G. Clark, *The Campden wonder*, Oxford 1959.

[120] Wrigley and Schofield, *Population history*, 486, 675–80.

landlord power which would inevitably accompany a Stuart Restoration was a price worth paying in order to be rid of religious strife. But those of Lower Slaughter, who realised what they could expect from their landlords, knew better.

6

Restoration Gloucestershire, 1660–72

The Restoration

1660 saw a restoration not just of the monarchy but also of the Anglican Church and of the gentry as a ruling class, determined that what they had suffered should never be allowed to happen again. It was also a pragmatic restoration, and many of the changes of the past twenty years were quietly left intact. The politics of Charles II's reign are amply covered by historians, but little has been written on relations between the central government and the provinces. The 'county community' school tends to break off in 1660 with Blankshire welcoming the Restoration and the yokels getting drunk around a maypole. The exceptions are works on Devon and Hampshire, and a recent article on Dorset, Somerset and Wiltshire.[1]

This chapter is not a direct comparison with any of them. Gloucestershire lacks the extensive local records of other western counties, and the depth of material in the state papers on Hampshire. Still, Andrew Coleby's work is intriguing because it goes so much against the grain of traditional historiography. He compares Interregnum and Restoration governments in three broad areas: office-holding, the enforcement of policy and relations between the centre and the county. Far from being the military despotism of received opinion, the former emerges as neither centralised nor efficient, vulnerably reliant on local elites who were not necessarily sympathisers for the execution of policy and quite often in the dark about events. By contrast, Charles II's regime, at least until the mid-1670s, was more successful in adjusting power structures in favour of its supporters and involving the people of the provinces in their own defence. Through better communications via lords lieutenant and other officers and sympathisers, and with a more pluralist, informal court, it remained more sensitive to local opinion.

No county can be taken to be representative of the others, as Coleby admits. But he does venture that the presence of the naval base at Portsmouth and the strategic importance of the Solent, which no government could possibly ignore, make Hampshire a good testing ground for the regime as a whole. One wonders if this is so. The military presence in Hampshire and the Isle of Wight and the important customs and excise operations at Southampton

---

[1] Roberts, *Devon*; Coleby, *Hampshire*; P. J. Norrey, 'The Restoration regime in action: the relationship between central and local government in Dorset, Somerset and Wiltshire, 1660–1678', *HJ* xxxi (1988), 709–812.

and Portsmouth meant that London wielded far more patronage there than in most areas. It does not follow that those who got it right where it mattered most did so everywhere else.

Naturally, both regimes did all they could to put trustworthy men into key positions. But Charles II could appeal to the whole ruling class, most of whom could not serve Cromwell because they had fought for Charles I. Security was a priority of both; that is what governments are there for. However, there is a major difference in what the word means to a regime backed by almost everyone and one whose partisans were a religious minority based on military service.

Charles II never had to appeal to moderates and time-servers, or to rely on an isolated group to enforce and even anticipate policy. On the contrary, he was deluged with support, mostly from suitors for offices and pensions. This enthusiasm, and the unrealistic expectation that 1660 would bring 'Peace and no Taxes', created problems in the long run. The regime could only satisfy a fraction of the claimants on its favour. Disillusion set in once Charles was clearly safe from attempts to overthrow him. A regime which was popular in principle rapidly became very unpopular in practice.

For convenience's sake, the rest of this chapter is divided in two, with one section on internal developments in politics and religion and another on relations between the 'county community' and central government. This can be a misleading division. The gentry could not regulate the corporations or persecute dissenters without central backing. And although the dispute over land carriage in the mid-1660s was essentially between the parishes of one region and a government agent, it also pitched different regions of the county against each other.

There was no hard and fast division between central and local politics, but certain matters were determined locally, albeit within the context of a national polity, others were not. This division makes it easier to hold on to the thread of events than in a continuous narrative. Again, many conclusions may be distorted because so much of the evidence relates to one man, John Smyth of Nibley. But if it is possible to trace the 'General crisis of the seventeenth century' and the rise of capitalism through the writings of his father, the historian, then it is surely not too ambitious to analyse the development of Restoration government through the career of the son![2]

Politics and religion, 1660–72

Restructuring local government proved easy in Gloucestershire. No member of the pre-war 'county' gentry had irrevocably compromised himself by supporting the republic or even the Protectorate, and, of the Royalists, only the Pooles were ruined by composition. Otherwise a mere handful of estates changed hands permanently as a direct result of the Civil War. Those who had

---

[2] Rollison, 'Bourgeois soul', passim.

remained in office had mostly demonstrated their antipathy to the local Independent ruling clique. In any case, none of the latter could normally expect to be named to high office anyway. There was a strong feeling in favour of reconciliation among the gentry, despite the way in which some of those who had done most to further the Restoration locally were elbowed aside.

The loyal address produced in the name of the gentry of Gloucestershire in 1660 was a roll-call of the county and middling gentry families; in all, of those who signed, thirty-three had been Royalists or were of royalist background, thirty were Parliamentarians or of parliamentarian background and thirteen were of no discernible allegiance. None of the old Independents signed. Whilst many of these were not of sufficient standing to do so or were republicans, the absence of others is surprising. One suspects that they were not allowed to sign. Thomas Pury junior had done more than anyone to aid the Restoration in Gloucestershire, and Neast publicly accepted Charles's general pardon. Both were to appear in the heralds' visitation in 1682–3 and Neast had as good a pedigree as some signatories.[3]

Equally significant was the fact that the loyal address and the new commissions of the peace could boast bluer blood than they had for many years. William, Lord Chandos, and Viscount Campden were no longer resident and the Chandos fortune had been largely dispersed, but Gloucestershire now had two resident lords for the first time in half a century. Henry Somerset, Lord Herbert of Raglan, the second son of the marquis of Worcester (to which title he acceded in 1667), had acquired Badminton by devise from a half-cousin and moved there in 1660. He had renounced his family's Catholic faith and was on good terms with Cromwell, but he was later involved in Massey's plot. In 1660 he became lord lieutenant of Gloucestershire, Herefordshire and Monmouthshire. Herbert was to prove an efficient lieutenant and a vital link between the counties and Whitehall.

Both Herbert and the young Lord Berkeley were among the commissioners who invited Charles to return on behalf of the Convention. George Berkeley succeeded his dilettante father in 1658. He moved back from London to Berkeley in 1661, was created *custos rotulorum* of Gloucestershire and later became an earl. Later, county politics were to revolve around the two poles of the Whig Berkeleys and the Tory Beauforts, but throughout the 1660s and 1670s the two families remained on good terms.[4]

If anything, the return of the gentry as a ruling group made local politics more factious, within the context of consensus support for the regime. This and the growing influence of the two young lords were exemplified in the elections, in 1661, to the new Parliament, whose initial ferocious loyalism earned it the title of 'Cavalier Parliament'.

---

[3] BL, 669 f25 (42), *The loyal addresse of the gentry of Gloucestershire*, n.p. 1660; GRO, TBR A1/3, fo. 72v; *Visitation of 1682–3*.

[4] *DNB, s.v.* Henry Somerset, first duke of Beaufort, George Berkeley, first earl of Berkeley; Robinson, 'Parliamentary representation', 78 and passim.

At least five candidates were mooted for the prestigious county seats. When Sir Thomas Overbury dropped out in February, Sir Baynham Throckmorton considered Herbert himself and the younger Howe to be the frontrunners. Although he disavowed any intention to stand, Throckmorton was probably already in contention, if only through dislike of Howe 'because he thinks himself above all men'. On 18 March, Lord Berkeley pitched in to 'engage my interest as far as I may for him [Throckmorton]', and asked Smyth to get his tenants and friends and the clothiers out to vote. Herbert, who could win any seat in his lieutenancy, opted to sit for Monmouthshire instead, but Sir Thomas Stephens was also in the field and Lord Berkeley refused to back any second candidate.

Evidently there was a poll before Throckmorton and Howe were elected on 17 April, for a petition against the return by an unnamed contestant was later rejected by the Commons' Committee of Privileges and Elections, on the grounds that these two had the majority of voices. In Gloucester's last free election, Massey and the recorder Evan Seys were returned. Tewkesbury and Cirencester, however, were already under the thumb of the gentry. The former again chose Dowdeswell and Capel, the latter John George and the new lord of the manor, James, earl of Newburgh. No contests were recorded in the boroughs.[5]

Parliamentary elections were of passing importance. The cornerstone of local authority and the true symbol of the revival of the gentry was their restoration as JPs. A total of seventy-one men, excluding honorific appointments, were named to the first two new commissions of the peace. Of these, at least forty-six appeared at one or more of eighteen sessions between 1661 and 1667 at which those in attendance were recorded (latecomers were simply noted as 'and others'). In addition, ten JPs who were added later also appeared, most of them only after 1664.[6]

The most active JPs at sessions were such middling gentry as Smyth, Philip Sheppard and Thomas Master, most of whom could not usually aspire to anything higher. Herbert appeared about once a year, which was as much as could be expected in his large lieutenancy. Most of the active JPs were of royalist backgrounds. Twenty in all had been nominated to Interregnum Commissions of the Peace, but they included those who had opposed the Independents in elections and over the decimation, such as Guise, Hodges and Lord Berkeley himself, and ex-Parliamentarians who had assisted Charles II, such as the Howes and William Cooke. All twenty were substantial gentlemen, mostly of pre-war JP families.

Little survives to illustrate the routine work of the JPs, other than in Smyth's papers. Most often we see them as commissioners, as persecutors of religious

5 Throckmorton to Smyth, 9 Feb. 1661, HMC, MSS Cholmondely, 365; Lord Berkeley to Smyth, 18, 31 Mar. 1661, Smyth of Nibley papers, ii. 99, 100; CJ viii. 410; Robinson, 'Parliamentary representation', 222–3, 267–8, 294.
6 PRO, C193/12/3; C220/9/4; GRO, QSIB 1, passim.

dissenters and dealing with central government. It is in this role that there is better evidence for their outlook and activity in general. Some JPs also acted together as deputy lieutenants. Six were nominated in each division. Of the twenty-four, twelve were of royalist backgrounds, nine of parliamentarian and the other three were new arrivals. They included old Cavaliers such as Sir Robert Poyntz, Thomas Chester and Lord Tracy, with the anti-republicans from the 1650s: Howe, Guise, William Cooke and John Stephens amongst others. Hardly any papers survive, but the appearance of the militia during the Second Dutch War greatly impressed observers. Not all counties, however, had the advantages of a resident lord lieutenant and so few seats in Parliament that most of the deputy lieutenants were still present at home.[7]

Despite public resentment, it proved necessary to retain the assessment as the basic form of direct taxation. Each county's fixed sum was raised under the supervision of local commissioners drawn from the gentry. The early commissions only added a leavening of poor Cavaliers to the March 1660 group, but Royalists were more dominant in the commissions for the Eighteen Months' Assessment in 1661 and the Four Subsidies of 1663. From the mid-1660s, and particularly with the four assessments that paid for the Second Dutch War, the tendency was to nominate the entire bench and more. These commissions comprised forty-nine men of royalist backgrounds, forty of parliamentarian and twenty others. In 1672 142 were nominated, including almost all of the gentry and quite a few unknowns. They seem to have taken their duties seriously, for no less than twenty-five appeared at a routine meeting at Cirencester to implement the Royal Aid in April 1666.[8]

Religion and politics were as much intertwined in the 1660s as before. The civilians and ministers who had been the mainstay of Cromwell's rule were rapidly swept out. Many had to answer Exchequer bills concerning their accounts: Thomas Jeynes of Tewkesbury, Giles Birt, the sequestration money agent, Neast and Crofts as soldiers and tax collectors, Thomas Rogers and Hancock as sequestration commissioners, Thomas Pury junior as receiver of royal rents in Wiltshire and Gloucestershire and Aldermen Thomas Hill and Luke Nurse as treasurers, along with a few other collectors and agents.[9] Hancock may have been particularly victimised, for he also had to answer to the Treasury for £500 outstanding in his accounts. Jeynes and Neast were accused of plotting against the regime in November 1661, and Nathaniel Cripps was frequently persecuted for his Quakerism.[10]

The younger Pury's services to Charles II were not entirely forgotten, for he

[7] SP 29/11, fo. 159; *CSPD* 1665–6, 480, 556; 1667, 234; Norrey, 'Restoration regime', 790.

[8] *Statutes of the realm*, v, London 1819, passim; Smyth of Nibley papers, i. 6.

[9] PRO, E112/565/300, 591; E112/2383 (unnum.); E113/5/1A (unfol.). For these processes in general see S. K. Roberts, 'Public or private? Revenge and recovery at the Restoration of Charles II', *BIHR* lix (1986), 172–88.

[10] *CSPD* 1661–2, 148, 348; *CTB* i. 395; Besse, *Sufferings*, i. 211, 215.

remained colonel of Lord Herbert's regiment by Monck's commission until its disbandment in November 1660. By an order of June 1661 he was allowed to keep certain fee farm rents he had purchased and he may still have been in service in October 1663. Solace was the only other leading figure from the 1650s to appear on the right side of the fence, bringing an indictment and serving as a juror at quarter sessions. Most, however, returned to the obscurity from which they had come. The only men prominent in the 1650s to remain in service for any length of time were the professionals, Wade and Furzer.[11]

Both the accounting process and the removal of the leading Independent ministers were the result of central official action. Parliament was determined to restore a national, exclusively Anglican Church, suitably shorn of Laudian pretension. Despite the king's personal inclination to toleration, moves to fulfil his promise of a 'liberty for tender consciences', either through official toleration of politically quiescent sects or through their comprehension in a broad Church, were wrecked. There were many 'ejected' clerics clamouring for reinstatement. Some of these managed to assert their right to their former livings immediately, while others had to wait until a vacancy could be found if they were unable to prove their case.

From 1662, however, there were more than enough vacancies, for under the Act of Uniformity all ministers who would not swear their conformity to the Church of England were ejected. In all, perhaps a tenth of England's ministry departed. Their fortunes have been chronicled by Edward Calamy. In Gloucestershire as many as twenty-three ministers were removed in 1660 (three of them may have left for other reasons). In addition, both Helme and Palmer were driven out of the county by force and later resurfaced as the heads of congregations in London variously described as Fifth Monarchist, Baptist and Independent. They remained hostile to the monarchy and were monitored by the government as potential rebels. Among the others went the heart of the Independent group – Beale, Tray, Wells, Harris and Forbes – plus the alleged Anabaptist, Richard Harrison, from Charlton Kings, Sheppard's friend, Jonathan Smith, from Hempstead and Palmer's assistant, Thomas Paxford, from his curacy in Clapton.[12]

The fact that the radical group had been so prominent in the 1650s may have made the retribution that much more complete, for it was unusual for more ministers to be removed from the county in 1660 than in 1662. It is also notable that more of the ejected radicals were nominated during the Protectorate than the Commonwealth. Of course, there were more factors involved in the choosing of a minister than central approval, but this may tell us something about Cromwellian religious policy. The eleven ejected in 1662 were more often conservative, long-established figures; Alexander Gregory

---

11 HMC, MSS Cholmondely, 361; Bodl. Lib., Wood 593 (33), *Mercurius Publicus*, no. 33, 9–16 Aug. 1660; CCSP v. 225, 340; GRO, QSIB 1, fos 47v, 142, 171.
12 Matthews, *Calamy revised*, passim; Capp, *Fifth Monarchy men*, 252, 257; Matthews, *Sheppard*, 63, 243; Thatch, *Gainsayer convinced*, 54.

had been at Cirencester since 1632. Five others were ejected at times unknown. Four conformed and were reinstated after initial refusals. These purges were important in terms of quality rather than quantity, for most ministers did conform in 1662 as readily as they had to every other innovation of recent years.[13] The back of the radical party was broken, and yet fear of dissent was not killed off.

All the JPs were now conforming Anglicans, as indeed were almost all the gentry, but the enforcement of religious conformity *per se* was not an immediate priority. Several other matters required attention. One issue was the authority of the Council in the Marches of Wales, an administrative court set up by the Tudors to bring order into a lawless region. Many gentlemen of the 'Four Shires' (Herefordshire, Shropshire, Gloucestershire and Worcestershire) had long objected to the council's jurisdiction in their counties, partly because of its use of torture and informers, partly out of dislike of a Welsh court having authority in England, and, no doubt, partly because the council's swift procedures were more to the advantage of the humble litigant than those of the common law courts. In 1640 this had been one of the first issues to which the MPs of the Four Shires turned, and an exemption bill was passed in July 1641.[14]

The issue was revived in 1660 when the council was restored. The Four Shires were not specifically included in the patent, although some assumed them to be comprehended under the title of 'the marches'. The Gloucestershire gentry had other ideas, and they deliberately provoked test cases to fight their cause. On 14 March 1662, the lord president, the earl of Carbery, wrote to the sheriff, Smyth, ordering him to enforce statutes concerning highway repair. At the assizes only eight days later, the Grand Jury, prodded by the JPs, petitioned that it was a 'great greevance' for the council thus to demand accounts of the execution of laws, and asked the JPs to seek redress. Twenty-one of them duly wrote to deny that Gloucestershire was within the council's jurisdiction.[15]

Smyth and others also resisted in more direct ways. In December 1662 one Thomas Carter tried to serve a council writ at Wotton-under-Edge. He found the mayor obstructive, and when the schoolmaster, Thomas Byrton, objected that the council's writ did not run there, Carter broke into a torrent of abuse and left. He returned in April to summon Byrton and another man to answer contempt charges in Ludlow. Matters got out of hand and the dispute had to be reconvened at an inn before the nearest available JPs, Smyth and Gabriel Lowe of Ozleworth.

Accounts differ about what ensued, but clearly Smyth supported the mayor, as he fined Carter for threatening behaviour and forced him to give security

---

[13] Matthews, *Calamy revised*, passim.
[14] R. E. Ham, 'The Four Shire controversy', *Welsh History Review* viii (1976–7), 381–400; C. A. J. Skeel, *The Council in the Marches of Wales*, London 1904, 137–45; *CJ* ii. 210, 216.
[15] Skeel, *Council*, 174; *CSPD 1671–2*, 218; BL, MS Add. 33, 589, fo. 16; PRO, ASSI 5/1/7, fo. 2; *HMC*, MSS Cholmondely, 338.

to appear at the quarter sessions. Carter alleged that Smyth openly refused to obey any council order and said that the lord president had no power to hold a plea of action of debt, which was the original cause of the case. The issue persisted for a while and the king himself ordered the sheriff, in December 1663, to assist the council's officers in apprehending twelve fugitives. In the long run, though, it was impractical to assert the council's authority in the teeth of gentry defiance.[16]

Did the common people have any strong feelings on the matter? Smyth evidently had support in Wotton and from the Grand Jury, and he spoke confidently of '[th]e universall dislike [th]e country hath to a subiection under [th]e Courte of Wales, takeing from them theire birthright of Englishmen'. Others disagreed. One petition was raised in and around Gloucester in 1661 with 183 signatures – the organisers reckoned they could have had 2,000, given time – to ask for the council's retention, praising the cheap, speedy justice it afforded to ordinary people. The signatories were mostly humble, although they included eight clerics and a number of common councillors of Gloucester.[17] Popular opinion cannot be measured accurately, but that is not the important point. The council gradually lost its authority in the Four Shires because the gentry there wanted it so.

War was waged on the enemy without and within at the same time. It was inevitable that Gloucester's record would be called in question by the restored monarchy, despite the city's hasty surrender of the fee farm rents. This gave the gentry the chance to renew the Inshire dispute, a long-running battle which had been given new urgency by increased levels of taxation. There may have been some truth in the stories of unfair rating by the aldermen – although co-operation was not unknown, for William Cooke, Christopher Guise and other Inshire gentlemen acted as trustees to repair the cathedral in 1656.[18] Certainly, though, the city's rule was anomalous in that the Inshire was not a true economic hinterland.

A lot of nonsense was talked about the issue too. Guise, who lived in a detached portion of the Inshire at Elmore and who might have known better, believed that Gloucester grew poor by neglecting trade and 'depending too much on theyr powers in the incounty, and leaviing monyes which . . . is . . . enough to make them odiouse and by consequence as much as may be hindered and depressed in theyr trade'.[19] He also blamed his father's sequestration in 1644 on the malice of the aldermen, when his own papers show that only two of the eleven who voted William Guise a delinquent on a six–five vote were Gloucester men. There were also complaints that Gloucester denied the Inshire gentry the right to vote in elections and to become JPs, but they were not truly disenfranchised, because they could vote and serve at county

---

16 Smyth of Nibley papers, v. 87–9; xii. 19; SP 29/37, fos 69–69ii.
17 BL, MS Add. 33,589, fo. 20; Smyth of Nibley papers, v. 89.
18 GRO, GBR B3/3, fo. 879.
19 *Guise memoirs*, 104–5.

level.[20] However, the accuracy of the beliefs of men like Guise mattered less than their determination to act on them.

The onslaught began in the Commons in 1661. Gloucester spent £160 fighting the bill through Massey and Seys, and several common councillors were sent to London to join the campaign, but it was passed in May 1662. The militia commissioners lost no time in pressing Gloucester to pay to equip the county's light horse, and the corporation fought to avoid creating a precedent by asking to compound and also for exemption from the county charge for indigent officers. (This, with the Poll Tax of 1667, was one of only two taxes in which Gloucester did not keep a separate commission.)[21]

Again, popular opinion cannot be traced. But one prediction of the writer who defended Gloucester's case, that the poor of the parishes containing suburbs of Gloucester and outlying hamlets would suffer if the Corporation lost control of charity there, proved quite correct. This is precisely what happened in 1663 when city and county overseers would not meet to set a rate, and it was still a problem in September 1664.[22]

Gloucester had other problems. Like other cities with anti-Stuart pasts, her walls were demolished by the king's orders. Then, in December 1661, Charles assented to the Act for the Well Governing and Regulating of Corporations. The object of this was to weed out officials elected illegally in the boroughs during the Interregnum and to restore men removed for Royalism. The task was entrusted to local commissioners, who were to call all borough officials before them to take the oaths of supremacy and allegiance. Any who did not swear to these before 25 March 1663 was to be removed from office immediately. The commissioners might also remove men willing to take the oaths if they deemed it 'expedient for the public safety'. Thereafter only communing Anglicans could be elected.

Extensive purges occurred all over the country, but in most cases this led to the reinstatement of old Royalists. In Gloucester, however, there were no old Royalists to restore. Every single alderman and common councillor in office had been properly elected. Hence the purge of 1662–3 can fairly be called savage. The fourteen active commissioners, led by Herbert, were mostly old Royalists, including Wintour and Throckmorton, or Inshire gentlemen with a grudge, like William Cooke and Guise, plus the Gloucester Royalist, Dr Robert Fielding.

The commissioners sat for three days in July and called in forty-seven men. Only three refused the oaths. None the less, six aldermen, seventeen common councillors and Dorney were removed. The elder Pury, who would certainly

[20] Ibid. 124–5; BL, K 816 m.16(5), *The state of the case for the city of Gloucester against the bill for dis-uniting the two hundreds of Dudston and Kings Barton from the said citie*, 1660.

[21] GRO, GBR B3/3, fos 187–9, 255, 266, 282, 300; *Statutes of the realm*, 14 Car. II c.8, Private Act 13, 18 & 19 Car. II c.1.

[22] *The state of the case*; PRO, ASSI 2/1, fos 105, 127.

have been another casualty, had already resigned, supposedly on the grounds of his advanced age and non-residence. In October another alderman and eight common councillors were also removed. As the expiry of their commission was drawing near, and no doubt spurred on by a letter from Herbert to encourage them not to risk leaving any 'ill humour' in Gloucester's body politic, the commissioners removed three more aldermen and one other on 12 March 1663. This included one of their previous nominees. In all, some three-quarters of the corporation's members were purged, almost all because the commissioners chose to do so in the name of public safety.[23]

Inevitably, Gloucester ceased to be governed by the men best able to bear the burden of office, as most of the veterans were removed, including both Singletons, Capel, Wise, Nurse, Nicholas Webb, Thomas Pierce, Toby Jordan and Town Clerk Dorney. There had already been considerable demoralisation and absenteeism in recent years. Fifty-two members did not appear on 6 December 1660, and after 1661 Dorney had ceased to record absentees, which is suggestive. However, this was not an exercise in cutting out dead wood – indeed, those who had been inactive in the 1650s did better than the activists. The extent of the purge forced the commissioners not only to dig deep but also to violate the principle of seniority. Most flagrantly, their particular favourites, Fielding, Henry Ockold, John Wagstaffe and Henry Fowler were first made common councillors without serving as stewards, then aldermen without serving as sheriffs.

Finally, the remodelled corporation was one of many hit by *Quo Warranto* actions by the crown. A new charter was obtained in 1664, at no little expense, which confirmed the detachment of the Inshire and the king's right to veto all appointments and to choose the town clerk and recorder himself. This was not necessary in the latter case, as the corporation had already elected a suitable man in Sir William Morton, now a prominent judge. There seems little doubt that the commissioners removed more men from office than was strictly necessary, and did so out of malice. The losers were the citizens, who were left with a council inadequate to the city's needs, which rarely met and which, before long, was torn by faction once more.[24]

The commissioners were equally thorough at Tewkesbury. Thirty-nine inhabitants had hastily declared their acceptance of the king's general pardon in June 1660, and, in October, six of Disbrowe's surviving victims petitioned for and won a letter from the Privy Council for their reinstatement. This was not enough. On 25 August 1662, Herbert, the commissioners and Tewkesbury's MPs displaced thirteen of twenty-four burgesses and put in nine in their stead. The victims included such radicals as Neast and John Batch, but most were not obviously party men and might safely have been left. Their replacements

23 R. Austin, 'The city of Gloucester and the regulation of corporations', *TBGAS* (1936), 257–74; GRO, GBR B3/3, fos 223–4; VCH, *Glos.*, iv. 113.
24 GRO, GBR B3/3, fos 164–5, 274–5, 286 and passim.

were mostly their natural successors, with a leavening of deserving royalist soldiers in Conway Whithorne and Thomas Nanfan.[25]

Although episcopal church government was restored in its entirety, the Church relied on lay support in Parliament and the localities to enforce Anglican supremacy. Bishop William Nicholson of Gloucester, the poorest of all English sees, was careful to cultivate sympathetic gentlemen. In the early 1660s, Parliament passed a series of acts aimed at eradicating dissent, such as the Conventicle Act, which banned religious meetings of more than five persons on pain of heavy fines, and the Five Mile Act, which restricted dissenters' freedom of movement. These were collectively labelled the Clarendon Code, though Clarendon himself was not the inspiration behind them.

How afraid of rebellion were Gloucestershire men? The existing evidence does not amount to very much. The only report of actual trouble came (probably) in January 1661, in a long, garbled letter by one James Long, wherein it was reported, amid other news, that 'Lord Herbert is active in Gloucestershire; the gates of Gloucester were shut, because the sectaries of the forest flocked in so fast.'[26]

There was another scare in November, after a letter from Thomas Jeynes to William Neast was intercepted, the cryptic language of which convinced a Worcestershire deputy lieutenant that there was a plot in it, possibly connected to other letters to old republicans in the region. Within days stories were abroad of men being arrested carrying 'fire balls' and of a design to burn Worcester. The panic spread to Gloucester and Bristol. Herbert, Howe, Fettiplace and others went to Gloucester to put the city in order, and thus 'hindered the fanaticks intention of securinge Gloster and burning it' – a rather unlikely aim, one would have thought![27]

This was the last time that there is any evidence of panic about sectarian revolt. In October 1663, after the discovery of the Northern Rising which supposedly targeted Bristol and Gloucester among cities to be secured by the plotters' (probably non-existent) southern allies, there was another flurry of security measures which yielded little more than a few books and a letter which spoke of thirty men 'engaged' in Stapleton.[28]

Attention was soon distracted from this to Bishop Nicholson's personal *bête noire*, when some pamphlets by Ralph Wallis, the famous 'cobbler of Gloucester', now living in Clapham, were discovered being handed to the carrier. The book in question, *More news from Rome, or Magna Charta*, was an entertaining sneer at 'popish' church ceremonies, combined with scatological

[25] Ibid. TBR A1/3, fos 6, 14–v, 71v.
[26] Long to Robert Long, 19 Jan. [1661?], *CSPD 1660–1*, 478.
[27] Henry Coker to Secretary Nicholas, 20 Nov. 1661, Anne Ba[ll] to Mr Sparry and to Andrew Yarrington, undated, SP 29/44/69–69i, 83–83ii.
[28] Nathaniel Cale to Williamson, 19 Dec. 1663–4, *CSPD 1663–4*, 287, 289, 297, 300, 381–2.

stories about local clerics. Nicholson was worried that Wallis had been able to sell it openly in the streets of Cirencester, Stow and Gloucester, where it was well received 'by a people [tha]t love to make [the]m selves merry with such stuffe', but in the event he and Alderman Wagstaffe hounded Wallis out of Gloucester easily enough.[29]

Little has survived of the dissenters' records, with the exception of the Quakers. Their records support this impression of a spate of anti-dissenter hysteria in 1660–2 which tapered off thereafter. The Restoration brought a flurry of persecution in the form of fines, imprisonment and disrupted meetings, particularly at Cirencester, Nailsworth, Tetbury and in and around Gloucester. However, only four more instances of persecution were recorded between 1663 and 1670.

The intensity of persecution depended very much on individual initiative – the only JPs recorded as persecutors in the 1660s were Lowe and John Guise; Overbury made plain his distaste for imprisoning men for refusing to swear against their conscience. Indeed, in the *Life* of John Roberts of Siddington, Bishop Nicholson appears as a rather sympathetic character, who regarded the Quakers with bemused tolerance and protected Roberts as best he could. The real villains were greedy priests and thuggish underlings. By the late 1660s, if not before, Nicholson had come to believe in comprehension within the Church.[30]

This pattern of early enthusiasm gradually declining is somewhat at variance with the pattern of quarter sessions indictments, although the rising tide of persecution at the end of the 1660s is unmistakeable. Between Epiphany 1661 and Epiphany 1669, there were seventy-seven presentments of 218 people, mostly for not attending church, though some for various other acts profaning the Sabbath. Hardly any occurred before Easter 1664, but they build up gradually thereafter. The indictment book is a problematic source, as the formulae used do not distinguish between those who were absent at a conventicle and the irreligious or apathetic. However, the nineteen inhabitants of Cirencester presented in the single largest indictment, in 1669, were definitely Quakers.[31]

Nicholson also grew concerned about conventicles in the late 1660s. In August 1669 he wrote to Herbert (now earl of Worcester) and seven JPs in Berkeley Division, asking them to act forcefully because dissenters were holding conventicles in Hawkesbury and Dursley deaneries 'in greater numbers and more dareing then formerly'. In ten of the twenty parishes he named it was only a matter of a few diehards, but in some there was a major problem:

[29] Ibid. 440, 446, 486, 623; 1664–5, 8, 19, 69; Bodl. Lib., Gough Clouc. 32 (6), R. Wallis, *More news from Rome or Magna Charta*, London 1666; ibid. Pamph. C125 (7), R. Wallis, *Room for the cobler of Gloucester and his wife*, London 1668, 29; SP 29/118, fo. 32.

[30] 'First publishers', 109; *Early Quaker letters*, 529; Besse, *Sufferings*, i. 210–16; Hutton, *Restoration*, 266.

[31] GRO, QSIB 1, fos 177v–80 and passim.

300 Presbyterians met at Marshfield, almost the entire parish of Iron Acton went to conventicles at Rangeworthy, and over fifty attended them in both Pucklechurch and Frampton Cotterell. One group of 300 at Wotton-under-Edge twice openly defied Lowe's orders to disperse in January 1670.[32]

The Compton Census of 1676 shows that although Stow deanery had the highest proportion of dissenters per head of the population, at 7.55 per cent, largely due to the survival of a congregation at Bourton-on-the-Water, Hawkesbury did indeed contain the largest numbers of dissenters, though not on the scale of the meetings encountered by Smyth and Lowe; for instance there were only fourteen nonconformists to 1,713 conformists at Wotton. Dissent was rather thinner in the Cotswolds and the Vales of Gloucester and Evesham, and it was very rare indeed in Gloucester and the Forest.[33]

Nicholson was right, then, to identify the south as a problem area, but he may not have realised the true scale and nature of the problem. Well before 1670, the Quakers were organised on a county-wide basis for mutual aid and quasi-ecclesiastical discipline. The monthly meetings were still based at Frenchay for the south, Nailsworth (also covering Cirencester and Tetbury), Gloucester and Tewkesbury. It was in 1670, in George Fox's presence, that eighteen rules were laid down for governing the congregations, ranging from the disciplining of immoral or wayward members, to the buying of burial grounds and registers.

The evidence of charitable donations, and the distribution of births, marriages and deaths recorded since 1656, suggest very strongly that the Quakers' numbers and wealth in 1670 were where they always had been, in the south, particularly in Winterbourne and Olveston. Only Nailsworth and Cirencester were on a par with any of the southern meetings; the Gloucester and Tewkesbury meetings were slightly smaller, but very small indeed relative to the size of the towns. Most of those around Gloucester and Tewkesbury and in the Cotswolds were both small and poor.[34]

Besse and Daniel Roberts agree in portraying a rising tide of anti-Quaker feeling from 1670 to match Nicholson's general concern. The cue for this was perhaps the passing of the Second Conventicle Act, which Parliament wrung out of the king, when many MPs had become alienated by his deceitful behaviour. Active persecution in Gloucestershire came from a new generation of JPs, such as Thomas Master, William Bourchier and the royalist zealots in the Gloucester corporation. And yet, apart from the distraint of some cattle at Olveston and Winterbourne in 1670, the main thrust of persecution was not against the areas of the Quakers' true strength but, once again, in the Cirencester and Gloucester areas. So it continued, sporadically, throughout the decade. Although persecution may have worked where it was concentrated, for several small congregations did go under in the late 1670s, it could

[32] BL, MS Add. 33, 589, fos 69, 75, 78–78v.
[33] Compton Census, 428–45.
[34] GRO, D1340 A1/M1, fos 1v, 4–5v, 8–17 and passim; A1/R1, R2, R3 passim.

not wholly succeed where it was so reliant on individual initiatives by JPs to coerce large numbers of the recalcitrant.[35]

Finally, what of the survival of dissent in general? In 1672 Charles II tried to make a decisive break with the Anglican exclusivists in Parliament by issuing a Declaration of Indulgence, by which Presbyterian, Congregational and Baptist groups could apply for licences to practise their faiths at specified places.

An examination of the distribution of licences in Gloucestershire and of Quaker meeting houses in 1670 (see Map 5) [36] seems to show that the Quakers were more numerous than the rest, although this was not necessarily true. The Baptists were numerically weak, but as well as the four licensed meetings there were also dwindling groups at Gloucester, Framilode and Wheatenhurst in 1674, which we know about because of their begging letters to their Bristol brethren. These did not bother to apply for a licence, although Horton, which was in no better shape, did.[37]

With this reservation in mind, Map 5 does hint at considerable survival of meetings since the 1650s. Presbyterianism was still in the old Puritan heartland in the Vale, but there was also a surprising growth on the fringes of Dean, which was not reflected in the Compton Census four years later. It may have been more extensive than these records show. For instance, no meeting houses were licensed at Dursley, but depite that parish's fulsome Royalism in 1660, Nicholson's secretary later groused 'That all the Dogs, Pigs, Cats, Rats, Mice, Fleas and Lice in Dursly were Presbyterian'.[38]

It has been suggested that in general Presbyterian and Independent groups tended to merge into each after the Restoration. This would make practical sense, and many of the issues which had divided them were no longer relevant. But other than in the case of the former minister of Longhope, Thomas Smith, who was licensed as a Congregational there and a Presbyterian in Huntley, this does not seem to have happened in Gloucestershire. Congregationalism largely maintained its Interregnum geography, being centred in Gloucester, the north and Tewkesbury. Among those licensed in 1672 were Forbes at Gloucester and Stinchcombe, Harris at Painswick and Tray, still at Oddington, among a total of fifteen previously ejected ministers.[39] This is an impressive tribute to the survival of dissent and to the ineffectiveness of spasmodic persecution.

Coincidentally, crisis also loomed at Gloucester in the early 1670s. Lack of space prevents any examination in depth of an incident which, though

35 Besse, *Sufferings*, i. 216–18; Roberts, *Life of John Roberts*, 42–8; GRO, D1340, A1/M1, passim.

36 *Original records of early nonconformity under persecution and indulgence*, ed. G. Lyon Turner, London 1914, 815–25; GRO, D968.

37 *Broadmead records*, 296–310.

38 Wallis, *Room for the cobler of Gloucester*, 30.

39 *Original records*, 815–25.

Map 5
The distribution of dissent, 1670–2

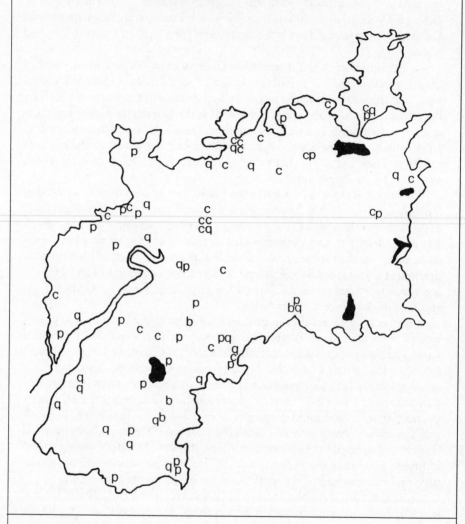

Key:

p – Presbyterian licensed, 1672

c – Congregationalist licensed, 1672

b – Baptist licensed, 1672

q – Quaker meeting place, 1670

interesting, was peripheral to the mainstream of county life.[40] Certain points, however, are worthy of note. The problem was rooted in the reshaping of the corporation, which thrust city government on men who did not have the customary years of preparation or the wealth to sustain their status. Meetings were few and their proceedings inconsequential; office was viewed increasingly as a burden to be avoided and, between 1666 and 1668, an alarming number of nominees chose to pay a fine rather than serve in office.[41]

Although Morton, the recorder, blamed 'A Presbyterian party headed by a discontented cavalier', the contending groups were both the product of the changes of 1662–3.[42] The 'loyal' party was headed by John Wagstaffe and Henry Fowler, who were raised from the dust in 1662–3, but then so were their main antagonists, Robert Fielding and Anthony Arnold. All the aldermen advanced in the late 1660s, however, were of the 'adverse' party, as was the survivor from the Interregnum, James Stephens. From the many close votes recorded, it is clear that neither had an absolute majority and that the votes of non-partisans had to be wooed.

The conflict rumbled in the late 1660s as the commissioners' favourites, Ockold and Wagstaffe, served in turn as mayor from 1668 to 1670. It exploded in October 1670, when the 'adverse' party tried to block the election of Fowler, who was probably already intriguing to have his enemies removed. In this instance, though, Fowler was in the right for he was next in line of seniority, and after Morton had procured a letter from the Privy Council to order that he be elected, the common council complied, with only five aldermen dissenting.

Fowler was an ostentatious, self-aggrandising loyalist, and as mayor he took down the insignia erected at the Southgate after the siege, 'A city assaulted by man but saved by God', as a symbol of rebellion. Moreover, he had Fielding disenfranchised, after another close vote, for a technical violation of the liberties of the mercers' company, and brought in as his replacement a local gentleman, Henry Norwood of Leckhampton. The intention was that Norwood should fine for his shrievalty and succeed Fowler as mayor.[43]

Fowler's actions were undoubtedly a violation of the city's customs, and Arnold's group fought back. With Fowler's party away at a service in the cathedral on election day, 4 October 1671, they hastily convened a meeting and elected as mayor William Bubb, who was next in line of seniority. There were violent scuffles as Fowler and Wagstaffe returned to elect Norwood, but Fowler managed to escape with the mace and sword, and so continued as mayor. The common council was split, with a narrow majority for Bubb, but Fowler

---

40 A. R. Warmington, ' "Madd, bedlam madd": an incident in Gloucester's seventeenth-century municipal history reconsidered', *TBGAS* cxi (1993), 165–73.

41 VCH, *Glos.*, iv. 375; GRO, GBR B3/3, fos 312–15, 334, 351–5, 363–5, 376–7, 382.

42 Morton to Williamson, 3 Sept. 1670, *CSPD* 1670, 419.

43 GRO, GBR B3/3, fos 446, 450, 473, 478, 483; *CSPD* 1670, 419, 428, 431, 448; 1671, 411–12, 419–20, 429.

held all the aces, for the information reaching the king, from him, Morton, Dean Vyner and Bishop Nicholson, was all one-way. Charles determined that the charter should be surrendered, and city government was in abeyance for eight months while Worcester and the Privy Council thrashed matters out in London.[44]

The new charter was a fatal blow to Gloucester's independence. Twenty members were removed, including eight aldermen. Of these, sixteen had supported Bubb's election, though two had opposed it.[45] Most unusually, the new common council was named in the charter, with Norwood as mayor, and four country gentlemen with no real connection to the city as aldermen: William Cooke, Duncombe Colchester, Henry Brett and William Selwyn. They each served as mayor in that order with the exception of Brett who died in 1674. Three were raised from the common council to make up the numbers. A succession of reliable mayors was ensured by inserting the purge survivors, William Russell, Thomas Price, Wagstaffe and Fowler, above these three, even though, according to the seniority principle, those men, who had already served once, should have waited until after the new men.[46]

Gloucester's parliamentary elections thereafter were not tame, but the party heats that occurred were entirely within the framework of gentry domination. The new order was exemplified as early as 1675, in a fiercely contested by-election fought between Norwood and Cooke after Massey's death.[47] Given the existence of two evenly balanced factions tearing each other apart and civic rule by men ill-equipped to bear the burden, the logical solution was either to recall the old Puritan mercantile elite or to call in the gentry. Norwood and the other gentry were reaping what Herbert and his commissioners had sown in 1662 and 1663, so in a way they now accepted responsibility for the consequences of that purge. They were also taking the prestige and power involved and reserving seats in Parliament for themselves.

In reality, the conflict of 1670–2 was shadow-boxing, because the government and the gentry already had the power to emasculate Gloucester at will. The 'loyal' party won the battle because they were able to portray themselves as such. And although Fielding's group opened hostilities, the real violators of Gloucester's traditions were Henry Fowler and Sir William Morton, who exploited their court contacts, promoted outsiders into the corporation and deliberately provoked their enemies into acting in a way which must cause their downfall.

[44] Ibid. 521–2, 531, 542; 1671–2, 24; GRO, GBR B3/3, fo. 347.
[45] P. J. G. Ripley, 'The city of Gloucester, 1660–1740', unpubl. M.Litt. diss. Bristol 1977, 187.
[46] GRO, GBR B3/3, fo. 498; VCH, Glos., v. 378.
[47] BL, LR 305(a) 7(7), The case of Mr William Cooke, n.p. 1675.

Carriers and chimneys: relations with central government

Various other issues were also at stake which were of continuous concern to the county as a whole, and which had their origins in the aims and interests of the regime and its servants as much as within the county itself. There was much continuity in policy with the Interregnum regimes. Charles II, like Cromwell, aimed to stamp out the growing of tobacco and to profit from his jurisdiction over the Forest of Dean. The county's other woodland, Kingswood Chase, also became a matter of interest, and a wealth of material survives relating to the collection of taxes. None of these were affairs of great importance or national security, yet they are worthy of consideration precisely because they were small parts in the jigsaw of national government.

The Convention Parliament lost no time prohibiting the cultivation of tobacco in England. This time there was no question but that pressure from the Virginia merchants was responsible. Late in 1660, they obtained an act banning the crop. The reasons cited were the importance of tobacco to the colonies and to English navigation, the inferior quality of English tobacco and the loss of customs revenue. It prescribed fines of 40s. per rod or pole of ground planted after 1 January 1661 and £5 for any who resisted the destruction of the crop, requiring all local officials to assist within ten days of being informed.[48] The regime tried harder than Cromwell had to involve the local community in the suppression of tobacco, and some responded. With an enthusiastic sheriff, like Sir Humphrey Hooke in 1661–2 and Sir Richard Cocks in 1667–8, good results could be obtained. At the Easter quarter sessions of 1664, orders were sent out to constables to cut down and destroy the crop, and over the next three sessions eight officials from Tewkesbury, Cheltenham and Prestbury were indicted for failing to do so.[49]

By 1667, in the face of annual complaints from the customs farmers, troops had to be used again. As a later note mentions the loss of a number of the Horse Guards' armour pieces in service of Winchcombe, it seems that the planters gave as good as they got.[50] Once again, military action without local support was ineffective. Part of the problem was that the act only required officials to take steps when specific complaint was made. More importantly, in the Tewkesbury area at least, there was 'scarce one of the Justices but on their land tob[acco] is planted', including the sheriff and Bishop Nicholson.

In August, the JPs were ordered to destroy all tobacco immediately on being informed of its existence. It was also suggested that the assize judges should charge the Grand Jury to present full details so that procedures could be tightened, and that the king should commission deputies with wide powers of entry, even that a proclamation be made against unlicensed buying and selling

---

[48] CJ viii. 179; CSPD 1660–1, 518; *Statutes of the realm*, 12 Car. II c.34.
[49] CSPD 1661–2, 602; CTB ii. 225, 338; iii. 998, 1314; GRO, QSIB 1, fos 49v, 54–v, 62, 65.
[50] CTB ii. 42, 59; iii. 428, 1025; CSPD 1667, 399; 1670, 321.

of tobacco. As a result, a new act was passed in in 1671, requiring JPs to issue warrants to constables and others to make full returns at quarter sessions of all tobacco growing in their parishes. Once filed by the clerk of the peace, such reports would be sufficient proof in law to convict the grower unless he prosecuted a traverse at the next sessions. Any constables, other officials or any who refused to assist in the destruction on demand was to forfeit 5s. for each offence.[51]

However, even the most generous provision for informers and involving local auxiliaries could not counter the dead weight of local opposition. More people who mattered had an interest in cultivating than in destroying tobacco in Gloucestershire. Annual complaints were made, orders issued and troops sent up to the late 1680s, but tobacco continued to be cultivated until growing public preference for Virginian leaf finally killed off English competition towards the end of the century.[52]

The Forest of Dean was another testing place for the regime. Here there were more claimants on the government's favour than elsewhere and not enough resources with which to reward them. There was a fine balance between rewarding old servants and making the Forest profitable. In 1660 a commission headed by Herbert, as Constable of St Briavel's, and including both Throck- mortons and both Cookes, recommended the resumption of all previous grants and the continuation of direct management. Likewise the commission of 1662, which included Wade, suggested that 4,000 acres be set aside for the inhabi- tants and 14,000 enclosed to supply the navy and ironworks on a fourteen-year rotation.[53]

But the government did not have a free hand. Many claimants had to be satisfied or bought out. Some were rejected and the inhabitants' role in restoring Charles was ignored, but Wintour and Throckmorton could not be overlooked. Wintour had lost £15,000 fighting for Charles I, and he had serious long-term debts, though he had managed to keep his estates intact by sales to his agents. To give up the bargain of 1640, he received £30,000, his nominees were granted the two remaining state ironworks for eleven years, and he was licensed to take 30,133 timber trees, reserving 11,335 tons of timber for the Navy. Throckmorton received a sub-lease from him of 805 cords of woods at 10s. each and the iron produced from 2,570 more cords.[54]

This settlement gave Wintour considerable scope to do more damage to the woods, but, as it was observed on his behalf, no one would enclose and defend a large area against popular hostility and it was worth less to him than the bargain of 1640. In the event, though, the freeholders' demands were modest enough and opposition was conducted in the Exchequer. Setting aside plots

---

[51] SP 29/212, fo. 108; *Statutes of the realm*, 22 & 23 Car. II c.26.
[52] Thirsk, 'New crops', 281.
[53] Hart, *Royal forest*, 154–7; Hammersley, 'Iron industry', 241–2.
[54] CTB i. 66, 256; Hammersley, 'Iron industry', 243–6; Hart, *Royal forest*, 153–8.

for the poor of each parish may also have soothed matters. In any case, the riot-prone elements had already been driven out by Wade and scarcely any cottagers remained.[55]

Thus ended the state ironworks. Furzer remained in Dean as shipwright and purveyor of timber. On 29 August 1660, the much-delayed *Princess* was finally launched. After some months trapped in Lydney by the wind and lack of supplies, she was finally brought down to King's Road in January 1661, and Furzer dispatched the *Elias* with a cargo of timber and iron. Removing one part of the project simplified matters, though it also meant that Furzer now had to go to Bristol for money. In practice, he was as short of money as Wade before him and he spent much of 1660 and early 1661 reminding the Navy Commissioners of his situation.[56] In May 1662 cutting was grinding to a halt. It seems that a decision was made to build no more ships, for Furzer twice asked the Navy Commissioners what to do with the yard. The business of purveying timber went smoothly at first, and in 1662 the *Elias* and the *Fortune* both sailed fully laden, but no more was shipped until 1664.[57] By then, Furzer was encountering the hostility of the county.

Land carriage proved to be the point at which local tolerance of the project ended. It seems a trivial issue, but the statute under which JPs were required to press men and carts to carry timber for the Navy was passed specifically to replace the hated royal right of Purveyance. Under the statute, carriages with sufficient horses or oxen could be pressed into service for hauling duties as specified in any warrant from the naval authorities to two local JPs. Furzer could not employ enough men for the seasonal job of hauling timber to Lydney, and he relied on the JPs to issue warrants to constables to conscript local men and plough teams. They were supposed to be paid 12*d.* per mile for this, but Furzer could not always pay and, in any case, the inconvenience was resented by the inhabitants.[58]

Furzer's dependence on the local gentry was emphasised when he needed their help in inspecting damage and employing guards to save timber in the aftermath of a great storm which destroyed 3,000 oaks and beeches in February 1662. With such a vast windfall in urgent need of carriage, and the business slowed down by Wintour's claim to the bark, Furzer complained for the first time of the carriers' 'backwardness' in June, and he asked that warrants be directed to Berrow and the younger Throckmorton, the nearest JPs.[59]

Summer drew on, the carriers went home for harvest work and Furzer spent his time going to and fro between JPs and constables, then 'uppon their delay

[55] *True narrative*, 6 and passim; Hart, *Royal forest*, 155–7; PRO, E112/565/555, 556, 557, 597; E112/569/1171.
[56] CSPD 1660, passim; 1660–1, 592; Furzer to Navy Commissioners, 10 Sept. 1660, SP 29/14, fo. 80.
[57] SP 29/55, fo. 10; SP 29/57, fo. 26; SP 29/21, fo. 7; SP 29/52, fo. 9; Hart, *Royal forest*, 158–9, 162–3.
[58] *Statutes of the realm*, 14 Car. II c.20.
[59] Furzer to Navy Commissioners, 3 Mar., 11 June 1662, SP 29/52, fo. 9; SP 29/56, fo. 46.

to the Justices Againe as far as bristoll for warrants to bringe both Constables and carriers before the Justices'. Attempts to rectify this by extending the warrant to Herefordshire came to nothing, as the local JPs interpreted the warrant so pedantically as to make their contribution worthless. When Furzer called a meeting over land carriage in September, no JPs turned up.[60]

By spring 1664, when the season for carriage drew near, a large quantity of timber lay squared in the forest, ready to be taken to Lydney for transportation to Portsmouth on the *Augustine*. The issue became whether parishes on both sides of the Severn or just the Forest were comprehended in the statutory requirement for all parishes within twelve miles of Lydney, the lading place, to supply carriage. The Severn's configuration meant that some parts of Whitstone and Berkeley Hundreds were nearer than parts of the Forest to Lydney, and the river could be forded by plough teams. John Smyth took up the cause of 'his side Severn' at law at some stage before October 1663, when he told Furzer that he must continue to find carriage from the Forest side.[61]

During 1664 Furzer continued to rely on the Forest side, but it proved difficult and sometimes impossible, for lack of JPs to issue warrants. The *Augustine* finally sailed in August, but when it arrived in Portsmouth, the commissioners were very displeased with the quality of the aged timber from Wintour's concession. This incident did at least serve to focus some overdue attention on Wintour's depredations in the Commons, although all the bills, orders and reports produced no tangible results for years.[62]

The battle intensified. As the nation slid ill-prepared into the Second Dutch War, it was decided to build another frigate in the Forest. However, Lydney pill had become so silted up that Furzer had to shift his operations to Conpill, in Tidenham, three miles downriver. Conpill was more convenient for building and tallowing ships, but the distance from the Forest made carriage that much greater a burden. Leaving Lydney also involved undignified haggling with Wintour over rent for the yard and damage done in lading ships, as well as the problem of selling large stocks of offal timber which, in the 1650s, might have gone straight to the ironworks.[63]

Despite the reissue of carriage warrants in October 1664 and a letter from the Privy Council, 280 loads of timber were still unmoved in December. Furzer decided to see the JPs at Gloucester on 21 December, where they had gathered to elect a new MP, the elder Throckmorton having died in June. There, however, 'I found noe great Incouragement from them about Carriage but rather a contest about, those of the other side Severne pleading by the river being in betweene they are free from carriage.' Hale refused to pass an opinion

[60] Furzer to Navy Commissioners, 18 Aug., 29 Sept., 11 Oct. 1662, SP 29/58, fo. 58; SP 29/60, fo. 35; SP 29/61, fo. 31.

[61] SP 29/67, fo. 92; Smyth to Furzer, 5 Oct. 1663, Smyth of Nibley papers, xii. 24.

[62] Furzer to Navy Commissioners, 13 Apr. 1664, SP 29/71, fo. 63; CSPD 1663–4, 194, 257, 348, 371, 532; Hart, *Royal forest*, 159–60.

[63] Furzer to Navy Commissioners, 17 Oct., 14 Nov. 1664, SP 29/103, fo. 76; SP 29/104, fo. 97; CSPD 1664–5, 55, 67, 92, 107.

and the Forest JPs, led by the younger Throckmorton, said they would not continue until the others shared the burden.[64]

This was, then, a genuinely triangular conflict between a government agent and two sections of the county. The by-election was portrayed to the world, in a private letter of Herbert to the earl of Elgin, and in the press, as 'the first (except in the times of the usurpation when few were prevailed, fewer to be chosen and the county had more knights) that ever was in the memory of man without opposition'. The younger Throckmorton, both said, was elected without opposition and to universal satisfaction. It was not for want of trying. Smyth, almost certainly in connection with the carriage controversy, had attempted to promote Overbury's candidature, but was left high and dry when he declined to stand.[65]

For some reason, Furzer did not report all the events of that day until a year later when he had been provoked beyond endurance. Smyth had at first refused to accept the letter from the Privy Council, and Furzer eventually pressed it on Herbert, who handed it to Smyth, Throckmorton and Colchester in turn to read. He toured their homes afterwards, but Throckmorton and Colchester palmed the matter off on Smyth, as the current chairman of the bench, because the warrant was not directed to any particular JP. Smyth himself denied receiving a previous warrant and blustered that at least he did not take money for opposing Furzer, unlike 'Mr Stephens of Lippet'. The most outrageous statement, however, came from Throckmorton, now an MP with responsibility for voting taxes to finance a war demanded by public opinion. He said that 'there was no need of building more ships; the King had ships enough'.[66] Within two years, the Dutch had sailed up the Medway, left the king with nowhere near ships enough, and forced him to make peace.

Gloucestershire's contribution to the war effort was small, and such episodes were insignificant in themselves, but if they were typical of the behaviour of local elites, it is no wonder the war went so badly. Furzer spent much of 1665 at Lydney and Bristol, fitting out a forge, buying anchors and keeping a worried eye on the progress of the two frigates being built by Baylie.[67] But by October 1665 land carriage again headed the agenda. Smyth and the Vale JPs continued to 'looke uppon it as a very slite matter', defying warrants from Forest JPs and letters from the Privy Council until the Forest JPs said 'that unles the other side carry as well as they, these will carry no more'. Unable to pay off his men for want of money or to give them work for want of timber when 180 loads awaited carriage in the forest, Furzer reported Smyth to the Navy Commissioners, revealing full details of his conduct in January. They in turn procured

---

64 Ibid. 7, 159; Furzer to Navy Commissioners, 2 Jan. 1665, SP 29/110, fo. 6.
65 Herbert to Elgin, 2 Jan. 1665, HMC, 15th report appendix, part vii (MSS of the marquis of Aylesbury), 174; BL, Burney 62A, The intelligencer, no. 101, 26 Dec. 1664; Overbury to Smyth, 25 June 1664, Smyth of Nibley papers, xii. 26.
66 Furzer to Navy Commissioners, 9 Dec. 1665, SP 29/138, fo. 78.
67 CSPD 1664–5, passim.

an angry letter from the Privy Council, who summoned Smyth to appear before them.[68]

Smyth was not idle either, for he wrote to Wintour, who was still secretary to the queen mother. Wintour wrote back on 7 December to tell him what to expect when he appeared, and to advise him to come to court at Oxford immediately. Smyth also cultivated his court contacts with the traditional Gloucestershire gifts of lamprey pies and cider. His intrigues evidently outweighed the anger of the Navy Commissioners, for he got his wish for a trial of whether oxen and waggons could cross the Severn at the next assizes. On 9 January 1666 he summoned representatives of all owners of plough in Whitstone Hundred to meet him and Stephen Fowler of Stonehouse to organise their defence. Meanwhile, Throckmorton refused to act, on the excuse that the warrants named Lydney and not Conpill as the destination for the timber, and the business stood still.[69]

The assizes took place on 4 April, prior to which Smyth's ally, Richard Stephens of Eastington, had sent a servant to attend the judges at Hereford lest Throckmorton attempt to pre-empt the issue there. Both sides put their case in a three-hour argument, then the judges watched a man ford the Severn with a plough team. But, as Furzer feared, this was not the end. Smyth wrote to Sir William Coventry to say the test was invalid as the places actually in contention were not the usual fords for waggons and that fording had hardly ever been possible before the last month, as the river was lower than ever in living memory, and even then grids were needed. He blamed everything on the other side's obstructiveness 'haveinge 10 [plough teams] for one to this side'. Smyth claimed Furzer's support in this, but it is notable that in March an anonymous correspondent tipped Smyth off about a complaint to be made against him in a dispute over the Hearth Tax by 'him that was a wellwisher to mr Furzer's buisnes'.[70] The issue of Gloucestershire's share in national defence was becoming embroiled in squabbles among the gentry.

From now on, the project was more integrated with Baylie's operations at Bristol, which eased Furzer's financial woes, but carriage continued to be a problem, as did the unsuitability of much of the timber for futtocks and floor timbers. Both Baylie and Furzer began to look further afield and were in a more optimistic mood by the end of the year.[71]

Their hopes were dashed as the project gradually fell victim to the paralysis of the war effort. In January 1667 Furzer was beset by creditors and his men

[68] Furzer to Navy Commissioners, 30 Oct. 1665, SP 29/135, fo. 107; CSPD 1665–6, 45, 54, 69; BL, MS Add. 33,589, fo. 29.

[69] Smyth of Nibley Papers, xii. 33–4, Wintour to Smyth, 7 Dec. 1665, 35–7, 41; Furzer to Navy Commissioners, 31 Jan. 1666, SP 29/146, fo. 76.

[70] Stephens to Smyth, 31 Mar. 166[6], Smyth of Nibley papers, xvi. 22; Smyth to Coventry, undated, ibid. xii. 42; Furzer to Navy Commissioners, 6 Apr. 1666, SP 29/153, fo. 37; anonymous to Smyth, 17 Mar. 1666, BL, MS Add. 33,589, fo. 41.

[71] CSPD 1665–6, 420, 570 and passim; 1666–7, 14, 84, 88, 111, 190, 225, 513 and passim; SP 29/170, fo. 24; SP 29/174, fo. 144.

refused to work on until money came. He clung to the planned launch date at Candlemas, if only the JPs would compel the carriage of thirty loads of timber in Dean, including vital beams and knees, which had been lying there for over a year. In the end, he was delayed again and the *St David*, a 638-ton frigate with sixty-four guns, was finally launched on 1 April 1667. Further delayed by repairs and shortage of money, she took no part in the war, having only reached Portsmouth when peace was signed, although she later did good service at Tobago in the Third Dutch War. Meanwhile, the *Princess* had seen action, and both she and the *Forester* remained in service until at least 1670.[72]

This proved the end of the project, as Furzer spent the rest of the year in Bristol. Here, still unpaid, he dodged his creditors and helped Sir John Knight to fit out several ships while the naval bureaucracy collapsed about their ears. At one stage in May, Knight found that it was costing more to keep the *St David* waiting for stores than the stores themselves were worth, when they could be had cheaper in Bristol anyway.[73] It was a fitting postscript.

The project had long diverted attention from other matters of concern in the Forest of Dean. Both Parliaments were concerned with the preservation of naval timber and were suspicious of Wintour as a papist and a known despoiler. In April 1663 a sub-committee was appointed. Their report made harsh criticisms of his patent, which was based solely on the surrender of that of 1641, for granting him almost unlimited power over 18,000 acres of prime forest for eleven years. During this time, they said, he had taken no care to preserve the saplings from damage during felling, which they thought enough to invalidate the grant. They recommended resumption and that the king enclose 14,000 acres for timber. This would ensure a clear profit of £6,257 5s. 4d. per year with proper management.[74]

No doubt the presence of two Throckmortons in succession in the Commons ensured that horror stories against Wintour lost nothing in the telling, and a bill was progressing through when a prorogation effectively killed it. However, Wintour had many friends at court, and the king remained favourable. When a new survey of his 18,000 acres was ordered in July 1665, the result was that Wintour was given a new grant of 8,000 acres and was allowed to manage the other 10,000 as a timber nursery, despite Herbert's fear that the 'numerous, lawless and very stout' inhabitants would riot to defend their common land.[75]

On 1 August 1667 Worcester, Throckmorton and thirteen others were commissioned to survey the state of the 10,000 acres. The return, in December,

---

[72] *CSPD* 1666–7, 547, 564; 1667, 3 and passim; F. H. Harris, 'Lydney ships', *TBGAS* lxv (1945), 243–4.
[73] *CSPD* 1666–7, 106–7 and passim; 1667, passim.
[74] *CJ* viii. 118, 156, 195, 312, 391, 587, 589–90.
[75] Ibid. viii. 528, 532; *CTB* i. 673; Hart, *Royal forest*, 160–1; Herbert to Clarendon, 2 June 1665, *CCSP* v. 490.

was gruesome: only 200 of Wintour's 30,133 trees were standing and barely 1,000 tons of naval timber had been delivered, with 500 more lying squared in the forest. It was standard practice to terminate leases in Dean with an exaggerated account of destruction. However, Wintour himself admitted the figures for naval timber were accurate, and both the Reafforestation Act of 1668 and Samuel Pepys's naval timber survey of 1671 affirmed that very little timber remained outside the Lea Baly. Certainly, Wintour's depressed finances had forced him to mortgage his ironworks and large areas of land to creditors in London, thus further reducing his control of affairs.[76]

The gentry of the Forest area, headed by Worcester and Throckmorton, and supported by the surveyor-general, Sir Charles Harbord, and the Commons, took the offensive in November 1667. They suggested that the best way to preserve timber and satisfy the commoners would be to enclose a third and reafforest the rest, allowing the commoners the rights of pannage and estboot there. Wintour evidently saw the end coming, for he tried to smuggle his iron out, but Throckmorton and Harbord reported this and the stocks were seized.[77]

On 9 May 1668, the Dean Forest (Reafforestation) Act received the king's assent. Largely based on the 1667 proposals and citing as a motive the total destruction of timber in the forest, this enacted that 11,000 acres, including the Lea Baly, should be enclosed as a timber nursery and all common rights extinguished there. It was hoped that the sale of decayed and non-timber trees would finance the fencing. The Forest was reafforested within the 1634 perambulation and the traditional offices were reactivated. Pannage, a right most useful to the indigent poor, was extinguished until 1687. In compensation, the rigours of Forest Law were not to be enforced. The inhabitants were allowed free rein on the lands outside the enclosure, without any need to procure licences to take wood.[78]

In practice, this meant that the Forest was handed back to the propertied inhabitants. The JPs gained the power to regulate felling and at least two had to be present before the enclosure commissioners could act. These men were, in any case, hand picked by Worcester from among the local gentry. Duncombe Colchester and the Cookes became the new verderers, while the regarders consisted of Pyrkes, Goughs, Worgans and other minor gentry of Dean. A mention of rioters pulling down hedges in June 1670 shows that, once again, not everyone was content. The riot was the result of moves towards enclosure, after a swanimote court agreed on a site to plant acorns. As early as July and August 1669, the Treasury remonstrated with the officials in Dean about the destruction of young trees by animals and the colliers' taking of wood, presumably from the enclosed area.[79]

The government evidently saw the act as another means to the end it had

76 CTB ii. 174; Hart, *Royal forest*, 291–7; Hammersley, 'Iron industry', 244–5.
77 CTB ii. 131, 268–70, 275–6, 284, 287, 289, 301; Hart, *Royal forest*, 166.
78 *Statutes of the realm*, 19 & 20 Car. II c.8.
79 CTB ii. 428, 439, 446, 448, 452, 454, 459, 467; iii. 112, 170, 262, 457.

always pursued, that of making Dean profitable through careful management. Despite the chaotic state of the naval administration, it was envisaged that ships should still be built and timber supplied out of Dean. In May 1668 the Privy Council ordered that another third-rate frigate be built there, 140 tons were marked out for another in 1670, and in August 1671 sixty beeches were felled for a ship to be built at Portsmouth.[80] Furzer remained in service in the area for several more years.

However, the idea crumbled in the face of the government's continued inability to pay its way and the stranglehold on Dean's resources that had been granted away. Furzer last met the Gloucestershire JPs in February 1668, and he never returned to the Forest after September. Most of the next two years he spent in Bristol continuing to avoid creditors and repairing assorted ships.[81] In November 1670 he estimated that he was owed £1,465 5s. 5d. for building the St David and fitting out the three other ships at Bristol over the course of several years. It is not clear whether or not he was ever paid, and it is very unlikely that the men who worked on the St David were ever paid. Furzer was redeployed to build and repair ships at Woolwich by March 1671.[82]

With Furzer gone, one half of the 1668 Act remained a dead letter. About 8,500 acres were actually fenced, but Dean ceased to supply naval timber. This was partly the result of a survey of naval timber made there by Samuel Pepys in 1671. He estimated that there were only 5,000 oaks left and of these barely 800 would be any use, few of which would yield knees or beams. 900 loads of squared and 500 of unsquared timber lay rotting on the ground from nobody knew how many years before. Moreover, there remained 'the great charge of conversion, land and water carriage to the place of use, the charge of sending materials from London and other places that cannot be had in these parts and seamen to bring the ship about when built'.[83]

But we should not underestimate the part played by sheer inertia and the resistance of the gentry and freeholders to continued government involvement. After 1669, the Forest almost disappears from the treasury minutes, except when local interests, in the form of Worcester and William Cooke, set the agenda. The main items were the felling of timber to rebuild the Speech House and to repair St Briavel's Castle, for which £200 apiece was allotted from the sale of dotard trees.[84]

Soon after, the local community campaigned on another crucial matter. In 1673 the lease of the king's ironworks to Wintour, which he sublet to two creditors and which was not affected by the reafforestation, expired. Worcester, Colonel Cooke and Throckmorton took up the fight against a proposal to lease them to Viscount Grandison, urging, once again, that they were destructive of

[80] Ibid. iii. 331, 682, 924.
[81] CSPD 1667–8, 232, 579; 1668–9, passim; CTB iii. 535, 543 and passim.
[82] CSPD 1670, 558–9; 1667–8, 349; 1671, passim.
[83] Cited in Hart, Royal forest, 296–7.
[84] CTB iii, passim.

timber. Persistent pressure paid off and, in March 1674, the two remaining furnaces and two forges were sold to Paul Foley, the Shropshire iron magnate, for scrap. The last ironworks of Dean fell victim to the mistaken belief that they were incompatible with the growing of timber trees. It was still possible to supply the Navy out of the Forest, despite all the depredations of recent years. Some coppices were only now growing to maturity. Yet in 1674, rational administration was abandoned and Dean became a 'secret society' once again. The casual destruction of the next century was to prove far worse than anything done by seventy years of iron-founding.[85]

Thus the government's efforts to use Dean and reward a servant were deliberately, if not consciously, thwarted by the gentry, probably with the support of the freeholders. What Dean could contribute in terms of ships, timber or iron was a tiny proportion of the Navy's needs, and the scale of resistance made it more trouble than it was worth. Dean was marginal in terms of national defence, the profits were not enough to justify the time and expense needed. In return for easing out the shipbuilding and timber project, Wintour's concession and the ironworks, the inhabitants conceded the perpetual enclosure of over half of the Forest. But eventually they had their way on every count. The most astonishing symbol of the capitulation was that the duke of York granted to John Smyth the reversion of two lighthouses in Kent 'for his care in the improvement of the Forest of Dean'.[86]

Dean was not the only Gloucestershire woodland to attract attention. Kingswood Chase (or Forest) covered 3,400 acres of the large parishes of Bitton, Mangotsfield and Stapleton and outlying parts of Bristol. Here the crown had certain ill-defined franchises, but the soil belonged to the lords of these manors, notably the Berkeleys of Stoke Gifford, the Newtons of Barrs Court, the Creswickes of Hanham, the Chesters of Almondsbury and the Players of Mangotsfield. They were a litigious lot, constantly at odds over access to the valuable coal seams in the chase – it was common practice to mine under each other's lands – and manorial boundaries were blurred. The mines and quarries in the area had for some time been attracting a burgeoning army of cottagers, whose presence put increasing pressure on the woods.[87]

The government's problem was to make the most of their rights in Kingswood before the mining operations and the growing population destroyed woods and deer alike. This pressure had been mounting for some time, and matters were not helped by the fact that all such offences were automatically pardoned at the Restoration. Because Kingswood lacked Dean's chartered liberties, there was no clear framework in which to act. As with any area in which the king had patronage to dispense, Kingswood was the subject of

85 Hammersley, *Iron industry*, 245–6, 348–57; Hart, *Royal forest*, 173–5.
86 *CSPD 1670*, 572; Hart, *Royal forest*, 171.
87 H. T. Ellacombe, *The history of the parish of Bitton*, Exeter 1881, 178–94; Sharp, *In contempt*, 189–90.

petitions for land and office in 1660. With the crown's franchises worth little more than their nuisance value, it was decided, in October 1661, to give Sir Gilbert Gerard and Sir Nicholas Throckmorton £2,500 to prosecute the crown's interest in the hope that the lords would compound for technical trespasses on crown property and agree to split the soil three ways with king and commoners in return for the disafforestation of Kingswood. This paid off for a while, for in January 1663 Gerrard and Throckmorton were granted £1,500 out of fines arising from the franchises.[88]

By 1665 the younger Baynham Throckmorton, as yet out of luck in Dean, had bought an interest in the office of ranger for the life of the incumbent, Humphrey Hooke. Throckmorton claimed to be acting for the family of his uncle, Sir Nicholas, who had just died heavily in debt. He managed to get treasury policy reversed, for in December 1665 he obtained a grant of the whole chase for £2,500, a nominal £20 annual rent and a composition for the ranger's fee. This change of attitude may have been the result of Lord Treasurer Southampton's report that it would not be worthwhile for the crown to purchase a stake in the soil at any price, however valuable the mines turned out to be.[89]

Throckmorton found the lords 'refractory' about compounding, as they did not believe he could enforce Forest Law, and he asked for a grant of the crown's franchise so that he could do so. He was opposed by many apart from the lords. A Quaker lawyer, Walter Clement of Olveston, said in November 1667 that three deputy lieutenants had released him from gaol, where Throckmorton had sent him for refusing the oath of allegiance, when they found that in reality Throckmorton acted out of malice because Clement opposed him over Kingswood.[90] Ironic that the head of the family of supposed champions of the commoners in Dean should play Wintour's role elsewhere.

Matters came to a head in 1670, when Throckmorton obtained a sixty-year lease. Under this, Kingswood was to be, in practice, reafforested. He was to restock it with deer for the king's hunting, build a lodge and suppress enclosures. On behalf of the lords, Sir John Newton, William Player, Thomas Chester and John Meredith petitioned that this went against all precedent and that Throckmorton was oppressing the commoners.[91] Kingswood rapidly spiralled out of control.

By September 1670, about 800 families were subsisting on the wastes. When Throckmorton and the sheriff's bailiffs came to arrest some miners on a quarter sessions indictment, about 300 or 400 'met at the sound of trumpet and drum in a tumultuous manner' and beat them out, almost killing some in the process. Newton lost no time in milking Throckmorton's plight. He blamed the riot on

88 CSPD 1660–1, 243, 529; 1667–8, 433; 1663–4, 29; CTB i. 293–4, 696.
89 Ibid. iii. 312; i. 696.
90 CSPD 1667–8, 141, 443–4; CTB ii. 133, 136.
91 Ellacombe, Bitton, 201–2; HMC, MSS Cholmondely, 5th Report, part i, appendix (MSS of the Revd H. T. Ellacombe), 324.

Throckmorton's oppression, and the threats and violence of his followers 'some of whom were formerly in the rebellion'. He also implied that Throckmorton, as ranger, was disrupting the inhabitants' peaceful enjoyment of the chase and that he would ruin the poor, threaten Bristol's coal supply and lose the king thousands of pounds.[92]

The self-interest in this complaint was obvious enough, but Newton may have touched a nerve. The government was deeply concerned about Bristol in the wake of corporation faction-fighting and religious riots. In July 1671 a commission was set up to enquire into the state of the chase and about offences committed there with regard to illegal tree-felling, mining, quarrying, building and destruction of game since 1660. This hinted that it was a losing battle. Before long, the crown gave up the unequal struggle. After Throckmorton's death in 1680 brought his long-running suit with Newton to an end, Kingswood was wholly abandoned to the lords and the perennially riotous miners.[93]

Despite the hope that the Restoration would bring 'Peace and no Taxes', the Commons always realised that it would be necessary to give the king suitable financial provision so that he need never resort to the dubious fiscal experiments which had discredited his father's rule. In practice the country came to accept levels of taxation which the pre-war generation would never have tolerated. The financial settlement of 1660 did not at first bring in the yearly target of £1,200,000, but it was not ungenerous. The most valuable part, raising between £300,000 and £400,000 in the early 1660s was the customs, a relatively popular tax with the Commons who did not yet see it as a hindrance to trade.[94] Gloucester had no customs base, and Bristol's was fairly small, with no wider regional significance in terms of crown patronage.

The excise, a wartime innovation of dubious legality, was far more contentious, but for lack of alternatives it survived to become the second major component of the public revenue. Of the £300,000 it raised annually, 90 per cent came from levies on liquor. It was administered through commissioners in London acting through sub-commissioners, usually impoverished ex-Cavaliers, in the shires. In the disputes that the collection of this unpopular and administratively complex tax inevitably engendered, the JPs had a vital role. Any two, other than brewers and maltsters, might determine cases and, although the sub-commissioners also had judicial powers, final appeal was to the quarter sessions, where the bench were unlikely to rule against their colleagues.[95]

---

[92] James Baskerville to Williamson, 12, 14 Sept. 1670, CSPD 1670, 433, 435–6; Newton to Williamson, 14 Sept. 1670, ibid. 443–4.
[93] CTB iii. 911, 1062; Ellacombe, Bitton, 207; R. W. Malcolmson, 'An ungovernable people: the Kingswood colliers in the eighteenth century', in J. Brewer and J. Styles (eds), An ungovernable people, London 1980, 85–127.
[94] C. D. Chandaman, The English public revenue, 1660–1688, Oxford 1975, 9–28.
[95] Ibid. 37–43, 49–55.

With three bad harvests and the teething troubles of a chaotic system, the yield of the excise up to October 1662 was disappointing, and the government decided to farm the tax on a county basis. The Gloucestershire sub-farm was taken by a deserving Cavalier, Colonel Edmund Chamberlain of Maugersbury, for £3,700 per year for three years, Henry Guise and Sir Gabriel Lowe withdrawing rival bids.

As so often, it was found that tax-farming increased the local antipathy to the tax. Early in 1663 Chamberlain complained that, because of the JPs' opposition, it would soon be impossible for him to continue. This reflected administrative problems as much as obstructions. Six JPs, including Smyth and Lowe, retorted that they had acted properly. The bench, chaired by Chamberlain's brother John, had deliberated for three hours before voting to return goods distrained from a Chipping Sodbury man, because Chamberlain had failed to keep a book in which producers could declare their goods, as by statute he should have done. All JPs, they claimed, were 'very forward in firthering the paym[en]t of the duty of Excise'.

This case may not have been the sole issue. In April 1663 Lord Treasurer Southampton reproved the JPs of Gloucestershire and Somerset for failing to help the Bristol farmers track down major frauds by brewers there, and in November 1664 there was violent resistance to Chamberlain's officers in parts of Dean. Smyth later expressed his hatred for the collectors for oppressing the poor, 'like the Egiptian taskmasters to make theyre burthens more heavy'.[96]

For many reasons, the first phase of county farming was not a success. In Bristol, where the controversy merged into other ongoing feuds, the results were quite disastrous. Consolidation of the county farms into blocks improved yields considerably. In 1665, when they were renewed for thirty-three months, Gloucestershire passed out of Chamberlain's sole control and was merged with the far more valuable Bristol sub-farm. The new farm, largely run by London merchants, was a measure of the rising value of the excise generally. Bristol alone had been worth £3,400 per year between 1662 and 1665; the new farm went for £8,000 per year in 1665 and £14,000 per year by 1671 when the Act for an Additional Excise raised rates by up to 50 per cent.[97] The evidence is much thinner after 1665. It seems that popular hostility was directed at the tax itself, rather than its efficiency or the total burden.

The most controversial tax of the day, out of all proportion to its value, was the hearth tax, which was hurriedly voted through Parliament to make up a £300,000 per year shortfall in revenue. From Lady Day 1662, 2s. per year was charged on the owner or occupier of a house for every hearth and stove in it. Although those too poor to pay rates and those worth less than £10 or twenty shillings per year were exempted, this crude property tax weighed heavily on

---

96 CTB i. 426, 517, 626; Smyth of Nibley papers, iii. 43–4; xii. 72. This memorandum was written in 1683.
97 Chandaman, *English public revenue*, 45–7, 55–6; Norrey, 'Restoration regime', 798; CTB i. 434, 482, 639–40, 832–3; iii. 831.

the poor. It was also resented as an intrusion into the home. At first the job of making lists of hearths, collecting the tax and distraining on refusers was entrusted to sheriffs, constables and other local officials, but the result was a dismally low yield, despite an act in 1663 to tighten up procedures. The highly unpopular decision had to be taken, in March 1664, to hand the collection over to professionals.

This made the tax a ground for conflict between centre and locality for the co-operation of local authorities was still vital. Ministers and churchwardens were to certify exemptions and constables and 'substantial' inhabitants were responsible for enforcing the law against those who refused to make proper returns or pay. At the final stage, JPs approved certificates and arbitrated in disputes. These tasks were not easy. Exemptions could be based on poverty or on having two hearths or fewer, which made many cases marginal. Similarly, it was not always clear what forms of hearth were liable; bakers' ovens and smiths' forges were often at issue. There was also a lot of conscious fraud, in the form of the walling up of chimneys and the dividing of houses, and there were instances of corruption among collectors and violence on both sides. In all, there was plenty of scope for resistance, particularly with the support of sympathetic JPs and constables.[98]

Charles II again showed his concern for the welfare of old Cavaliers by making Colonel Thomas Veel of Symondshall county receiver of the tax. Veel had already been granted a series of favours by the king. These scarcely rebuilt his fortunes, but when he died in 1663 his sons Thomas and Nicholas inherited the receivership of the hearth tax.[99] The paucity of early Treasury papers hampers our knowledge, but there was certainly mounting resistance to the tax in Gloucestershire, as in other western counties, by November 1665, when the arrest of twenty-four men was ordered in parishes all over the Vales of Berkeley and Gloucester for abusing Thomas Veel in the course of his duties. In December, the sheriff was among fourteen arrested because of growing arrears.[100]

Then, in 1666, resistance mounted on the Veels' doorstep. On 1 March two of Nicholas Veel's collectors came to blows with householders at Berkeley. The constable detained the collectors on a felony charge, returned the distrained goods and fetched Smyth. Smyth heard the cause at a petty sessions at Wotton-under-Edge. According to the collectors, he returned the distrained goods on the grounds that the collectors had not been there an hour before taking them, and declared that 'the Justices of the peace had power to heare & finally to determine' all disputes concerning the tax. Smyth and Lowe had already been active in the matter. Indeed, later in the month an exasperated collector told a complainant 'you returne & goe to your god Smyth &

98 Chandaman, *English public revenue*, 77–85; L. M. Marshall, 'The levying of the hearth tax, 1662–1688', *EHR* li (1936), 628–46.
99 *CSPD* 1660–1, 46; 1660–70 addenda, 668; *CTB* i. 14–15, 76–7, 436.
100 Ibid. i. 689, 694; PRO, T51/13, 73.

Complaine. But my Lord Chancelour hath couled [sic] him'. It was soon after this that 'a wellwisher to Mr Furzer's buisnes' reported Smyth to the Privy Council.[101]

There were conflicting accounts on both sides. The collectors seem to have become cynical towards deserving cases, and in one instance Nicholas Veel backed them up, in a frosty exchange of notes with Smyth, against allegations of extorting payment, despite his own promise of exemption. Smyth detailed many others of the 'numberless' complaints of the poor, of whom he estimated there were 10,000 within ten miles of Nibley: Veel's men tried to exact all arrears since 1662, charged both owners and occupiers in rented houses, carried swords and pistols to intimidate people, enforced the prescribed double duty even on those who could prove they had stopped up chimneys for genuine reasons before the act of 1664, and habitually broke into houses to distrain even if the owners were easily available, without allowing the constables their two pence in the pound for so doing.[102]

Given the many grey areas in procedure, Smyth's attitude was not outrageous, though it certainly reflected a one-sided view of his duty. Not all his decisions went against collectors, and his letter to Lord Ashley in April 1666, after an appeal from the Veels, shows that his major concern was for the authority of the JPs. He complained that despite a meeting between JPs and collectors to smooth over problems, Nicholas Veel contemptuously ignored restitution orders, claiming over-riding orders from the Privy Council, and saying that 'he was the kings servant and priviledgd from any arrest or question therefore'. As a result, most JPs were refusing to act again until the government had intervened to discipline the Veels.[103]

This was part of a wider crisis. Nationwide, receipts hit new annual lows of £112,500 between Michaelmas 1664 and Lady Day 1666. In desperate need of ready money to fight the war, the government farmed the tax out for seven years, but amid growing hostility in the provinces and in the Commons, the ill-prepared contract collapsed within a year and when it was finally wound up in 1669, it had yielded only £103,000 per year. The winter of 1666–7 was a high point of resistance. Although most of the evidence relates to Berkeley Hundred, other regions were involved. A riot was reported at Winchcombe, and, in January 1667, a petition from the Cirencester blacksmiths prodded the Commons into investigating abuses by collectors.[104]

The hearth tax was not the only problem. Despite the intention to provide for the king through indirect taxes, direct taxation was a roughly equal burden between 1660 and 1668, firstly to pay off the Commonwealth's forces and then to pay for the Second Dutch War. And despite firm intentions to abandon the assessment, a return in 1663 to the preferred formula of subsidy was a failure.

---

101 BL, MS Add. 33,589, fos 38, 41, 43–v, 52–3; Smyth of Nibley papers, i. 41–4.

102 Ibid. i. 41; BL, MS Add. 33,589, fos 50–1.

103 Ibid. fo. 49.

104 Chandaman, English public revenue, 91–5; Marshall, 'Hearth tax', 629, 632–3; CJ ix. 15.

The war was paid for by a 'Royal Aid' for three years from December 1664, supplemented by an 'Additional Aid' for the final two years, two other assessments for a year from December 1667, with a poll tax in January 1667. Gloucestershire's share in the four assessments totalled £136,079 2s. 9d., and Gloucester's was £2,965 13s. 9d.[105]

Over four years when the hearth tax was in crisis and trade disrupted, this was no little burden for society and government alike. In Gloucestershire, problems with all these taxes tended to go together, not least because Nicholas Veel was also collector of the two 'aids'. Again, little early material survives, but Veel clearly did not satisfy the Treasury for in June 1667, he was £4,000 in arrears on the aids and was replaced by another son of a debt-ridden Cavalier, Lawrence Bathurst of Lechlade. Both Veels, amongst many other provincial officers, spent much of the next two years being hauled up before the Treasury, and they were in and out of custody several times.

The arrears were hardly disastrous by contemporary standards, but ready money was desperately short. Nicholas Veel blamed corrupt and incompetent collectors, two of whom, William Lavington in Langley and Swineshead, Henbury and Barton Regis Hundreds and Thomas Davis in Dean, faced questions in 1667 for arrears which were still not fully satisfied in 1672. In fact, there were arrears in almost every part, though these two areas and Upper Kiftsgate Hundred were the worst.[106] Meanwhile, Thomas Veel faced an enquiry into his hearth tax account. One collector had to be threatened with arrest before paying in £1,600 owing from 1666. Not until April 1668 did Thomas secure a stay of the process against him.[107]

In purely fiscal terms, the two aids were a success. But although Bathurst managed to clear up most of the arrears, the combination of delays and continued resistance to the hearth tax ruined the Veels. The Eleven Months' Assessment may have been the proverbial last straw. By May 1670, four months after it lapsed, nearly £12,000, about one third of the total imposed, was uncollected or in the hands of Nicholas Veel and Bathurst. Bathurst also had to juggle the receipts of this tax to make up the £3,877 6s. still outstanding from Veel on the additional aid, and some of this, plus other sums were still owing in the summer of 1671 when an extent was threatened on Veel's lands. In the end, all bar £587 6s. 5d. from six collectors of various taxes dotted all over the county was collected by August 1672.[108] In the interim, though, the government had not received the county's share of the burden when it was most needed.

The hearth tax remained an acute problem. In October 1669, when the tax was in abeyance, the arrears of Anthony Maux's sub-farm stood at £3,747 11s.

---

[105] *Statutes of the realm*, 16 & 17 Car. II c.1; 17 Car. II c.1, c.9; 18 & 19 Car. II c.1; 18 & 19 Car. II c.13.
[106] CTB ii. 20, 26, 173, 185, 295, 395; iii. 1299–1300 and passim; PRO, T51/34, 16.
[107] CTB ii. 58, 66, 71, 79, 542.
[108] Ibid. iii. 72, 571–2, 859–60, 914, 1299–1300.

In May 1670 farming was abandoned and collection resumed, with a Londoner, Nathaniel Whetham, as receiver.[109] Inevitably, the attempt to raise three half-year's collections at once to make up for the missing year sparked off smouldering anger. July saw disputes between collectors and inhabitants at Wotton-under-Edge and probably elsewhere too.

The JPs, headed by Sir William Ducie, wrote to complain of the collectors again ignoring their exemption certificates, charging smiths' furnaces and forges, collecting one sixth more than they should and generally 'alienating the harts of the people'. For good measure they added that the collectors were men of so low 'quality' that they would surely defraud the Treasury. The Treasury Commissioners replied that smiths' forges and furnaces were indeed chargeable and that the collectors would have to make a new return because of the insufficiency of the old. They ended with a pointed reminder to 'distinguish between an injurious proceeding and a vigorous one where the obstinacy of such as ought to pay the duty doth necessitate it'. At some time before February 1672, a letter, probably to the same effect, was sent to the JPs about bakers' ovens.[110]

In the 1670s the hearth tax gradually became more and more productive, though it only approached its full capacity in the 1680s, just before it was abolished. To some extent, though, the JPs who had opposed the Veels' corrupt and arbitrary implementation of the tax had their way. In June 1671 Whetham was removed, having failed to pass his accounts, and was replaced by Christopher Smyth of Nibley. His father, John Smyth, stood surety for him, together with Thomas Veel. It would be too cynical to assume that Smyth had always been angling for this, but there was a nice irony when, in October 1672, Christopher Smyth complained of John George and Henry Powle discharging smiths' forges from the tax.[111]

The nature of the evidence makes it easy to forget that most taxes were paid in full and not very late. Delays and shortfalls probably owed as much to the rudimentary apparatus of collection and corruption as to active obstruction. But these obstructions were significant precisely because they were not to be taken for granted. In the case of the hearth tax in particular, the evidence strongly suggests that, whatever the rights and wrongs of the tax itself, most resistance was consciously fraudulent and not discouraged by the gentry. This was partly out of genuine sympathy for the poor and partly out of fear that their right to interpret the vagaries of statutes and to act as the link and arbitrator between government and people was being infringed by collectors whose sole allegiance was to the government and their own pockets.

A JP could only resist the government to a limited extent. None would

---

109 Chandaman, *English public revenue*, 94–6; CTB iii. 281, 288, 296, 306, 359–60, 386, 532.
110 JPs to Treasury Commissioners (draft), 5 Aug. 1670, BL, MS Add. 33, 589, fos 89–90, 91; CTB iii. 668, Treasury Commissioners to JPs, 1 Oct. 1670., 1031.
111 Ibid. iii. 887, 914, 921, 934, 1106; BL, MS Add. 33,589, fos 93–5.

willingly go so far as to procure their own downfall or to help destabilise a regime of which they all approved in principle. But they made their point. It is not insignificant that in October 1671, not long before Charles II embarked on a desperate gamble in fiscal, religious and foreign policy to break the stranglehold of the Cavalier–Anglican party in the Commons, the Privy Council wrote to the Gloucestershire JPs about the hearth tax for the last time. Abandoning their previous hectoring tone, they disavowed any intention to restrain the exercise of legal powers by the JPs, blamed ministers, church-wardens and overseers for granting too many exemptions and lamely asked the JPs to prevent abuses by examining claims in public at the petty sessions 'for it cannot bee supposed that [th]e Law intends to oblidge the Justices to allow whatsoever shall bee offered to them without examining the truth thereof'.[112] John Smyth must have read those lines with a wry smile.

Between 1660 and 1672, Gloucestershire probably became more of a county community than it had been before the Civil War. Party differences disap-peared as the gentry were reunited into one group which acted together as JPs, deputy lieutenants, assessment commissioners and so forth. This does not mean that faction-fighting was unknown. The gentry of Berkeley and Whitstone Hundreds confronted those of Dean over their respective duties regarding land carriage; those of Dean confronted Wintour over his role there; Newton and others fought against Throckmorton in a similar battle over Kingswood. Different gentlemen had diverging interests in the tobacco issue. Fierce rival-ries persisted, not least over seats in Parliament, but only within the context of consensus support for the regime in Whitehall and the knowledge that gentry rule within the provinces could be taken for granted.

In some ways, the government succeeded where its Interregnum predeces-sors failed. It could appeal to men of many different outlooks, almost all of whom could find some sympathy and support in a court which embraced all kinds of men with all kinds of views, from former Cromwellian soldiers to Cavaliers who had shared Charles's poverty-stricken exile. No one could be absolutely sure of official support, few could wholly despair of it. Political battles could be fought through a number of channels: through Herbert, who was a useful representative of local opinion, through courtiers with local ties, and ultimately through the Treasury and the Privy Council. It is certainly striking how many more Gloucestershire men were in the corridors of power in the 1660s than before: Morton, Sir Robert Atkyns and Hale as jurists, Wintour and Sir William Ducie, a gentleman of the Privy Chamber, and Henry Powle, who was later the Speaker.[113]

But any comparison between Interregnum and Restoration styles of govern-ment must be put in context. There was another side to this 'success'. In

112 Ibid. fo. 96.
113 DNB, s.v. Sir Robert Atkyns, Sir Matthew Hale; GRO, D34A/X6A; Williams, Parlia-mentary history, 62.

Gloucestershire, between 1660 and 1672, the power of the Council in the Marches of Wales was overthrown, Gloucester was stripped of the Inshire and the bulk of her experienced rulers were removed from office, leaving an inadequate, faction-ridden corporation that was again dismantled in 1672 for the gentry to step in, thus destroying her independence and integrating her into county politics.

At the same time, the government's attempts to build ships in Dean were effectively frustrated, as were their attempts to reward a favoured servant from the resources of Dean and to manage it profitably. Both Dean and Kingswood were effectively abandoned to their inhabitants. Other crown nominees were harassed in their attempts to raise taxes, which limped in years late, tobacco continued to grow despite sporadic moves against it, dissent was marginalised but not effectively persecuted. All these things may or may not have made county government more efficient, but the reason why they happened was because the gentry, or to be precise the weight of the gentry who took any opinion in each case, wanted them to happen.

There was a limit to how far local obstruction could defy a powerful government. Many of the actions of the gentry class in Gloucestershire were with official licence, but others went against the king's wishes. In some cases defiant JPs found some support at court, not so much because one or other of the king's ministers wanted to undermine him but because, in the context of national policy, Gloucestershire did not matter very much. Its tax revenue was only a part of a far greater whole – indeed, the single most important part of the revenue was not levied in Gloucestershire at all.

It would have been useful to have been able to build ships at Lydney, but the operation was dwarfed by Chatham and Portsmouth and the return was simply not worth the amount of attention that had to be devoted to it. It would not have come amiss to have profited from Dean and Kingswood, but even the most optimistic estimates of their value amounted to pin money. The colonies might have benefited from tobacco being suppressed in England, but America was far away. And what did it really matter who ruled Gloucester compared to London, or even Bristol?

This is why it is fallacious to assume that a regime's overall success can be measured in terms of the most strategically important areas. No government could possibly overlook the defence of the south coast, nor could the ruling groups there ignore their responsibilities in national defence. The gentry of Gloucestershire, like those of most other counties, one suspects, could easily combine support for the measures of which they approved with selfish and irresponsible behaviour in matters pertaining to their county's share in the burdens of national policy, confident that the government was unlikely to bring the full weight of its disapproval to bear on them.

Bibliography

Unpublished primary sources

Bristol Records Office
36074/136 papers of Thomas Smyth

Cambridge University Library
MS Dd 8.1 *liber pacis*, 1653

Gloucester Public Library
Smyth of Nibley papers, i–v, x–xii, xvi

Gloucestershire Records Office
Family and other collections
D36 Colchester of Westbury-on-Severn
D45 Whitmore of Slaughter
D128, 326 Guise of Elmore
D149 Clifford of Frampton
D225 Berkeley of Berkeley Castle and Veel of Symondshall
D269A Rogers of Dowdeswell
D269B Coxwell of Ablington
D340 Ducie of Frocester and Tortworth
D421 Wintour of Lydney
D547 Stephens of Eastington
D621 Chamberlain of Maugersbury
D979A Daunt of Owlpen
D1340 Quaker Records
D1571 Estcourt of Shipton Moyne
D1844C Newton of Barr's Court
D2071 Borough of Chipping Sodbury
D2510 Smyth of Nibley

Gloucester Borough Records
GBR B3/2, B3/3 Common Council minute books

Tewkesbury Borough Records
TBR A1/2, A1/3 Common Council minute books
A14/2 Indenture, 1656
D2688 Giles Geast charity book

Churchwardens', Vestry and Overseers' Records
P34 CW2/1 Barnsley
P107 CW2/1 Daglingworth
P124 CW2/4 Dursley
P127 CW2/1 Eastington

P154 CW2/7 St Michael's, Gloucester
P154/11 CW2/1–2 St Mary de Crypt, Gloucester
P197 CW2/1 Lechlade
P230 CW2/1 Nibley
P298A OV2/1 Slimbridge
P343 VE2/1 Twining

Diocesan Records
GDR 97, 100, 108, 111, 114, 116 Depositions, 1605–16

Quarter Sesssions Indictment Books
QSIB1 (1661–8)

Miscellanea
CG46, D115, D640, D1867, D2768, EL140, 968

London, British Library
MS Add. 5,494 Sequestration papers
MSS Add. 11,044, 11,055 Scudamore papers
MSS Add. 18,980–2 Prince Rupert's Civil War correspondence
MS Add. 34,012 Major-General Disbrowe's list of suspects, 1655–6
MS Add. 34,014 Suspects travelling to London, 1655–6
MSS Add. 38,588–9 Smyth of Nibley papers
MSS Harleian 477, 480 Sir John More's parliamentary diary
MS Harleian 5013 Survey of crown lands, 1650
MSS Harleian 6,802, 6,804, 6,851–2 Royalist papers
MSS Lansdowne 822–3
MSS Loan 29/174, 29/176, 206 Harley papers
MS Stowe 577 *liber pacis*, 1651–2
Thomason Tracts

London, Public Records Office
ASSI 2/1, 5/1/7 Assize records

Chancery
C3 Chancery cases
C193/12–13 *libri pacis*
C231/5–7 Crown Office docquet books

Exchequer
E112/564, 565, 659, 2383, E113/5/1A Bills and answers against defaulting
accountants
E372/490–506 Exchequer Pipe Rolls, 1645–62
E178/6080 Survey of the Forest of Dean, 1660

State paper office
SP 16 Charles I
SP 18, 25 Interregnum
SP 19 Committee for the Advance of Money
SP 20 Committee for Sequestration
SP 23 Committee for Compounding with Delinquents

SP 24 Committee for Indemnity
SP 28 Assorted Interregnum papers
SP 29 Charles II

Treasury
T51 Treasury papers, 1660–72

Northamptonshire Records Office
MSS Finch-Hatton 133 Commission of Array, 1642

Oxford, Bodleian Library
MS Carte 1
MSS Clarendon 27, 62–3, 68–71
MS Dugdale 19 Docquets passed under the Great Seal at Oxford, 1643–6
MSS Firth C6–C8
MSS Rawlinson A23, A27, A33, A34, A39, A40, D1099
MSS Tanner 51, 57, 59–62, 147, 303
MSS Walker C3, C7

Published primary sources

Offical publications
Acts and ordinances of the Interregnum, ed. C. H. Firth and R. S. Rait, London 1911
Acts of the Privy Council, London 1899–1964
Calendar of the Clarendon state papers, iii, ed. W. D. Macray, Oxford 1876; iv–v, ed. F. J. Routledge, Oxford 1932, 1970
Calendar of the proceedings of the Committee for Advance of Money, ed. M. A. E. Green, London 1888
Calendar of the proceedings of the Committee for Compounding with Delinquents, 1642–1660, ed. M. A. E. Green, London 1892
Calendar of state papers, domestic, ed. M. A. E. Green, London 1867–95
Calendar of state papers, Venetian, xxviii–xxx (1647–72), London 1927–34
Calendar of treasury books, ed. W. A. Shaw, London 1904–8
Clarendon state papers, ed. T. Monkhouse, Oxford 1786
A collection of the state papers of John Thurloe, ed. J. T. Birch, London 1742
Commons journals, ii–ix (1640–72)
Lords journals, iv–x (1640–9)
The statutes of the realm, v, London 1819, repr. 1963

Historical Manuscripts Commission
HMC, 4th Report, MSS House of Lords 1640–1, appendix, part i (MSS Denbigh and De la Warr)
HMC, 5th Report, MSS Cholmondely, part i, appendix (MSS House of Lords and MSS of the Revd H. T. Ellacombe)
HMC, 6th Report, part i, appendix (MSS House of Lords, 1644–7)
HMC, 7th Report, part i, appendix (MSS House of Lords, 1648–65)
HMC, 8th Report, part i (MSS of the duke of Marlborough)
HMC, 9th Report, MSS Salisbury, part xxii

HMC, 12th Report, part ix (records of the corporation of Gloucester)
HMC, 13th Report, appendix, part ii (MSS Portland iv)
HMC, 14th Report, appendix, part i (MSS Portland i)
HMC, 15th Report, appendix, part vii (MSS of the marquis of Aylesbury).

Civil War periodicals from the Thomason Tracts

Certaine informations from severall parts of the kingdom, Feb.–Mar. 1643, Dec. 1643–Oct. 1644
Certaine passages of each dayes intelligence, June 1654
Chief heads of each dayes proceedings in Parliament, May 1645
A continuation of certaine speciall and remarkable passages, February 1643–Apr. 1644
A diary, or an exact journall, Dec. 1644–Jan. 1645
England's memorable accidents, Dec. 1642
An exact and true diurnall, Aug. 1642
The intelligencer, Dec. 1664.
The kingdomes weekly intelligencer, Jan. 1643–Feb. 1649
The kingdoms weekly post, Oct. 1645, Mar. 1648
The London post, Sept. 1644–Jan. 1645
The loyall scout, July–Aug. 1659
Mercurius Anglicus, Jan.–Feb. 1644
Mercurius Aulicus, Jan. 1643–Sept. 1645
Mercurius Aulicus againe, Mar.–Apr. 1647
Mercurius Britannicus, Sept. 1643–Feb. 1646
Mercurius Civicus, Sept. 1643–Oct. 1646
Mercurius Elenthicus, Apr.–Nov. 1648
Mercurius Melancholicus, Sept. 1647–Aug. 1648
Mercurius Militaris, Oct. 1648
Mercurius Politicus, June 1650–Mar. 1660
Mercurius Pragmaticus, Nov. 1647–Dec. 1648
Mercurius Publicus, Dec. 1659–Oct. 1660
Mercurius Rusticus, Jan.–Aug. 1643
Mercurius Veridicus, Jan.–Feb. 1644, Jan. 1645, Mar. 1646.
The moderate, July 1648–Jan. 1649
The moderate intelligencer, Apr. 1645–Aug. 1648
Occurrences of certain speciall and remarkable passages, Feb. 1644
Packets of letters, Oct. 1648
The parliamentary intelligencer, Dec. 1659–May 1660
The Parliament scout, Jan. 1644–Jan. 1645
A perfect diurnall of some passages in Parliament, June 1646–June 1647, July 1648–Jan. 1649, Aug. 1649–Jan. 1650, Oct.–Nov. 1652.
A perfect diurnall of the passages in Parliament, Dec. 1642–Sept. 1643
Perfect occurrences, Apr. 1644, Aug.–Dec. 1646
Perfect occurrences of each dayes iournall in Parliament, Jan.–Aug. 1647
Perfect passages of each dayes proceedings in Parliament, Dec. 1644–Jan. 1645, Feb. 1646
Perfect proceedings of state affairs, Mar.–June 1655
The perfect weekly account, Oct. 1647–Nov. 1648
The publick intelligencer, Dec. 1655–Jan. 1657, Sept 1658–July 1659
The Scottish dove, Dec. 1643–Feb. 1646

Several proceedings in Parliament, Sept. 1652, July–Oct. 1654
Several proceedings of Parliament, Aug. 1653
Several proceedings of state affairs, Apr. 1654
Speciall passages, Dec. 1642–May 1643
The true informer, Oct. 1643–Dec. 1644, Sept.–Nov. 1645
The weekly account, Oct. 1643–Apr. 1645, Feb. 1646, Jan.–Apr. 1647
The weekly intelligencer, Apr.–Oct. 1654, July–Aug. 1659
The weekly post, July 1659–Jan. 1660

Contemporary books and articles

The autobiography of Richard Baxter, ed. N. H. Keeble, London 1974
Autobiography of Thomas Raymond and memoirs of the family of Guise, ed. G. E. Davies (Camden 3rd ser. xxviii 1917)
Bacon, R., *The spirit of prelacie yet working, or truth from under a cloud*, London 1646
Barksdale, C., *The disputation at Winchcombe*, London 1653
———— *The Winchcombe papers revived*, London 1658
Besse, J., *A collection of the sufferings of the people called Quakers*, London 1753
Bibliotheca Gloucestrensis: a collection of scarce and curious tracts relating to the county and city of Gloucester, illustrative of and published during the Civil War, ed. J. Washbourne, London 1823
Bishop, G., *A modest check to part of a scandalous libell*, London [1650]
Blome, R., *Britannia*, London 1673
Bromwich, I., *The spoiles of the Forrest of Deane asserted*, London 1650
Bruce, J., 'Extracts from the accounts of the churchwardens of Minchinhampton', *Archaeologia xxv* (1883)
Burnet, G., *The life and death of Matthew Hale, Kt.*, London 1682
The case of Mr William Cooke, n.p. 1675
A catalogue of the lords, knights and gentlemen that have compounded for their estates, London 1655
Clark, R., *The lying wonders or rather the wonderful lyes*, London 1660
The Clarke papers: selections from the papers of Sir William Clarke, ed. C. H. Firth (Camden ns il, liv, lxi, lxii, 1894–1901)
The committee at Stafford: the order book of the Staffordshire committee, 1643–1645, ed. D. H. Pennington and I. A. Roots, Manchester 1956
The Compton Census of 1676: a critical edition, ed. E. A. O. Whiteman, London 1986
Coppin, R., *Truth's testimony: and a testimony of truth's appearing in power, life, light and glory*, London 1654
Corbet, J., *A vindication of the magistrates and ministers of the city of Gloucester*, London 1646
A declaration concerning his majesties royall person, London 1648
A declaration of the city and county of Gloucester, London 1659
A declaration from the city of Bristol, London 1643
The declaration of Lieutenant Generall Cromwell, London 1648
A declaration of the sufferings of above 140 persons of the people of God . . . called . . . Quakers, London 1659
Defoe, D., *A tour thro' the whole island of Great Britain*, London 1725
Diary of the marches of the Royal Army, ed. C. E. Long (Camden os xxiv, 1859)
Diary of Thomas Burton esquire, ed. J. T. Rutt, London 1828.

Dorney, J., A briefe and exact relation of the most materiall and remarkable passages . . ., London 1644

——— Certain speeches made upon the day of the yearly election of officers in the city of Gloucester, 1653

Dover R., and others, Annalia Dubriensa, London 1635

Early Quaker letters from the Swarthmore MSS to 1660, ed. G. F. Nuttall, London 1952

Eben-Ezer: a full and exact relation of the severall remarkable and victorious proceedings . . . of Colonell Massey, London 1644

England's glory: or an exact catalogue of the lords of His Majestie's most honourable Privy Council, London 1660

Eniantos Terastios: mirabilis annus, or the year of prodigies and wonders, London 1661

'The first publishers of truth', ed. N. H. Penney, London 1907

A full declaration of all particulers concerning the march of the forces under Collonell Fiennes to Bristol . . . also a relation of the late bloody abominable conspiracy against the city of Bristol, London 1643

Fuller, T., The history of the worthies of England, London 1662

The Gloucester-shire ministers testimony to the truth of Jesus Christ and to the Solemne League and Covenant, London 1648

Harman, S., Vox populi or Glostersheres desire, London 1642

Harry Hangman's honour: or, Gloucester-shire hangman's request to the smoakers or tobacconists in London, London 1655

Harris, F., Some queries proposed to the . . . Quakers, London 1655

Harrison, S. E., The Cirencester vestry book in the seventeenth century, Gloucester 1914

Higford, W., Institutions, or advice to a grandson, London 1658

Historical and genealogical memoirs of the Dutton family of Sherborne, privately printed, 1899

Hyde, E., earl of Clarendon, The history of the rebellion and Civil Wars in England, ed. W. D. Macray, Oxford 1969

The illustrated journeys of Celia Fiennes, 1685–c.1712, ed. C. Morris, London 1892

J[essey], H[enry], The Lord's loud call to England, London 1660

The journal of George Fox, ed. N. H. Penney, Cambridge 1911

Journal of Sir Samuel Luke, ed. I. G. Philip (Oxfordshire Record Society xxix, xxxi, xxxiii, 1950–3)

The journal of Sir Simonds d'Ewes, ed. W. H. Coates, New Haven 1970

To the kings most excellent majestie the humble petition of the inhabitants of the county of Gloucester, London 1641

Leigh, E., England described, London 1659

The letter book of John, Viscount Mordaunt, 1658–1660, ed. M. Coate (Camden 3rd ser. lxix, 1945)

The letter books of Sir Samuel Luke, ed. H. G. Tibbutt (Bedfordshire Historical Record Society xlii, 1963)

A letter from an eminent person at Gloucester to a friend in London, London 1660

A letter from the mayor of Bristoll and others, London 1643

A letter from an officer in His Majesty's army to a gentleman in Gloucestershire, Oxford 1643

A letter sent to a worthy member of the House of Commons, concerning the Lord Shandois coming to Cisseter, London 1642

The life of Marmaduke Rawdon of York, ed. R. Davies (Camden os lxxxv, 1923)

The life of Robert Frampton, bishop of Gloucester, ed. T. S. Evans, London 1876

The life and times of Anthony Wood, antiquary, of Oxford, 1632–1695, ed. A. Clark, Oxford 1891

A list of the names of the members, London 1648

The loyal addresse of the gentry of Gloucestershire, n.p. 1660

Matthews, A. G., *Calamy revised*, Oxford 1934

—— *Walker revised*, Oxford 1948

The memoirs of Edward Ludlow . . . , *1625–1672*, ed. C. H. Firth, Oxford 1894

Memoirs of Prince Rupert and the Cavaliers, ed. E. Warburton, London 1849

Memorials of the Great Civil War in England from 1646 to 1652, ed. H. Cary, London 1842

Military memoir of Colonel John Birch, written by Roe, his secretary, ed. J. Webb and T. W. Webb (Camden ns vii, 1873)

Mirabilis annus secundus or, the second year of prodigies, n.p. 1662

Mirabilis annus secundus or, the second part of the second years prodigies, n.p. 1663

Mr Thomas Pury, alderman of Gloucester, his speech, n.p. 1641

The names of the justices of peace in England and Wales . . . this Michaelmas terme 1650

The Nicholas papers, ed. G. F. Warner (Camden n.s. xl, l, lvii; 3rd ser. iv, 1886–97)

Originall letters and papers of state, addressed to Oliver Cromwell, ed. J. Nickolls jr, London 1743

Original records of early nonconformity under persecution and indulgence, ed. G. Lyon Turner, London 1914

Palmer, A., *The gospel new-creature*, London 1658

—— *A scripture rale to the Lord's table*, London 1654

Panarmonia: or, the agreement of the people, n.p. 1659

A perfect relation of all the passages and proceedings of the Marquesse of Hartford, London 1642

A perfect wonder of the phanatick wonders seen in the west of England, n.p. 1660

The petiton of the inhabitants of Cyrencester, Oxford 1643

A petition presented unto His Maiestie at his court at Bristoll on the 7 day of August 1643 by Sir Baynham Throckmorton baronet, Oxford 1643

Powell, W., *Newes for newters*, London 1648

The prisoner's report, Oxford 1643

The private journals of the Long Parliament, 3 January to 5 March 1642, ed. W. H. Coates, A. S. Young and V. F. Snow, New Haven 1982

Reasons inducing the justice in equity of Mr Pury's petition in Parliament, London 1659

The records of a church of Christ meeting in Broadmead, Bristol, 1640–1687, ed. E. B. Underhill, London 1847

Records of early English drama: Cumberland, Westmorland and Gloucestershire, ed. A. Douglas and P. Greenfield, Toronto 1986

A relation from Portsmouth . . . likewise sixteen propositions presented at the generall meeting of the gentry of the county of Gloucester, the 25 and 26 of August 1642, London 1642

A relation of the cruell and unparallel'd oppression . . . , 1647

A relation of a short survey of 26 counties observed in a seven weeks journey begun on August 11 1634, ed. L. G. Wickham Legg, London 1904

A relation of the taking of Cicester, London 1643

The remonstrance of the knights, gentlemen and freeholders of the county of Gloucester, n.p. 1660

Roberts, D., *Some memoirs of the life of John Roberts*, 2nd edn Bristol 1747

The Royalist ordnance papers, ed. I. Roy (Oxfordshire Record Society xliii, 1964)

Rudge, H., J. Adeane, J. Berrow and J. Wade, *Certaine reasons . . . why those iron-works in the Forest of Deane should be in honour and justice of the House speedily demolisht*, London 1650

S[tephens], E[dward], *A letter of advice from a secluded member*, n.p. 1648

The second part of the narrative, n.p. 1648

Secunda pars de comparatis comparandis, London 1648

The severall examinations and confessions of the treacherous conspirators against the citie of Bristoll, London 1643

The Short Parliament (1640) diary of Sir Thomas Aston, ed. J. T. Maltby (Camden 4th ser. xxv, 1988)

A short relation of some part of the sad sufferings . . . inflicted on the . . . Quakers, n.p. 1670

Smyth of Nibley, J., *A description of the hundred of Berkeley*, ed. Sir J. Maclean, Oxford 1885

Speed, J., *England, Wales, Scotland and Ireland described and abridged*, 1627

The state of the case for the city of Gloucester against the bill for dis-uniting the two hundreds of Dudston and King's Barton from the said citie, n.p. 1661

'N.T.', *Strange and true newes from Gloucester*, London 1660

Stuart royal proclamations, II: Royal proclamations of King Charles I, 1625–1646, ed. J. F. Larkin, Oxford 1983

T[hatch], T[homas], *The gainsayer convinced*, London 1649

Taylor, J., *John Taylor's last voyage*, London 1641

—— *A short relation of a journey through Wales*, ed. J. O. Halliwell, London 1859

Tertia pars de comparatis comparandis, London 1648

A true and exact relation of the marching of the trained bands of the city of London, London 1643

A true and impartiall relation of the battaile . . . of Newbury, London 1643

A true narrative concerning the woods and iron-works of the Forrest of Deane, n.p. [1661?]

A true relation of disbanding the supernumarary forces, London 1648.

The true relation how Sir John Wintour . . . made a wicket attempt on certain soldiers, n.p. 1642–3

A true relation of the late attempt made upon the town of Ciceter, London 1643

A true relation of the several passages which have happened to our army since it advanced towards Gloucester, London 1643

A true relation of a wicked plot . . . against the city of Gloucester . . . discovered by Captain Backhouse, London 1643

Two diaries of the Long Parliament, ed. M. Jansson, Gloucester 1984

Two letters from Colonell Morgan, London 1646

Two letters read in the House of Commons on Munday 24 Jan: 1647 of a great bloody plot discovered at Broadway in Worcestershire, London 1648

The victorious and fortunate proceedings of Sir William Waller, London 1643

The vindication of Richard Atkyns, in *Military memoirs of the Civil War*, ed. P. Young, London 1967

The visitation of the county of Gloucester, taken in the year 1623 . . . , ed. Sir J. Maclean and W. C. Hearne, London 1865

The visitation of the county of Gloucester [1682 and 1683], ed. T. Fitz-Roy Fenwick and W. C. Metcalfe, Exeter 1884

Wallis, R., *More news from Rome or, Magna Charta*, London 1666

———— *Room for the cobler of Gloucester and his wife*, London 1668

A warning-piece to all His Maiesties subjects of England, Oxford 1643

Whitelocke, B., *Memorials of the English affairs*, London 1682

[Wintour, Sir J.], *A true narrative concerning the woods and iron-works of the Forrest of Deane, and how they have been disposed since the year 1635*, London [1661]

The writings and speeches of Oliver Cromwell, ed. W. C. Abbott, Cambridge, Mass. 1937

Secondary sources

Adair, J., *Roundhead General: a military biography of Sir William Waller*, London 1969

Adlard, E., *Winchcombe cavalcade*, London 1939

Atkyns, R., *The ancient and present state of Gloucestershire*, Gloucester 1712

Austin, R. A., 'The city of Gloucester and the regulation of corporations, 1662–1663', *TBGAS* lviii (1936), 257–74

Aylmer, G. E., *The king's servants: the civil service of Charles I*, London 1961

———— 'Who was ruling in Herefordshire from 1645 to 1661?', *Transactions of the Woolhope Club* xl (1972), 373–87

———— *The state's servants: the civil service of the English republic*, London 1973

———— *The Interregnum: the quest for settlement*, London 1974

Baddley, W. St C., *A Cotteswold manor . . . Painswick*, Gloucester 1929

Bennett, J., *A history of Tewkesbury*, Tewkesbury 1830

Bigland, R., *Historical, monumental and genealogical collections relative to the county of Gloucester*, Gloucester 1791

Blackwood, B. G., *The Lancashire gentry and the Great Rebellion, 1640–1660*, Manchester 1978

Blunt, J. H., *Dursley and its neighbourhood*, Gloucester 1975

Braithwaite, W. C., *The beginnings of Quakerism*, Cambridge 1955

Brunton D. and D. H. Pennington, *Members of the Long Parliament*, London 1954

Capp, B. S., *The Fifth Monarchy men*, London 1972

Casada, J. A., 'Dorset politics in the Puritan Revolution', *Southern History* iv (1982), 107–22

Chandaman, C. D., *The English public revenue, 1660–1688*, Oxford 1975

Clark, Sir G., *The Campden wonder*, London 1959

Clark, P., ' "The Ramoth-Gilead of the Good": urban change and political radicalism at Gloucester, 1540–1640', in P. Clark, A. Smith and N. Tyacke (eds), *The English Commonwealth: essays presented to J. Hurstfield*, Leicester 1979, 167–87

Cliffe, T., *The Yorkshire gentry from the Reformation to the Civil War*, London 1964

Coate, M., *Cornwall in the Great Civil War and Interregnum: a social and political study*, Oxford 1933

Cockburn, J. S., *A history of English assizes*, Cambridge 1972

Coleby, A. M., *Central government and the localities: Hampshire, 1649–1689*, Cambridge 1987

Cooke, J. N., 'On the great Berkeley law suit of the fifteenth and sixteenth centuries: a chapter of Gloucestershire history', *TBGAS* iii (1878–9), 304–24

Cust, R. P., *The forced loan and English politics, 1626–1628*, Oxford 1987

Davies, W. H. S., 'Some notes on Chavenage and the Stephens family', *TBGAS* xxii (1899), 128–37

Dent, E., *Annals of Winchcombe and Sudeley*, London 1872

Dictionary of national biography

Ellacombe, H. T., *The history of the parish of Bitton*, Exeter 1881

Elrington, C. R., 'The survey of church livings in Gloucestershire in 1650', *TBGAS* lxxxiii (1964), 85–98

Everitt, A. M., *The community of Kent and the Great Rebellion, 1640–1660*, Leicester 1966

—— *The local community and the Great Rebellion* (Historical Association Pamphlet G70, 1969)

Eward, S., *No fine but a glass of wine: cathedral life at Gloucester in Stuart times*, Salisbury 1975

Finberg, H. R. P., *Gloucestershire studies*, Leicester 1957

Fletcher, A. J., *A county community in peace and war: Sussex, 1600–1660*, London 1975

—— *The outbreak of the English Civil War*, London 1981

—— 'National and local awareness in the county communities', in H. Tomlinson (ed.), *Before the English Civil War*, London 1983, 151–74

—— and J. Stevenson (eds), *Order and disorder in early modern England*, Cambridge 1985

Friedman, J., *Miracles and the pulp press during the English Revolution*, London 1993

Gloucestershire historical studies, Bristol University, Department of Extra-Mural Studies, 1967–82

Gloucestershire notes and queries, Gloucester 1881–1914

Gordon, M. D., 'The collection of ship money in the reign of Charles I', *TRHS* 3rd ser. iv (1910), 147–62

Gruenfelder, J. K., 'The election to the Short Parliament, 1640', in H. S. Reinmuth, Jr (ed.), *Early Stuart studies*, Minneapolis 1970, 180–230

—— 'Gloucester's parliamentary elections, 1604–1640', *TBGAS* xcvi (1978), 53–9

Haley, K. H. D., *The first earl of Shaftesbury*, Oxford 1968

Ham, R. E., 'The Four Shire controversy', *Welsh History Review* viii (1976–7), 381–400

Hammersley, G. F., 'The revival of the Forest Laws under Charles I, *History* xlv (1960), 85–102

—— 'The crown woods and their exploitation in the sixteenth and seventeenth centuries', *BIHR* xxx (1977), 136–61

Harris, F. H., 'Lydney ships', *TBGAS* lxvi (1945), 238–45

Hart, C. E., 'The metes and bounds of the Forest of Dean', *TBGAS* lxvi (1945), 166–207

—— *The free miners of Dean Forest*, Gloucester 1953

—— *Royal forest: a history of Dean's woods as timber producers*, Oxford 1960

Hill, C., *The world turned upside-down*, London 1972

Hill, M. C., 'The borough of Stow-on-the-Wold', *TBGAS* lxv (1944), 175–86

Hilton, R., *A medieval society*, London 1966

Hirst, D., *The representative of the people? Voters and voting in England under the Early Stuarts*, Cambridge 1975

Hodgson, E., *A history of Tetbury*, Dursley 1976

Holmes, C., *The Eastern Association in the English Civil War*, Cambridge 1974

—— 'The county community in Stuart historiography', *JBS* xix (1980), 54–73

Hughes, A., 'The king, the Parliament and the localities in the English Civil War', *JBS* xxiv (1985), 236–63

—— 'Parliamentary tyranny? Indemnity proceedings and the impact of the Civil War: a case study from Warwickshire', *Midland History* xi (1986), 49–78

—— *Politics, society and Civil War in Warwickshire, 1625–1660*, Cambridge 1987

Hutton, R. E., *The Royalist war effort, 1642–1646*, London 1982

—— *The Restoration: a political and religious history of England and Wales, 1658–1667*, Oxford 1985

Ingram, M., *Church courts, sex and marriage in England, 1570–1640*, Cambridge 1987

Jeayes, I. H., *Descriptive catalogue of the charters and muniments . . . at Berkeley Castle*, Bristol 1908

Johnson, J., *Stow-on-the-Wold*, Gloucester 1980

—— *Tudor Gloucestershire*, Gloucester 1985

Jones, C., M. Newitt and S. K. Roberts (eds), *Politics and people in revolutionary England*, Oxford 1986

Keeler, M. F., *The Long Parliament 1640–1641: a biographical study of its members*, Philadelphia 1954

Kishlansky, M. A., *Parliamentary selection: social and political choice in early modern England*, Cambridge 1986

Latimer, J., *The annals of Bristol in the seventeenth century*, Bristol 1900

Little, B., *Cheltenham*, London 1952

Liu, T., *Discord in Zion: the Puritan divines and the Puritan Revolution*, The Hague 1973

Malcolm, J. L., *Caesar's due: loyalty and Charles I*, London 1983

Malcolmson, R. W., 'A set of ungovernable people: the Kingswood colliers in the eighteenth century', in J. Brewer and J. Styles (eds), *An ungovernable people*, London 1980, 85–127

Manning, B. S., *The English people and the English Revolution: 1640–1649*, London 1976

—— *1649: The crisis of the English Revolution*, Manchester 1992

Marshall, L. M., 'The levying of the hearth tax, 1662–1688', *EHR* li (1936), 628–46

Matthews, N. L., *William Sheppard, Cromwell's law reformer*, Cambridge 1984

Morgan, B. (ed.), *Historical and genealogical memoirs of the Dutton family of Sherborne*, privately printed 1899

Morrill, J. S., 'Mutiny and discontent in the English provincial armies, 1645–1647', *P&P* lvi (1972), 49–74

—— *Cheshire 1630–1660: county government and society during the Puritan Revolution*, Oxford 1974

—— *The revolt of the provinces: conservatives and radicals in the English Civil War, 1630–1650*, London 1974

—— *The nature of the English Revolution: essays by John Morrill*, London 1993.

Norrey, P. J., 'The Restoration regime in action: relations between central and local government in Somerset, Dorset and Wiltshire, 1660–1678', *HJ* xxxi (1988), 789–812

Pennington, D. H., 'The accounts of the kingdom, 1642–49', in F. J. Fisher (ed.), *Essays in the economic and social history of Tudor and Stuart England*, Cambridge 1961, 182–203

Perry, R., 'The Gloucestershire woollen industry, 1100–1690', *TBGAS* lxvi (1945), 49–137

Phillips, C. B., 'County committees and local government in Cumberland and Westmorland, 1642–1660', *Northern History* v (1970), 34–66

Playne, A. T., *Minchinhampton and Avening*, Gloucester 1978

Prestwich, M., *Cranfield: politics and profits under the early Stuarts*, Oxford 1966

Reay, B., *The Quakers and the English Revolution*, London 1985

Richardson, R. C. (ed.), *Town and countryside in the English Revolution*, Manchester 1992

Roberts, S. K., *Restoration and recovery in an English county: Devon local administration, 1649–1670*, Exeter 1985

—— 'Public or Private? Revenge and recovery at the Restoration of Charles II', *BIHR* lix (1986), 172–88

Rollison, D. P., 'Property, ideology and popular culture in a Gloucestershire village, 1660–1740', *P&P* xciii (1981), 70–97

—— 'The bourgeois soul of John Smyth of Nibley', *Social History* xii (1987), 309–30

—— *The local origins of modern society: Gloucestershire, 1500–1800*, London 1992

Roy, I., 'The English Civil War and English society', in B. S. Bond and I. Roy (eds), *War and society: a yearbook of military history*, London 1975, 25–43

—— 'England turned Germany? The aftermath of the Civil War in its European context, *TRHS* 5th ser. xxviii (1978), 127–44

Rudd, M. A., *Historical records of Bisley with Lypiatt, Gloucestershire*, Dursley 1977

Rudder, S., *A new history of Gloucestershire*, Cirencester 1777

Sharp, B., *In contempt of all authority: rural artisans and riot in the west of England, 1586–1660*, Berkeley 1980

Skeel, C. A. J., *The Council in the Marches of Wales*, London 1904

Soden, G. I., *Godfrey Goodman, bishop of Gloucester, 1583–1656*, London 1953

Tawney, A. J. and R. H. Tawney, 'An occupational census of the seventeenth century', *EcHR*, 1st ser. v (1934–5), 25–64

Taylor, C. S., 'The northern boundary of Gloucestershire', *TBGAS* xxxii (1909), 107–11

Taylor, J. K. G., 'The civil government of Gloucester, 1640–1646', *TBGAS* lxvii (1947–8), 59–118

Thirsk, J. (ed.), *The agrarian history of England*, v, London 1984

—— *The rural economy of England*, London 1984

Thomas, K. V., 'Another Digger broadside', *P&P* xlii (1969), 57–68

Underdown, D., *Royalist conspiracy in England, 1649–1660*, New Haven 1960

—— 'Party management in the recruiter elections, 1645–1648', *EHR* lxxxiii (1968), 235–64

—— *Pride's purge: politics in the Puritan Revolution*, Oxford 1971

—— *Somerset in the Civil War and Interregnum*, Newton Abbot 1973

———— 'The chalk and the cheese: contrasts among the English Clubmen', *P&P* lxxxv (1979), 25–48

———— *Revel, riot and rebellion: popular politics and culture in England, 1600–1660*, New York 1987

VCH *Gloucestershire*, ii, iv, vi–viii, x–xi, London 1965–88

VCH *Oxfordshire*, ix, London 1969

VCH *Shropshire*, iii, London 1979

VCH *Warwickshire*, v, London 1953

VCH *Wiltshire*, v, London 1957

VCH *Worcestershire*, iii, iv, London 1971

Warmington, A. R., 'Frogs, toads and the Restoration in a Gloucestershire village', *Midland History* xiv (1989), 30–42

———— ' "Madd, bedlam madd": an incident in Gloucester's seventeenth-century municipal history reconsidered', *TBGAS* cxi (1993), 165–73

White, B. R., 'The organisation of the Particular Baptists, 1644–1660', *JEH* ii (1966), 209–26

Whitfield, C., *A history of Chipping Campden and Captain Robert Dover's olympick games*, Eton–Windsor 1958

Whitley, W. T., *A history of British Baptists*, London 1923

Willan, T. S., 'The river navigation and trade of the Severn valley, 1600–1750', *EcHR* 1st ser. viii (1937–8), 68–79

Willcox, W. B., *Gloucestershire: a study in local government, 1590–1640*, New Haven 1940

Williams, W. R., *The parliamentary history of the county of Gloucester*, Hereford 1898

Wood, A. C., *Nottinghamshire in the Civil War*, London 1937

Woolrych, A. M., *Commonwealth to Protectorate*, Oxford 1972

Worden, A. B., *The Rump Parliament*, Cambridge 1974

Wrigley, E. A. and R. S. Schofield, *The population history of England, 1541–1871*, London 1981

Wyatt, J. W., 'How accurate is "Men and Armour"?', *Gloucestershire Historical Studies* ix (1978), 19–30.

Unpublished works

Beats, L., 'Politics and government in Derbyshire, 1640–1660', unpubl. Ph.D. diss. Sheffield 1978

Hamilton, P., 'Patterns of rural settlement in Gloucestershire, Herefordshire and Worcestershire', unpubl. MA diss. Reading 1960

Hammersley, G. F., 'The history of the iron industry in the Forest of Dean region, 1562–1660', unpubl. Ph.D. diss. London 1972

Harrison, G. A., 'Royalist organisation in Gloucestershire and Bristol 1642–1646', unpubl. MA diss. Manchester 1961

———— 'Royalist organisation in Wiltshire, 1642–1646', unpubl. Ph.D. diss. London 1973

Horn, J. P. P., 'Social and economic aspects of local society in England and the Chesapeake: a comparative study of the Vale of Berkeley, Gloucestershire, and the lower western shore of Maryland, c.1660–1700', unpubl. D.Phil. diss. Sussex 1982

Hryniewicz, E. A., 'The MPs for Wiltshire, 1640–1649', unpubl. M.Litt. diss. London 1982

Lynch, G. J., 'The risings of the Clubmen in the English Civil War', unpubl. MA diss. Manchester 1973

McParlin, G. E., 'The Herefordshire gentry in county, society and government, 1625–1661', unpubl. Ph.D. diss. Aberystwyth 1981

Moreton-Jackson, M., 'The dissolution of the monasteries in Worcestershire and Gloucestershire', unpubl. MA diss. Bristol 1978

Porter, S., 'The destruction of urban property in the English Civil Wars, 1642–1651', unpubl. Ph.D. diss. London 1983

Redmond, M. F., 'The borough of Tewkesbury, 1575–1714', unpubl. MA diss. Birmingham 1950

Reece, H. M., 'The military presence in England, 1649–1660', unpubl. D.Phil. diss. Oxford 1981

Ripley, P. J. G., 'The city of Gloucester, 1660–1740', unpubl. M.Litt. diss. Bristol 1977

Robinson, R. P., 'The parliamentary representation of Gloucestershire, 1660–1690', unpubl. Ph.D. diss. Yale 1975

Saul, N. E., 'The Gloucestershire gentry in the fourteenth century', unpubl. D.Phil. diss. Oxford 1978

Silcock, R. H., 'County government in Worcestershire, 1603–1660', unpubl. Ph.D. diss. London 1974.

Tann, J., 'Aspects of the development of the Gloucestershire woollen industry', unpubl. Ph.D. diss. Leicester 1964

Zweigman, L. J., 'The role of the gentleman in county government and society: the Gloucestershire gentry, 1625–1649', unpubl. Ph.D. diss. McGill 1987

Index